THE COMMON LAW JURISPRUDENCE OF THE CONFLICT OF LAWS

This book presents a collection of leading common law cases in private international law ranging from the 18th to the 21st century. The cases traverse issues of jurisdiction, choice of law and the recognition and enforcement of foreign judgments. Questions of marital validity, domicile, foreign immovable property and choice of law in contract are just some of the topics that this collection examines. The 'unusual factual situations' of some 18th- and 19th-century English cases also reveal compelling human interest stories and political controversies worthy of further exploration.

Drawing on a diverse team of contributors, this edited collection showcases the research of eminent conflicts scholars together with emerging scholars from the United Kingdom, Australia, Canada, Ireland and South Africa.

The Common Law Jurisprudence of the Conflict of Laws

Edited by
Sarah McKibbin
and
Anthony Kennedy

•HART•
OXFORD • LONDON • NEW YORK • NEW DELHI • SYDNEY

HART PUBLISHING

Bloomsbury Publishing Plc

Kemp House, Chawley Park, Cumnor Hill, Oxford, OX2 9PH, UK

1385 Broadway, New York, NY 10018, USA

29 Earlsfort Terrace, Dublin 2, Ireland

First published in Great Britain 2023

A catalogue record for this book is available from the British Library.

A catalogue record for this book is available from the Library of Congress.

ISBN: HB: 978-1-50995-427-8
ePDF: 978-1-50995-429-2
ePub: 978-1-50995-428-5

Typeset by Compuscript Ltd, Shannon

FOREWORD

This collection of essays, focused as it is on the common law underpinnings of the conflict of laws, fittingly reflects the varied international backgrounds of its contributors. The collection brings together a range of established and emerging scholars from the United States, Canada, Ireland, England, South Africa and Australia, who span all stages of their respective careers in practice and academia. Each of the twelve chapters provides a thorough and engaging analysis of a different landmark private international law case, and thoughtfully draws out the implications of each case for the development of a coherent mode of common law reasoning in resolving complex disputes of an international character. What emerges is a fascinating depiction of parallel yet interdependent legal systems, at times moving in synchronicity and at other times starkly diverging, but all appealing to the same shared conceptual foundations of private international law norms.

The variety of this collection comes not only from the international perspective of its contributors, but also from the broad range of legal doctrines that fall within its purview. The chosen cases touch upon, among other things, developments in choice of law rules for contract disputes (chapters 2 and 4), marriage validity (chapter 1) and tort claims (chapter 8); comparative common law approaches to *forum non conveniens* and stay applications (chapters 5 and 10); the enforcement of governmental interests by foreign states beyond territory (chapter 6); attempts to impugn the acts of foreign states within territory (chapter 9); the recognition and enforcement of foreign judgments at common law (chapters 11 and 12); and what can be learnt from *intra*-national conflict of laws disputes in federal common law countries (chapters 3 and 7). Through their scholarly analyses of principle, the contributors also shed light on the more fundamental (and at times competing) *values* that inform the common law's approach to conflict of laws cases, including international comity, party autonomy, decisional uniformity, finality of outcome and, in certain cases, the protection of forum public policy and fundamental common law rights.

For much of its history, the common law has been one of the great harmonising forces in the development of a coherent international body of legal norms governing the conflict of laws. It continues to play a critical role in transnational litigation, notwithstanding the growth in legislative and international instruments regulating the field. The common law world of course encompasses many of the most important global hubs for international commerce and dispute resolution, including London, Singapore, New York, Hong Kong, and my own home city of Sydney.

Yet the need to grapple with issues of private international law is not limited to these commercial centres. It is now trite to observe that, as the world grows smaller, and as global markets for capital, goods, services, labour and information grow ever more integrated, conflict of laws issues will arise in an increasing number of courtrooms, boardrooms and legislative assemblies across the globe (and far beyond the established commercial hubs to which I have referred). Speaking on the topic of 'The Future of Private International Law in Australia' a number of years ago, I made the observation that:

> ... it follows, as night follows day, and as the world becomes more and more integrated – through technology; through electronic payment systems; through improved and vastly cheaper travel; through the liberalisation of trade barriers – that there will be more international movement and more international trade and, of course, as there is more international movement and more international trade, there will be more and more disputes of an international character. It is inevitable.[1]

In hindsight, perhaps I should not have been so unequivocal in my remarks about increased international movement and trade (not to mention 'vastly cheaper travel'!), had I an inkling of the immense disruption that would be caused by the COVID-19 pandemic. The pandemic, however, sparked an acceleration in other forms of transnational activity – notably, that involving digital communications and the information economy. With the worst effects of the pandemic now largely behind us, the international community has returned to its trajectory of integration. All of this is to say: it will be crucial for the lawyer of the 21st century, no matter their *locus domicilii*, to have a robust working familiarity with the principles of the conflict of laws, including its common law underpinnings.

Of course, for many years, the majority of the countries discussed in this collection (with the exception of the United States) were tethered together by the unified appellate structure of the Commonwealth, with an apex court – the Privy Council – bringing a measure of uniformity to the common law jurisprudence of the conflict of laws. That is no longer the case. As time has passed, and as the former colonies of Britain have forged their own judicial paths, the common law rules of the conflict of laws have diverged in important respects. Perhaps one of the most prominent examples of this phenomenon has arisen in the Australian context, in the approach taken to the doctrine of *forum non conveniens* in *Voth v Manildra Flour Mills Pty Ltd*.[2] This is only one example among many. A number of the chapters of this book discuss cases in which the courts of one country have been faced with the question of whether or not to follow the approach taken by a superior court of another common law country in dealing with various aspects of private international law.

[1] Andrew Bell, 'The Future of Private International Law in Australia' (2012) 19 *Australian International Law Journal* 11, 11.

[2] (1990) 171 CLR 538.

In this context, scholarship plays a critically important part in the development of a coherent, if not necessarily uniform, body of common law private international law. The role of academic research and commentary in informing the development of conflict of laws rules is, of course, not novel. In the first chapter of this book, Dr Sarah McKibbin provides a compelling account of, among other things, the influence of scholarship in 19th century Britain in the development of modern choice-of-law rules relating to marriage. Today, research in the field of private international law occupies a similarly important role. Just as considerable academic attention is devoted to initiatives to harmonise private international law rules by means of international instruments and co-ordinated legislative reform, it is important that scholars continue to scrutinise developments and variances in underlying common law principles between common law jurisdictions.

Notwithstanding some doctrinal divergence between jurisdictions, one common thread which emerges from the cases discussed in this collection concerns the role of *adaptive common law reasoning* in complex disputes of an international character. The strength of the common law is, to adopt the words of Anthony Kennedy and Andrew Moran in the twelfth and final chapter of this collection, its ability to "evolve over time and … shape conclusions to ensure that they accord with principle".

This attribute of common law systems is of particular significance in a field as multifaceted as the conflict of laws. One consequence of the trajectory of global integration already referred to is that transnational disputes will continue to grow not only in volume but also in *complexity*. In particular, commercial and social activity involving digital platforms – much of which may be difficult to locate within geographical borders at all – will continue to throw up increasingly challenging and novel fact scenarios for courts and practitioners to digest. Where developments in commerce and technology outstrip the pace of regulation, as they inevitably will from time to time, it will frequently fall to common law courts to determine how best to fashion existing principle to address the new challenges of private international law. The emergence of bitcoin is a case in point.

Another characteristic of the conflict of laws which emerges from the commentaries in this book is its place at the nexus of private and public law. That is to say, what is often termed "private international law" is in many cases inextricably tied to questions of governmental authority and public policy. In chapter 6, Reid Mortensen offers a fascinating account of the formulation and ultimate success of the policy-based argument which found favour with the High Court of Australia in *Attorney-General (UK) v Heinemann Publishers Australia Pty Ltd [No 2]*[3] (the Spycatcher case). Similarly, in chapter 9, Michael Douglas illustrates the significance of *Kuwait Airways Corp v Iraqi Airways Co*[4] in developing English common

[3] (1988) 165 CLR 30.
[4] [2002] 2 AC 883.

law as to the non-enforcement of foreign laws which are contrary to public international law.

Yet even where foreign states or their instrumentalities are not directly implicated in a dispute, the study and practice of the conflict of laws involves the interaction between private and public law norms. Scholars and practitioners of the conflict of laws fundamentally grapple with an intractable (and endlessly interesting) issue of law and policy: namely, how to reconcile the often competing interests of, on the one hand, the freedom of sovereign governments to determine the content and enforcement of rights and duties between their subjects, and on the other hand, the important objectives of promoting certainty, party autonomy and, where possible, uniformity in the resolution of international disputes.

Finally, something should be said about the importance of edited collections such as this one in a legal practitioner's modern 'online' world. For today's lawyers, there is of course no such thing as an unreported decision. Any decision of a superior court throughout the common law world (and beyond) may be accessed with only a few keystrokes and a basic grasp of online research tools. Particularly in the field of private international law, the volume of available case law is so vast that, for a busy practitioner (or, might I add, judicial officer), it is impossible fully to digest, comprehend and absorb the vast body of case law without the aid of thorough, high-quality commentary and analysis. Collections of essays of the kind gathered in this book play an important role in enabling modern lawyers to engage with conceptual and comparative discussions of private international law practices in different jurisdictions, and to stay abreast of developments and points of interest abroad.

This collection of thoughtful and engaging analyses is a significant addition to the literature. It traverses a wide variety of contemporary issues in private international law, and its authors are to be congratulated on the originality and thoroughness of their scholarship.

Andrew Bell
Chief Justice's Chambers
Supreme Court of New South Wales
20 February 2023

EDITORS' PREFACE

In a world which has, over the last few years, been heir to more than its fair share of natural shocks, there has been something comfortingly familiar in working on, and presenting, a collection of papers considering the common law jurisprudence on the conflict of laws. Environmentally, politically and, at least from an English private international lawyer's perspective, legally, all has been a unique kind of chaos; to hear the voices of the contributors to this collection speak again of the cases which have moulded the development of private international law in several jurisdictions across the common law world has offered something of a balm.

Prior to, at least, the environmental and political chaos, there seemed to us to be a gap in the scholarly literature on the conflict of laws, which gap a collection like this one is designed to fill. The idea having been conceived, and the idea having been encouraged, an online symposium was held in January 2022, at which various of the contributors to this collection presented their draft papers and discussed how the questions to which their chosen cases gave rise might be answered by courts situated in different outposts of the common law world. Not to be able to meet in person because of various travel restrictions brought about by the pandemic was a great shame, but to hold the symposium in the dead of the Australian night and the cool of the Canadian morning was a very clear reminder not only of the ancestral and continuing connections which common law courts have to one another but also the connections which scholars writing about the common law jurisprudence of the conflict of laws maintain.

The various contributions to this collection focus on the decisions of the Australian, American, Canadian. Irish and South African courts. From the collection, one can see clearly how the traditional topics of private international law, such as jurisdiction, choice of law and the recognition and enforcement of foreign judgments, have developed differently in each of the jurisdictions addressed. Of course, aspects of a shared heritage remain visible but the contributors to this collection have also demonstrated how that shared heritage has given rise to quite sharp divergence between the approaches which several common law courts can adopt to fundamental questions of private international law theory and practice. We are very grateful to each of the contributors to this collection for their hard work and the generosity with which they have shared their knowledge.

We are also exceptionally grateful for the support given us by Hart Publishing and, in particular, Kate Whetter and Sinead Moloney, without whom this collection would not exist in its present form or, indeed, at all. To be able to research on, and present this collection concerning, the common law jurisprudence on the conflict of laws is an immense privilege; we hope that this collection adds to the development of that subject in its own small way.

Sarah McKibbin
Anthony Kennedy
Toowoomba, Qld and London, UK
August 2022

TABLE OF CONTENTS

Foreword .... *v*
Editors' Preface .... *ix*
List of Contributors .... *xiii*
Table of Cases .... *xv*
Table of Legislation .... *xxix*

1. Brook v Brook: *Rethinking Marriage Choice of Law* *1*
   Sarah McKibbin

2. *The Mixed Blessing of* Vita Food Products: *The Impact and Influence of the Privy Council's Decision* *23*
   Helen Morton

3. Erie Railroad Company v Tompkins *in a Private International Law Context* *43*
   Michael S Green

4. *Good Stock? The Enduring Influence of the 'Proper Law' Rule in* Bonython v Commonwealth of Australia *65*
   Ian McDonald

5. M/S Bremen v Zapata Off-Shore Company: *US Common Law Affirmation of Party Autonomy* *85*
   Ronald A Brand

6. *Lucy's Argument: The* Spycatcher *Case in Australia* *111*
   Reid Mortensen

7. *Conflicts and Public Law Concerns: A New Way of Conceiving the Conflict of Laws:* Morguard Investments Ltd v De Savoye *137*
   Angela Swan OC

8. Tolofson v Jensen: *Reframing the Canadian Common Law Choice of Law Rule for Torts* *151*
   Joost Blom

9. *The Limits of Our Tolerance for Acts of Foreign States: The Legacy of* Kuwait Airways (Nos 4 and 5) *171*
   Michael Douglas

10. Bid Industrial Holdings (Pty) Ltd v Strang and Another (Minister of Justice and Constitutional Development, Third Party)*: An Analysis*............*191*
Elsabe Schoeman

11. Re Flightlease *and Common Law Judgment-Recognition in Ireland*..............*207*
Máire Ní Shúilleabháin

12. Vizcaya Partners Limited v Picard*: Implications for the Recognition and Enforcement of Foreign Judgments at Common Law and Beyond*..................*225*
Anthony Kennedy and Andrew Moran

Index..*245*

LIST OF CONTRIBUTORS

Joost Blom is Professor Emeritus at the Peter A Allard School of Law at the University of British Columbia, where he taught 1972–2017 and served as Dean 1997–2003. His teaching subjects were private international law, contracts, torts and intellectual property, and he has published widely in those areas. He served as an elected bencher of the Law Society of British Columbia 2004–11 and is now a Life Bencher.

Ronald A Brand is the Chancellor Mark A Nordenberg University Professor of Law, John E Murray Faculty Scholar, and the founding Director of the Center for International Legal Education (CILE) at the University of Pittsburgh School of Law. He regularly teaches courses in international business transactions, international arbitration and litigation, and matters of private international law.

Michael Douglas is Senior Lecturer at UWA Law School, Australia, and a barrister and solicitor in Western Australia. His research includes co-authorship of the 10th edition of *Nygh's Conflict of Laws in Australia*. Michael was previously a visiting scholar at the Hague Conference on Private International Law.

Michael S Green is the Dudley W Woodbridge Professor of Law at the College of William and Mary in Williamsburg, Virginia.

Anthony Kennedy is a Retained Fee Lecturer in Roman Law at Somerville College, Oxford, and a lecturer on the Bar Training Course at BPP University in London. He is also an Associate Member of Serle Court Chambers, 6 New Square, Lincoln's Inn.

Ian McDonald is a barrister at 4 New Square Chambers in London and a member of the Middle Temple. He has a keen interest in private international law and has worked as a teaching assistant on the Conflict of Laws module on the Bachelor of Civil Law at the University of Oxford and delivered tutorials in the subject to visiting students at St Catherine's College, Oxford.

Sarah McKibbin is a Lecturer in Law at the University of Southern Queensland.

Andrew Moran is a barrister and Queen's Counsel practising at Serle Court Chambers, 6 New Square, Lincoln's Inn, London, and is a Master of the Bench of Middle Temple.

Reid Mortensen is a Professor of Law, and Head of the School of Law and Justice, at the University of Southern Queensland, Toowoomba, Australia. He specialises in private international law.

Helen Morton is a barrister practising at Essex Court Chambers in London. Her practice often requires her to engage with questions of private international law.

Máire Ní Shúilleabháin is an Associate Professor in Law at University College Dublin specialising in private international law.

Elsabe Schoeman is Dean of the Faculty of Law, University of Pretoria, South Africa. She is a former Deputy Dean of Auckland Law School in New Zealand. She is an Alexander von Humboldt Fellow and specialises in private international and comparative law. She has published widely in her areas of interest and has also made contributions to international legal encyclopaedias, as well as submissions to law commissions (in South Africa and New Zealand/Australia).

Angela Swan is a Life Member of the Law Society of Ontario. She is Counsel and a member of the Capital Markets and Corporate/Commercial Practice Groups at Aird Berlis LLP in Toronto and an Adjunct Professor at the Osgoode Hall Law School of York University, where she teaches courses on contracts. Her areas of expertise include contract law, corporate law, and the conflict of laws. She was appointed an Officer of the Order of Canada in 2021.

TABLE OF CASES

United Kingdom

Adams v Cape Industries plc [1990] 1 Ch 433 ....211, 213, 231
Adelaide Electrical Supply Co Ltd v Prudential Assurance Co Ltd [1934] AC 122 (HL) 71–73
Amin Rasheed Shipping Corp v Kuwait Insurance Co [1984] AC 50 (HL) 31, 33, 77–80
Armadora Occidental SA v Horace Mann Insurance Co [1977] 1 WLR 1098 (CA) 77
Armadora Occidental SA v Horace Mann Insurance Co [1977] 1 WLR 520 77
Attorney-General v Guardian Newspapers Ltd (No 2) [1990] 1 AC 109 112
Attorney-General (Canada) v Schulze (1901) 9 SLT 4 118
Attorney-General (New Zealand) v Ortiz [1984] AC 1 ....118–20, 123, 125, 127–28, 130–32, 134
Banco de Vizcaya v Don Alfonso de Bourbon y Austria [1935] 1 KB 140 118
Bank of Australasia v Harding (1850) 9 CB 661, 137 ER 1052 ....227–28, 230–31, 238, 240–41
Bank of Australasia v Nias (1851) 16 QB 717, 117 ER 1055 ....227–28, 230–31, 238, 240
Belhaj v Straw [2017] UKSC 3, [2017] AC 964 .... 179–81, 183–84, 186–88
Blohn v Desser [1962] 2 QB 116 ....230–32, 237
Boissevain v Weil [1949] 1 KB 482 ....27, 31, 74
Bonython v The Commonwealth [1951] AC 201 (PC) 31, 65–83
Boys v Chaplin [1971] AC 356 (HL) 157, 174, 177
British South Africa Co v Companhia de Moçambique [1893] AC 602 (HL) 184
Brokaw v Seatrain UK Ltd [1971] 2 QB 476 120
Broken Hill Proprietary Co v Latham [1933] Ch 373 71
Brook v Brook (1858) 3 Sm & G 481, 65 ER 746 ....9, 1–22
Brook v Brook (1861) 9 HL Cas 193, 11 ER 703 ....1, 7, 12–16
Butler v Forbes [1811–17] Ferg 209 4
Butler v Freeman (1756) Amb 301, 27 ER 204 3
Buttes Gas and Oil Co v Hammer (No 3) [1982] AC 888 (HL) 182
Cammell v Sewell (1860) 5 H & N 728, 157 ER 1371 175
Castrique v Imrie (1870) LR 4 HL 414 175
Chartbrook Ltd v Persimmon Homes Ltd [2009] 1 AC 1101 (HL) 79

Compagnie d'Armement Maritime SA v Compagnie Tunisienne de Navigation SA [1971] AC 572 (HL) 79
Compton v Bearcroft (1769) 2 Hag Con 444 5
Conway v Beazley (1831) 3 Hag Ecc 639, 162 ER 1292 5–6
Cooper v Stuart (1889) 14 App Cas 286 (PC) 114
Copin v Adamson (1875) 1 Ex D 17 ....228–30, 237
Cotton v R [1914] AC 176 (HL)....118
Dalrymple v Dalrymple (1811) 2 Hag Con 54, 161 ER 665....3
De Reneville v De Reneville [1948] P 100 (CA)....2
Don Alonso v Cornero (1792) Hob 212; 80 ER 359 120
Duntze v Levett [1811–17] Ferg 68....4
Edmonstone v Lockhart [1811–17] Ferg 168 4
Emanuel v Symon [1908] 1 KB 302 (CA) 209, 229–32, 236–39
Enka Insaat Ve Sanayi AS v OOO Insurance Company Chubb [2020] 1 WLR 4117 (UKSC).... 78–81
Fenton v Livingstone (1856) 18 D 865 (IH) 7
FS Cairo (Nile Plaza) LLC v Brownlie [2021] UKSC 45, [2021] 3 WLR 1011 (UKSC) 237
Government of India v Taylor [1955] AC 491 (HL)....118
Government of the Islamic Republic of Iran v The Barakat Galleries Ltd [2009] QB 22....134
Harford v Morris (1776) 2 Hag Con 423, 161 ER 792....5
Harris v Hicks (1692) 2 Salk 548 9
Holman v Johnson (1775) 1 Cowp 341....118
Huntington v Attrill [1893] AC 150 (HL)....118–19, 123, 127–28, 132
Husayn v Foreign and Commonwealth Office [2022] EWCA Civ 334 (CA) 178
Ilderton v Ilderton (1793) 2 H Bl 145, 126 ER 476 5
Ilyssia Compania Naviera SA v Bamaodah [1985] 1 Lloyd's Rep 107 (CA)....198
Indian and General Investment Trust Co Ltd v Borax Consolidated Ltd [1920] 1 KB 539....118
Inglis v Robertson [1898] AC 616 (HL) 175
Jacobs v Crédit Lyonnais [1884] 12 QBD 589 .... 24, 75
James Miller & Partners Ltd v Whitworth Street Estates (Manchester) Ltd [1970] AC 583 (HL)....77
JSC BTA Bank v Ablyazov [2011] EWHC 202 (Comm), [2011] 2 All ER (Comm) 10....179
Kenward v Kenward [1951] P 124 (CA) 1
Kibblewhite v Rowland [1811–17] Ferg 226 4
King of Italy v Marquis Cosimo de Medici Tornaquinci (1918) 34 TLR 623 120
Kuwait Airways Corporation v Iraqi Airways Co [1992] EWHC 67 (Comm)....174
Kuwait Airways Corporation v Iraqi Airways Co [2000] 2 All ER (Comm) 360....174

Kuwait Airways Corporation v Iraqi Airways Co (No 1) [1994] 1 Lloyd's Rep 276 (CA) 174
Kuwait Airways Corporation v Iraqi Airways Co (No 1) [1995] 1 WLR 1147 (HL) 172
Kuwait Airways Corporation v Iraqi Airways Co (No 5) [1999] CLC 31 174
Kuwait Airways Corporation v Iraqi Airways Co (Nos 4 and 5) [2001] 3 WLR 1117 (CA) 172
Kuwait Airways Corporation v Iraqi Airways Co (Nos 4 and 5) [2002] 2 AC 883 (HL) 171
L Schuler AG v Wickman Machine Tool Sales [1974] AC 235 (HL) 79
Lawlor v Sandvik Mining and Construction Mobile Crushers and Screens Limited [2013] 2 Lloyd's Rep 98 77–78
Lawrence v Lawrence [1985] 2 WLR 86 (Fam D) 19
Lloyd v Guibert (1865) LR 1 QB 115 .... 24, 75
Luther v Sagor [1921] 3 KB 532 (CA) 175
M'Carthy v De Caix (1831) 2 Cl & F 568, 6 ER 1268 4
Machado v Fontes [1897] 2 QB 231 (CA) 151
Maduro Board of the Central Bank of Venezuela v Guaido Board of the Central Bank of Venezuela [2021] UKSC 57, [2022] 2 WLR 167 (UKSC) 182, 184–85
Marks & Spencer plc v BNP Paribas Securities Services Trust Co (Jersey) Ltd [2015] UKSC 72, [2016] AC 742 (UKSC) 228
Mayor of Auckland Corporation v Alliance Assurance Co Ltd [1937] AC 587 (PC) 68, 72–73
Mbasogo v Logo Ltd [2007] QB 846 134
Mette v Mette (1859) 1 Sw & Tr 416, 164 ER 792 19
Middleton v Janverin (1802) 2 Hag Con 437, 161 ER 797 3
Mohammed v Secretary of State for Defence [2017] UKSC 1, [2017] AC 821 (UKSC) 182
Mount Albert Borough Council v Australasian Temperance and General Mutual Life Assurance Society [1938] AC 224 (PC) 24, 31, 69
Municipal Council of Sydney v Bull [1909] 1 KB 7 118
Nachimson v Nachimson [1930] P 217 (CA) 2
Nigeria v JP Morgan Chase Bank NA [2019] EWHC 347 (Comm) 79
Nissan v Attorney General [1970] AC 179 (HL) 184
Okura & Co Ltd v Forsbacka Jernverks AB [1914] 1 KB 715 213
Oppenheimer v Cattermole [1976] AC 249 (HL) 176–78, 189
Padolecchia v Padolecchia [1968] P 314 (PDA) 2
Payne v Deputy Federal Commissioner of Taxation [1936] AC 497 (PC) 72
Phillips v Batho [1913] 3 KB 25 210
Phillips v Eyre (1870) LR 6 QB 1, Ex Ch 151–52, 154, 174
Princess Paley Olga v Weisz [1929] 1 KB 718 120
Pugh v Pugh [1951] P 482 (PDA) 2
R v Brentwood Marriage Registrar [1968] 2 QB 956 (QB) 1–2

R v Cuthbertson [1981] AC 470 (HL) 118
R v Dibdin [1910] P 57 (CA)....................9
R v Governor of Pentonville Prison; Ex part Budlong [1980] 1 WLR 1110....................119
R v International Trustee for the Protection of Bondholders A/G [1937]
AC 500 (HL) 69
R v Jones (Margaret) [2007] 1 AC 136 (HL)....................186
R v Lolley (1812) Russ & Ry 237, 168 ER 779 4
Radwan v Radwan (No 2) [1972] 3 WLR 939 (Fam D)....................2, 19
Re Lord Cable, Deceased [1977] 1 WLR 7 119
Re Missouri Steamship Company (1889) 42 Ch D 321....................24, 36, 75
Re Paine [1940] Ch 46 (Ch) 1–2, 19
Re Spectrum Plus Ltd (in liquidation) [2005] UKHL 41, [2005] 2
AC 680 (HL) 215
Re State of Norway's Application [1987] QB 433....................120
Re Visser [1928] 1 Ch 877.................... 118–19
Red Sea Insurance Co Ltd v Bouygues SA [1995] 1 AC 190 (PC) 152
Regazzoni v KC Sethia Ltd [1958] AC 301 (HL)....................40–41, 119
Reliance Industries Ltd v Union of India [2018] EWHC 822 (Comm),
[2018] 1 Lloyd's Rep 562....................184
Richardson v Mellish (1824) 130 ER 294, 2 Bing 229 180
Robinson v Bland [1558–1774] All ER Rep 177....................24, 74–75
Rodriguez v Speyer Brothers [1919] AC 59 (HL) 180
Royal Bank of Scotland v Etridge (No 2) [2001] UKHL 44; [2002] 2
AC 773 (HL) 215
Rubin v Eurofinance SA [2012] UKSC 46; [2013] 1 AC 236 (UKSC)....................210–11,
217, 226–27, 237, 242–43
Ruding v Smith (1821) 2 Hag Con 371, 161 ER 774....................3, 8
SA Consortium General Textiles v Sun and Sand Agencies Ltd [1978] QB 279....................236
Salaman v Secretary of State for India [1906] 1 KB (CA) 181
Schemmer v Property Resources Ltd [1975] Ch 273....................118
Schibsby v Westenholz (1870) LR 6 QB 155....................209
Scrimshire v Scrimshire (1752) 2 Hag Con 395, 161 ER 782 3
Sfeir & Co v National Insurance Company of New Zealand [1964]
1 Lloyd's Rep 330....................231–32, 235, 237, 239–41
Shergill v Khaira [2014] UKSC 33, [2015] AC 359 181
Showlag v Mansour [1995] 1 AC 431 223
Simonin v Mallac (1860) 2 Sw & Tr 67, 164 ER 917....................7
Sirdar Gurdyal Singh v Rajah of Faridkote [1894] AC 670 (PC)....................229
Société Générale de Paris v Dreyfus Brothers (1885) 29 Ch D 239....................198
Sottomayer v De Barros (No 2) (1879) 5 PD 94 (PDA) 17–20, 22
Sottomayor v De Barros (1877) 2 PD 81 (PDA) 17
Sottomayor v De Barros (No 1) (1877) 3 PD 1 (CA) 2, 17–18, 21
South African Breweries Ltd v King [1899] 2 Ch 173 74

Spiliada Maritime Corp v Cansulex Ltd [1987] AC 460 (HL)....... 115, 195, 197–99, 201, 203–06
Szechter v Szechter [1971] P 286 (PDA)..2
The Assunzione (No 1) [1954] P 150 (CA)...76, 149–50
The Komninos S [1991] 1 Lloyd's Rep 370 79
The Law Debenture Trust Corporation plc v Ukraine [2017] EWHC 655 (Comm), [2017] QB 1249 187
The Law Debenture Trust Corporation plc v Ukraine [2018] EWCA Civ 2026, [2019] QB 1121 187–88
The Metamorphosis [1953] 1 WLR 543..76
The Philippine Admiral (1976) 2 WLR 214 (HL)...189
United States Securities and Exchange Commission v Manterfield [2010] 1 WLR 172 134
Unterweser Reederei GmbH v Zapata Off-Shore Co ('The Chaparral') [1968] 2 Lloyd's Rep 158 (CA)... 94–95
Valleé v Dumergue (1849) 4 Ex 290, 154 ER 1221.. 227, 229
Vervaeke v Smith [1983] 1 AC 145 (HL)...19
Vita Food Products Inc v Unus Shippping Co Ltd [1939] AC 277 (PC)...... 23–42, 76
Vizcaya Partners Limited v Picard [2016] UKPC 5, [2016] 3 All ER 181...... 225–44
Vogel v R & A Kohnstamm Ltd [1973] QB 133 ....232, 237–38, 240–41
Warrender v Warrender (1835) 2 Cl & Fin 488, 6 ER 1239 3–5
Wasa International Insurance Co Ltd v Lexington Insurance Co [2010] 1 AC 180 (HL) 79
Westminster City Council v C [2008] EWCA Civ 198, [2009] 2 WLR 185.............19
Williams & Humbert Ltd v W&H Trade Marks (Jersey) Ltd [1986] AC 387 (HL) 118
Yukos Capital Sarl v OJSC Rosneft Oil Co (No 2) [2011] EWHC 1461 (Comm), [2011] 2 Lloyd's Rep 443 179

Australia

Akai Pty Ltd v The People's Insurance Company Ltd [1996] HCA 39, (1996) 188 CLR 148 81
Al-Kateb v Godwin [2004] HCA 37, (2004) 219 CLR 562............................... 186–87
Applicant S v Minister for Immigration and Multicultural Affairs [2004] HCA 25, (2005) 217 CLR 387 179
Attorney-General (United Kingdom) v Heinemann Publishers Australia Pty Ltd (1987) 8 NSWLR 341 ....112, 121–24
Attorney-General (United Kingdom) v Heinemann Publishers Australia Pty Ltd (1987) 10 NSWLR 86 ....112, 125–26, 130–31
Attorney-General (United Kingdom) v Heinemann Publishers Australia Pty Ltd (1987) 75 ALR 461...130

Attorney-General (United Kingdom) v Heinemann Publishers Australia Pty Ltd [1988] HCA 25, (1988) 165 CLR 30 178
Bath v British and Malayan Trustees Ltd [1969] 2 NSWR 114 119
Bonython v Commonwealth [1948] HCA 2, (1948) 75 CLR 589 .... 31, 65–83
Breavington v Godleman [1988] HCA 40, 169 CLR 41 .... 114, 139, 142, 152, 159, 163
CGU Insurance Ltd v Blakeley [2016] HCA 2, (2016) 259 CLR 339 181
Clubb v Edwards [2019] HCA 11, (2019) 267 CLR 171 179–80
Commonwealth of Australia v John Fairfax & Sons Ltd (1980) 147 CLR 39........126
Cook v Cook (1986) 162 CLR 376...114
Dunbee Ltd v Gilman & Co (Australian) Pty Ltd [1968] 2 Lloyd's Rep 394 (NSWCA)..236–37, 239
Firebird Global Master Fund II Ltd v Republic of Nauru [2015] HCA 43, (2015) 258 CLR 31 187
Goldsbrough, Mort & Co Ltd v Hall [1948] VLR 145.. 72–73
Goldsbrough, Mort & Co Ltd v Hall [1949] HCA 2, (1949) 78 CLR 1 72–73
Habib v Commonwealth of Australia [2010] FCAFC 12, (2010) 183 FCR 62......184
Hobart International Airport Pty Ltd v Clarence City Council [2022] HCA 5 (HCA)..181
In the Marriage of Barriga (No 2) (1981) 7 Fam LR 909 (FamCA) 2
In the Marriage of El Oueik (1977) 29 FLR 171 133
John Pfeiffer Pty Ltd v Rogerson [2000] HCA 36, (2000) 203 CLR 503 .... 114, 135, 168, 177
Jumbunna Coal Mine v Victorian Coal Miners' Association (No 2) [1908] HCA 95, (1908) 6 CLR 309 187
Kok v Resorts World at Sentosa Pte Ltd [2017] WASCA 150, (2017) 323 FLR 95...178
Lange v Australian Broadcasting Corporation (1997) 189 CLR 520......................135
Mabo v Queensland [No 2] [1992] HCA 23, (1992) 175 CLR 1 (HCA) 114, 187
Marriage of Teves and Compomayor (1995) FLC 92-578 (FamCA) 2
Maudsley v Colonial Mutual Life Assurance Society Ltd [1945] VLR 161 71
McKain v RW Miller (South Australia) Pty Ltd (1988) 174 CLR 1........................114
McLelland v Trustees Executors and Agency Co Ltd [1936] HCA 45, (1936) 55 CLR 483 74
Merwin Pastoral Co Pty Ltd v Moolpa Pastoral Co Pty Ltd (1933) 48 CLR 565...74
Miller v Teale [1954] HCA 68, (1954) 92 CLR 406 19
Neilson v Overseas Projects Corp of Victoria Ltd [2005] HCA 54, (2005) 223 CLR 331 ....38, 168, 180, 188
Oceanic Sun Line Special Shipping Company Inc v Fay (1988) 165 CLR 197 115
Palmer v Western Australia [2021] HCA 5, (2019) 95 ALJR 229 180
Petrotimor Companhia De Petroleos SARL v Commonwealth [2003] FCAFC 3, (2003) 126 FCR 354.. 134, 183

Privatbrauerei Erdinger Weissrau Werner Brombach GMBH v World Brands Australia Pty Ltd [2016] WASC 9 239
Régie National des Usines Renaut SA v Zhang [2002] HCA 10, (2002) 210 CLR 491 .... 168, 177
Robb Evans & Associates v European Bank Ltd (2004) 61 NSWLR 75 134
Scarffe & OBannon [2020] FamCA 77 185
Stevens v Head (1993) 176 CLR 433 114
Surgibit IP Holdings Pty Limited v Ellis (No 2) [2017] NSWSC 1379 134
Victoria Aircraft Leasing v United States [2005] VSCA 76, (2005) 12 VR 340 183
Voth v Manildra Flour Mills Pty Ltd (1990) 171 CLR 538 .... 115, 205

British Virgin Islands

JSC VTB Bank v Katunin (unreported, Eastern Caribbean High Court, British Virgin Islands, 22 March 2022) 189

Canada

Amchem Product Inc v British Columbia (Workers' Compensation Board) [1993] 1 SCR 897 (SCC) 115, 155
Avenue Properties Ltd v First City Development Corp Ltd (1986) 32 DLR (4th) 40 (BCCA) 169
Barrick Gold Corp v Goldcorp Inc 2011 ONSC 3725 166
Beals v Saldanha 2003 SCC 72, [2003] 3 SCR 416 (SCC) 207–08, 210, 214–16, 219–20, 242
Bezan v Vander Hooft 2004 ABCA 44 .... ??
Breeden v Black 2012 SCC 19, [2012] 1 SCR 667 (SCC) 144, 166
Brill v Korpach Estate 1997 ABCA 205 165
British Columbia v Imperial Tobacco Canada Ltd 2004 BCCA 269, *aff'd* 2005 SCC 49, [2005] 2 SCR 473 (SCC) 161
Castillo v Castillo 2005 SCC 83, [2005] 3 SCR 870 .... 140, 144, 149–50, 162
Central Sun Mining Inc v Vector Engineering Inc 2013 ONCA 605 166
Club Resorts Ltd v Van Breda 2012 SCC 17, [2012] 1 SCR 572 (SCC) 144, 165, 167, 169
Committee for the Equal Treatment of Asbestos Minority Shareholders v Ontario (Securities Commission) 2001 SCC 37, [2001] 2 SCR 132 (SCC) 141
Das v George Weston Ltd 2018 ONCA 1053, *leave to appeal to SCC refused*, 38529 (8 August 2019) 164–65
Éditions Écosociété Inc v Banro Corp 2012 SCC 18, [2012] 1 SCR 636 (SCC) 144, 166

Gillespie Management Corp v Terrace Properties (1989) 62 DLR (4th) 221 (BCCA)....................148–49
Greenshields Inc v Johnston (1981) 119 DLR (3d) 714, [1981] 3 WWR 313, (Alta SC); *aff'd* (1981) 131 DLR (3d) 234, [1982] 2 WWR 97 (Alta CA) 144–46, 148
Greta Inc v Robert De Lange 2013 ONSC 3086 165
Grimes v Cloutier (1989) 61 DLR (4th) 505 (Ont CA) 152–54
Gulevich v Miller 2015 ABCA 411 165
Haaretz.com v Goldhar 2018 SCC 28, [2018] 2 SCR 3 (SCC)....................144, 166–67
Hanlan v Sernesky (1998) 38 OR (3d) 479 (OCA) 164
Hertz Corp v Friend 130 S Ct 1192 (2010) 51
Holt Cargo Systems Inc v ABC Containerline NV (Trustees of) [2001] 3 SCR 907, 207 DLR (4th) 577 147–48
Hunt v T&N plc [1993] 4 SCR 289, 109 DLR (4th) 16 (SCC)........ 139, 155–56, 167
Hurst v Société Nationale de l'Amiante (2008) 93 OR (3d) 338, 53 BLR (4th) 10 (OCA)....................141
Imperial Life Assurance Co of Canada v Colmenares [1967] SCR 443 (SCC)........81
JP Morgan Chase Bank v Lanner (The) 2008 FCA 399, 305 DLR (4th) 442 148
Kazi v Canada (Minister of Citizenship and Immigration) [2014] CanLII 83460 2
Lapointe Rosenstein Marchand Melançon LLP v Cassels Brock & Blackwell LLP 2016 SCC 30, [2016] 1 SCR 851 (SCC)....................167
Lilydale Cooperative Ltd v Meyn Canada Inc 2015 ONCA 281....................81
Long v Dundee Resort 2013 ONSC 4238 164
Lucas v Gagnon (1992) 11 OR (3d) 422 (Ont CA) 151–55, 161, 168–69
Mattar v Public Trustee [1952] 3 DLR 399 (Alta CA).................... 236, 239
McLean v Pettigrew [1945] SCR 62 (SCC) 152–54, 157–58
Moran v Pyle National (Canada) Ltd [1975] 1 SCR 393, 43 DLR (3d) 239 (SCC) 138, 142–43, 148, 150, 167
Morguard Investments Ltd v De Savoye [1990] 3 SCR 1077 (SCC)....................137–50
Moses v Shore Boat Builders (1993) 106 DLR (4th) 654 ....215, 219
Nevsun Resources Ltd v Araya 2020 SCC 5, [2020] SCJ No 5 (SCC) 160, 183
Pearson v Boliden Ltd 2002 BCCA 624, 222 DLR (4th) 453, *leave to appeal to SCC refused*, 29578 (18 September 2003) 166
Québec (Attorney General) v A 2013 SCC 5, [2013] 1 SCR 61....................143
Québec (Sa Majesté du Chef) v Ontario Securities Commission (1992) 10 OR (3d) 577, 97 DLR (4th) 144....................140
Québec Procureur général) c Comité pour un traitement égal des actionnaires minoritaires de la société Asbestos ltée 1999 CanLII 13813 (QCCA) ....??
Re Dwelle Estate (1969) 69 WWR 212 ()....................119
Re Marriage Laws [1912] SCR 132 (SCC)....................2
Reference re Securities Act 2011 SCC 66, [2011] 3 SCR 837 (SCC)....................142
Sangi v Sangi [2011] BCSC 523 178
Somers v Fournier 2002 CanLII 45001 (ONCA), 214 DLR (4th) 611 164

Spar Aerospace Ltd v American Mobile Satellite Corp 2002 SCC 78, [2002] 4 SCR 205 (SCC) 167
Sparling v Québec (Caisse de Dépôt et Placement du Québec) [1988] 2 SCR 1015, 55 DLR (4th) 63 (SCC) ....??
SSAB Alabama Inc v Canadian National Railway Co 2020 SKCA 74 167
The Strandhill v Walter W Hodder Company [1926] SCR 680, [1926] 4 DLR 801 147
Thomson v Thomson [1994] 3 SCR 551 155
Thorne v Hudson 2016 ONSC 5507 166
Todd Shipyards Corp v Altema Compania Maritima SA [1974] SCR 1248, 32 DLR (3d) 571 147–48
Tolofson v Jensen 1992 CanLII 931 (BCCA), 89 DLR (4th) 129; *on appeal* 3 SCR 1022, 102 DLR (4th) 289 ....139–40, 142, 149, 151–70
Unifund Insurance Co v Insurance Corpn of BC 2003 SCC 40, [2003] 2 SCR 63 161
United States of America v Harden [1963] SCR 366 119
Wong v Lee 2002 CanLII 44916, 58 OR (3d) 398 (Ont CA) 164
Wong v Wei 1999 CanLII 6635 (BCSC) 164

European Union

Owusu v Jackson (Case C-281/02) [2005] ECR I-1383 202

Gibraltar

Picard and Bernard L Madoff Investment Securities LLC (in liquidation) v Vizcaya Partners 2013–14 Gib LR 209 233–34
Vizcaya Partners Limited and Asphalia Fund Limited v Picard (as Trustee for Bernard L Madoff Investment Securities LLC (in Liquidation) 2015 Gib LR 282 225–44

Hong Kong

Chen Li Hung v Ting Lei Miao [2000] 1 HKC 461, [2000] 1 HKLRD 252 (CFA) 178, 180
Suen Toi Lee v Yau Yee Ping (2001) 4 HKCFAR 474 2

Ireland

Bussoleno v Kelly [2011] IEHC 220 ....??
Dyer v Dolan (10 June 1993, Irish High Court, unreported) 208

H v H [2015] IESC 7; [2015] 1 ILRM 453 223
In the matter of Flightlease (Ireland) Limited (in voluntary liquidation) and in the matter of an application for directions pursuant to s 280 of the Companies Act 1963; Paul McCann and Stephen Akers, Joint Liquidators [2006] IEHC 193, [2012] IESC 12, [2012] 1 IR 722 207
Murphy v Att Gen [1982] IR 241 215
Rainford, Boston and Graham v Newell-Roberts [1962] IR 95 ....208–12, 214–15, 219, 221–22, 224
Salo v Tarutin [2019] IEHC 240 ....??
Steele v Braddell [1837] Milw 1 (Ir) 5
W v W [1993] 2 IR 476 223

Malaysia

Re Maria Huberdina Hertogh; Adabi v Hertogh [1951] MLJ 164 2

New Zealand

Attorney-General (United Kingdom) v Wellington Newspapers Ltd [1988] 1 NZLR 129 124
Attorney-General (United Kingdom) v Wellington Newspapers Ltd (No 2) [1988] 1 NZLR 180 124
Deng v Ye [2018] NZAR 560 2
Kawasaki v Kawasaki [1997] NZFLR 932 (DC) 2
McConnell Dowell v Lloyd's Syndicate 396 [1988] 2 NZLR 257 115

Singapore

Ah Kiu v Central Provident Fund Board [1992] 2 SLR(R) 440 2
Brinkerhoff Maritime Drilling Corp v PT Airfast Services Indonesia [1992] 2 SLR 776 115

South Africa

Bid Industrial Holdings (Pty) Ltd v Strang and Another (Minister of Justice and Constitutional Development, Third Party) 2008 (3) SA 355 (SCA) 191–206
Cargo Laden and Lately Laden on Board the MV Thalassini Avgi v MV Dimitris 1989 3 SA 820 (A) 192

Dias Compania Naviera SA v MV AL Kaziemah 1994 3 All SA 4 (D) 192
Ex parte Spinazze 1985 (3) SA 650 (A) 192
Government of the Republic of Zimbabwe v Fick [2013] ZACC 22, 2013 (5) SA 325 (CC) 224, 242
Great River Shipping Inc v Sunnyface Marine Ltd 1992 4 SA 313 (C) 192
M T Tigr Bouygues Offshore SA v Owners of The M T Tigr 1998 4 SA 740 (C) 192
Multi-Links Telecommunications Ltd v Africa Prepaid Services Nigeria Ltd 2014 3 SA 265 (GP) 199–201
Standard Bank v Butlin 1981 (4) SA 158 (D) 239
Veneta Mineraria Spa v Carolina Collieries (Pty) Ltd (In Liquidation) 1987 (4) SA 883 (A) 195, 202

United States

AAR International Inc v Nimelias Enterprises SA 250 F3d 510 (7th Cir 2001) 105
Abadou v Trad 624 P2d 287 (Alaska 1981) 99
Abbott Laboratories v Takeda Pharmaceutical Co Ltd 476 F3d 421 (7th Cir 2007) 108
Abela v Gen Motors Corp 677 NW2d 327 (Mich 2004) 61
Aceequip Ltd v Am Eng'g Corp 153 F Supp 2d 138 (DC Conn 2001) 106
Arguss Communications Group Inc v Teletron Inc 2000 WL 36936 (DNH 1999) 104
Arthur Young & Co v Leong 383 NYS2d 618 619 (App Div), *appeal dismissed*, 390 NY2d 927 (1976) 107
Babcock v Jackson 191 NE 2d 279 (NY Ct Apps) 157–58, 162
Banco De Sonora v Bankers' Mut Cas Co 100 N 532 (Iowa 1904) 48
Barrielle v Bettman 199 F 838 (SD Ohio, 1912) 48
Black & White Taxicab & Transfer Co v Brown & Yellow Taxicab & Transfer Co 276 US 518 (1928) 47
Black v Rebstock Drilling Co 837 F Supp 200 (WD La 1993) 60
Blanco v Banco Industrial de Venequela SA 997 F2d 974 (2d Cir 1993) 106
Bodum USA Inc v La Cafetiere Inc 621 F3d 631–36 (7th Cir 2010) 61
Bonny v Society of Lloyd's 3 F3d 156 (7th Cir 1993) 105–06
Boyle v United Techs Corp 487 US 504 (1988) 47
Bromely v Crisp 561 F2d 1354 (10th Cir 1977) 62
Bryant Electrical Co v City of Fredericksburg 762 F2d 1192 (4th Cir 1985) 108
Burford v Sun Oil Co 319 US 336 (1943) 51
Cambridge Nutrition AG v Fotheringham 840 F Supp 299 (SDNY 1994) 106
Can Malting Co v Paterson SS Ltd 285 US 413 (1932) 92
Carbon Black Export Inc v The Monrosa 254 F2d 297 (5th Cir 1958), *cert dismissed*, 359 US 180 (1959) 89, 91–92, 95–96

Caribe BMW Inc v Bayerische Motoren Werke Aktiengesellschaft 821 F Supp 802, *set aside, vacated and remanded on other grounds,* 19 F2d 745 (1st Cir 1994) 106
Carnival Cruise Lines Inc v Shute 499 US 972 (1991) 87–88, 91, 102
City of New York v Pullman Inc 477 F Supp 438 (SDNY 1979), *affirmed,* 662 F2d 919 (2d Cir 1981), *reh'g denied,* 28 Sep 1981, *cert denied,* 454 US 1038, 102 S Ct 1038 (1982) 99
Clearfield Trust Co v United States 318 US 363 (1943) 47
Commonwealth v Lane 113 Mass 458, 469 (1873) 13
Coon v The Medical Ctr Inc 797 SE2d 828 (Ga 2017) 58
Cooper v Aaron 358 US 18–20 (1958) 61
Danner v MBNA Am Bank NA 255 SW3d 868 (Ark 2007) 61
Davison v Gibson 56 F 443 (8th Cir 1893) 48
Dentsply International Inc v Benton 965 F Supp 574 (MD Pa 1997) 102
Doe 1 v AOL LLC 552 F3d 1077 (9th Cir 2009) 108
Elia Corp v Paul N Howard Co 391 A2d 214 (Del Super Ct 1978) 99
Erie RR Co v Tompkins 304 US 64 (1938) 108
Evolution Online Sys Inc v Koninklijke PTT Nederland NV 145 F3d 505 (2d Cir 1998) 105–06
Faulkner v Hart 82 NY 413 (1880) 57
Fid Union Trust Co v Field 311 US 177 (1940) 60
FIL Leveraged US Gov't Bond Fund Ltd v TCW Funds Management Inc 156 F3d 1236 (9th Cir 1998) 107
Florida Polk County v Prison Health Servs Inc 170 F3d 1081 (11th Cir 1999) 104
Forepaugh v Del Lackawanna & W RR 128 Pa 217 (1889) 58
Freeman v Lane 962 F2d 1258 (7th Cir 1992) 62
Fru-Con Const Corp v Controlled Air Inc 574 F3d 527 (8th Cir 2009) 108
Gelpcke v City of Dubuque 68 US 175 (1863) 60
General Elec Co v G Siempelkamp GmbH & Co 29 F3d 1095 (6th Cir 1994) 106
Ginter ex rel Ballard v Belcher, Prendergast & Laporte 536 F3d 439 (5th Cir 2008) 108
Gough v Hamburg Amerikanische Packetfahrt Aktiengesellschaft 158 F 174 (SDNY 1907) 91
Green v Clinic Mawsters Inc 272 NW2d 813 (SD 1978) 99
Greenough v Munroe 2 F Supp 104 (SDNY 1932) 60
Guaranty Trust Co v York 326 US 99 (1945) 52
Gulf Oil Corp v Gilbert 330 US 501 (1947) 92, 95
Hauenstein & Bermeister Inc v Met-Fab Indus 320 NW2d 886 (Minn 1982) 108
Healey v Eastern Building and Loan Association 17 Pa Super 385 (Pa Super 1901) 90
Heller Financial Inc v Midwhey Powder Co 883 F3d 1286 (7th Cir 1989) 106
Hi Fashion Wigs Profit Sharing Trust v Hamilton Inv Trust 579 SW2d 300 (Tex Civ App 1979) 99

Home Ins Co v Morse 87 US 445 (1874) 90
Hulin v Fibreboard Corp 178 F3d 318–19 (5th Cir 1999)....................60
Hull 753 Corp v Flugzeugwerke 58 F Supp 2d 925 (ND Ill 1999) 102
Hunter Distrib Co v Pure Beverage Partners 820 F Supp 284
(ND Miss 1993) 106
International Text-Book Co v Connelly 99 NE 722 (NY 1912)....................48
Johnson v St Paul Mercury Ins Co 256 La 296–97 (1970) 60
Jones v Western Union Telegraph Co 18 F2d 650 (WD La, 1926) 48
Jumara v State Farm Ins Co 55 F3d 873 (3d Cir 1995) 108
Koontz v Baltimore & Ohio RR Co 163 A 212 (Pa 1932) 43
Krenger v Pennsylvania RR 174 F2d 556 (2d Cir), *cert denied*,
338 US 866 (1949) 91
Kuhnhold v Compagnie Generale Transatlantique 251 F 387 (SDNY 1918) 91
Kulukundis Shipping Co v Amtorg Trading Corp 126 F2d 978;
1942 AMC 364 (2d Cir 1942) 90
Lawler v Schumacher Filgters Am 832 F Supp 1044 (ED Va 1993) 106
Lockhart v Fretwell 506 US 376 (1993) 62
Loucks v Standard Oil Co of New York 120 NE 198 (1918) 178
M/S Bremen and Unterweser Reederei GmbH v Zapata Off-Shore Co
407 US 1 (1972) 85–109
Manetti-Farrow Inc v Gucci America Inc 858 F2d 509 (9th Cir 1988)....................108
Medway v Needham 16 Mass 157 (1819)....................6
Mercier v Sheraton International Inc 981 F2d 1345 (1st Cir 1992)....................105
Metcalf v City of Watertown 153 US 678 (1894)....................60
Mitsui & Co (USA) Inc v Mira M/V 111 F3d 33, 37 (5th Cir 1997)....................105
National Equipment Rental Ltd v Szukhent 375 US 311 (1964).................... 92, 97
Northwestern National Ins Co v Donovan 916 F2d 372, 378 (7th Cir 1990)....................105
Nute v Hamilton Mutual Insurance Co 72 Mass 174 (1856)....................90
Nutter v New Rents Inc 945 F2d 398 (4th Cir 1991) 108
Omron Healthcare v Maclaren Exports 28 F2d 600 (7th Cir 1994) 106
P & S Business Machines Inc v Canon USA Inc 331 F3d 804 (11th Cir 2003)....................108
Pearcy Marine v Seacor Marine 847 F Supp 57 (SD Tex 1993) 106
Phillips v Audio Active Ltd 494 F3d 378 (2d Cir 2007) 108
Plum Tree Inc v Stockment 488 F2d 754 (3d Cir 1973) 101, 106
Poddar v State Bank of India 79 F Supp 2d 391 (SDNY 2000) 106
Prince Steam-Shipping Co v Lehman 39 F 704 (SDNY 1889) 91
Prudential Resources Corp v Plunkett 583 SW2d 97 (Ky Ct App 1979) 108
Re Unterweser Reederei GmbH 428 F2d 888 (5th Cir 1970) 95–96, 98
Richards v United States 369 US 1 (1962) 162
River Paper Co v Hammermill Paper Co 223 Mass 8, 111 NE 678 (1916)....................90
Rivera v Centro Medico de Turabo Inc 575 F3d 10 (1st Cir 2009) 108
Royal Bed & Spring Co Inc v Famossul Industria e Comercio de Moveis Ltda 906 F2d 45 (1st Cir 1990).................... 105–06

S Pacific Co v Jensen 244 US 222 (1917) 46
Santamauro v Taito do Brasil Industria e Comercia 587 F Supp 1312 (ED La 1984) 99, 106
Scherk v Alberto-Culver Co 417 US 506 (1974) 88, 100, 108
Shelp v National Surety Company 333 F2d 431 (5th Cir 1964) 60
Skyline Steel Corp v RDI/Caesars Riverboat Casino LLC 44 F Supp 2d 1337, 1338 (ND Ala 1999) 106
Smith, Valentino & Smith Inc v Superior Court 131 Cal Rptr 374, 551 P2d 1206 (Cal 1976) 99, 107
Societe Jean Nicolas et Fils JB v Mousseux 123 Ariz 59, 597 P2d 541 (1979) 99
St Charles Ventures LLC v Albertsons Inc 265 F Supp 2d 686–87 (ED La 2003) 60
St Nicholas Bank v State National Bank 27 NE 851 (NY 1891) 57
Stalker v McDonald 6 Hill 93 (NY 1843) 51
Steffel v Thompson 415 US 482 (1974) 62
Steve Weiss & Co Inc v INALCO SpA 1999 WL 386653 (SDNY 1999) 102, 104
Sudduth v Occidental Peruana Inc 70 F Supp 2d 691 (ED Tex 1999) 102, 105–06
Swift v Tyson 41 US 1 (1842) 43–63
TUC Electronics Inc v Eagle Telephonics Inc 698 F Supp 35 (D Conn 1988) 106
Underhill v Hernandez 186 US 250 (1897) 189
US Asphalt ReF Co v Trinidad Lake Petroleum Co 222 F 1006 (SDNY 1915) 90
Volkswagenwerk AG v Klippan GmbH 611 P2d 498 (Alaska), *cert denied*, 449 US 974 (1980) 99
Wm H Muller & Co v Swedish American Line Ltd 224 F2d 806 (2d Cir 1955) 91
Wong v PartyGaming Ltd 589 F3d 821 (6th Cir 2009) 108
Yavuz v 61 MM Ltd 465 F3d 418 (10th Cir 2006) 108

TABLE OF LEGISLATION

United Kingdom

Statutes

Administration of Justice Act 1920 .... 231, 239
Australia Act 1986 113
Australian Constitutions Act 1842 113
Australian Constitutions Act 1850 113
British North America (Quebec) Act 1774 143
Carriage of Goods by Sea Act 1924 .... 25, 39
Carriage of Goods by Sea Act 1971 .... 35, 40
Clandestine Marriages Act 1753 5
Commonwealth of Australia Constitution Act 1900 113
Contracts (Applicable Law) Act 1990 .... 31, 37, 80
Court of Chancery Act 1851 10
Family Law (Scotland) Act 2006 20
Foreign Judgments (Reciprocal Enforcement) Act 1933 239
Foreign Limitation Periods Act 1984 167
Marriage Act 1835 .... 7, 9–14, 16, 19, 21
Marriage (Enabling) Act 1960 20
Marriage (Scotland) Act 1977 20
Matrimonial Causes Act 1857 .... 3–4, 10
Matrimonial Causes Act 1973 20
Merchant Shipping Act 1894 27
Official Secrets Act 1939 .... 123–24, 126–28, 134
Private International Law (Miscellaneous Provisions) Act 1995 .... 152, 224
Royal Marriages Act 1772 .... 7, 11, 13
State Immunity Act 1978 174
Statute of Westminster Adoption Act 1942 113

Statutory Instruments

Civil Procedure Rules 1998 1998/3132 204
Law Applicable to Contractual Obligations and Non-Contractual
Obligations (Amendment etc.) (EU Exit) Regulations 2019/834 .... 32, 80

Canada

Statutes

Canada Business Corporations Act 1985 142
Carriage of Goods by Sea Act 1932 (Newfoundland) 25–29, 37
Constitution Act 1867 .... 137, 139, 142
Conflict of Laws (Traffic Accidents Act) 2002 (Yukon) 158
Court Jurisdiction and Proceedings Transfer Act 2003 (British Columbia) 165
Criminal Code 1985 .... 139, 145
Foreign Extraterritorial Measures Act 1985 139
Guarantees Acknowledgment Act 1970 (Alberta) 144–46
Highway Traffic Act 1937 (Ontario) 152
Limitations Act 2000 (Alberta) 162
Limitations Act 2002 (Ontario) 149
Water Carriage of Goods Act 1910 28

Provincial Codes

Civil Code 1991 (Quebec) 143, 168

Australia

Australia Act 1986 113–14
Bank of Australia Act 1833 228
Commonwealth of Australia Constitution Act 1900 113
Foreign Judgments Act 1991 239
The Judiciary Act 1903 .... 129, 140
Privy Council (Appeals from the High Court) Act 1975 113
Privy Council (Limitation of Appeals) Act 1968 113
Service and Execution of Process Act 1901 120
Service and Execution of Process Act 1992 138

New Zealand

Historic Articles Act 1962 119–20
Property (Relationships) Act 1976 35

Republic of Ireland

Companies Act 1963 .... 213, 218

South Africa

Admiralty Jurisdiction Regulation Act 105 of 1983 .... 192, 201
Constitution of the Republic of South Africa, 1996 .... 191, 195, 206
Superior Courts Act 10 of 2013 193
Supreme Court Act 59 of 1959 .... 193, 196

United States of America

Constitution of the United States 138
Harter Act 1893 28
Judiciary Act 1789 47
US Federal Arbitration Act 1925 .... 85, 90–91, 233

Codes

28 USC 91–92, 94, 101, 106, 108

European Union

European Convention on Jurisdiction and Enforcement of Judgments in Civil and Commercial Matters, done at Brussels, 27 September 1968 85
Regulation (EC) No 864/2007 of the European Parliament and of the Council of 11 July 2007 on the law applicable to non-contractual obligations 80
Regulation (EC) No 593/2008 of the European Parliament and of the Council of 17 June 2008 on the law applicable to contractual obligations 31–32, 36–38, 80–83, 85
Regulation (EU) No 1215/2012 of the European Parliament and of the Council of 12 December 2012 on jurisdiction and the recognition and enforcement of judgments in civil and commercial matters (Brussels recast) 85–86, 99, 101, 203, 207

International

Hague Convention on the Law Applicable to Traffic Accidents 1971 .... 158, 164
Hague Convention on Choice of Court Agreements 2005 .... 86–88, 109, 241

Hague Convention on the Recognition and Enforcement of Foreign Judgments in Civil or Commercial Matters 2019 .... 221–24, 241, 243
Hague Principles on Choice of Law in International Commercial Contracts 2015 86
Lugano Convention on jurisdiction and the recognition and enforcement of judgments in civil and commercial matters 2007........................207, 213, 221

1

Brook v Brook: Rethinking Marriage Choice of Law

SARAH McKIBBIN*

I. Introduction

Until the latter half of the nineteenth century, English courts deferred to the law of the place of celebration (the *lex loci celebrationis*) to determine the validity of marriages with a foreign element.[1] *Brook v Brook*[2] was a 'turning point'.[3] In 1861, the House of Lords unanimously invalidated a marriage celebrated outside England even though it was valid under the *lex loci*. The dominant scholarly view of *Brook* is that Lord Campbell LC developed a bifurcated choice of law rule demanding the formal and essential validity of a marriage. The choice of law rule for formal validity – the form and ceremonies required to solemnise a marriage – is the *lex loci*.

The choice of law rule for questions of capacity or essential validity said to have emerged from *Brook* is less clearly stated. Questions of capacity include questions of marriageable age, consanguinity and affinity, marital status, and lack of consent. Lord Campbell referred this question to the 'the law of the country in which the parties are domiciled at the time of marriage, and in which the matrimonial residence is contemplated'.[4] This passage suggests two possible choice of law rules. The first, popularised by AV Dicey, is the dual domicile theory: each party must have capacity to marry under the law of their respective domiciles at the time of marriage.[5] The second is the intended matrimonial home theory, favoured

* I thank Reid Mortensen, Anthony Kennedy, Jeremy Patrick and Katie Murray for their comments on this chapter. Any errors are my own.

[1] Collins (ed), *Dicey, Morris and Collins on the Conflict of Laws*, 15th edn, 5th supp (Sweet & Maxwell, 2018) [17–059].

[2] (1861) 9 HL Cas 193, 11 ER 703 ('*Brook v Brook* (HL)').

[3] Sykes and Pryles, *Australian Private International Law*, 3rd edn (The Law Book Company Ltd, 1987) 391.

[4] *Brook v Brook* (HL) (n 2) 207.

[5] For support for Dicey's dual domicile test, see: Dicey, *Digest of the Law of England with Reference to the Conflict of Laws*, 2nd edn (Stevens and Sons, 1908) 613 ('2nd edn'); Dicey and Morris (eds), *Conflict of Laws*, 6th edn (Sweet & Maxwell, 1949) 762; Law Commission, 'Private International Law: Choice of Law Rules in Marriage' Law Com No 165 (1987) para 2.3. See also England: *Re Paine* [1940] Ch 46 (Ch) 49–50; *Kenward v Kenward* [1951] P 124 (CA) 144–46 (Denning LJ); *R v Brentwood Marriage Registrar*

by Cheshire:[6] the law of the intended matrimonial home governs capacity to marry. Applying one's *lex domicilii* to determine capacity to marry was a novelty at the time of *Brook*, but is now well-established.[7]

This chapter examines *Brook* not only to explore the evolution of the common law choice of law rules on marriage,[8] but also to highlight the influential role played by scholars in this area. The chapter begins by examining the law applicable to foreign marriages before *Brook*. The civilian doctrine of 'evasion of the law' is identified as a way in which English scholars challenged the place-of-celebration rule. The chapter then analyses *Brook* and concludes by considering the symbolic value of *Brook*. It is argued that the bifurcated choice of law rule demanding formal and essential validity was not (as conventionally believed) established in *Brook*. The form-capacity distinction, incongruously represented as 'well-established' in the Court of Appeal's decision of *Sottomayor v De Barros (No 1)*,[9] became fully fledged in 'scholarly portrayals of doctrine'[10] and in subsequently decided cases.[11] The highest court of appeal in England has never revisited this question; only High Court or Court of Appeal decisions have subsequently mentioned or applied *Brook*.[12]

II. Before *Brook*: The Law Applicable to Foreign Marriages

A. The Influence of Case Law and Scholarship

i. The Lex Loci

By the early nineteenth century, Anglo-American courts were well-equipped to identify which law would determine the validity of a marriage taking

[1968] 2 QB 956 (QB) 968; *Padolecchia v Padolecchia* [1968] P 314 (PDA) 336 (Sir Jocelyn Simon P); *Szechter v Szechter* [1971] P 286 (PDA) 295; Australia: *In the Marriage of Barriga (No 2)* (1981) 7 Fam LR 909 (FamCA) 912; *Marriage of Teves and Compomayor* (1995) FLC 92–578 (FamCA) 81735–36; New Zealand: *Kawasaki v Kawasaki* [1997] NZFLR 932 (DC) 934; *Deng v Ye* [2018] NZAR 560; Canada: *Re Marriage Laws* [1912] SCR 132; *cf Kazi v Canada (Minister of Citizenship and Immigration)* [2014] CanLII 83460; Singapore: *Re Maria Huberdina Hertogh; Adabi v Hertogh* [1951] MLJ 164; *Moh Ah Kiu v Central Provident Fund Board* [1992] 2 SLR(R) 440; Hong Kong: *Suen Toi Lee v Yau Yee Ping* (2001) 4 HKCFAR 474.

[6] Cheshire, *Private International Law*, 1st edn (Clarendon Press, 1935) 154–56.

[7] Law Commission (n 5) para 2.6.

[8] Fentiman, 'The Validity of Marriage and the Proper Law' (1985) 44 *CLJ* 256; Adams, 'Same-Sex Relationships and Anglo-Canadian Choice of Law: An Argument for Universal Validity' (1996) 34 *Canadian Yearbook of International Law* 103, 110–15.

[9] *Sottomayor v De Barros (No 1)* (1877) 3 PD 1 (CA) 5–6.

[10] Pontin, 'A Room with a View in English Nuisance Law: Exploring Modernisation Hidden within the "Textbook Tradition"' (2018) 38 *Legal Studies* 627, 627.

[11] *Re Paine* (n 5); *Szechter v Szechter* (n 5).

[12] *Nachimson v Nachimson* [1930] P 217 (CA) 221, 226; *De Reneville v De Reneville* [1948] P 100 (CA) 114 (Lord Greene MR); *Pugh v Pugh* [1951] P 482 (PDA) 486–90 (Pearce J); *Radwan v Radwan (No 2)* [1972] 3 WLR 939 (Fam D) 946–47.

place abroad.[13] The *lex loci* governed all questions of marital validity. American scholar and jurist Joseph Story, in a locus classicus on the validity of foreign marriages, stated:

> [B]etween persons, sui juris, marriage is to be decided by the law of the place, where it is celebrated. If valid there, it is valid everywhere. It has a legal ubiquity of obligation. If invalid there, it is equally invalid everywhere.[14]

This rule had been firmly established by a line of English decisions in the church courts.[15] These decisions mostly involved British subjects – typically minors – who had solemnised their marriages abroad in contravention of local law. In *Scrimshire v Scrimshire*, Mr Scrimshire and Miss Jones – two English minors with dependent domiciles in England – married clandestinely in France.[16] In Jones' suit for restitution of conjugal rights, Scrimshire argued that the marriage was invalid. Neither party had obtained parental consent as required under French law, the *lex loci*, for persons under the age of 25. In judging the marriage invalid, Sir Edward Simpson observed that 'all nations have consented, or must be presumed to consent, for the common benefit and advantage, that such marriages should be good or not, according to the laws of the country where they are made'.[17] As English barrister Hosack observed in 1847, the marriage was invalid 'not on the ground that they were incapacitated from marrying by the law of their own domicile, but solely because the marriage was void by the law of France'.[18] Civilian scholars held a different view. If the parties married in a foreign place 'with the view of evading [the law] of their own domicile', the marriage was void.[19]

ii. The Question of Domicile

The 1835 House of Lords' divorce decision, *Warrender v Warrender*, foreshadowed the potential for domicile to assume greater importance in cases involving the

[13] English courts had determined cross-border cases raising issues of domicile, succession, and marriage. See, eg, on marriage: *Scrimshire v Scrimshire* (1752) 2 Hag Con 395, 161 ER 782; *Dalrymple v Dalrymple* (1811) 2 Hag Con 54, 161 ER 665. See generally Harrison, *On Jurisprudence and the Conflict of Laws* (OUP, 1919) 118.

[14] Story, *Commentaries on the Conflict of Laws, Foreign and Domestic: In Regard to Contracts, Rights, and Remedies, and Especially in Regard to Marriages, Divorces, Wills, Successions, and Judgments*, 1st edn (Hilliard, Gray & Co, 1834) 103–04 §113.

[15] See, eg, *Scrimshire v Scrimshire* (n 13) 413, 789 (Sir Edward Simpson); *Middleton v Janverin* (1802) 2 Hag Con 437, 446–47, 448; 161 ER 797, 801 (Sir W Wynn), quoting *Butler v Freeman* (1756) Amb 301, 303; 27 ER 204, 205 (Lord Hardwicke LC); *Dalrymple v Dalrymple* (n 13) 59, 667 (Lord Stowell); *Ruding v Smith* (1821) 2 Hag Con 371, 390–91; 161 ER 774, 781 (Lord Stowell). The ecclesiastical courts possessed exclusive jurisdiction over marriage until the Matrimonial Causes Act 1857 transferred its jurisdiction to the new Court for Divorce and Matrimonial Causes.

[16] *Scrimshire v Scrimshire* (n 13).

[17] ibid 790.

[18] Hosack, *A Treatise on the Conflict of Laws of England and Scotland*, vol 1 (William Blackwood & Sons, 1847) 151.

[19] ibid 151.

validity of marriages with a foreign element.[20] The issue in *Warrender* – whether a Scottish court had jurisdiction to dissolve an English marriage – had vexed English and Scottish courts for decades. The English courts' position, expressed in *R v Lolley*, was that Scottish courts could not dissolve an English marriage.[21] In *Lolley*, Ann Sugden secured a divorce in Scotland against her Liverpool-based husband, William Lolley, on the grounds of adultery. When Lolley remarried in England, English law treated his second marriage as bigamous for which he was convicted of bigamy and sentenced to seven years' transportation. In effect, only the legal system in which the marriage contract originated (the *lex loci*) could dissolve it. This was a moot point: in England, judicial divorce was not possible until 1857.[22] Scottish courts were still prepared to grant divorces to English couples, provided that one party had some physical, usually temporary, connection with Scotland to ground jurisdiction.[23]

Invoking domicile in *Warrender* could reconcile these conflicting legal positions. The English marriage of Sir George Warrender and Anne Boscawen could be validly dissolved in Scotland because the husband's domicile throughout was Scottish.[24] In contrast, from the House of Lords' perspective, the earlier refusal in *Lolley* to recognise a Scottish divorce of an English marriage was explicable under English law. The wife, domiciled in England, had temporarily repaired to Scotland to establish jurisdiction.[25] Yet, in giving judgment in *Warrender*, Lord Brougham – counsel for the defendant in *Lolley* – addressed a larger question: would the English courts uphold the *lex loci* as the general rule for 'all personal contracts'[26] in matters affecting the 'essence' of the contract?[27] Whilst compliance with the forms and solemnities of the *lex loci* indicated intention to enter the contract, personal disqualifications and conditions precedent were of the essence, negating one's consent to make the contract.[28] Lord Brougham therefore thought that English courts would hesitate to uphold a foreign marriage between close relatives (eg, uncle and niece or brother and sister-in-law) validly celebrated and enforceable

[20] (1835) 2 Cl & Fin 488, 6 ER 1239.

[21] *R v Lolley* (1812) Russ & Ry 237, 168 ER 779. See also *M'Carthy v De Caix* (1831) 2 Cl & F 568, 6 ER 1268.

[22] Matrimonial Causes Act 1857 (20 & 21 Vict c 85).

[23] See, eg, *Duntze v Levett* [1811–17] Ferg 68; *Edmonstone v Lockhart* [1811–17] Ferg 168; *Butler v Forbes* [1811–17] Ferg 209; *Kibblewhite v Rowland* [1811–17] Ferg 226, cited in *Warrender v Warrender* (n 20) 555, 1263. See discussion in Leneman, *Alienated Affections: The Scottish Experience of Divorce and Separation, 1684–1830* (Edinburgh University Press, 1998) ch 11.

[24] Shelford, *A Practical Treatise of the Law of Marriage and Divorce; Containing Also the Mode of Proceeding on Divorces in the Ecclesiastical Courts and in Parliament; the Right to Custody of Children; Voluntary Separation Between Husband and Wife; the Husband's Liability to Wife's Debts; and the Conflict Between the Laws of England and Scotland Respecting Divorce and Legitimacy* (John S Littell, 1841) 465.

[25] ibid 477.

[26] *Warrender* (n 20) 529, 1254.

[27] ibid 532, 1255.

[28] ibid 531, 1255.

under the foreign *lex loci*.[29] The parties, being under a personal disqualification, could not consent to marry in the first place.

The parties' matrimonial domicile would regulate the incidents of marriage. The wife's argument in *Warrender* that indissolubility was essential to the marriage contract begged the question – by 'confound[ing] incidents with essence'.[30] In Lord Brougham's view, 'the contract and all its incidents, and the rights of the parties to it … *must be dealt with by the Courts of the country where the parties reside, and where the contract is to be carried into execution*'.[31] Where the parties' matrimonial domicile differed from their place of marriage, they would not have expected the *lex loci* to forever regulate the rights and obligations of their marriage.[32] The marriage contract was considered to be 'emphatically one which parties make with an immediate view to the usual place of their residence'.[33] The husband married in contemplation of the newlyweds' domicile – 'their home'[34] – under which law the incidents of marriage would be judged.[35]

Before *Brook*, neither the civilian preference for 'domicile'[36] nor evasion of the law had a major foothold in judging the validity of a foreign marriage which was, like all other contracts, determined by the *lex loci*.[37] In civilian jurisdictions, 'evasion and fraud upon the law of the country to which the parties *belong*' were recognised as limits to the place-of-celebration rule.[38] In contrast, English case law consistently upheld the validity of Scottish marriages 'contracted by English parties in the face and in fraud of the English law'.[39] In *Compton v Bearcroft*, the Court of Delegates upheld an evasive marriage solemnised in Scotland between an English couple.[40] While considered good by the *lex loci*, the marriage would not have satisfied the requirements of Lord Hardwicke's Act 1753 as applicable to England.[41] The underage bride – a ward of court – required her guardian's permission to marry. As Lord Brougham noted in *Warrender*, subsequent English courts were powerless to intervene against so-called Gretna Green marriages practised 'daily by the English people'.[42]

[29] ibid 531, 1255.
[30] ibid 533, 1255.
[31] ibid 533–34, 1255 (emphasis added).
[32] ibid 516, 1249. Lord Brougham considered this conclusion 'too absurd'.
[33] ibid 535, 1256.
[34] ibid 536, 1256.
[35] ibid 535–36,1256.
[36] *Conway v Beazley* (1831) 3 Hag Ecc 639, 652; 162 ER 1292, 1297 (Dr Lushington).
[37] Anonymous, *On the Present State of the Law as to Marriages Abroad Between English Subjects Within the Prohibited Degrees of Affinity* (E Spettigue, 1840) 18–19; Hosack, *A Treatise* (1847) 150.
[38] Shelford, *A Practical Treatise of the Law of Marriage and Divorce* (1841) 120 (emphasis added). See also Anonymous (n 37).
[39] *Warrender* (n 20) 542–43, 1258–59 (Lord Brougham), citing *Compton v Bearcroft* (1769) 2 Hag Con 444; *Ilderton v Ilderton* (1793) 2 H Bl 145, 126 ER 476. See also *Harford v Morris* (1776) 2 Hag Con 423, 161 ER 792; *Steele v Braddell* [1837] Milw 1, 32–35 (Ir).
[40] *Compton v Bearcroft* (n 39).
[41] Clandestine Marriages Act 1753 (26 Geo II c 33).
[42] *Warrender* (n 20) 542, 1259 (Lord Brougham).

Strict deference to the place of celebration, notwithstanding evidence of evasion, was also accepted elsewhere. In an 1819 decision, *Medway v Needham*, the Massachusetts Supreme Judicial Court validated an evasive, interracial marriage between two Massachusetts residents celebrated in the neighbouring province of Rhode Island, where the parties had temporarily gone to evade Massachusetts anti-miscegenation law.[43] Parker CJ emphasised the 'general convenience and security' of the *lex loci* principle 'even when it appears that the parties went to another state to evade the laws of their own country, the marriage in the foreign state shall nevertheless be valid in the country where the parties live'.[44]

A few English legal treatise writers, clearly inspired by civilian scholarship on evasion, signalled a break from the *lex loci*. In his *Commentaries on Colonial and Foreign Laws Generally* (1838), William Burge argued a position resembling the modern-day distinction between the formal and essential validity of marriage.[45] Using the civilian scholarship of Huber, Müller, Pothier and Paul Voet,[46] Burge insisted on the *lex domicilii*'s application in cases where:

> [T]he party retains his domicile in the country where the prohibitory law prevails, but quits it, and resorts to another country, for the single purpose of evading that law, and of doing that which the law of the latter country permits, or rather does not prohibit.[47]

Where parties have 'no *bonâ fide* domicile in *loco contractus*, but have resorted thither to evade a prohibitory law',[48] the personal incapacity of the *lex domicilii* continued to apply.[49] Contemporary Shelford made a similar argument.[50] These scholarly views were not, at that point, supported by English case law. Only from the late-1850s, however, did domicile become 'a most important and distinguishing feature' in English case law.[51] Domicile positioned marriage as more closely assimilated to status than contract, reinforcing the state's continued interest in the marriage of its domiciled subjects.[52]

iii. Exceptions to the Lex Loci

The possibility of exceptions to the place-of-celebration rule was foreseen in legal treatises and case law. Exceptions were canvassed in successive editions of Story's

[43] 16 Mass 157 (1819).
[44] ibid 159 (Parker CJ).
[45] Burge, *Commentaries on Colonial and Foreign Laws*, 1st edn (Saunders and Benning, 1838) vol 1, 199–200.
[46] ibid 190–92.
[47] ibid 191.
[48] ibid 200.
[49] ibid 192.
[50] Shelford (n 24) 119–20. After *Brook*, parental consent was recast as an issue of formal validity for the *lex loci*'s determination.
[51] *Conway v Beazley* (n 36) 652, 1297; Shelford (n 24) 480. This period coincides with Sir Cresswell Cresswell's appointment as the first judge ordinary of the Court for Divorce and Matrimonial Causes.
[52] See Taylor, 'Marriage, Work, and the Construction of the Family in Nineteenth-Century English Law and Legal Thought' (SJD thesis, University of Toronto 2019) 336, 340.

Conflict of Laws[53] and English private international law treatises, such as Hosack's *A Treatise on the Conflict of Laws of England and Scotland* (1847).[54] A selection of English and Scottish decisions, together with continental scholarship, shaped this discussion.[55] Story's three exceptions to the place-of-celebration rule, supported by continental scholarship as well as Anglo-American and Scottish case law, offered the groundwork for analysis.

The first exception – marriages violating natural law – captured polygamous and some incestuous marriages.[56] Only marriages deemed incestuous 'by the general consent of Christendom' qualified under this first category of exception.[57] Incest could result from a blood relationship (consanguinity), or a relationship created by marriage (affinity). Marriages between blood relatives 'in the lineal ascending or descending line' were 'unnatural and unlawful' according to 'the common, the canon, and the civil law'.[58] Conversely, prohibitions on affinity marriages had a less certain foundation by the law of nature and Christianity with considerable variation apparent between Christian states.[59] In Story's second edition (1841), a new English law prohibiting marriage to a deceased wife's sister (Lord Lyndhurst's Act 1835) – incest by affinity – was criticised for lacking 'Scriptural authority'.[60] In many American states and Protestant countries of Europe, Story noted, these marriages were not only civilly lawful but 'deemed in a moral, religious, and Christian sense lawful, and exceedingly praiseworthy'.[61] Leading nineteenth-century American treatise writers did not however present a united front on the legality of affinity marriages.[62]

Statutory public policy, applicable 'only to the subjects of a country', gave a second exception to the place-of-celebration rule.[63] For example, the now-repealed Royal Marriages Act 1772[64] rendered void marriages contracted by descendants of King George II without the monarch's consent and, in other cases, without giving 12 months' notice to the Privy Council.[65] Likewise, under the Napoleonic

[53] The first edition was published in 1834, followed by an 'enlarged' second edition in 1841.

[54] See especially Burge, *Commentaries on Colonial and Foreign Laws*, 1st edn (Saunders and Benning, 1838); Hosack (n 18) 142–43.

[55] See especially *Fenton v Livingstone* (1856) 18 D 865, 878 (Lord Curriehill) (IH); *Brook v Brook* (HL) (n 2); *Simonin v Mallac* (1860) 2 Sw & Tr 67; 164 ER 917.

[56] Story, '1st edn' (n 14) 104.

[57] ibid 104.

[58] ibid 105.

[59] ibid 104.

[60] Story, *Commentaries on the Conflict of Laws, Foreign and Domestic: In Regard to Contracts, Rights, and Remedies, and Especially in Regard to Marriages, Divorces, Wills, Successions, and Judgments* (2nd edn, Hilliard, Gray & Co, 1841) 180 ('2nd edn').

[61] Story, '2nd edn' (n 60) 180–81.

[62] See generally Fernandez, 'American Treatise Writers and the Nineteenth-Century Debate on Marriage with a Deceased Wife's Sister in Transatlantic Context' (2019) 59 *American Journal of Legal History* 324.

[63] Story, '1st edn' (n 14) 108.

[64] (12 Geo 3 c 11) ss 1, 2.

[65] Story, '1st edn' (n 14) 108.

Code, marriages validly celebrated by French subjects abroad could be avoided based on a pre-existing incapacity under French law.[66]

The third exception focused on marriages 'celebrated in foreign countries by subjects entitling themselves under special circumstances to the benefit of the laws of their own country'.[67] Under this exception, a marriage celebrated abroad was valid where compliance with local forms was impossible but the English common law requirements of marriage were met.[68] In *Ruding v Smith*, two British subjects were married at the Cape of Good Hope in 1795 authorised by a marriage licence issued by the commander-in-chief of the occupying British forces. Neither party had secured their parents' or guardians' consent to marry as required by the Cape's Dutch law.[69] The husband, arguing noncompliance with local forms, sought an annulment. Lord Stowell upheld the 'marriage of twenty-five years' standing noting the '*the insuperable difficulties of obtaining any marriage conformable to the Dutch law*'.[70] The third exception also took in marriages of English subjects solemnised in British factories abroad, including St Petersburg, Livorno (Leghorn), Aleppo, and İzmir (Smyrna).[71]

B. Closing Remarks

By the 1840s, English legal opinion was sharply divided on whether domestic prohibitions on affinal and consanguineous marriages travelled with British subjects choosing to solemnise their marriages abroad.[72] Some solicitors opined that the domestic prohibition operated as 'a personal disqualification between the parties which nothing can remove'.[73] Others thought that establishing a domicile in the *locus celebrationis* removed the disability. The sufficiency of the *lex loci* was asserted by others. These solicitors nevertheless agreed that it was a 'highly inexpedient' situation 'calculated to create doubts as to the legitimacy of children, to promote litigation among the nearest relatives, and to place the titles to numerous estates upon an insecure footing'.[74]

[66] ibid.

[67] ibid.

[68] ibid 109; *Ruding v Smith* (n 15). This is equivalent to the modern exception to the general rule that the *lex loci* determines the formal validity of a marriage.

[69] *Ruding v Smith* (n 15) 777 (Lord Stowell).

[70] ibid 782 (Lord Stowell) (emphasis added).

[71] Story, '1st edn' (n 14) 109–13.

[72] Hayward, *Remarks on the Law regarding Marriage with the Sister of a Deceased Wife* (W Benning & Co Law Booksellers, 1845) [9].

[73] ibid.

[74] ibid.

III. Litigation in *Brook*

A. The Case

The validity of a marriage solemnised abroad between a man and his deceased wife's sister, a Victorian *cause célèbre*, was central to the *Brook* litigation.

Between 1692 and 1835,[75] unions within prohibited degrees of consanguinity and affinity were challengeable in the ecclesiastical courts by suit of any interested party, but only during the lifetime of both parties to the marriage.[76] Once a party to the marriage died, the jurisdiction 'ceased'.[77] This practice changed in 1835 with the passage of Lord Lyndhurst's Act. Section 1 retrospectively validated marriages within the prohibited degrees celebrated before 31 August 1835. Section 2 rendered future marriages of this kind void. Under section 3, the statute did not apply to Scotland. The prohibited degrees of affinity and consanguinity were not defined in Lord Lyndhurst's Act; however, relationships within the Levitical degrees and those outlined in Archbishop Parker's Table of Kindred and Affinity (1563) were at the very least contemplated.[78] This included marriage with a deceased wife's sister.

In 1850, William Leigh Brook married his deceased wife's sister, Emily Armitage, at Wandsbek in the Duchy of Holstein.[79] The couple, British subjects domiciled in England at the time of the marriage and afterwards, had temporarily gone to the Duchy knowing they could legally marry there. Wandsbek and nearby Altona in the Duchy of Holstein were popular wedding destinations for well-to-do British couples seeking to evade the 1835 statute.[80] Theoretically, these kinds of marriages could take place abroad because Lord Lyndhurst's Act had, it was thought, no extraterritorial effect.[81] Critically, the Act never addressed the choice of law issues that would inevitably arise when English couples to whom the 1835 statute applied shopped for sympathetic wedding venues abroad.

Merely five years after their wedding, William and Emily were dead. While on a European holiday, they contracted cholera and died within two days of each other.

[75] See, for example, *Harris v Hicks* (1692) 2 Salk 548. See also Tolstoy, 'Void and Voidable Marriages' (1964) 27 *MLR* 385, 387.

[76] See Hosack (n 18) 122. For background, see Frew, 'Marriage to a Deceased Wife's Sister in Australia and England, 1835–1907' (PhD thesis, Macquarie University 2012); Frew, 'The Marriage to a Deceased Wife's Sister Narrative: A Comparison of Novels' (2012) 24 *Law and Literature* 265.

[77] *R v Dibdin* [1910] P 57 (CA) 108; Tolstoy, 'Void and Voidable Marriages' (1964) 387 fn 15.

[78] See Shelford, *A Practical Treatise of the Law of Marriage and Divorce* (John S Littell, 1841) 140.

[79] 'Charlotte Brook' (1847) West Yorkshire, England, Church of England Deaths and Burials, 1813–1985, West Yorkshire Archive Service, WDP167/1/2/6; 'Marriages' *The Hull Packet and East Riding Times* (Hull, 14 June 1850) 5.

[80] See a similar comment in Kuper, *Incest and Influence: The Private Life of Bourgeois England* (Harvard University Press, 2009) 69.

[81] *Brook v Brook* (1858) 3 Sm & G 481, 524–25; 65 ER 746, 765.

Just before his death on 19 September 1855, William executed a will by which he divided his real estate between his two sons and his personal property between his five children. An English clergyman, 'who happened to be present',[82] drafted the will mindful of the uncertain state of the second marriage and the legitimacy of its children. He described the second marriage's three children as the testator's 'reputed' children 'commonly so called'.[83] Less than a year later, the youngest child and only son of the second marriage died, setting in train the proceedings that followed.

B. The Vice-Chancellor's Court

During the administration of William Brook's will, a question arose as to the validity of Mr and the second Mrs Brook's marriage. In November 1857, the case was heard in the Vice-Chancellor's Court before Stuart V-C with a common law judge, Cresswell J, assisting.[84] Cresswell J delivered his opinion,[85] with which Stuart V-C agreed, that the second marriage was void and the children of that marriage were illegitimate. The deceased child's share in his father's estate escheated to the Crown. Cresswell J's opinion and the Vice-Chancellor's concurring judgment responded to two questions. The subject of the first question was the statutory construction of Lord Lyndhurst's Act 1835.[86] The second question was whether the *lex loci* – the law of Holstein – continued to govern the validity of the Brooks' marriage.[87]

In answer to the first question, both judges were agreed that Lord Lyndhurst's Act was a personal statute prohibiting all British subjects wherever they may be from contracting a marriage in violation of the statute.[88] Section 2 of Lord Lyndhurst's Act provided that '*all* marriages which shall hereafter be celebrated between persons within the prohibited degrees of consanguinity or affinity shall be absolutely null and void to all intents and purposes whatsoever'.[89] In their 'common and ordinary sense', those words were meant to cover 'marriages wherever celebrated; otherwise some only and not all would be rendered void'.[90] The statutory prohibition 'would attach upon the persons of British subjects, and accompany them to all parts of the world'.[91] Lord Lyndhurst's Act had 'a personal

[82] '*Brook v Brook* – Marriage with a Deceased Wife's Sister' *London Evening Standard* (17 March 1857) 1.
[83] Will of William Leigh Brook, 1–2.
[84] Court of Chancery Act 1851 (14 & 15 Vict c 83), s 8. Interestingly, Cresswell J was appointed the first judge-in-ordinary of the Court for Divorce and Matrimonial Courts. The Matrimonial Causes Act 1857 (20 & 21 Vict c 85) commenced on 1 January 1858 with Cresswell J's appointment commencing on 11 January 1858.
[85] Court of Chancery Act 1851 (14 & 15 Vict c 83), s 8.
[86] *Brook v Brook* (1858) (n 81) 511, 759 (Cresswell J); 525, 765 (Stuart V-C).
[87] ibid 766 (Stuart V-C).
[88] ibid 523, 764 (Cresswell J); 525, 765, 527, 766 (Stuart V-C).
[89] Quoted in ibid 522, 764 (Cresswell J) (emphasis added).
[90] ibid 522, 764 (Cresswell J).
[91] ibid.

quality which, according to Huber and other jurists, travels round everywhere with the persons; inseparable from them as their shadows'.[92] The House of Lords' 1844 decision in the *Sussex Peerage Case* lent further support to this construction.[93]

In the *Sussex Peerage Case*, Sir Augustus d'Este's claim to the dukedom of Sussex depended on the validity of his parents' marriage. Prince Augustus Frederick, George III's sixth son and the first Duke of Sussex, had twice married Lady Augusta Murray in 1793 without his father's knowledge or consent. Augustus d'Este, born in 1794, was their eldest child and only son. The Royal Marriages Act 1772 prohibited descendants of George II from marrying 'without the previous consent of his Majesty, his heirs or successors'.[94] The House of Lords found the marriage void, concluding that the Royal Marriages Act included 'all marriages, in whatever part of the world they may have been contracted or celebrated'.[95] Tindal CJ, delivering the Lords' opinion, noted that the statute was

> free from ambiguity. The prohibitory words of it are general … The statute does not enact an incapacity to contract matrimony within one particular country and district or another, but to contract matrimony generally and in the abstract. It is an incapacity attaching itself to the person of A B, which he carries with him wherever he goes.[96]

Likewise, the prohibition in Lord Lyndhurst's Act was not geographically limited; it applied to future marriages 'between English subjects' within the prohibited degrees.[97]

As to the second question, public policy excluded the place-of-celebration rule.[98] Conflicts scholars agreed that public policy formed 'an exception from the principle of comity and respect due to foreign laws'.[99] For Stuart V-C, the statutory prohibition on marriage to a deceased wife's sister was 'an integral part of our law and public policy'.[100] Lord Lyndhurst's Act had mandatory effect: its prohibitions could not 'be evaded by having resort to the laws of any foreign country'.[101] Cresswell J acknowledged the place-of-celebration rule as a general principle, but believed that exceptions applied to this case.[102] Under English law, marriage to a deceased wife's sister was 'prohibited by Holy Scripture, … within the degrees of affinity prohibited by God's law, and punishable as incestuous'.[103] The Brooks'

[92] ibid 527; 766 (Stuart V-C).
[93] ibid. See *Sussex Peerage Case* (1844) 11 Cl & F 85, 8 ER 1034.
[94] Royal Marriages Act 1772 (12 Geo 3 c 11), s 2, quoted in *Brook v Brook* (1858) (n 81) 522, 764 (Cresswell J).
[95] *Sussex Peerage Case* (n 93) 144, 1057 (Tindal CJ), quoted in *Brook v Brook* (1858) (n 81) 523, 764 (Cresswell J).
[96] ibid.
[97] *Brook v Brook* (1858) (n 81) 523, 764 (Cresswell J); 525–26, 765 (Stuart V-C).
[98] ibid 531, 767 (Stuart V-C).
[99] ibid.
[100] ibid 531, 768.
[101] ibid.
[102] ibid 513; 760 (Cresswell J).
[103] ibid.

marriage was captured by 'the exceptions stated in Story (Conflict of Laws, s 113), and not to be recognised in this Christian country'.[104]

Story's first exception on incest 'by the general consent of Christendom' was criticised, but nevertheless applied, by Cresswell J. The appropriate role of English judges lay at the heart of Cresswell J's criticism. This criticism, repeated in the appeal to the House of Lords,[105] underscored the practical problem of discerning the legal positions of different countries on incestuous marriage when 'the law of his own country has already settled what is incestuous or the contrary'.[106] A domiciled Englishman, cohabiting with his deceased wife's sister, could not simply 'by taking a short voyage to Denmark [ie, Holstein], and celebrating a marriage there, … acquire the privilege of returning to this country and maintaining an intercourse by our law deemed incestuous, with perfect impunity'.[107] What was voidable before 'was absolutely void to all intents and purposes' after Lord Lyndhurst's Act.[108] The Brook siblings appealed to the House of Lords.

C. The House of Lords

Delivering judgment in March 1861, the House of Lords affirmed the Vice-Chancellor's decree. Four grounds for decision are discernible from the concurring speeches of Lord Campbell LC, Lord Cranworth, Lord St Leonards, and Lord Wensleydale. Despite *Brook*'s four speeches, Lord Campbell LC's leading speech has attracted the most judicial and scholarly attention,[109] inspiring the two choice of law rules outlined in the Introduction.

i. *Ground 1: A Personal Statute*

The first reason for decision, which had been advanced by Cresswell J and Stuart V-C in the court below, was that Lord Lyndhurst's Act was a personal statute binding British subjects worldwide. In the House of Lords, only Lord St Leonards supported this ground.[110] For Lord St Leonards, the issue was 'purely an English question' that 'depends wholly upon our own laws, binding upon all the Queen's subjects'.[111] As Mr and Mrs Brook were British subjects and domiciled in England, they were bound by English law. Lord Lyndhurst's Act had made 'general

[104] ibid.
[105] See, for example, *Brook v Brook* (HL) (n 2) 209–10, 710 (Lord Campbell LC); 723–24 (Lord Wensleydale).
[106] *Brook v Brook* (1858) (n 81) 513, 760 (Sir John Stuart V-C).
[107] ibid 514 (Cresswell J).
[108] ibid.
[109] See Sawer, 'Conflict of Laws – Essential Validity of Marriage' (1939–41) 2 *Res Judicatae* 125, 127–28.
[110] *Brook v Brook* (HL) (n 2) 234–28, 719–21 (Lord St Leonards).
[111] ibid 230, 718.

and unqualified' use of the words '*all* marriages', demonstrating that the legislature meant to render '*all* such marriages … null and void'.[112] The House of Lords' decision in the *Sussex Peerage Case* on the Royal Marriages Act's interpretation strengthened his conclusion that the marriage was void.[113] The Royal Marriages Act and Lord Lyndhurst's Act were not 'exactly alike'; however, they 'have the same object, viz, the annulling and rendering void a marriage contract contrary to their provisions'.[114]

Lord Campbell, Lord Cranworth and Lord Wensleydale roundly rejected this personal construction of Lord Lyndhurst's Act.[115] This interpretation was, according to Lord Campbell and Lord Wensleydale respectively, 'incorrect' and 'wrong'.[116] For Lord Campbell, the 1835 statute did not fix a personal incapacity 'on all Englishmen … all over the world' nor did it affect 'the law of marriage in any conquered colony in which a different law of marriage prevailed'.[117] Lord Cranworth limited the application of Lord Lyndhurst's Act to 'the inhabitants of Great Britain and Ireland'.[118] The statute did not 'operate throughout all our colonies, and on all who owe allegiance to the British Crown wheresoever they may be'.[119]

ii. Ground 2: Incestuous Marriage

The second reason, 'suggested by Mr Justice Cresswell and Lord Wensleydale only',[120] was that the place-of-celebration rule was subject to Story's first exception involving polygamous and incestuous marriage.[121] Lord Wensleydale agreed that the incest and public policy exceptions were engaged; however, he also sought to make the Christendom qualification in Story's first exception 'unobjectionable'.[122] He argued that 'it is by no means improbable, that Story's meaning was to apply his first exception only to those cases to which the second could not apply … to those cases, namely, in which there was no particular law in the country of the domicile of the parties to such marriage'.[123] In *Commonwealth v Lane*, Gray CJ of the Massachusetts Supreme Judicial Court pointed out that this interpretation was contrary 'to all the American authorities'.[124]

[112] ibid 235–36, 719.
[113] ibid 235–38, 720–21.
[114] ibid 238, 721.
[115] ibid 214, 712 (Lord Campbell LC), 222, 715 (Lord Cranworth), 240, 722 (Lord Wensleydale).
[116] ibid 214, 712 (Lord Campbell LC); 240, 722 (Lord Wensleydale).
[117] ibid 214, 712 (Lord Campbell LC).
[118] ibid 222, 715 (Lord Cranworth).
[119] ibid.
[120] *Commonwealth v Lane*, 113 Mass 458, 469 (1873).
[121] *Brook v Brook* (HL) (n 2) 241–42, 722–23 (Lord Wensleydale).
[122] ibid.
[123] ibid 242, 722–23.
[124] *Commonwealth v Lane* (n 120) 469.

iii. Ground 3: Against God's Law

The third ground for decision, agreed by all Law Lords, was that Parliament proscribed marriages within the prohibited degrees of consanguinity and affinity as 'contrary to God's law'.[125] For Lord Campbell, the decision depended on whether the marriage was illegal, and could have been annulled in the ecclesiastical courts during Mr and Mrs Brook's lifetime, before the passage of Lord Lyndhurst's Act.[126] The answer was yes: 'Such a marriage was expressly prohibited by the legislature of this country, and was prohibited expressly on the ground that it was "contrary to God's law"'.[127] Lord Lyndhurst's Act ensured that future marriages within the prohibited degrees, previously voidable in the ecclesiastical courts, were void.[128]

Lord Cranworth agreed. Before 1835, the ecclesiastical courts had jurisdiction to determine the validity of a foreign marriage.[129] Brooks' marriage was prohibited under English legislation 'on the grounds of it being contrary to God's law'.[130] English law would only 'interfere with or regulate the marriages of … those who are subject to its jurisdiction', which certainly covered Mr and Mrs Brook.[131] The general rule in favour of the *lex loci* applied with one qualification: 'that such marriages are not contrary to the laws of the land to which the parties contracting them *belong*'.[132] The marriage, prohibited 'wheresoever celebrated' under various Henrician statutes, was rendered 'absolutely void' by Lord Lyndhurst's Act.[133]

Lord St Leonards concurred that the marriage was void 'upon the rule that we do not admit any foreign law to be of force here, where it is opposed to God's law, according to our view of that law'.[134] In accordance with Henrician-era statutes, marriage to a deceased wife's sister was 'plainly prohibited and detested by the laws of God'.[135] English statute, assimilating cases of consanguinity and affinity, had 'already declared' such marriage to be 'against God's law' – 'and we must obey the law'.[136] For Lord Wensleydale, the marriage was 'prejudicial to our social interest and of hateful example',[137] being 'forbidden in this country on the ground of its being against the law of God deduced from Holy Scripture'.[138]

[125] *Brook v Brook* (HL) (n 2) 206, 709, 214, 712, 215, 712 (Lord Campbell); 225, 716 (Lord Cranworth).
[126] ibid 206 (Lord Campbell).
[127] ibid.
[128] ibid.
[129] ibid 223, 715 (Lord Cranworth).
[130] ibid 226, 717.
[131] ibid.
[132] ibid 226–27, 717 (emphasis added).
[133] ibid 229–30, 718.
[134] ibid 231, 718.
[135] ibid 233, 719 (Lord St Leonards).
[136] ibid.
[137] ibid 245, 724 (Lord Wensleydale).
[138] ibid 243, 723.

iv. Ground 4: Formal and Essential Validity

A two-pronged choice of law rule – the orthodox interpretation of *Brook* – is the fourth possible ground for decision.[139] This rule, suggested in Lord Campbell's speech, refers the formalities required to enter marriage (formal validity) to the *lex loci* and the essentials (essential validity) to 'the *lex domicilii*, the law of the country in which the parties are domiciled at the time of the marriage, and in which the matrimonial residence is contemplated'.[140] Lord Cranworth agreed: while the *lex loci* governed the solemnities of the marriage contract, 'no law but our own can decide whether the contract is or is not one in which the parties to it, being subjects of Her Majesty domiciled in this country, might lawfully make'.[141]

The distinction drawn by Lord Campbell in this passage is complicated by its lack of scholarly support. Relying on 'the writings of many eminent jurists who have discussed the subject',[142] Lord Campbell quoted from the third axiom of Ulrik Huber's *De Conflictu Legum* and sections 113 and 114 of Story's *Conflict of Laws*.[143] Huber's third axiom, translated into English from its original Latin, reads:

> Sovereigns will so act by way of comity that rights acquired within the limits of a government retain their force everywhere *so far as they do not cause prejudice* to the power or rights of such government or of its subjects.[144]

Huber referred the validity of marriage to the *lex loci* 'with the reservation that its example is not too revolting – for example … an incestuous marriage'.[145] The words 'prejudice' and 'revolting' give every indication of Huber's limitation being a traditional public policy exception.

Lord Campbell's subsequent discussion of the law set out in Story's *Conflict of Laws* confirmed that the *lex loci* was subject to three exceptions.[146] While Lord Campbell rejected Story's incest exception – 'What means am I to resort to for the purpose of ascertaining the opinions of foreign nations?'[147] – he thought the *Brook* case clearly fell within Story's second exception of 'marriages positively prohibited by the public law of a country, from motives of policy'.[148]

[139] See, for example, Fentiman, 'The Validity of Marriage' (1985); Adams, 'Same-Sex Relationships and Anglo-Canadian Choice of Law' (1996) 110–15.
[140] *Brook v Brook* (HL) (n 2) 207, 709 (Lord Campbell).
[141] ibid 224, 715–16 (Lord Cranworth).
[142] ibid 208, 709 (Lord Campbell).
[143] ibid 208–09, 709-10 (Lord Campbell).
[144] ibid 208, 709. For the leading Latin–English translation of Huber's *De Conflictu Legum* from which this translation is drawn, see Lorenzen, 'Huber's *De Conflictu Legum*' (1918–19) 13 *Illinois Law Review* 374 (emphasis added).
[145] *Brook v Brook* (HL) (n 2) 208, 709 (Lord Campbell).
[146] ibid 209, 710.
[147] ibid.
[148] ibid.

D. Concluding Remarks: The Ratio

The previous section identified four grounds upon which the House of Lords decided that the Brooks' marriage was void. Of the four grounds, only the third ground was accepted by all Law Lords. That is, English statute proscribed marriages within the prohibited degrees of consanguinity and affinity, having declared these unions to be against God's law. Lord Lyndhurst's Act applied only to those subject to English law's jurisdiction. The statutory prohibition found in the parties' *lex domicilii* evinced a fundamental public policy, binding British subjects resident in England and Ireland. Lord Lyndhurst's Act itself reflected a fundamental English policy, grounded in Scripture, regulating the marriage of closely related couples. Using modern conflicts language, the statute had mandatory effect. The Wandsbek marriage was not sufficient to place Mr and Mrs Brook – British subjects resident and domiciled in England before and after the marriage – beyond the reach of English law.

And yet this is not the view of *Brook* that has prevailed: the distinction between formal and essential validity, advanced by Lord Campbell and supported by Lord Cranworth, has. One reason for that may be the prominence attached to the distinction in Clark and Finnelly's headnote of the House of Lords case, beginning with:

> The forms of entering into the contract of marriage are regulated by the *lex loci contractus*, the essentials of the contract depend upon the *lex domicilii*. If the latter are contrary to the law of the domicile, the marriage (though duly solemnised elsewhere) is there void.[149]

IV. After *Brook*: The Law Applicable to Foreign Marriages

The form-capacity distinction suggested to have emerged in *Brook* lay dormant in English courts for a decade. First applied in the 1874 decision of *Re Alison's Trusts*,[150] the rule invalidated a marriage solemnised at Tehran between a British subject and an Armenian woman, Vardine Rafael. Pregnancy prohibited Miss Rafael from marrying in the Armenian Church, so the parties were wed in a Roman Catholic ceremony. Because neither party was Catholic, the marriage was not lawfully solemnised in accordance with the law of the Roman Catholic Church. The marriage was invalid: neither the local form nor the religious law of Miss Rafael had been satisfied. Malins V-C explained that the ceremony of marriage is 'determined by the law of the country where it has been celebrated, in the absence of any incapacity in either part'.[151]

[149] ibid 193, 704.
[150] (1874) 31 LT 638.
[151] *Re Alison's Trusts* (n 150) 640. Malins V-C was counsel for the plaintiffs in *Brook*.

An inability to contend with separate premarital domiciles seems to have settled the bifurcated choice of law rule in marriage, as demonstrated by the *Sottomayor v De Barros* litigation of the late 1870s.[152] The three decisions in *Sottomayor* promoted two unwieldly rules for marriage choice of law.[153] For traditional conflicts writers, the Court of Appeal's decision in *Sottomayor v De Barros (No 1)* demanded a bifurcated choice of law rule for marriage, requiring consideration of formal and essential validity.[154] Despite the Court of Appeal's assertion that this two-pronged rule was 'well-recognised',[155] only Lord Campbell and Lord Cranworth's speeches in *Brook* provided support for this view. The rule in *Sottomayer v De Barros (No 2)* is the second rule, which applies as an exception to the dual domicile theory. Kahn-Freund argued that it was 'a crystallised rule of public policy',[156] because its use inevitably leads to forum law being applied.[157]

The *Sottomayor* litigation concerned the validity of an 1866 marriage celebrated in England between first cousins of Portuguese extraction, Ignacia Sottomayor and Gonçalo de Barros. Ignacia petitioned for an annulment, arguing that her domicile of dependence at the time of marriage, Portugal, prohibited the marriage of first cousins unless papal dispensation was obtained. Dispensation was not obtained. At first instance, Sir Robert Phillimore upheld the marriage.[158] The Court of Appeal reversed the first instance decision in *Sottomayor v De Barros (No 1)*, remitting the matter to the Probate, Divorce and Admiralty Division to determine questions of fact. On the remittal reported as *Sottomayer v De Barros (No 2)*, Sir James Hannen P upheld the marriage. New evidence of the parties' respective antenuptial domiciles was central to these different outcomes.

In *Sottomayor v De Barros (No 1)*, the parties were assumed to have had a common Portuguese domicile at the time of marriage. The first instance judge, Sir Robert Phillimore, concluded that the *forum celebrationis* was not 'bound to recognize the incapacities affixed by the law of the domicile on the parties

[152] *Sottomayor v De Barros* (1877) 2 PD 81 (PDA) 86–87 ('*Sottomayor* (PDA)'); *Sottomayor (No 1)* (n 9) 5–6; *Sottomayer v De Barros (No 2)* (1879) 5 PD 94 (PDA) ('*Sottomayer (No 2)*'). See also Davis, 'The Marriage Amendment Act 1985 – The Reason Why' (1987) 11 *Adelaide Law Review* 32, 53. Unfortunately, the law reports were not consistent in the spelling of Sottomayor's name. So, when referring to the litigation as a whole, I use 'Sottomayor'. In discussing the rule in *Sottomayer (No 2)*, I revert to the law report's spelling of 'Sottomayer'.

[153] See, eg, Morris (ed), *Dicey's Conflict of Laws*, 6th edn (Stevens and Sons, 1949) 758 r 168, 784 (exception 1). See also Graveson, 'Matrimonial Domicile and the Contract of Marriage' (1938) 20 *Journal of Comparative Legislation and International Law* 55, 65; Sawer, 'Conflict of Laws' (1939–41) 126. *cf* Sykes, 'The Essential Validity of Marriage' (1955) 4 *ICLQ* 159, 161.

[154] See, for example, Sawer (n 109) 126; Graveson, 'Matrimonial Domicile' (1938) 65; Sykes, 'Capacity and the Conflict of Laws' (1950) 1 *University of Western Australia Annual Law Review* 266, 268–69.

[155] *Sottomayor (No 1)* (n 9) 5. *cf Sottomayer (No 2)* (n 152) 100.

[156] Kahn-Freund, 'Reflections on Public Policy in the English Conflict of Laws' (1953) 39 *Grotius Society* 39, 53, 55.

[157] ibid. See comment about it creating 'an ungainly exception to the dual domicile theory', here: Smart, 'Interest Analysis, False Conflicts, and the Essential Validity of Marriage' (1985) 14 *Anglo-American Law Review* 225, 229.

[158] *Sottomayor* (PDA) (n 152).

to the contract, when those incapacities do not exist according to the *lex loci contractus*'.[159] The marriage was not void because the law of Portugal considered the union incestuous; nor was the union, in light of Story's *Conflict of Laws*, 'incestuous according to the general consent of Christendom'.[160] This is an orthodox interpretation of the *lex loci* as the governing law. On appeal, this decision was reversed.[161] The Court of Appeal determined that the parties' personal law – the law of their common domicile of Portugal – governed the essential validity of marriage. Cotton LJ pronounced that 'it is a well-recognised principle of law that the question of personal capacity to enter into any contract is to be decided by the law of domicile'.[162] As the *lex domicilii* governed essential validity, the marriage was invalid because the parties' common domicile considered it incestuous.[163] In doing so, on the analysis outlined earlier, the Court of Appeal misconstrued *Brook*. The House of Lords' decision depended on the mandatory application of an English statute on British subjects resident and domiciled in England and Ireland. Instead, the Court of Appeal imported domicile as a connecting factor in all circumstances of capacity.

By the time of the decision in *Sottomayer v De Barros (No 2)*, newly adduced evidence suggested that the husband had an English domicile at the time of marriage. The incapacity under Portuguese law only affected the wife. Despite the Court of Appeal's pronouncement on personal capacity, Hannen P referred the validity of the marriage to the *lex loci* and upheld the marriage.[164] The earlier Court of Appeal decision was not applied because it was, in the language of the Court of Appeal, 'confined to the case where both the contracting parties are at the time of their marriage domiciled in a country the laws of which prohibit their marriage'.[165]

To this end, Hannen P bridled at the proposition advanced by the Court of Appeal that the law of domicile governed personal capacity to marry.[166] His Lordship observed:[167]

> [T]he doctrine thus laid down has not hitherto been 'well recognised.' On the contrary, it appears to me to be a novel principle, for which up to the present time there has been no English authority. What authority there is seems to me to be the other way.

The Court of Appeal's decision 'has only been to define a further condition imposed by English Law, namely, that the parties do not both belong by domicil to a country the laws of which prohibit their marriage'.[168] The case before Hannen P was

[159] ibid 87.
[160] ibid 86.
[161] *Sottomayor (No 1)* (n 9).
[162] ibid 5 (Cotton LJ).
[163] ibid 5–6.
[164] *Sottomayer (No 2)* (n 152) 104. See also Morris (ed), *Dicey's Conflict of Laws*, 7th edn (Stevens and Sons, 1958) 264 fn 41; Collins et al (n 1) [17–061].
[165] ibid 99–100.
[166] ibid 100.
[167] ibid.
[168] ibid 101.

distinguishable because it involved 'the marriage of a British subject in England, where the marriage is lawful, with a person domiciled in a country where marriage is prohibited'.[169] Accordingly, Hannen P felt that the authorities, which referred the question of validity to the *lex loci*, 'remain[ed] with undiminished effect'.[170]

The rule that emerged from *Sottomayer v De Barros (No 2)* effectively validated any marriage lawfully celebrated in England between a person domiciled in England and a person with a foreign domicile, whose law imposes an incapacity unknown to English law.[171] The High Court of Australia in *Miller v Teale* hesitantly accepted the rule, but only where 'a specified consent or consents' would remove the incapacity.[172] The rule's bias towards the forum has led to its criticism as 'anomalous', 'illogical', 'xenophobic', and 'unfortunate'.[173] It emerged not because Hannen P misapprehended the Court of Appeal's form-capacity distinction,[174] but rather because he took issue with the claim that the distinction was 'well-established'. The law on capacity to marry that was subsequently to develop would have seen the marriage in *Sottomayer* invalidated.[175]

English law is not entirely free from doubt on the theory courts are to apply for questions of capacity to marry.[176] Case law on essential validity is sparse. Conventional wisdom has it that Lord Campbell's speech in *Brook* suggested two choice of law rules for capacity to marry: the dual domicile theory and – but only incidentally[177] – the intended matrimonial home theory.[178] While the weight of common law authority supports the dual domicile theory,[179] in some English case law capacity to marry has depended upon nationality,[180] the intended matrimonial home theory,[181] and the real and substantial connection test.[182] The tendency

[169] ibid.
[170] ibid 102.
[171] ibid 105.
[172] For the High Court of Australia's statement of the rule in these terms, see: *Miller v Teale* (1954) 92 *CLR* 406, 414 (Dixon CJ, McTiernan, Fullagar and Taylor JJ).
[173] See Clarkson, 'Marriage in England: Favouring the *Lex Fori*' (1990) 10 *Legal Studies* 80, 85 (and sources cited therein); Collins et al (n 1).
[174] Collins et al (n 1) [17–061].
[175] See, eg, *Re Paine* (n 11) 49.
[176] Law Commission, 'Private International Law: Choice of Law Rules in Marriage' Law Com No 89 (1985) para 3.3.
[177] Sawer (n 109) 127. Sawer describes Lord Campbell's reference to the intended matrimonial home as 'merely argumentative': at 127.
[178] *Brook v Brook* (n 1) 207, 709 (emphasis added): 'the essentials of the contract depend upon the *lex domicilii*, the law of the country in which the parties are domiciled at the time of the marriage, *and in which the matrimonial residence is contemplated*'.
[179] (n 5) and the cases therein set out.
[180] *Mette v Mette* (1859) 1 Sw & Tr 416, 164 ER 792. Born in Hesse-Kassel, the deceased was a naturalised British subject who had married his deceased wife's sister in Germany with whom he had several children. Sir Cresswell Cresswell held that the second marriage was in contravention of s 5 of Lord Lyndhurst's Act to which the deceased 'as a natural liege subject, owed obedience': at 796. This decision was however handed down before the House of Lords' decision in *Brook*.
[181] *Radwan v Radwan (No 2)* (n 12) 953–54.
[182] *Vervaeke v Smith* [1983] 1 AC 145 (HL) 164–66 (Lord Simon); *Lawrence v Lawrence* [1985] 2 WLR 86 (Fam D) 91. See discussion in *Westminster City Council v C* [2008] EWCA Civ 198, [2009] 2 WLR 185.

of the dual domicile theory to invalidate a marriage spawned these alternative validating tests. Several statutory provisions nonetheless give force to the idea that the law of a person's pre-nuptial domicile governs questions of capacity.[183]

Despite some initial scholarly reservations, the bifurcated rule set out in *Sottomayer* has become entrenched in scholarly portrayals of marriage choice of law doctrine. Writing before the House of Lords' decision in 1861, Westlake in the first edition of his *Treatise on Private International Law* (1858) regretted how the certainty of the *lex loci* had yielded to the uncertainty of domicile thanks to the 'dangerous example' of marriage with a deceased wife's sister.[184] He deprecated the failure of the first instance decision in *Brook* to clarify 'whether it is on domicile or allegiance that the binding force of the British marriage laws is in future to rest'.[185] From the revised first edition (1880) until the sixth and final edition (1922), Westlake's *Private International Law* asserted that the *lex loci* governed formal and essential validity.[186] But, in addition, 'the personal law of each party be satisfied so far as regards his capacity to contract it, whether absolute, in respect of age, or relative, in respect of the prohibited degrees of consanguinity or affinity'.[187]

The first edition of Dicey's *Conflict of Laws* (1896) maintained that marital validity depended on the parties' capacity to marry and the form of celebration.[188] Capacity was to be governed by 'the law of a person's domicil'.[189] In Dicey's second edition (1908), the marriage choice of law rule (rule 172) and its accompanying commentary were rewritten to remove any doubt about the rule's two elements. This outline remained consistent from the second (1908) to the fifth edition (1932) with few changes made to case law.[190] For essential validity, '*each* of the parties' had to have capacity to marry the other 'according to the law of his or her respective domicil'.[191] The rule applied whether the parties 'belong to the same country or

[183] Marriage (Enabling) Act 1960, s 1(3); Matrimonial Causes Act 1973, s 11(d); Marriage (Scotland) Act 1977, ss 1(1), 2(1)(b), (3)(a), 5(4)(f); Family Law (Scotland) Act 2006, s 38(2), (4).

[184] Westlake, *Treatise on Private International Law, or the Conflict of Laws, with Principal Reference to its Practice in the English and Other Cognate Systems of Jurisprudence* (W Maxwell, 1858) 323.

[185] Westlake (n 184) 323.

[186] Westlake, *Treatise on Private International Law, with Principal Reference to its Practice in England*, 1st edn rev (William Maxwell & Son, 1880) 52 §13, 53 §14, 53 §15 ('Revised 1st edn'); Westlake, *Treatise on Private International Law, with Principal Reference to its Practice in England*, 3rd edn (Sweet and Maxwell, 1890) 55 §17, 56 §18, 56 §19, 57 §21; Westlake and Bentwich, *A Treatise on Private International Law, with Principal Reference to its Practice in England*, 6th edn (Sweet and Maxwell, 1922) 57 §19, 57 §20.

[187] Westlake, 'Revised 1st edn' (n 186) 54; Westlake, '6th edn' (n 186) 57 §21.

[188] Dicey, *Digest of the Law of England with Reference to the Conflict of Laws*, 1st edn (Stevens and Sons Ltd, 1896) 642.

[189] Dicey (n 188) 642.

[190] See Dicey and Keith, *Digest of the Law of England with Reference to the Conflict of Laws*, 3rd edn (Stevens and Sons, 1922) 661–65; Dicey and Keith, *Digest of the Law of England with Reference to the Conflict of Laws*, 4th edn (Stevens and Sons, 1927) 686–91; Dicey and Keith, *Digest of the Law of England with Reference to the Conflict of Laws*, 5th edn (Stevens and Sons, 1932) 732–37.

[191] Dicey, '2nd edn' (1908) 613.

to different countries'.[192] As to formal validity, the marriage had to comply with 'any one of the following conditions', including marriage in accordance with local forms.[193]

V. Conclusion

This chapter used the House of Lords' landmark decision in *Brook* as a focal point to chronicle the early development of English choice of law rules for marriage. Before *Brook*, the validity of a foreign marriage depended exclusively on the *lex loci*. The marriage contract was treated like any other personal contract. When well-to-do British couples started to evade domestic law by marrying abroad, it raised uneasy questions about their validity and supplied no easy answers. Lawyers offered conflicting opinions. While English case law seemed to suggest the *lex loci* was alone sufficient, contemporary legal treatises proposed exceptions that remained untested before English courts until *Brook*.

By examining the Vice-Chancellor's Court judgments and the four speeches comprising the House of Lords' decision, this chapter has argued against the orthodox interpretation of *Brook*. It contended that the House of Lords preserved the *lex loci* as determinative of essential validity except where a prohibition contained in the parties' *lex domicilii* is construed to have mandatory effect. The late Mr and Mrs Brook were captured by the prohibition in Lord Lyndhurst's Act, which manifested a fundamental forum policy: it was against God's law (as that was defined by statute) for a man to marry his deceased wife's sister.[194] The subsequent Court of Appeal decision in *Sottomayor (No 1)* arguably misread *Brook*, first, by holding that a foreign marriage's validity depended on satisfying formal and essential validity and, secondly, by importing domicile as a relevant connecting factor for essential validity. The introduction of domicile reinforced the state's continued interest in marital affairs.

The two-pronged choice of law rule suggested to have emerged from the House of Lords' decision in *Brook* is now well-established in the common law jurisprudence of the conflict of laws. The rule has not been without problems. These problems have centred on the applicable choice of law rule governing essential validity. Formal validity is a more straightforward question to answer. While the invalidating tendency of the dual domicile theory has encouraged the development of alternative validating tests, neither the intended matrimonial home theory nor the real and substantial connection test commands any real support outside

[192] ibid 615.
[193] ibid 613.
[194] The posthumous invalidation of Mr and the second Mrs Brook's marriage had devastating effects on their children. The children of the second marriage were considered illegitimate and prevented from inheriting any of their father's substantial estate.

English case law. The passage of just over 160 years has not freed the common law from uncertainty: English law remains wedded to the bifurcated choice of law rule for marriage.

Complications with this rule were bound to emerge when couples' prenuptial domiciles diverged.[195] The common law's fragmentation prompted international efforts to simplify the private international law of marriage. The resulting Hague Convention on Celebration and Recognition of the Validity of Marriage 1978, which restores the *lex loci* as determinative of marriage validity,[196] has not been a success. Of the three countries to have entered it into force, only one – Australia – is a common law country following the authority of *Brook*.[197] One way forward for England and common law countries abiding by the authority of *Brook* may be to follow Australia's example and adopt a position reflecting that of the 1978 Hague Marriage Convention.

[195] See esp *Sottomayer (No 2)* (n 152).

[196] See Fisher, 'The Australian Adoption of the Hague Convention on Celebration and Recognition of the Validity of Marriages' (1986) 2 *Queensland Institute of Technology Law Journal* 17, 18; Davis, 'The Marriage Amendment Act 1985' (1987) 2 *Adelaide Law Review* 32 fn 4.

[197] Part VA of Australia's Marriage Act 1961 gives effect to the Hague Marriage Convention.

2

The Mixed Blessing of *Vita Food Products*: The Impact and Influence of the Privy Council's Decision

HELEN MORTON

I. Introduction

Vita Food Products Inc v Unus Shipping Co Ltd (In Liquidation)[1] has had mixed reviews. On the one hand, it is a beacon for party autonomy for (i) express choice of law and (ii) the validity of a contract according to the law of the forum despite its illegality under the law of another place, with modern cases still referring back to its precedent. On the other, it has been roundly criticised by commentators and in the courts, partly because – on a first read at least – the reader may be left somewhat bemused. Lord Diplock opined more strongly in 1983, when he concluded that analysis of at least some of the judgment can amount to 'an unrewarding task of trying to ascertain precisely what those dicta meant'.[2] Nevertheless, it still merits its place in a collection charting the development of the common law jurisprudence of the conflict of laws and the ins and outs of the judgment itself deserve close scrutiny. Indeed, it has been said that it answers – or purports to answer – two maritime and up to 11 conflict of laws questions.[3]

II. Choice of Law before *Vita Food*

Prior to the decision of the Privy Council in *Vita Food*, English law had progressed from an initial focus on the *lex loci contractus* to a search for the parties' intention.

[1] [1939] AC 277 (PC) ('*Vita Food*').

[2] *The Hollandia* [1983] 1 AC 565, 577–78. Even more strongly, Morris apparently liked to say in university lectures that all the parties, including Lord Wright, were 'drunk' at the time: Reynolds, 'Adrian Briggs and the Conflict of Laws in Oxford' in Dickinson and Peel (eds), *A Conflict of Laws Companion* (OUP, 2021) li. This does not provide the most auspicious start to this chapter. Happily, at least for these purposes, it appears that this view has not gained widespread acceptance.

[3] Tetley, '*Vita Food Products* Revisited (Which Parts of the Decision are Good Law Today?)' (1992) 37 *McGill Law Journal* 292.

An early statement that the common law focused on the *lex loci contractus* unless the parties had agreed otherwise can be found in *Robinson v Bland*.[4] In that case, the question was whether a gambling debt which had been won in France was recoverable in an action in England. Gambling debts were void under English law but not French.[5] Lord Mansfield stated:

> [T]he general rule established *ex comitate et jure gentium*, is that the place where the contract is made, and not where the action is brought is to be considered in expounding and enforcing the contract. But this rule admits of an exception when the parties at the time of making the contract had a view to a different kingdom.[6]

Where there was no such intention, the *lex loci contractus* prevailed,[7] but this was on the basis of a presumption of the parties' intention which could be refuted in certain circumstances, with a particular focus on the country in which the contract had its most real connection.[8]

By 1938, only a year before *Vita Food*, Lord Wright was able to summarise the position which the law had reached thus:

> English law in deciding these matters has refused to treat as conclusive, rigid or arbitrary, criteria such as *lex loci contractus* or *lex loci solutionis*, and has treated the matter as depending on the intention of the parties to be ascertained in each case on a consideration of the terms of the contract, the situation of the parties, and generally on all the surrounding facts. It may be that the parties have in terms in their agreement expressed what law they intend to govern, and in that case prima facie their intention will be effectuated by the Court. But in most cases they do not do so.[9]

This reasoning was a precursor to his later analysis in *Vita Food*: in *Mount Albert Borough Council v Australasian Temperance and General Mutual Life Assurance Society* '*prima facie*' the parties' expressed intention would be applied by the Court. A year later the '*prima facie*' had disappeared.[10]

[4] (1760) 1 WM Bl Rep 234.

[5] There are at least two different versions of this case, no doubt due to the differences in notes taken at the time, but in the 97 ER 717 report Wilmot J referred to the 'marshals of France', who proceeded personally against 'gentlemen' on matters of honour, and in which the gambling debt was recoverable, as a 'wild, illegal, fantastical Court of Honour … contrary to the universal and general laws even of the country where the transaction happened, and contrary to the genius and spirit of our own law too'. The Court held that whilst the money won was not recoverable, despite the 'marshals of France', the money lent to gamble with was recoverable under the laws of both England and France.

[6] (1760) 1 WM Bl Rep 234, 258.

[7] *Allen and Carberry v Kemble* 13 ER 704.

[8] See Bentwich, *Westlake's Private International Law*, 7th edn (Sweet & Maxwell, 1925) 302; *Lloyd v Guibert* (1865–66) LR 1 QB 115, 122–23 referring to situations including where the contract is to be entirely performed elsewhere and the subject matter is immoveable property situated in another country; see also *Jacobs v Crédit Lyonnais* (1884) 12 QBD 589, 596–97; in *In Re Missouri Steamship Company* (1889) 42 Ch D 321 the Court emphasised that the starting point was the law of the place where the contract was made but that this could be affected by the intention of the parties.

[9] *Mount Albert Borough Council v Australasian Temperance and General Mutual Life Assurance Society* [1938] AC 224 (PC) (a case which did not involve an express choice of law clause).

[10] [1938] AC 224 (PC).

III. The Decision in *Vita Food*

A. Facts

The appellant, Vita Food, purchased three lots of herrings in barrels from MG Basha to be shipped from Middle Arm, Newfoundland to New York in January 1935 on the *Hurry On*.[11]

Bills of lading for herrings were dated 15 January 1935 which acknowledged receipt on board of the goods in apparent good order and condition and provided for delivery in good order and condition at New York. The difficulty in the case arose, however, from the precise form of Bills used: instead of up-to-date forms taking into account the requirements of the Newfoundland Carriage of Goods by Sea Act 1932 ('1932 Act'), which incorporated the Hague Rules, old versions were inadvertently used. As a result, they did not contain the 'clause paramount' required by the 1932 Act, which clause should have contained 'an express statement that it is to "have effect subject to the provisions of the said rules as expressed" in the 1932 Act'.[12]

Had it contained that clause, and subjected the Bills to the Hague Rules, any clause relieving the carrier from liability for negligence was void. In this instance, the non-confirming Bills did indeed contain a clause exempting liability for damage due to the negligence of the shipowners' servants.

The Bills also contained a term that the contract 'shall be governed by English law'. At the time, English law had incorporated the Hague Rules, just like the 1932 Act, but herein lay the problem: the Bills were governed by English law (and not Canadian law), but the English Carriage of Goods by Sea Act 1924 applied the Hague Rules only to outward shipments. Thus, the Hague Rules were neither incorporated by the application of the 1932 Act (because the clause paramount had been omitted) nor by the application of English law (because this was not an outward shipment from England). As a result, the case fell through a 'gap' in what was intended to be (a semblance of) international uniformity.

During the voyage, the *Hurry On* ran ashore in Nova Scotia through negligence of the captain. The herrings were unloaded and forwarded on another ship to New York but were received by Vita Food in a damaged condition. The *Hurry On* was registered at the port of Halifax, Nova Scotia so the claimant brought an action for damages in Nova Scotia; the carriers resisted on the grounds that the Bills contained an exemption for liability for damage caused by the negligence of their captain. The main thrust of the claimant's argument was that the failure to include the clause paramount, as required by section 3 of the 1932 Act, rendered the Bills null and void. This, in turn, meant that the carrier was a common carrier,

[11] It is important to note that at this time Newfoundland was not a province of Canada. It achieved self-governing dominion status in 1907, although it gave up its self-governing status in 1934 to the British Government. Its union with the Canadian Confederation did not occur until 1949.

[12] Newfoundland Carriage of Goods by Sea Act 1932, s 3.

independent of any contract or bill of lading, and subject to all the liabilities which that entailed. Importantly, it would also mean that the carrier could not avail itself of the exceptions in either the Bills or the provisions of the 1932 Act.

B. The Decisions of the Canadian Courts

The Chief Justice at first instance, Chisholm CJ, found for the carriers.[13] Having ascertained that there was in fact a contract between the parties, evidenced by the bill of lading,[14] he found that section 3 of the 1932 Act was directory, and that the Bills were to be construed as containing the clause paramount.[15] The failure to do so did not render the Bills illegal, and the provisions of the 1932 Act, and therefore the Hague Rules, applied. He then rejected arguments of unseaworthiness[16] and that valid 'suit' was brought within the year-long time-bar in art III 6 of the Hague Rules[17] so that the claim failed.[18]

That decision was affirmed on appeal to the Supreme Court but for different reasons.[19] It was common ground that if the Bills were valid then they provided a complete defence to the carrier, but the Supreme Court found that they were not: section 3 of the 1932 Act was obligatory, and allowing parties to fail to comply and contract out of the 1932 Act would have defeated its purpose.[20] However, that illegality worked both ways: if the Bills were illegal, the carrier could not rely on the exceptions therein, but that also meant that the claimants could not found their action on them.[21] In other words: the parties were in *pari delicto* so the action failed. Any claim in tort, in particular bailment, would only lie independently of the Bills where the alleged wrongful act was also independent of the contract, which was not the case here.[22] This effectively meant that (i) if the Bills were legal, then the action failed, and (ii) if the Bills were illegal, the action also failed.[23]

C. The Decision of the Privy Council

The claimants appealed to the Privy Council. Counsel for the claimants once again argued that the failure to comply with the 1932 Act rendered the Bills null and

[13] [1938] 2 DLR 372.
[14] ibid [13]–[20].
[15] ibid [25].
[16] On the grounds that the allegedly unseaworthy part was in fact unnecessary, §26; the argument was abandoned thereafter.
[17] [1938] 2 DLR 372 [28].
[18] ibid [30]. Chisholm J was not confident of his opinion however, finding it difficult to 'free oneself from doubt in coming to any definite opinion', §13. If ever there was an invitation to appeal, this was it.
[19] *Vita Food Products v Unus Shipping Co (The Hurry On)* [1938] 2 DLR 372, 382 ff.
[20] ibid [34], [49].
[21] ibid [8], [88].
[22] ibid [71]–[72].
[23] For short summaries of the proceedings in both courts, see the judgment of the Privy Council (n 1) 288–89.

void, and the carrier would be subject to the rights and duties of a common carrier in bailment. The contract should be construed according to the *lex loci contractus*, ie Newfoundland law, and that would regard the contract as illegal. Legislation passed in various countries following the introduction of the Hague Convention was intended to protect the cargo-owner, and that if parties could contract out of their application, this would run contrary to their intention. Further, the claimants were not parties to the illegality, and should be entitled to rely on bailment, which was not subsequently destroyed by an illegal contract.

Counsel for the carrier, on the other hand, argued that the Bills were not void and that the Hague Rules contained in the 1932 Act applied to them. In particular, those Rules were incorporated by the clause that the contract was governed by English law, and English law would regard the 1932 Act as incorporated. If they were not incorporated, then English law would not regard the Bills as illegal. But even if the Bills were illegal, no cause of action could arise from it and the claim of bailment could not lie independently of the parties' contract.

Having heard these arguments over the course of four days, Lord Wright gave the judgment of the Privy Council on the fifth: that the Bills were not illegal but were in fact valid documents, hence the action failed (again).

In order to determine the effect of section 3 of the 1932 Act on the Bills, Lord Wright first asked what was the proper law of the contract. In an oft-cited passage, His Lordship determined that the proper law was English law as it was:

> [W]ell settled that by English law (and the law of Nova Scotia is the same) the proper law of the contract is 'the law which the parties intended to apply'. That intention is objectively ascertained and, if not expressed, will be presumed from the terms of the contract and the relevant surrounding circumstances … But where there is an express statement by the parties of their intention to select the law of the contract, it is difficult to see what qualifications are possible, provided the intention is bona fide and legal, and provided there is no reason for avoiding the choice on the ground of public policy.[24]

Crucially, and contrary to one of the traditional views,[25] '[c]onnection with English law is not as a matter of principle essential',[26] so that the objection that the transaction had nothing to connect it with English law did not impact the choice. Lord Wright recognised that the provisions in the contract for English arbitration[27] importing English law were frequent in international business despite the parties having no connection with England, but in any event found a link with England by virtue of the registration of the vessel under the Merchant Shipping Act 1894

[24] *Vita Food*, 289–91.

[25] See Westlake, *Private International Law* (1925) 302: 'it may be said that the law will be selected in England on substantial considerations, the preference being given to the country with which the transaction has the most real connection, and not to the law of the place of contract as such'; cited by Lord Denning in *Boissevain v Weil* [1949] 1 KB 482, 490.

[26] *Vita Food* 290.

[27] Meant, presumably, to mean the litigation of the dispute as opposed to the modern process.

(so that the underwriters were likely to be English).[28] Further, a choice of English law could also coexist with the incorporation of foreign law (for instance the provision in the Bills for the Canadian Water Carriage of Goods Act 1910 or the US Harter Act to apply in certain situations), and respected its application where necessary (for instance, where performance of the contract would be illegal in the place of performance[29]), but neither affected the application of English law as the governing law, and it was that which must be applied to determined whether the Bills were illegal by failure to comply with section 3 of the 1932 Act.[30]

It must be said that this section of the judgment is not as clear as it might have been. The section of the judgment from which the points discussed in the previous paragraph are taken may also be interpreted to mean that the choice of English law as the proper law of the contract includes its conflict of laws rules, ie the doctrine of *renvoi*.[31] Indeed, Lord Wright did state: 'English rules *relating to the conflict of laws* must be applied to determine how the bills of lading are affected by the failure to comply with s 3 of the Act' (emphasis added).[32]

In any event, the effect of the passage is broadly that if the Bills were illegal under Newfoundland law, this would not necessarily render the Bills illegal under the governing law. But before deciding whether or not that was the case, Lord Wright considered whether the Bills would in fact be illegal under Newfoundland law. He decided that no, they were not so illegal: section 3 was directory, and not mandatory or obligatory. There was no provision that bills of lading which did not contain the required statement were illegal and void, no penalties for failure to comply or prohibition of the same.[33] Further, importing a public policy flavour into the reasoning, finding that such bills of lading were illegal would seriously impair business dealings if they could not be taken at face value.[34]

Having concluded thus and so having decided in favour of the carrier, Lord Wright went on to hold that even if the Bills were in fact illegal under Newfoundland law, the result would be the same. Specifically: 'If [the Court] has before it a contract good before its own law or by the proper law of the contract, it will in proper cases give effect to the contract and ignore the foreign law'.[35] This rather begs the question why Lord Wright devoted a good part of the judgment

[28] *Vita Food* 291. This is about as tenuous a link as one finds in this context, and, it is submitted, should not detract from the general principle of the case that no connection is needed; see also n 44.

[29] For example: *Ralli Bros v Compania Naviera Sota y Aznar* [1920] 2 KB 287.

[30] *Vita Food* 291–92.

[31] Falconbridge, 'Bills of Lading: Proper Law and Renvoi' (1940) 18 *Canadian Bar Review* 77, 83–85.

[32] *Vita Food*, 292. Lord Wright, earlier in the paragraph, also referred to 'that part of English law which is commonly called the conflict of laws required, where proper, the application of foreign law' but the examples given are those referred to already, ie illegality in the place of performance and so forth. Although Falconbridge (n 31) 84 considers this reference also to refer to *renvoi*, the sentence is ambiguous.

[33] *Vita Food* 294.

[34] ibid 294–95.

[35] ibid 296.

to ascertaining the position Newfoundland law would take if it was not in fact the proper law of the contract.[36] In any event, Lord Wright's proclamation was subject to the proviso that there are matters of foreign law of 'such a character that it would be against the comity of nations for an English Court to give effect to the transaction'.[37] To translate: English law rules unless there is an important public policy reason to apply foreign law.

Finally, Lord Wright dealt expressly with a Court of Appeal case which had been decided seven years earlier, *The Torni*.[38] In that case, the bills of lading for a cargo of oranges had been issued in Jaffa, Palestine in which a Sea Carriage of Goods Ordinance applied in similar terms to the 1932 Act. Those bills contained a provision that they were 'to be construed in accordance with English law', and the Court of Appeal found that the provision in the Ordinance, that bills of lading must contain a clause paramount, was not defeated by the reference to English law. In particular, the English law clause did not mean that the whole contract was to be governed by English law, but rather the parties 'made it just as much subject to [the Ordinance] as if they had expressly stated so in the document'. Instead, the English law provision only directed that the words of the Ordinance should be construed according to English rules of construction.[39] It should be noted that there was a difference in *The Torni* (with *Vita Food*), in that the Ordinance stated expressly that where such a clause was not present in the bill of lading it 'shall be deemed to have effect subject thereto, notwithstanding the omission of such express statement'. Slesser LJ, having referred to this provision, noted that it would be contrary to comity to allow parties to contract out of the Ordinance.[40]

Lord Wright[41] firstly considered that the difference between the two choice of law phrases: 'construed in accordance with English law' and 'governed by English law' were too similar to make any material difference. Secondly, he did not agree with the Court of Appeal's conclusion in *The Torni* on the grounds that there was no reason to refuse to give effect to the express intention of the parties that the proper law of the contract should be English law (and referring to the 'fundamental principle of the English rule of conflict of laws that intention is the general test of what law to apply').[42] And so the Court of Appeal, in reading the bill of lading as it is expressly provided that it was to be governed by the law of Palestine, was wrong.

Incidentally, Langton J at first instance provided an alternative conclusion based on the intention test,[43] that because many of the facts connected with Palestine, it must have been the intention of the parties that they contracted upon

[36] See Morris, 'The Proper Law of a Contract in the Conflict of Laws' (1940) 56 *LQR* 320, 326–27.
[37] In the same way as the rule in *Ralli Bros v Compania Naviera Sota y Aznar* [1920] 2 KB 287.
[38] [1932] P 78 (CA) (hereafter, '*The Torni*').
[39] *The Torni*, 87.
[40] ibid 92.
[41] *Vita Food* 298–300.
[42] ibid 300.
[43] [1932] P 27.

the footing that the law of Palestine should apply to the contract.[44] With respect to the Court of Appeal, this is a more understandable and theoretical basis on which to rest the decision than creating what is essentially a fiction that the bills did in fact expressly provide for the relevant Palestinian law to apply.[45] The alternative course, with which Slesser LJ grappled[46] but did not rest his reasoning on, would have been to invoke a general principle of public policy and/or comity requiring international uniformity in respect of the Hague Rules (see section VII below). But this was not the course which the Court of Appeal chose.

Before leaving the reasoning of the Privy Council in *Vita Food*, it is worth noting that, at the end of his judgment,[47] Lord Wright dealt with the (moot) alternative case in bailment, holding that if the Bills were illegal, the parties would be in *pari delicto* and could not rely on an action in tort.

IV. The Influence of *Vita Food* on Express Choice of Law

A. England and Wales

Following *Vita Food* the principle of party autonomy was generally accepted,[48] but it did not go without criticism. Dr Cheshire dismissed it entirely, saying that 'It is scarcely credible that it will survive as an authority'.[49] Similarly, Dr John Morris opined that Lord Wright's assessment was 'indefensible in principle and unworkable in practice',[50] and hung much of his reasoning on the purported 'evasion' by the parties of the law of the country with which the contract has the closest factual connection.[51] This was particularly acute in *Vita Food* since the result of the Privy Council's judgment created a gap, later known as 'The Vita Food Gap': the contract was from a country which had adopted the Hague Rules, to a country that had adopted the Hague Rules but the expression for English law allowed the contract to escape the Hague Rules. In such circumstances, one can understand Morris's view that this was 'manifestly absurd' which did not promote the goal of commercial certainty.[52]

[44] ibid 41.

[45] See *The Torni*, 92 per Slesser LJ for words to this effect.

[46] ibid.

[47] *Vita Food* 300–01.

[48] See for instance *Whitworth Street Estates (Manchester) Ltd v James Miller and Partners Ltd* [1970] AC 583, 603 and *Akai Pty Ltd v People's Insurance Co Ltd* [1998] 1 Lloyd's Rep 90, 100:1; note that this refers only to where the parties have expressed an intention. Where they have not, see the analysis offered by Ian McDonald in his contribution to this collection.

[49] Cheshire, *International Contracts* (Jackson, Son & Company, 1948) 33.

[50] Morris, 'The Proper Law of a Contract' (1940) 322.

[51] ibid 329; Mann, 'The Proper Law in the Conflict of Laws' (1987) 36 *ICLQ* 437, 446.

[52] Morris (n 36) 329 and 331; see below for further discussion at section VII; Morris also addressed the somewhat half-hearted attempt by Lord Wright to link the contract with England so as to find a

This reasoning also supported the 'sudden'[53] detour from *Vita Food* in one line of cases from about 1950 to the mid-1980s where the choice of law was treated as one factor to be thrown into the pot when deciding on governing law, but it failed to gain mainstream traction. In *Boissevain v Weil*[54] Lord Denning expressly disagreed with *Vita Food* when he said that 'intention is only one of the factors to be taken into account', which was then accepted by Viscount Simmons in *Bonython v Commonwealth of Australia*.[55] Upjohn J tried to harmonise matters in *Re Helbert Wagg & Co Ltd*[56] by deeming *Vita Food* as consistent with a two-stage approach involving starting with the parties' intention and then checking whether or not the stipulated law has any 'real or substantial connection with the contract as a whole'.[57] Lord Diplock in *The Hollandia*[58] drew a similar conclusion in the context of an arbitration clause, and, as noted above, was somewhat perplexed by Lord Wright's judgment in *Vita Food*.

Thereafter, the position reverted to the modern line of thinking: the expressed intention of the parties was, in general, conclusive.[59] The position was overtaken in any event with the advent of the Rome Convention 1980, which came into force in 1991, and enshrined the express choice of law by the parties.[60] As is further explained below, the paramountcy of the express choice is tempered in the Regulations, but it is interesting to note that the UK refused to adopt Article 7(1) of the Rome Convention which allowed account to be taken of 'overriding provisions' or 'mandatory rules' of a country with a 'close connection' to the situation. Rome I dropped the provision altogether; perhaps it can be optimistically be said that the effect of *Vita Food*'s influence has seeped into European policy.

Putting aside the paramountcy of the parties' express choice as compared to other legal systems, there are three (apparent) qualifications to this choice: that it be bona fide, legal and in accordance with public policy.[61] In English jurisprudence, all three have been treated with indifference, Morris noting that they are

'connection' (the apparent likelihood that the underwriters of the Vessel were English. He opined that law of the flag of the Vessel (Nova Scotia), the lack of any true likelihood of English underwriters and the inconsequentiality of the fact that the contract was written with reference to 'English legal terms' were insufficient for such a connection. That appears correct, and it is difficult not to agree with his reference to the American legal scholar, Joseph H Beale, in his Treatise on the Conflict of Laws 1935, who said 'The remarkable fact which is noticed after reading many of the cases is the great regularity with which the English Courts find, by various methods, that it was the law of England which was intended by the parties' (at 333).

[53] Mann, 'The Proper Law' (1987) 444.

[54] [1949] 1 KB 482.

[55] [1951] AC 201 (PC).

[56] [1956] Ch 323.

[57] [1956] Ch 323, 340–41, derived from *Mount Albert Borough Council* and *The Torni*.

[58] [1983] 1 AC 565 (HL).

[59] A year after *The Hollandia*, Lord Diplock smoothed the inconsistencies in the case law and emphasised the importance of the parties' expressed intention in *Amin Rasheed Shipping Corporation v Kuwait Insurance Co* [1984] AC 50.

[60] Enacted into UK law by the Contracts (Applicable Law) Act 1990.

[61] *Vita Food* 290.

'so vague and indeterminate as to be practically useless as a basis for decision',[62] and no English case has ever examined their meaning or application. Indeed, Mann characterised these 'limits' on the freedom of choice as simply the limits that are imposed on every freedom, ie the 'limits of reason'.[63] It is nonetheless intriguing to contemplate how these requirements would work in practice, and particularly in respect of *Vita Food* itself.

The concept that the choice must be 'legal' is perplexing, because – as Morris pointed out – there is no indication as to how that is tested and by what law. That issue is no longer in play because of the impact of the Rome Convention, Rome I and the subsequent English adaptation post-Brexit which provides for the law which the parties purported to choose.[64] But before that, the position was not settled, and the balance seemed to weigh in favour of the *lexi fori* instead.[65]

As to the bona fide nature of the choice, Cheshire and North considered that it may speak to the situation where parties who realised that a provision was invalid according to the law with which the contract had its closest connection then agreed to subject the contract to another law.[66] This would not be considered as a bona fide choice. It is difficult to support this contention given the modern paramountcy on express choice. Insofar as it may hold true in some situations, it is better expressed as a rule of public policy with reference to the specific provision and rules in question. Indeed, Morris' argument that a later attempt to contract out of the application of the Hague Rules is contrary to public policy, which in turn renders the question of whether the choice was bona fide unnecessary, is a better formulation of the limits involved.

On that note, Mann considered the third requirement, that the choice is not contrary to public policy, as 'so obvious that it will not be mentioned again',[67] but it had particular significance in *Vita Food* itself and the application of the Hague Rules.[68] The general rule is that English law will not enforce or recognise a right arising under the law of a foreign country if it is inconsistent with a fundamental public policy of English law.[69] This, of course, does not mean that every provision of foreign law which diverges from English law will not be given effect and to do so would undermine the process of giving effect to choice of law clauses.[70]

[62] Morris (n 36) 336; see also Briggs, *The Conflict of Laws*, 4th edn (OUP, 2019) 196 fn 1 and Briggs, *Agreements on Jurisdiction and Choice of Law* (OUP, 2008) at 2.31 and 10.02.

[63] Mann (n 51) 447.

[64] See Art 3 of Regulation (EC) No 593/2008 of the European Parliament and of the Council of 17 June 2008 on the law applicable to contractual obligations (Rome I) [2008] OJ L177/6 and the Law Applicable to Contractual Obligations and Non-Contractual Obligations (Amendment etc.) (EU Exit) Regulations 2019/834.

[65] Briggs, *Agreements on Jurisdiction* (2008) at 10.29; *Mackender v Feldia AG* [1967] 2 QB 590 at 598, 603.

[66] Cheshire and North, *Private International Law*, 11th edn (Butterworths, 1987) 454.

[67] Mann (n 51) 446.

[68] As for the Vita Food Gap itself, see below at section VII.

[69] *Dicey, Morris & Collins on the Conflict of Laws*, 15th edn (Sweet & Maxwell, 2012) 5R-001.

[70] Mills, *Party Autonomy in Private International Law* (CUP, 2018) 488.

Instead, those laws which 'outrage [the English courts'] sense of justice or decency' will not be followed or enforced.[71] However, this is concerned with particular provisions of foreign law, as opposed to the choice of foreign law itself, and the question fits more neatly into whether the English court will enforce or recognise mandatory rules of law, rather than whether public policy will operate to strike down the choice of law as a whole.[72]

B. Elsewhere

It stands to reason that when assessing the position of other commonwealth states in the context of *Vita Food*, one should start with Canada. The jurisprudence follows English common law, insofar as *Vita Food* remains authority for the importance of the express choice of law, as cemented by Lord Diplock in *Amin Rasheed Shipping Corp v Kuwait Insurance Co.*

There are two respects in which Canadian law diverges, at least to some extent, from its English counterpart. In respect of what law is used to determine the validity of the choice of law clause, the Canadian position appears to adopt the modern European one, namely the law purportedly chosen by the parties.[73] However, that conclusion is thrown into doubt by the approach taken to the three limits imposed by *Vita Food*. Indeed, Canadian jurisprudence has a good deal more to say on these than anyone has had in England. One of the leading Canadian textbooks on the subject opines that the choice of a 'randomly selected country' for the purposes of a choice of law clause would likely not be a good faith choice, or where parties 'mischievously' choose the law of a country 'with no connections to the transaction'.[74] The choice of a law with no such connection is said to be a 'concern' that the choice is not bona fide. This rather flies in the face of the trajectory of the common law on the topic where the express choice of law was regarded as conclusive, and harks back to Morris and the detour discussed above.

This view has been adopted in the Canadian courts. In *2106701 Ontario Inc v 2288450 Ontario Limited*[75] Faieta J decided that one of the reasons that the choice of Nova Scotian law to govern an Aircraft Management and Operating Agreement was not bona fide was that there was no connection between that agreement and Nova Scotia.[76]

[71] *Dicey, Morris & Collins* (n 69) [5–005]; see also the Court of Appeal in *XX v Whittington Hospital NHS Trust* [2021] AC 275 [77] where a public policy against surrogacy was insufficient for this rule (the Supreme Court upheld the decision on slightly different grounds).

[72] As to which, see section V below.

[73] Pitel and Rafferty, *Conflict of Laws*, 2nd edn (Irwin Law, 2016) 287–88; see also *Uber Technologies Inc v David Heller* 2020 SCC 16 [50].

[74] Pitel and Rafferty (n 73) 288.

[75] 2016 ONSC 2673.

[76] ibid [27]–[30].

It is even more intriguing that Pitel and Rafferty regard New York and English law choices, despite any connection to the transaction, as prima facie bona fide on the grounds that the contract law of those countries is 'stable, developed and well understood'.[77] Whilst that may hold true for both English and New York law, it is difficult to envisage how this could be practically assessed when looking at other regimes. There is no further elucidation of what a 'stable, developed and well understood' legal system would look like, nor how to assess it. It does, however, produce a number of questions. To be assessed thoroughly, it would presumably involve detailed expert evidence, a review of the legislature, court system and enforcement procedures plus analysis of both historical and recent substantive law and decisions. Or would it be a lighter touch? Perhaps turning it upside down and using an approach analogous to the jurisdiction cases – in which the claimant contends they will not obtain substantial or practical justice in the 'natural' forum[78] – would suffice; for instance, whether the system is materially 'unstable, undeveloped and not well understood'.[79] Further, by what law would this be assessed? The *lex fori*, the purported *lex contractus*[80] (the latter said to determine the applicable law as in the European system) or even the law which would have applied absent the choice?[81] Use of the *lex contractus* seems circular in this particular instance; how can one undertake an assessment of a legal system by the law that underpins it? And use of the law which would have applied absent choice gives perhaps unwarranted primacy to that law in circumstances where it might not otherwise apply at all.

Turning to the third limit, public policy, and turning away from the law of Canada, the Australian courts have addressed the concept in one case, *Golden Acres Ltd v Queensland Estates Pty Ltd*,[82] which involved an agreement for the sale of land in Queensland which provided that it should be deemed to have been made in Hong Kong. Interpreting this as a Hong Kong choice of law clause, Hoare J held that it was contrary to public policy because it 'stultified' the legislative intention of a relevant Queensland statute (which Hoare J had determined applied to contracted governed by Queensland law) and the parties had chosen it to avoid the statute's application.

Although both the judge at first instance in that case, and Pitel and Rafferty, view the decision as a public policy decision,[83] Australian commentary and – it

[77] This requirement was supported by Faieta J in *2106701 Ontario Inc v 2288450 Ontario Limited* [33].

[78] See, for example, *Cherney v Deripaska* [2009] EWCA Civ 849 and *AK Investment CJSC v Kyrgyz Mobil Tel Ltd* [2011] UKPC 7, [2012] 1 WLR 1804.

[79] Although that line of case law was primarily concerned with corruption and the ability to receive a fair trial, whereas it might well be the case that a corrupt legal system is nonetheless technically 'stable, developed and well understood'.

[80] As per Pitel and Rafferty (n 73) 289.

[81] As is suggested in Hook and Wass, *The Conflict of Law in New Zealand* (LexisNexis Butterworths, 2020) [4.161].

[82] [1969] Qd R 378.

[83] ibid, 385 and Pitel and Rafferty (n 73) 289.

appears – the High Court of Australia have taken a different approach: (i) the High Court in *Golden Acres Ltd* decided that the choice of law was irrelevant because the Queensland statute applied to all contracts for the sale of land in Queensland, and (ii) Nygh, in *Nygh's Conflict of Laws in Australia*,[84] view the case as an application of mandatory law, as opposed to public policy striking down the entire choice of law clause. *Golden Acres* appears to be the only attempt in Australia to distil the limits propounded in *Vita Food*, and Australian law supports the broad entitlement to select the law governing their contractual obligations.[85]

New Zealand law does not diverge significantly. It also follows the general principle that parties have freedom to choose the governing law of a contract, following *Vita Food*, but there is some suggestion that the legislature (at least) casts mandatory rules slightly differently to the European attitude. Instead of the principle that the express choice of law will make way for those mandatory rules, the New Zealand approach, at least in some instances, takes down the choice of law clause entirely.[86] This bears resemblance to the position taken in *The Hollandia* where the choice of Dutch law in a bill of lading was invalid on the grounds that Dutch law would have applied the Hague Rules as opposed to the Hague-Visby Rules, which were law in England pursuant to the Carriage of Goods by Sea Act 1971.[87] However, unlike English law, the limits from *Vita Food* do make an appearance, for example in the Property (Relationships) Act 1976, which allows the court to disapply an express choice of law in relation to property if it would be 'contrary to justice or public policy'.[88]

V. Contractual Validity: English Law v Foreign Law

The second main issue for which *Vita Food* is still seen as authority is the enforceability of a contract which is valid and enforceable under English law even if it was unenforceable as contrary to public policy in which it was made. This (arguably) crosses two areas, albeit they are dealt with together here: (i) illegality at the place of contracting and its effect on contractual validity; and (ii) the operation of foreign mandatory rules (which is touched upon above). At common law the validity of a contract was determined by the governing law, and only the rules of the governing law applied, with three exceptions: where the contract in question was governed by foreign law (i) mandatory rules and (ii) public policy of English law would apply; and (iii) the English court would not enforce a contract insofar as its performance would be unlawful by the law of the country in which it

[84] Davies et al, *Nygh's Conflict of Laws in Australia*, 10th edn (LexisNexis Butterworths, 2020) [19.19]–[19.20].

[85] ibid [19.15]–[19.19].

[86] Hook and Wass (n 81) [4.158].

[87] Although this was not always the case: see *Dicey, Morris & Collins* (n 69) [32–092].

[88] Section 7A(3).

was to be performed.[89] Prior to *Vita Food* there was some suggestion of a fourth: that a contract would be regarded as invalid if it were invalid at the place where the contract was made (irrespective of whether it was valid according to its governing law).

This principle is drawn from *The Torni* in which the Court of Appeal characterised the lack of provision for the Hague Rules in a bill of lading as required by Palestinian Ordinance as illegal, and so the Court read the relevant provision into the bill.[90] This conclusion was expressly disapproved by Lord Wright in *Vita Food* on the grounds that the validity of the contract was determined by its governing law, and because the Palestinian Ordinance in any event did not render the contract illegal so as to nullify the contract.[91]

The position taken in *Vita Food*, that illegality or invalidity pursuant to the place of contracting is generally irrelevant to the enforceability of a contract, has been upheld in the English common law where it is still applicable,[92] despite obiter comments by Lord Diplock in *The Hollandia*.[93]

The issue of foreign mandatory rules is in any event a wider issue, and the general English approach is that foreign mandatory rules are not relevant to an English court unless the foreign law is the proper law of the contract. The main 'exception' to this is the rule in *Ralli Bros*,[94] that a contract was invalid insofar its performance was unlawful by the law of the country in which it was to be performed. However, whether this is a conflicts rule or one borne of public policy is a matter for debate, and it has been argued that it is a domestic rule only so that the English courts need not pay heed to the rule where English law does not govern the contract.[95]

The European legislation gives a more prominent role to 'mandatory rules' and of countries whose law is not chosen by the parties. Article 3(3) of both the Rome Convention and Rome I provide for the application of the rules which cannot be derogated from by agreement of a country (which is not the choice of law country) where all other elements relevant to the situation at the time of the choice are located there. This is a departure from the common law position,[96] since it expressly provides for the application of law which is neither the *lex fori* nor the *lex contractus*. However, the UK did not permit the principle to be widened even further: although Article 7(1) of the Rome Convention provided that effect may

[89] *Ralli Bros v Compania Naviera Sota y Aznar* [1920] 1 KB 614.

[90] Relying on Lord Halsbury's exception in *Re The Missouri Steamship Company Ltd* (1888) 42 Ch D 321 that 'where a contract is void on the ground of immorality, or is contrary to such positive law as would prohibit the making of such a contract at all, then the contract would be void all over the world and no civilised country would be called on to enforce it': at 336.

[91] *Vita Food* 299–300.

[92] See *Ecobank Transnational Inc v Tanoh* [2015] EWCA Civ 1309 [49] for one of the most recent (relevant) expressions of this principle and the cases referred to therein.

[93] *The Hollandia* [1983] 1 AC 565, 576.

[94] *Ralli Bros v Compania Naviera Sota y Aznar* [1920] 2 KB 287.

[95] See *Dicey, Morris & Collins* (n 69) [32–100].

[96] And the product of some debate, see *Dicey, Morris & Collins* (n 69) [32–084].

be given to the mandatory rules of the law of another country 'with which the situation has a close connection', the UK made a reservation to it and it did not come into force in the UK.[97]

Rome I includes a materially similar version of Article 3(3) and added in a mirroring provision in Article 3(4) which provided for the application of provisions of Community law where all other elements were located in a Member State. It did not, however, include a provision akin to Article 7(1) and instead contains what is in effect the *Ralli Bros* principle in Article 9(3): this provides that effect may be given to 'overriding mandatory provisions'[98] of the law of the country where contractual obligations have to be or have been performed if they render that performance unlawful.

As for the validity of a contract, the Rome Convention and Rome I indicates that material validity is governed by the applicable law of the contract (Articles 8 and 10 respectively), and formal validity by the applicable law or the law of the country in which the contract was made, and when the parties are in different countries, by the law of either country.

Canadian, Australian and New Zealand law all take the same approach as the English courts to illegality under the law of the place of contracting: it is generally irrelevant.[99]

VI. *Renvoi*

A. England and Wales

The next area of general importance dealt with by the Privy Council in the *Vita Food* judgment was the doctrine of *renvoi*. Lord Wright indicated that a choice of English law included English rules of the conflict of laws when he said that 'English rules relating to the conflict of laws must be applied to determine how the bills of lading are affected by the failure to comply with s 3 of the 1932 Act'.[100]

Falconbridge called this a '*lapsus calamai*' (slip of the pen) at the time for two reasons, neither of which detailed the pros and cons of the doctrine of *renvoi* itself.[101] Firstly, he said it was circular in practice because Nova Scotian conflict

[97] Contracts (Applicable Law) Act 1990, s 2(2).

[98] Defined in Art 9(1) as 'provisions the respect for which is regarded as crucial by a country for safeguarding its public interests, such as its political, social or economic organisation'; the New Zealand Court of Appeal termed overriding mandatory provisions as 'crystallised rules of public policy' in *New Zealand Basing Ltd v Brown* [2016] NZCA 525 [36].

[99] Pitel and Rafferty (n 73) 301–02; *Nygh's Conflict of Laws in Australia* (n 85) [19.84]; Hook and Wass (n 81) [4.76].

[100] *Vita Food* 292.

[101] Falconbridge, 'Bills of Lading' (1940), albeit he alluded to the difficulties with the doctrine. His position in general is neatly summarised by Morris in 'Falconbridge's Contribution to the Conflict

rules ought to have applied (and not English, albeit they were identical for these purposes) which would have applied English domestic law. Secondly, the reference, if it was intended to be a wholesale projection of *renvoi* across the subject, was rather too casual to be taken as a solution for such a difficult problem. Given that the doctrine of *renvoi* has generated heated debate and numerous writings, Falconbridge's second criticism holds considerable force. Indeed, there is no room here to do this complex and intriguing subject adequate justice.[102] It suffices to say that English law and commentary has broadly regarded *renvoi* with distaste,[103] and its application has been limited to specific contexts such as intestate succession, the validity of wills and legitimation by subsequent marriage. In any event, it has been specifically excluded in contract by Article 20 of Rome I (which reproduces Article 15 of the Rome Convention), and so this disposes with the uncertainty in *Vita Food*.

B. Elsewhere

The Canadian position appears to reflect the English law position,[104] whereas the Australian High Court applied the doctrine in a tortious context in *Neilson v Overseas Projects Corp of Victoria Ltd*.[105] The claim was for personal injury following a fall down a flight of stairs which had no balustrade in Wuhan, China, and came before the High Court of Australia on the issue of *renvoi*. The question was whether, in circumstances where Chinese law applied to the tort as the *lex loci delicti*, the choice of law meant the whole of Chinese law including its conflict rules or only its domestic rules. The Court favoured the former by a majority of six to one, but made it clear that this was applied to the facts of the case alone and not a 'single overarching theory of renvoi'.[106] There does appear to have been a difference amongst the majority as to whether this meant single or double *renvoi*, but it was not a point they had to decide.[107] The result of this decision is that in Australia, at least,[108] *renvoi* (probably double *renvoi*) is to be applied where the choice of law rule points to the *lex loci delicti*. Whilst this scenario stands alone in

of Laws' (1957) 35 *Canadian Bar Review* 610; the Court of Appeal in *Re United Railways of Havana and Regla Warehouses Ltd* [1960] Ch 52, 96 was also of the obiter view that this was an error of Lord Wright (the Court of Appeal decision was overturned in the House of Lords [1961] AC 1007 but there was no mention of Lord Wright's approach to *renvoi*).

[102] For discussion and reference, see *Dicey, Morris & Collins* (n 69) ch 4.

[103] Although there are proponents of a more flexible regime where the doctrine would be applied in some instances if useful, see Briggs '*In Praise and Defence of Renvoi*' (1998) 47 *ICLQ* 877; *Dicey, Morris & Collins* (n 69) [4–024].

[104] Pitel and Rafferty (n 73) 229–30.

[105] (2005) 223 CLR 331.

[106] *Neilson v Overseas Projects Corp of Victoria Ltd* (2005) 223 CLR 331, [99], [111] and [175].

[107] See *Nygh's Conflict of Laws in Australia* (n 85) [15.9] for further discussion.

[108] New Zealand law has yet to consider the doctrine separately from English or Australian law, see Hook and Wass (n 81) [4.51]–[4.55].

the law of obligations (the remaining *renvoi*-applicable situations involving things like wills and succession) the discussion in both the commentaries and the courts is far from over.

VII. The Hague Rules, Uniformity and Public Policy

Finally, *Vita Food* was hugely significant in maritime law in that it itself created (or rather identified) a loophole or 'gap' in the international application of the Hague Rules: despite the fact that the Hague Rules apply in both the law of the country of shipment and the applicable law of the contract, parties could evade their application because the Hague Rules in those countries applied *only* to outward shipments. So the law of the country of the outward shipment did not apply at all, by express choice, and the law of the country which did apply by that choice did not apply the Hague Rules to all shipments, only to outward shipments. As the shipment did not depart from the country of the applicable law, the Hague Rules did not apply.

It can reasonably be assumed that this oversight was unintended; after all, it does appear to be bizarre that in circumstances where both relevant[109] countries had considered, drafted and enacted their respective laws so that the Hague Rules applied, they did not in fact so apply. Even more so when one of the purposes of contracting into the Hague Rules was to help provide a uniform and predictable regime across the shipping industry. It should therefore be unsurprising that this particular aspect of the decision attracted criticism. For instance, Morris was stalwart in his view that the attempt to contract out of the Hague Rules in the *Vita Food* situation ought to have been frustrated, and supported wholeheartedly the conclusion arrived at by Langton J and the Court of Appeal in *The Torni*.[110] The result drawn by the Privy Council in *Vita Food* was 'manifestly absurd and scarcely creditable to judicial administration of the principles of the conflicts of laws',[111] and it is difficult to imagine more strongly worded criticism. Falconbridge was more measured, albeit barely, in his regret that the Privy Council had 'without apparent necessity seriously impaired the efficacy of the effort made … to give effect to an international convention'.[112] So too said Gutteridge who pointed out that a system of unified law cannot work unless the courts of the countries concerned give effect to the corresponding legislation of other countries.[113] And Tetley QC more recently provided a method: that the Carriage of Goods by Sea Act 1924 was

[109] This is said glibly, notwithstanding the previous discussion on the irrelevance of the law of the place of contracting.

[110] Morris (n 36) 328.

[111] Morris (n 36) 329.

[112] Falconbridge (n 31) 82.

[113] HC Gutteridge (1939) 55 *LQR* 323, 326.

mandatory and should have been incorporated by law, making necessary adjustments *mutatis mutandis*.[114]

Despite prompts from commentators to rectify the situation forthwith,[115] 47 years passed before it was statutorily corrected. The Hague-Visby Rules were enacted into English law by the Carriage of Goods by Sea Act 1971, which came into effect in 1977. Article X provides that the Rules apply to outward shipments from a contracting state, bills of lading issued in a contracting state and cases where the contract provides for the law of a contracting state. In short, it is broadly comprehensive in its application to cases which involve contracting states,[116] and so the gap was closed.

Prior to the Hague-Visby Rules, the common law attempted to close the gap itself, usually by the 'clause paramount' technique by contractually incorporating the Hague Rules into bills of lading. Lord Denning recommended that the courts 'strive' to give effect to these clauses and make 'all reasonable implications to this end' in *The Agios Lazaros*[117] to ensure the Rules' application.

Given those efforts, the criticism and the entire purpose of the Hague Rules, it is perhaps curious that Lord Wright did not find a way to apply them on public policy grounds. He commented on the role of public policy in his judgment, noting that public policy in the context of the *Vita Food* circumstances was to be understood in a wide sense with the English courts refusing to nullify a bargain except on 'serious and sufficient grounds'. Which begs the question why the international uniformity of the Hague Rules was not sufficiently serious or sufficient to warrant the application of public policy. As noted above, this may have been a better way of interpreting the result in *The Torni*, and that would have paved the way for fashioning a rule of public policy providing for the application of the Hague Rules either where English law applied, or – more specifically – where the country of shipment and the country of applicable law were both contracting states. And so the intention of the Convention would be preserved and no loophole would be allowed.

The English courts have not been reluctant to apply rules of public policy to achieve the 'right' result. Indeed, *Ralli Bros* is one example; *Foster v Driscoll* (the 'flip side' of *Ralli Bros*) is another,[118] and the House of Lords in *Regazzoni v KC Sethia* summarised them neatly as matters of public policy grounded in comity.[119] The instances of further application of public policy are numerous and diverse, and the underlying purposes range from: (a) protecting comity between nations

[114] Tetley (n 3).
[115] See, for instance, Gutteridge (n 113) 326, and Falconbridge (n 31) 82.
[116] Although it does not apply to shipments *to* contracting states, since this would be horribly complicated given the nature of the shipping industry and has no proper principle behind it; importantly, it does not apply to shipments from a non-contracting state (or country in which bills were issued or where the law of a non-contracting state applies), see *The Kominos S* [1991] 1 Lloyd's Rep 370 and case comment *Vita Food resurgent* LQR 1992, 108 (Jul) 395–98.
[117] [1976] QB 933.
[118] [1929] 1 KB 470.
[119] [1958] AC 301.

(as per *Ralli Bros, Foster* and *Regazzoni*); to (b) achieving the balance between public policies which always need application and those which should only apply domestically (for example in *Lemenda Trading Co Ltd v African Middle East Petroleum Co Ltd*);[120] and (c) where the interests of the English court must come first (for instance, in a procedural context, *Bank Mellat v HM Treasury*).[121]

Canadian, Australian and New Zealand courts proceed along similar lines, often following English jurisprudence. The New Zealand Court of Appeal summarised the point neatly in *New Zealand Basing Ltd v Brown* in saying that 'The touchstone is whether the result of applying the foreign law would be wholly alien to the fundamental requirements of justice as administered by a New Zealand court'.[122]

On the other hand, there is another argument which draws on public policy in support of *Vita Food*. Every first-year law student learns that one of the bedrocks of the law is certainty, and party autonomy in choosing the applicable law is now broadly accepted. On that basis alone, one can see the merits of Lord Wright's decision: ignoring the fact that the parties in *Vita Food* probably did not turn their minds to the precise legal position at the time, Lord Wright's decision was technically correct. Whilst it is easy to say with hindsight (which, of course, has 20:20 vision) that the commonsense approach would be to engineer the application of the Hague Rules to the facts by way of a sensible rule of public policy, the law as it stood at the time had a gap. Despite Morris' view that Lord Wright's decision did not promote commercial certainty, it did promote legal certainty.

In such circumstances the parties – or one party – took advantage of that gap. This was a legislative, not a common law, gap and one can see that the principle of legal certainty weighs heavily against the 'public policy' of fixing the holes that a variety of legislative authorities and committees failed to spot. As Holloway J said in the US case *Tucker v RA Hanson Co, Inc*:[123]

> Since every law is an expression of the public policy of the state, some higher threshold is needed to prevent the forum's law from being applied in every case. A strict construction of the public policy exception [is] necessary to prevent the whole field of conflicts of law from collapsing in on itself.[124]

VIII. Conclusion

It is clear that *Vita Food* has endured in modern English and Commonwealth law. If one ignores the more questionable aspects of the decision (for instance, the casual reference to *renvoi*) its catalytic effect on the development of the express

120 [1988] QB 448, 461.
121 [2019] EWCA Civ 449.
122 *New Zealand Basing Ltd v Brown* [2016] NZCA 525 [67].
123 And as quoted in Hook and Wass (n 81) [4.19].
124 956 F2d 215 (10th Cir 1992) 218.

choice of law cements its importance in the development of this area of conflict of laws. And whilst the refusal to apply the Hague Rules seems to favour technicality over practicality, it helped pave the way for international legislative reform. Given the strength of some of the criticisms levelled against it, that is really rather remarkable for a judgment which baffles the reader on a first read and bemuses on a second.

3

Erie Railroad Company v Tompkins in a Private International Law Context

MICHAEL S GREEN*

I. Introduction

In *Erie Railroad Co v Tompkins*,[1] Tompkins, a Pennsylvanian, sued Erie Railroad Co, a New York corporation, in federal court in New York. The source of federal jurisdiction was diversity: the plaintiff and defendant were citizens of different states.[2] Tompkins's arm had been severed in an accident in Pennsylvania involving a train owned by Erie. But because he was trespassing at the time, there was a question of the common law standard of care the railroad owed to him. The Pennsylvania Supreme Court had previously held that the standard of care to a trespasser was the absence of wanton and wilful negligence.[3] But the federal trial court, following the approach adopted by the US Supreme Court almost 100 years earlier in *Swift v Tyson*,[4] did not consider these Pennsylvania decisions to be binding and concluded that a simple negligence standard should be used.

Under *Swift*, federal courts sitting in diversity and entertaining common law actions arising in a state were required to defer to decisions of the relevant state's courts only concerning 'local usages' (such as matters involving real property). If the matter fell under the 'general' common law, they were free to ignore state court decisions. Such decisions were, at best, evidence of the general common law standards prevailing in the state – they were not the standards themselves. The federal trial court treated the railroad's standard of care as a general common law matter and the Second Circuit, on appeal, agreed.[5] But the US Supreme Court reversed, overturning *Swift*. Federal courts were bound by the decisions of the Pennsylvania Supreme Court.

* Thanks to the participants in the Conference on the Common Law Jurisprudence of the Conflict of Laws and especially Sarah McKibbin. Thanks also to Tom McSweeney and Alex Mills for their help.

[1] 304 US 64 (1938).

[2] 28 USC §1332.

[3] *Koontz v Baltimore & Ohio RR Co* 163 A 212 (Pa 1932).

[4] 41 US 1 (1842).

[5] *Tompkins v Erie RR Co* 90 F 2d 603 (2d Cir 1937).

If one is to measure the importance of a Supreme Court decision by the number of prior decisions it overturned, *Erie* is very likely the most important decision the Court has ever rendered, for in one fell swoop it overturned not just *Swift*, but countless federal court decisions articulating federal views about the general common law.

Despite, or because of, its iconic status in the American legal system, *Erie* is generally understood parochially, as tied to the unique concerns of that system. As American jurists see it, *Erie* is about *federalism*, particularly the relationship between the federal and state court systems in the US. But the truth is that *Erie* is about a much broader problem in private international law, which can arise within the American legal system or internationally. An *Erie* problem concerns the extent to which the court of one sovereign (the interpreter), when determining the content of the law of another sovereign (the target), should defer to the decisions of the target's courts (and especially its highest court of appeals). The interpreter does not have to be a federal court. It can be a state court or the court of a foreign nation. And the target does not have to be the common law of an American state. It can be the statutory law of a state or the law, whether common or statutory, of the US or of a foreign nation.

As a fundamental matter, the answer to *Erie* problems is easy. The interpreter should interpret the target's law the way the target's officials want it to. (Call this the *solution* to *Erie* problems.) The solution does not mean that the interpreter's interests do not count for anything. For example, if determining the views of the target's officials is too difficult, the interpreter might be permitted to use a rule of thumb. But the lodestone is fidelity to the views of the target.

The solution concerns how the interpreter should determine the content of the target's law. It is a different question whether the interpreter is obligated to use the target's law in the first place. For American courts, such limits have their source in the US Constitution and international law. Similar limits undoubtedly apply to foreign courts. They are not our concern here. The question, to which the solution is the answer, is the following: When a court has decided (or is legally compelled) to use another jurisdiction's law, what counts as correct interpretation of that law?

The solution follows from what might be called a *positivist* view of the law, according to which a standard is the law of a jurisdiction only if the jurisdiction's officials say so.[6] Pennsylvania law is up to Pennsylvania officials,[7] which means that they are the authority on how the courts of other jurisdictions should go about interpreting such law. When the law at issue is Pennsylvania common law, the relevant Pennsylvania authority is presumably the Pennsylvania Supreme Court. Thus, the answer in *Erie* was straightforward: the federal court should interpret the common law in Pennsylvania the way the Pennsylvania Supreme Court wants it to.

[6] In fact, this approach is not necessarily positivist in the sense in which Anglophone philosophers of law use the term. These details can be ignored here.

[7] Subject to constitutional limits that are not a concern here.

One might think that it follows from the solution that *Erie* was right, and *Swift* was wrong. But that is not so. Although it is true that a common law standard is the law of Pennsylvania only if the Pennsylvania Supreme Court says it is, the question remains *what that standard is*. And the Pennsylvania Supreme Court may think that the standard is independent of its interpretations.[8] If so, it will conclude that the courts of other jurisdictions are bound to adjudicate events in Pennsylvania according to *that standard*, not its interpretations. And that means that they are free to disagree with its interpretations of the standard. *Swift* will be the right approach for them to take.[9] Conversely, if it thinks the standard in Pennsylvania common law *is* its interpretation, *Erie* is the right approach. The answer to any *Erie* problem, therefore, is whether the relevant officials of the target (such as the target's supreme court) want the interpreter to use a *Swift* or an *Erie* approach concerning the target's law. As it turns out, however, that is difficult to determine, because the target's officials will usually have no occasion to make their views on the matter known (and sometimes would not know how to answer if they were asked, because their choice depends upon other jurisdictions' choices).

The main problem is the impossibility of appeal from the interpreter to the target, even when the issue concerns the target's law. Because the interpreter and the target belong to different sovereigns, appeal is usually impossible. Just as an Uzbek court cannot take a question of Uzbek law on appeal from a Brazilian court, so a state supreme court cannot take a question concerning the state's law on appeal from a federal court, or a court of a sister state, or a foreign court. It takes appeal only from lower courts of its own state. It therefore generally has occasion to opine only about the binding effect of its decisions on lower state courts, not on federal, sister state, or foreign courts. The courts of those other sovereigns will usually have to guess what its views are. *Swift* was one such guess. *Erie* was another.

Both Justice Brandeis, in *Erie*, and Justice Story, in *Swift*, probably accepted the solution. They both thought that federal courts should respect a state supreme court's views when interpreting the common law prevailing in the state. What they disagreed about was what those views were.

This chapter will begin by describing, and then criticising, the arguments against *Swift* offered by Justice Brandeis in *Erie*. *Swift* will emerge, not as the welter of errors that Brandeis made it out to be, but as a guess, like *Erie*, about how a state supreme court thinks the courts of other jurisdictions should interpret the common law within the state's borders.[10]

[8] See Sachs, 'Finding Law' (2019) 107 *California Law Review* 527.

[9] The possibility that the US Constitution prohibits a state supreme court from freeing federal and sister state courts of the duty to follow its decisions, discussed in Green, 'Erie's Suppressed Premise' (2011) 95 *Minnesota Law Review* 1111, is ignored here.

[10] For simplicity's sake, this chapter assumes that a jurisdiction's law applies only within its borders. This is a simplification, because a state or nation's lawmakers can have extraterritorial (and so overlapping) lawmaking power.

The chapter will then offer a comprehensive account of how *Erie* problems, in whatever context they might arise, should ideally be answered, by describing the variety of views the target might have. It will reach two main conclusions. First, there are more possible views than has generally been assumed, making *Erie* problems even more difficult and disorienting. The second is that a jurisdiction's choice of a *Swift* or an *Erie* approach for its own law can be subject to a coordination problem: it has a reason to choose an approach only if it can be reasonably assured that there are enough other jurisdictions that have chosen the approach as well. With such assurances in place, a *Swift* or *Erie* system is stable. But once doubt is introduced, as was the case in the late nineteenth to early twentieth centuries concerning the *Swift* system, one system can shift to the other.

This abstract discussion will be followed by a description of how a variety of *Erie* problems in a private international law context have been answered, based on the interpreters' guesses concerning the targets' views. Although it will look beyond the classic *Erie* scenario – in which a federal court entertains a common law action arising within a state – the focus, with one exception, will still be on *Erie* problems within the American legal system.

The chapter ends by discussing two areas where *Erie* problems did not have to be answered by speculation, because appeal from the interpreter to the target was possible. The first concerns how state courts should interpret federal law. Because appeal from state courts to the US Supreme Court on issues of federal law can occur, the Supreme Court has made it clear that the proper approach for state courts is *Erie*, not *Swift*. The second area concerns how a court of a member of the British Commonwealth (such as Australia) should interpret the common law of another member (such as Canada). One might suspect that Commonwealth courts, like American courts, began with a *Swift* system and later shifted to *Erie*. But they apparently never thought of a *Swift* approach as a possibility at all. It seems that the reason, once again, was the availability of appeal – in this case, to the Privy Council.

II. Brandeis on *Swift*

In his opinion in *Erie*, Brandeis identified four mistakes that he saw in *Swift*. The first was philosophical.[11] *Swift* took the general common law to be 'a transcendental body of law outside of any particular State but obligatory within it unless and until changed by statute'.[12] As Justice Holmes had earlier put it, *Swift* understood the general common law as a 'brooding omnipresence'[13] – as natural law that

[11] These mistakes are not listed in the order that they were presented in Brandeis's opinion. Some liberties have also been taken in reformulating them, in the interest of clarity and coherence with subsequent positions taken by the Court.

[12] *Erie* (n 1) 79.

[13] *S Pacific Co v Jensen* 244 US 222 (1917).

exists in a jurisdiction independently of what the courts and other officials in that jurisdiction think. Brandeis, by contrast, adopted a positivist understanding of the law, including the common law. Under this view, law exists in a jurisdiction due to the decisions of the jurisdiction's officials.

The second mistake he saw was constitutional. Because *Swift* allowed federal courts to ignore state court decisions concerning the common law prevailing in the state, the result was a federal encroachment upon state sovereignty that was incompatible with the constitutional division of lawmaking authority in the American legal system.[14] True, when there are sufficient federal interests (and Congress has not already spoken), federal courts can create federal common law.[15] But the existence of diversity jurisdiction does not, on its own, generate sufficient federal interests. Furthermore, federal common law binds state as well as federal courts. Under *Swift*, by contrast, federal decisions concerning the general common law did not purport to bind state courts. They were simply federal courts' opinions about the general common law prevailing in a state. Thus, *Swift* could not be justified as a constitutionally permissible assertion of federal lawmaking power. It was instead a constitutionally impermissible refusal to respect state lawmaking power in an area that had been left to state regulation.

The third mistake was practical. *Swift* granted a plaintiff who is diverse from the defendant the option of choosing the interpretation of the common law that was in his favour, by choosing between federal and state court.[16] A notorious example of such forum shopping is *Black & White Taxicab & Transfer Co v Brown & Yellow Taxicab & Transfer Co*,[17] in which the plaintiff, originally incorporated in Kentucky, reincorporated in Tennessee in order to be diverse from the Kentucky defendant, thereby allowing it to take advantage of a federal court's favourable interpretation of the common law in Kentucky. By encouraging such forum shopping, *Swift* violated the federal policy that a case should turn out similarly whether it is brought in federal or state court.

The fourth mistake Brandeis saw was statutory: Justice Story misread the scope of the Rules of Decision Act, originally section 34 of the Judiciary Act of 1789, which states that 'the laws of the several states, except where the constitution, treaties or statutes of the US shall otherwise require or provide, shall be regarded as rules of decision in trials at common law in the courts of the US in cases where they apply'.[18] Story wrongly read the term 'laws' in the Act as not including state court decisions concerning general common law matters.[19] Brandeis adopted

[14] *Erie* (n 1) 78–79.

[15] For example, *Clearfield Trust Co v United States* 318 US 363 (1943); *Boyle v United Techs Corp* 487 US 504 (1988). When federal interests are sufficient is a matter of enormous academic debate, which will not be discussed here.

[16] *Erie* (n 1) 74–75. Defendants usually have the same option through removal from state to federal court.

[17] 276 US 518 (1928).

[18] For the Act in its current form, see 28 USC §1652.

[19] *Swift* (n 4) 18.

a more reasonable reading of the Act, under which 'laws' means *laws*. Since no federal statute, provision of the federal constitution, or treaty was at issue in *Erie* (and no federal common law rule was being made), the laws of the several states – in particular, the common law of Pennsylvania as decided by Pennsylvania courts – was the rule of decision.[20]

A. Positivism

But Brandeis's reading of *Swift* was wrong about almost everything, even if the ultimate decision in *Erie* can be justified. Consider his claim that under *Swift* the general common law was understood as a brooding omnipresence that exists in a jurisdiction independently of the views of the jurisdiction's officials. If that were true, a federal court entertaining an action that arose in a civil law jurisdiction (such as Louisiana or France) would presume that the general common law prevailed there, whatever its officials might say about the matter. But that is not so. During the *Swift* regime federal courts did not take the general common law to prevail in civil law jurisdictions.[21]

One might try to salvage Brandeis's argument by saying that federal courts took the general common law to prevail in civil law jurisdictions as an original matter but concluded that it had been displaced by the jurisdictions' comprehensive statutory regimes. But assume that a federal court was interpreting the law of a jurisdiction that had a customary legal system, like a Native American tribe. Under Brandeis's account of *Swift*, the court should presume that the general common law prevailed in the tribe, since it had no displacing statutes. But it would not.[22] And that is because the general common law was *not* understood as a brooding omnipresence. It was thought to exist in a jurisdiction only if officials in that jurisdiction had chosen to adopt it. The evidence that they had made such a choice was their decision to have a common law system. *Swift* was no less positivist than *Erie*.

B. State Sovereignty

Nevertheless, Brandeis might argue, his second criticism remains valid. *Swift* involved a federal court in New York adjudicating an event that arose in New York. Assume that Story thought that any common law standards for adjudicating the

[20] *Erie* (n 1) 71–73.

[21] *Jones v Western Union Telegraph Co* 18 F2d 650 (WD La, 1926); *Barrielle v Bettman* 199 F 838 (SD Ohio, 1912). The same is true of state courts interpreting civil law systems: *International Text-Book Co v Connelly* 99 NE 722 (NY 1912); *Banco De Sonora v Bankers' Mut Cas Co* 100 N 532 (Iowa 1904). An exception is the law merchant (nn 27–29 below and the accompanying text).

[22] *Davison v Gibson* 56 F 443 (8th Cir 1893). For a further discussion of *Davison*, see Green, 'Law's Dark Matter' (2013) 54 *William & Mary Law Review* 856 fn 48.

case were the law in New York only because New York officials said so. That means that Story understood the common law at issue in *Swift* as, fundamentally, the law of New York. But that just proves why *Swift* violated the constitutional division of lawmaking power in the American legal system. *Swift* allowed federal courts to ignore decisions by the New York Court of Appeals (the highest court of appeals in the New York state court system[23]) *concerning New York law.*

Brandeis's second criticism also fails, however, for he assumes, without argument, that New York officials (which we can, for simplicity's sake, restrict to the New York Court of Appeals) thought that the courts of other legal systems should always follow the New York Court of Appeals' interpretations when determining the content of the common law in New York. And there is another possibility: the Court of Appeals might have thought that some common law standards in New York were independent of its interpretations of those standards, even though it was the case that those uninterpreted standards were the law in New York only because it (or other New York officials) said they were. It therefore thought that the courts of other jurisdictions should adjudicate events in New York by looking to the identified standards, not its interpretations of those standards.[24]

That was how Story understood the New York law at issue in *Swift*. It is true that he did not speak of it as 'New York law'. He spoke instead of the 'general commercial law'.[25] But one can use the term 'X law' or 'the law of X' (where X identifies one or more jurisdictions) in two senses. In the first sense, X identifies the jurisdiction or jurisdictions *where* the standards at issue are the law. That is the sense in which Story would have used the term. He therefore did not describe the law in *Swift* as 'New York law', because it was not the law only in New York. It was *general* law – standards that were the law, he thought, in all common law jurisdictions. In the second sense, however, X identifies the sovereign responsible for the standards being the law in the case at issue. (That is how the term is used here.) In that sense, Story would have said that *Swift* was about New York law. General common law standards prevailed in New York only because the New York Court of Appeals (or other relevant New York officials) said so.

To say that the New York Court of Appeals thought that New York law was independent of its interpretations might sound odd, however. After all, its interpretations were not just idle speculation. They were binding on lower New York state courts, even if they were not binding on other court systems. If so, how can they not be New York law?

Here it is helpful to rely on the familiar distinction in private international law between substance and procedure. If one wants to know the substance of a jurisdiction's cause of action, denuded of procedural elements that concern only how

[23] In fact, this description contains a simplifying anachronism, because the New York Court of Appeals was created a few years after *Swift* was decided, in 1846.

[24] For other readings that make sense of *Swift* in positivist terms see Goldsmith and Walt, '*Erie* and the Irrelevance of Legal Positivism' (1998) 84 *Virginia Law Review* 673.

[25] *Swift* (n 4) 18.

that cause of action should be litigated in that jurisdiction's courts, one considers what the jurisdiction's officials want to be used *in other court systems*.

For example, assume New York has a one-year statute of limitations for wrongful death actions. The limitations period is substantive – that is, part of a New York action for wrongful death – only if the New York Court of Appeals thinks it should be used in other court systems when entertaining the New York action. If it thinks that those other courts can use whatever limitations period they see fit, the period is procedural. To be sure, the New York Court of Appeals will rarely have a reason to make its views on the matter known. Because it takes appeals only from lower New York state courts, it will have no occasion to opine on what the courts of other legal systems should do with the period. The courts of the other legal systems will have to guess.[26] Nevertheless, the substantive or procedural nature of the period is fundamentally determined by whatever the New York Court of Appeals *would* say on the issue, as difficult as its views are to determine.

One way of putting Story's reading of New York law in *Swift*, therefore, is that the New York Court of Appeals' interpretations of the general common law standards prevailing in New York were procedural law, binding only on New York state courts. The substance of New York law was the general common law standards themselves, independent of its interpretations. The matter was one of speculation because the New York Court of Appeals never had occasion to say explicitly whether Story's reading was right.

Story – and federal courts during the *Swift* regime generally – tended to assume that a jurisdiction had a *Swift* approach to its common law if its officials adopted a common law system. That assumption was probably right when *Swift* was decided. But it is not necessarily true. A jurisdiction with a common law system might have an *Erie* approach, under which all common law standards within its borders are the decisions of its supreme court. Common law jurisdictions can reject the general common law.

What is more, a *civil law* jurisdiction can accept the general common law. Its officials might accept as law within their borders standards that are independent of any interpretations provided by their courts and that are also the law in other jurisdictions. For example, both civil and common law jurisdictions generally recognised the *law merchant*,[27] which was arguably understood as general commercial custom, independent of any interpretations of that custom that might be provided by a jurisdiction's courts.[28] Indeed, the law merchant might have been the very general commercial law at issue in *Swift*.[29]

[26] See generally: Green, 'Law's Dark Matter' (2013).

[27] Juenger, 'The Lex Mercatoria and Private International Law' (2000) 60 *Louisiana Law Review* 1133, 1135.

[28] For an account that questions the extent to which the law merchant was understood independently of courts' decisions, see Kadens, 'The Myth of the Customary Law Merchant' (2012) 90 *Texas Law Review* 1153, 1193.

[29] For the story of how the law merchant became part of the common law – a process in which Story played a role – see Bane, 'From Holt and Mansfield to Story and Llewellyn and Mentschikoff: The Progressive Development of Commercial Law' (1983) 37 *University of Miami Law Review* 351, 352–67.

Since the mid-twentieth century, the supreme courts of most states in the US have allowed what is known as *certification*, in which questions concerning their law can be presented to them by federal and sister state courts for answers. As a result, there is now a way for them to ask a state supreme court whether its statute of limitations is substantive or procedural. By the same token, they can now ask whether a state has a *Swift* or *Erie* view of its common law. But during the *Swift* regime, and for quite a while after *Erie*, there was no avenue to ask state supreme courts about the matter. The interpreting court had to guess.

Given the absence of any direct evidence from New York courts that they had a *Swift* view about their common law, and the fact that their choice of a common law system does not necessarily mean they had such a view, was there any other indirect evidence in favour of Story's reading?

Consider *Stalker v McDonald*,[30] issued one year after *Swift* was decided. A New York state court entertaining a common law action arising in New York faced an issue similar to that in *Swift*. It acknowledged that if the issue had concerned federal law, it would have been bound by the decision of the US Supreme Court. It also noted that if the issue had concerned a local usage, the decisions of New York state courts would have bound federal courts. But because the issue concerned 'commercial law', it thought New York and federal courts were free to come to their own interpretations of such law – although uniformity would, of course, be preferable. It then respectfully rejected *Swift*'s interpretation. That is evidence that Story's guess was right: New York officials had a *Swift*, not an *Erie*, view of New York common law.

C. Vertical Uniformity and the Rules of Decision Act

To sum up, Brandeis's second criticism of *Swift* is predicated upon a controversial theory about New York's views concerning the binding effect of New York courts' decisions on other court systems when adjudicating events in New York, a theory that was very likely false at the time *Swift* was decided. Concerning Brandeis's final two criticisms, I can be brief.

Brandeis's third criticism – that *Swift* violated a federal policy in favour of 'vertical' uniformity between federal and state court – has some merit. When federal and state courts are allowed to come to different conclusions about the content of a state's law, there will be substantial vertical forum shopping (that is, forum shopping between federal and state courts in a particular state), as occurred in *Black and White Taxicab*. And that is not merely a bad thing – it is also arguably contrary to the purpose Congress had in giving diversity jurisdiction to federal courts. Diversity jurisdiction exists to provide a forum in a state that is free of the prejudice that the state's courts might show toward those from outside the state.[31]

[30] 6 Hill 93 (NY 1843).

[31] *Hertz Corp v Friend* 130 S Ct 1192 (2010); *Burford v Sun Oil Co* 319 US 336 (1943) (Frankfurter J dissenting).

Given this purpose, there is an argument for procedural uniformity between a federal court and the courts of the state where it is located. Without such vertical uniformity, an out-of-state plaintiff who is worried about prejudice in state court might be discouraged from seeking the protection of the federal court in that state because of disadvantageous federal procedure. Conversely, a plaintiff who is diverse from the defendant but who is not worried about prejudice in state court might choose the federal court solely to take advantage of its favourable procedure, thereby wasting federal judicial resources on a case unrelated to the purposes of diversity.[32]

Consider the goal of vertical uniformity as it applies to statutes of limitations. Assume the New York Court of Appeals has said that its one-year statute of limitations for New York wrongful death actions is procedural, meaning that federal and sister state courts are free to use their own limitations period when entertaining such actions. The goal of vertical uniformity will give a federal court in New York entertaining a New York wrongful death action a reason to use New York's one-year limitations period anyway, even though New York officials do not care whether it is used.[33]

Similar considerations extend to the way state law is interpreted. If a federal court in New York interprets New York law differently from the way a state court in New York would, the result would be vertical forum-shopping that frustrates the purpose of diversity. One reason for a federal court to choose *Erie* over *Swift*, therefore, is independent of questions of interpretive fidelity. Even if the New York Court of Appeals has a *Swift* view of its common law, federal courts in New York have a reason to follow its interpretations anyway to vindicate this federal jurisdictional policy. This is an example where the interests of the interpreting court are sufficiently strong to override the goal of perfect interpretive fidelity.

As for Brandeis's fourth argument, recent historical work has cast doubt on his reading of the Rules of Decision Act.[34] But even if the Act is understood as compelling the federal court in *Swift* to apply New York law, New York law *was* applied in *Swift*. The important question in *Swift* was how New York officials wanted New York common law to be interpreted by federal courts. And nothing in the Act answers *that*.

III. *Erie* Problems: The Essentials

At its highest level of abstraction, an *Erie* problem concerns how the court of one sovereign (the interpreter) should interpret the content of the law of another

[32] Green, 'The Twin Aims of *Erie*' (2013) *Notre Dame Law Review* 1865, 1891–1900.

[33] *Guaranty Trust Co v York* 326 US 99 (1945).

[34] Ritz, *Rewriting the History of the Judiciary Act of 1789: Exposing Myths, Challenging Premises and Using New Evidence* (University of Oklahoma Press, 1990).

sovereign (the target). The interpreter should look to the *substance* of the target's law, denuded of the *procedural* elements that concern only how the target's law is litigated within the target's courts. What counts as the substance of the target's law is up to the target's officials, although they will not generally have occasion to answer the question, forcing the interpreting court to guess. *Erie* and *Swift* are different guesses about whether the interpretations of the target's common law provided by its highest court of appeals are substantive or procedural. But *Erie* problems can arise concerning other aspects of the target's law.

Assume that the target's legislature takes certain considerations into account – whether it is commercial custom, or economic efficiency, or moral values – and passes a statute. One can ask an *Erie* question about whether the statute is substantive or procedural. Perhaps the substantive law of the target consists of the considerations the legislature took into account, and the statute is for use only in the target's courts. If so, the interpreter would be required to look to the considerations when adjudicating events in the target, without being bound by the statute itself.

No interpreter has ever entertained this possibility, in part because of the difficulty it would have in identifying the considerations the legislature took into account in passing the statute. But it is important to remember that such an approach cannot be rejected on a priori grounds. It is the choice of the target's officials just how free or constrained the interpreter is when adjudicating events within the target's borders, although they will rarely have reason to say what their choice is.

Let us set aside such worries and assume that the target's legislature considers its statute to be substantive. A further *Erie* question is the extent to which the interpreter should look to how the statute has been read by the target's highest court. Note that the question is not how courts *within the target system* should treat such readings. Readings by the target's highest court might be binding upon lower target courts going forward (as is the case in common law systems) or they might be binding only in the case appealed, with lower courts remaining free to come to their own view of the statute in future cases (as is the case, at least to some extent, in civil law jurisdictions). Whatever approach is taken, the current question is different, namely, what the target's officials think courts of *other jurisdictions* should look to when adjudicating events within the target's borders.

One option is that the interpreter is bound only by the language of the statute, not interpretations by the target's highest court. It is the statute, not the interpretations, that is the target's substantive law. That means that the interpreter is free to come to its own conclusion about the statute's meaning. It can ignore how the target's highest court has interpreted the target's statute. This is a *Swift*-like approach to statutory interpretation.

Another option – the *Erie* one – is that the interpreter is bound by how the target's highest court has read the statute. What the interpreter should do when the target's highest court has not yet provided a reading, or its reading is so old that it would likely decide differently if it addressed the matter now, is more difficult.[35] But for current purposes, one can assume that if the target's officials have adopted an *Erie* approach to their statute, the interpreter should read the statute as it predicts the target's highest court would read the statute now.

Now consider interpretation of a target's common, or judge-made, law. Assume the target's highest court takes certain considerations into account – commercial custom, economic efficiency, moral values – and announces a common law decision. One possibility is that the target has an *Erie* view of its common law, under which the substantive common law standard within its borders is that decision. That would mean that the interpreter should respect the decision. Again, what the interpreter should do if the target's highest court has not yet decided the matter or its decision is so old that it would likely decide differently if it addressed the matter now is more difficult. But one can assume that if the target takes an *Erie* approach to its common law, the interpreter should decide as it predicts the target's highest court would.

But the target might take a *Swift* view of its common law. There appear to be two main possibilities here. First, the target's substantive law might be the considerations (custom, economic efficiency, moral values) that were relevant to the highest court when coming to its decision. If so, the interpreter is bound to look to those considerations, but not the court's decision, when adjudicating events within the target. Let us call this the *fact* approach to *Swift*.

The considerations the target's highest court took into account might exist only within the target's borders. For example, the relevant consideration might be custom that is local to the target.[36] Story calls this a local usage and assumes that the target would take an *Erie* approach to it, under which the target's substantive law is the decision of its highest court. But the target could take a fact approach, under which the interpreter is bound to look to the local considerations that the target's highest court took into account, without being bound by its decision. The reason Story rejects this is undoubtedly the difficulty the interpreter would have coming to its own conclusion about the considerations, given that they are local to the target. The problem is not just the burden of getting evidence about the considerations. It would also have had no prior experience with the considerations, since they are irrelevant to its adjudication of events arising within its own borders. It would be easier for it to just look to the decision of the target's highest court. And that is a reason for the target itself to adopt an *Erie* approach and make the decision its substantive law. As a guess about states' views, Story was probably right.

But the considerations that the target's highest court took into account might exist in many, or even all, jurisdictions. For example, the target's officials might

[35] See Green, 'Horizontal Erie and the Presumption of Forum Law' (2011) 109 *Michigan Law Review* 1237, 1247–51.

[36] This occasionally arises in cases interpreting the law merchant. Although the law merchant is understood by the target as what is, in fact, commercial custom, the relevant commercial custom might be unique to the target. Bellia and Clark, 'The Federal Common Law of Nations' (2009) 109 *Columbia Law Review* 21–22 fn 84.

choose general commercial custom (not the target courts' interpretation of that custom) as the standard that is the law within the target's borders. Such custom exists within the interpreter's borders as well.

If the interpreter's own officials do not make general commercial custom the law within their borders (but, say, make the language of a statute their law instead) the situation will still be somewhat like a local usage, for the interpreter will still struggle to interpret the target's law. It will have no familiarity with determining what general commercial custom is, even though such custom exists within its own borders, because such determination is irrelevant to its adjudication of domestic events.

Things are much easier if general commercial custom is the interpreter's law too. It will adjudicate events within the target the same way it adjudicates events within its own borders, by using its own interpretation of general commercial custom (which might, of course, differ from the interpretation of such custom by the target's courts).

The second reason that the target might consider the standard within its borders to be independent of the decisions of its courts can be called the *negotiation* approach. Under this approach, the officials of the target admit that the relevant standard within their borders consists of court decisions. But because they expect the standard to be shared across multiple jurisdictions, they want it to be a matter of informal negotiation between their courts and the courts of those other jurisdictions. To negotiate, the other jurisdictions' courts must have the latitude to come to their own suggestion about the common standard, even when adjudicating events within the target's borders. It follows that the courts of other negotiating jurisdictions can come to their own conclusion about the content of the target's law.

Whether a *Swift* jurisdiction has a fact or negotiation approach can be unclear. But the fact approach is more likely when there is one salient consideration, like general commercial custom, to which the target's highest court looked in its decision. That is because the target can reasonably expect other jurisdictions' officials to have made that same consideration their law. But if the target's highest court came to its decision by balancing multiple considerations, the assumption that interpreters make those same considerations their law is less likely. In such a case, the target should probably choose a negotiation approach, in which there is a court-created standard that is negotiated between multiple jurisdictions – or an *Erie* approach, in which the standard in its borders is the decision of its highest court.

When a negotiating interpreter adjudicates an event arising within a negotiating target, its interpretation of their common standard is, in effect, an overture in a process of negotiation with the target. The target, in subsequent cases, can either accept the interpreter's overture or, by offering its own reasoning for an alternative, hope that the interpreter will accept its alternative in a subsequent case.

Things are more problematic if the interpreter is not a negotiator, because the standard in the interpreter's borders is a statute or the decision of its highest court. The first problem is how it should interpret the negotiating target's law since it is not a partner to the negotiation. Assume a court of a civil law jurisdiction, with a statute as the standard within its borders, is interpreting the common law prevailing in A, which the interpreter knows to have adopted the negotiation approach with a third jurisdiction, B. Should the civil law court do its best to predict how an A court would interpret the common A/B standard, even if disagreement between A and B concerning the standard remains? That might not be compatible with A officials' views about the substantive standard within their borders, which they arguably take to be a common negotiated standard, not A's current position in the negotiation. The civil law court should perhaps determine what the final agreement between A and B would be. Of course, the proper approach the interpreter should use is, in the end, whatever the target's officials want (although that will be hard to determine). But there is a second problem. Whatever approach the target wants, it will be an unfamiliar and difficult process for the interpreter, for it will have nothing to do with how the interpreter adjudicates events within its own borders.

It has been assumed so far that a jurisdiction's highest court could, if asked, answer whether it has a *Swift* or *Erie* approach to its common law. But it may not know how to answer, because whether it should adopt an approach depends upon whether other jurisdictions adopt the same approach. Assume, for example, that all other jurisdictions have an *Erie* approach in which the substantive common law within their borders is the decision of their highest court. For one jurisdiction to demand a *Swift* approach of the fact variety for its own common law, in which interpreters have to figure out, say, what is in fact general commercial custom, puts an unusual burden on them. It would be easier if they just had to look at the decision of the target's highest court. And, of course, for the target to demand a *Swift* approach of the negotiation variety would be irrational, since there are no other negotiators.

On the other hand, assume all other jurisdictions have a *Swift* approach of the fact variety, in which standards in their borders is what is in fact general commercial custom. For a jurisdiction to demand an *Erie* approach also puts an unusual burden on interpreters, for they will be required to figure out how that jurisdiction's highest court has (or will) decide, rather than just relying on their views about general commercial custom that they have used for domestic cases.

In short, the choice between a *Swift* and an *Erie* system is, to some extent, a coordination problem. Each jurisdiction has a reason to adopt the approach the others have, although it is difficult to figure out what approach that is. But there are also independent arguments for one system over another. For example, a *Swift* system (of the fact variety) is better if interpreters have little access to information about the decisions of the target's courts and jurisdictions' regulatory concerns are relatively limited to, say, enforcing general commercial custom. Conversely, an *Erie* system allows jurisdictions to pursue more nuanced regulatory purposes within their borders. Another reason to prefer an *Erie* system was identified by Justice Brandeis: its ability to avoid the problem of forum shopping to reach a favourable interpretation of the target's law.

IV. The History of *Erie* Problems in a Private International Law Context

The above is a rough sketch of how a variety of *Erie* problems should ideally be answered, based on the possible views that the target might have – keeping in mind that the target's choice can itself depend upon other jurisdictions' choices. Let us now consider the history of how concrete *Erie* problems in a private international law context have been answered by interpreting courts. With one exception, the focus will be on *Erie* problems within the American legal system.

A. State Courts' Interpretation of a Sister State's Common Law

It is best to begin with horizontal *Erie* cases, that is, cases in which a state court interprets the common law of a sister state. That is because in the US the common law within states' borders is usually up to state officials. It is they who determine whether they have a *Swift* system or an *Erie* system or a muddled mixture of both.[37] Federal courts sitting in diversity, by contrast, are mere observers of these exercises of state sovereignty.

Assume, therefore, that a New York state court, rather than a federal court, is entertaining Tompkins's action. Should it defer to the decisions of the Pennsylvania Supreme Court concerning the railroad's standard of care in Pennsylvania? The Pennsylvania Supreme Court took certain considerations (custom, economic efficiency, moral values) into account when it announced its decision about a railroad's standard of care. Its decision is binding on lower Pennsylvania courts. But what does it consider to be substantive Pennsylvania law, to be used in other court systems? Its decision (the *Erie* view)? The considerations it took into account (the fact approach)? Or was its decision an overture in negotiation with other states, with substantive Pennsylvania law being the outcome of the negotiation (the negotiation approach)? There is no way to tell from the Pennsylvania Supreme Court's decision itself and, to repeat, no way for the New York state court to ask the Pennsylvania Supreme Court what its views are.[38]

During the nineteenth century, the New York court's guess would be that Pennsylvania had adopted a *Swift* approach (whether of the fact or negotiation variety) and thus that it could come to its own conclusion about the content of Pennsylvania common law.[39] The only exception would be for local usages. Indeed,

[37] Only a small number of matters are governed by federal common law, which is understood, in *Erie* fashion, to consist of the Supreme Court's decisions.

[38] Certification to the Pennsylvania Supreme Court was not available until 1999. Schultz Newman, 'Certification of State Law Questions: Pennsylvania's Experience in the First Five Years' (2004) 75 *Pennsylvania Bar Association Quarterly* 47.

[39] *St Nicholas Bank v State National Bank* 27 NE 851 (NY 1891); *Faulkner v Hart* 82 NY 413 (1880).

most state courts used a *Swift* approach for sister state common law at the time that *Swift* was decided. But there was at least one exception: Connecticut state courts used an *Erie* approach for sister state common law.[40]

Such horizontal *Erie* cases provide indirect evidence of what the interpreter thinks about its own common law. To be sure, this evidence is not perfect. The fact that New York courts use a *Swift* approach for Pennsylvania common law might be evidence only that they think Pennsylvania has a *Swift* approach, while thinking that their own common law consist of the New York Court of Appeals's decisions. Indeed, it is possible that everyone (except for Connecticut) was wrong during the *Swift* regime. Everyone had an *Erie* approach to their own common law, but they all wrongly thought that everyone else had a *Swift* approach.

But, in general, a state's guess concerning sister state common law reveals its view of its own. One reason is the coordination problem that has already been identified: if a state has a reason to choose the approach that other states have chosen, its conclusion that other states have chosen a certain approach is a reason to think it has chosen that approach too.

This coordination problem faced by a jurisdiction in determining whether to adopt a *Swift* or *Erie* approach for its own law is of great importance in understanding why the *Swift* system was able to be maintained. When *Swift* was decided, a sufficient number of states could reasonably assume that a sufficient number of other states had the *Swift* approach to keep the *Swift* system going.

Over the course of the late nineteenth and early twentieth centuries, however, state courts began to shift to an *Erie* approach to sister state law.[41] An example is the Pennsylvania Supreme Court's forceful adoption of such an approach in 1889, when adjudicating a common law action arising in New York.[42] It insisted on deferring to the decisions of the New York Court of Appeals. By the time *Erie* was decided, states had almost completely moved to an *Erie* system. But there was at least one holdout: Georgia. Indeed, in 2017 the Georgia Supreme Court pointedly reaffirmed its *Swift* approach to sister state law, refusing to defer to Alabama decisions concerning the common law prevailing in Alabama.[43]

One reason for the shift is that the independent advantages of an *Erie* system became greater (for example, states now had more nuanced regulatory goals, even concerning their common law) and its disadvantages became smaller (it was easier to access the decisions of sister state courts). But another reason for the shift was coordination. As other states moved to an *Erie* approach for their own law, a state had a reason to adopt an *Erie* approach itself. The system at the time *Swift* was decided was probably the fact approach, with the negotiation approach as a transition stage before the final transformation to an *Erie* system.

[40] Green, 'Suppressed Premise' (2011) 1125.
[41] ibid 1121–27.
[42] *Forepaugh v Del, Lackawanna & W RR* 128 Pa 217 (1889).
[43] *Coon v The Medical Ctr Inc* 797 SE2d 828 (Ga 2017).

B. Federal Courts' Interpretation of a State's Common Law

Now consider federal courts' interpretation of state common law, that is *Swift* and *Erie* themselves. Because the evidence of horizontal *Erie* cases (as well as other indirect evidence) shows a largely *Swift* system in the states at the time *Swift* was decided and a largely *Erie* system in the states at the time *Erie* was decided, each decision was, roughly, right for its time. But each made mistakes that a more nuanced jurisdiction-by-jurisdiction approach would have avoided. During the *Swift* regime federal courts failed to respect the decisions of the courts of those states, like Connecticut, that had apparently adopted an *Erie* approach to their common law. And under the current *Erie* regime, federal courts mischaracterise the views of the common law held by states, like Georgia, that have retained a *Swift* view.

One reason that a jurisdiction-by-jurisdiction approach was never adopted is undoubtedly the great administrative difficulty of divining whether a particular state has adopted a *Swift* or an *Erie* approach to its common law. Getting matters right was simply too costly, so a rule of thumb was used instead. This is an example of the interests of the interpreting court becoming sufficiently strong to override the goal of perfect interpretive fidelity.

But another reason that federal courts did not use a jurisdiction-by-jurisdiction approach has to do with the role of federal courts in diversity cases. It is important to remember that the *Swift*, *Erie*, or muddled system that was in place was up to the states. So, for example, if there was a *Swift* system of the negotiation variety in place, federal courts were not genuine negotiators, since they were not responsible for the common negotiated standards being the law in any territory. In that sense they were like a civil law court interpreting the law of a negotiating common law jurisdiction. That said, their experience with states' common law, combined with the fact that they had no regulatory skin in the game, might have made them the ideal arbitrators in the negotiation – the best courts to offer positions on which the negotiating states might agree. Certainly, federal courts saw themselves that way during the *Swift* regime.[44]

That can help explain why they used a general approach (whether *Swift* or *Erie*) rather than a jurisdiction-by-jurisdiction approach. Their choice was a signal to the states that they should coalesce around a *Swift* or *Erie* system. Thus, Story's opinion in *Swift* was not just a recommendation to the states that they adopt the particular interpretation of the general common law he articulated. It was also a recommendation that they adopt a *Swift* system in which they can each come to their own views about the general common law within one another's borders.

So much for federal courts interpreting the common law of states. There are, of course, other *Erie* questions faced by federal and state courts in a broader private

[44] Nelson, 'A Critical Guide to *Erie Railroad Co v Tompkins*' (2013) 54 *William & Mary Law Review* 948–49.

international law context. For example, how did American courts interpret the common law of non-American jurisdictions? In particular, did they ever use a *Swift* approach? Would they come to their own conclusion about the common law prevailing in England, in defiance of the decisions of English courts?[45] As fascinating as these questions are, they must be set aside.

C. Interpretation of a State's Statute

Now consider how *Erie* problems have played out when the interpreter is a federal or state court and the target is a state's statute. Given that interpreting courts were unable to ask the state supreme court whether it wanted them to follow its decisions when interpreting the state's statutes, we should not be surprised that there was disagreement about whether a *Swift* or *Erie* approach was appropriate. True, federal courts during the *Swift* regime generally deferred to state decisions concerning a state's statutes.[46] But they did not appear to recognise deference as an obligation.[47] It was rather late, and particularly after *Erie*, that deference was seen as required.[48] The history is sketchier for state courts interpreting sister state statutes, although now all of them (even Georgia) adopt an *Erie* approach.[49]

The only exception concerns the one American state with a (largely) civil law system: Louisiana. The fact that a state supreme court's interpretation of the state's law is binding on lower state courts does not mean that it is meant to bind the courts of other jurisdictions. But what inferences can one draw from the fact that lower Louisiana state courts are *not* bound by the Louisiana Supreme Court's interpretations of Louisiana statutes, except in the particular case in which the decision was made?[50] Doesn't that suggest the substantive law of Louisiana is the statute itself, not the Louisiana Supreme Court's interpretations of the statute, and thus that federal and sister state courts are free to come to their own conclusions about the statute's content? Some federal courts have indeed come to this conclusion,[51] although others disagree.[52]

[45] Research revealed one case in which a federal court entertaining a common law action arising in England said, concerning two English cases relied upon by a party, 'Both those rulings are in accordance with what I deem to be the law,' thereby suggesting that the court was exercising its own judgment about what the common law prevailing in England in fact was: *Greenough v Munroe* 2 F Supp 104 (SDNY 1932).

[46] *Metcalf v City of Watertown* 153 US 678–79 (1894).

[47] See *Gelpcke v City of Dubuque* 68 US 175 (1863); Roosevelt, 'Resolving Renvoi: The Bewitchment of our Intelligence by Means of Language' (2005) 80 *Notre Dame Law Review* 1821, 1841 fn 69.

[48] *Fid Union Trust Co v Field* 311 US 177 (1940).

[49] See generally: Green (n 35).

[50] *Johnson v St Paul Mercury Ins Co* 256 La 296–97 (1970) (overruled on other grounds).

[51] *Black v Rebstock Drilling Co* 837 F Supp 200 (WD La 1993); *Shelp v National Surety Company*, 333 F2d 431 (5th Cir 1964).

[52] *St Charles Ventures LLC v Albertsons Inc* 265 F Supp 2d 686–87 (ED La 2003); *Hulin v Fibreboard Corp* 178 F3d 318–19 (5th Cir 1999). Green (n 9) 1147 fn 155.

The same problem can arise with respect to the statutory law of foreign civil law jurisdictions. But here federal and state courts, although generally now able to take judicial notice of foreign law,[53] rely on the testimony of experts – whose own method of interpreting foreign law is unclear.[54] This makes it less likely that any American court will explicitly adopt a *Swift* approach to a civil law jurisdiction.

D. State Courts' Interpretation of Federal Law

Now consider two *Erie* problems that were not matters of speculation, because they could be answered through appeal. The first concerns federal law – including federal common law. One might ask an *Erie* question here too: are state courts bound by the decisions of the US Supreme Court concerning federal law or are such decisions binding only in lower federal courts? But the question has been answered, because the Supreme Court can take cases on appeal from the state court systems concerning issues of federal law and has thereby made it clear that it wants its decisions to bind state as well as federal courts.[55]

Notice that the mere existence of appeal, in which the US Supreme Court can reverse state court judgments, does not on its own mean that an *Erie* approach has been taken. The fact that a Supreme Court decision is binding on state courts in the particular case at hand does not mean it is binding on state courts going forward. The Supreme Court might have indicated to state courts that a system like that in civil law jurisdictions is appropriate. That would be like a *Swift* approach. But it chose *Erie* instead.

It is worth saying that because appeal from *foreign* court systems to the US Supreme Court cannot occur, an *Erie* question can still arise there. It is theoretically possible, however unlikely, that the US Supreme Court does not consider its interpretations of federal law to bind foreign courts.

Curiously, another area where an *Erie* problem arises concerns the interpretation of federal law by federal intermediate courts of appeals. Assume the Federal Court of Appeals for the Second Circuit, which encompasses the state of New York, takes a case on appeal from a federal trial court in New York and comes to an interpretation of federal law. The interpretation is binding, of course, on federal trial courts in the Second Circuit going forward. But is it binding on New York state courts? Here most state courts have adopted a *Swift* approach. Such decisions are not binding on them, the way they are binding on lower federal courts.[56]

[53] Miller, 'Federal Rule 44.1 and the "Fact" Approach to Determining Foreign Law: Death Knell for a Die-Hard Doctrine' (1967) 65 *Michigan Law Review* 697–702.

[54] For a criticism of the reliance on experts, especially when interpreting the law of civil law jurisdictions, see *Bodum USA Inc v La Cafetiere Inc* 621 F3d 631–36 (7th Cir 2010) (Posner J concurring).

[55] For example, *Cooper v Aaron* 358 US 18–20 (1958).

[56] *Danner v MBNA Am Bank NA* 255 SW3d 868 (Ark 2007); *Abela v Gen Motors Corp* 677 NW2d 327 (Mich 2004).

And some federal courts of appeals,[57] as well as some Justices of the US Supreme Court, have agreed.[58]

E. Interjurisdictional Interpretation of Common Law within the British Commonwealth

Now consider the *Erie* problem that arises when the interpreter is the court of one jurisdiction in the British Commonwealth (say, Australia) and the target is another Commonwealth jurisdiction (say, Canada). Does the interpreter use a *Swift* or *Erie* approach? One might expect things to have proceeded similarly to the US, with Commonwealth courts starting with *Swift* and then moving to *Erie*. But during the conference associated with this volume, all the participants from Commonwealth jurisdictions insisted that nothing like *Swift* arose.

There are two distinguishable questions here. The first is whether there is a unity to the common law in the Commonwealth (or whether, instead, each jurisdiction has its own common law). That question is independent of whether the Commonwealth had an *Erie* or *Swift* approach. The second – the *Erie* question – is the extent to which common law standards (whether general or particular to a jurisdiction) are understood as independent of the decisions of any highest court. In the US the answers to the two questions were seen as connected. *Swift* claimed there was a general common law in the US,[59] whose content was independent of the interpretations of that law by any highest court of appeals. *Erie*, by contrast, said that each state had its own common law, which was what the highest court of appeals in the state said it was. Of course, there was widespread disagreement in the US about which view was right. While the US Supreme Court had the *Swift* view, some states (such as Connecticut or, after 1889, Pennsylvania) had an *Erie* view. And when the Supreme Court moved to an *Erie* view, some states (such as Georgia) kept a *Swift* view. The reason for this disagreement was that there was no possibility of appeal to a highest court with unified authority over the matter.

Deferring to those who know more about these matters, it appears that in the Commonwealth, there was little or no disagreement about the answer to the two questions, because of appeal from Commonwealth courts to the Privy Council in the United Kingdom. First, the Council made it clear the extent to which there was a unity to the common law, for it could decide when a jurisdiction's local conditions would allow for local common law (akin to local usages under *Swift*) and when the

[57] *Freeman v Lane* 962 F2d 1258 (7th Cir 1992); *Bromely v Crisp* 561 F2d 1354 (10th Cir 1977).

[58] *Lockhart v Fretwell* 506 US 376 (1993) (Thomas J concurring); *Steffel v Thompson* 415 US 482 fn 3 (1974) (Rehnquist J concurring).

[59] Concerning the law merchant, the unity was broader – including all jurisdictions (even civil law jurisdictions) that recognised law merchant standards. It is also possible that general common law standards beyond the law merchant were understood by American courts as prevailing in common law jurisdictions outside the US (n 45).

standard for the jurisdiction was a general one throughout the Commonwealth.[60] Furthermore, when a jurisdiction chose to end appeal to the Council (as was the case in Australia in 1986[61] and in Canada in 1949[62]) that decision was also strong evidence that the jurisdiction now had its own common law.

It follows that if an Australian court in, say, 1910 was interpreting the 'general' common law prevailing in Canada – that is, common law that was unitary across the Commonwealth – it could reject interpretations provided by Canadian courts. That might make it seem as if a *Swift* system was in place. But there could still be an *Erie* system, for Commonwealth common law might be understood, in *Erie* fashion, as consisting of the *Privy Council's* decisions. If so, Commonwealth common law would be like federal common law in the US. If a New York state court were to interpret federal common law prevailing in Pennsylvania, it could reject the interpretations of that law provided by the Pennsylvania Supreme Court. But that does not mean there is a *Swift* system in place for federal common law, for the New York state court could not reject interpretations of such law provided by the US Supreme Court. There is an *Erie* system in place – federal common law standards consist of the US Supreme Court's decisions.[63]

To see whether there was a *Swift* or *Erie* system in place in the Commonwealth, therefore, one must answer the second question. Were Commonwealth common law standards understood as independent of the decisions of the Privy Council? Could an Australian court in 1910 interpreting the common law prevailing in Canada reject not just Canadian decisions but also decisions by the Privy Council? It appears that the answer is no. The Privy Council made it clear that Commonwealth common law standards were its decisions. That is what participants in the conference meant when they said that nothing like *Swift* ever existed in the Commonwealth.[64] When jurisdictions in the Commonwealth severed their relationship to the Privy Council, they nevertheless retained their *Erie* conception of the common law, with the common law in their borders consisting of the decisions of the relevant domestic highest court.

Of course, if there was no Privy Council decision on point, or its decision was sufficiently antiquated that it might decide differently now, the Australian court in 1910 would be forced, to some extent, to rely on its own judgment about what Commonwealth common law standards were. But its goal would apparently be to identify how the Privy Council would decide if asked.

The question remains whether the jurisdictions within Canada (such as Alberta or Ontario) and Australia (such as Queensland or New South Wales) have their own common law, or whether there is a unitary Canadian and Australian common law. Here too the ability of appeal from the constituent jurisdictions to

[60] See generally Keith, 'The Unity of the Common Law and the Ending of Appeals to the Privy Council' (2005) 25 *ICLQ* 197.

[61] ibid 206.

[62] ibid 204.

[63] Thanks to Alex Mills for helping me clarify these matters.

[64] Some questions remain concerning the law merchant, but they will not be pursued here.

one appellate body (the Supreme Court of Canada and the High Court of Australia) resulted in both unification (there is only Australian and Canadian common law) and the adoption of an *Erie* approach to such law.[65]

One might understand appeal from Australian or Canadian courts to the Privy Council as appeal within one British sovereign. If so, then interjurisdictional interpretation within the Commonwealth did not involve *Erie* problems as defined here. To repeat, an *Erie* problem is when a court of one sovereign interprets the law of another sovereign. But the role played by the Privy Council can be understood solely in terms of its coordinating function, independent of questions of sovereignty. For example, the Caribbean Court of Justice, created due to dissatisfaction with the Privy Council, currently takes appeals in common law cases from what are undoubtedly independent sovereigns, such as Jamaica and Belize.[66] And yet, due to its coordinating role, people now speak of a Caribbean or West Indian common law,[67] consisting, fundamentally, of the Court of Justice's decisions.

[65] See generally Leeming, 'Common Law Within Three Federations' (2007) 18 *Public Law Review* 186.

[66] Caserta and Madsen, 'Between Community Law and Common Law: The Rise of the Caribbean Court of Justice at the Intersection of Regional Integration and Post-Colonial Legacies' (2016) 79 *Law and Contemporary Problems* 89.

[67] Robinson, 'A Caribbean Common Law' (2007) 49 *Race & Class* 118.

4

Good Stock? The Enduring Influence of the 'Proper Law' Rule in *Bonython v Commonwealth of Australia*

IAN McDONALD

I. Introduction: Financial Woe, Fundraising and Federation

Times were tough in 1890s Australia. The real-estate bubble of the 1880s had burst, and the inflow of British capital had run dry.[1] Corruption was evident; corporate governance was weak; decision-making was questionable.[2] That perfect storm precipitated the collapse of the Federal Bank of Australia in January 1893, with many other financial institutions across the colonies following suit. The resulting depression – intensified and protracted by drought in 1895 – remains amongst the worst in Australia's history.[3]

The situation in Queensland, it must be said, was not quite as dire as that in New South Wales or Victoria.[4] Nevertheless, in 1894 legislation was passed authorising the Governor of Queensland to raise money for public services by way of loans of up to £2 million. The incumbent, the former British Indian Army officer and colonial administrator Sir Henry Wylie Norman, wasted little time in doing so, raising the sums of £1.25 million and £750,000, via loans in London and Australia respectively, the following year.

In respect of those sums, debentures were issued in 'pounds sterling'. Their holders included the Australian Mutual Provident Society, to which £250,000

[1] See, for example, Tolmie Merrett, 'The Australian Bank Crashes of the 1890s Revisited' [2013] *Business History Review* 407.

[2] ibid 407–08.

[3] Fitz-Gibbon and Gizycki, 'A History of Last-Resort Lending and Other Support for Troubled Financial Institutions in Australia' Reserve Bank of Australia Research Discussion Paper (October 2001) 21, available at www.rba.gov.au/publications/rdp/2001/pdf/rdp2001-07.pdf.

[4] ibid 31.

worth of debentures, in denominations of £1,000 and £500, were assigned. Such holders were entitled to be repaid the amount specified therein, plus three per cent interest, secured against the revenue of Queensland. The debentures provided that the principal sum was repayable on 1 January 1945, 'either in Brisbane, Sydney, Melbourne or London at the option of the holder'. They stated, also, that the holders were to notify the colonial Treasurer of Queensland, on or before 1 July 1944, at which of these locations they intended to seek repayment.

Federation soon came, however, and in 1927 the governments of the newly formed Commonwealth of Australia and the six Australian states agreed to coordinate and centralise their borrowing.[5] The Commonwealth duly took over Queensland's public debt, including its liability under the debentures, and in 1932 issued inscribed 3½ per cent stock in their place.[6] That inscribed stock was issued subject to the condition that it conferred upon its holders 'rights which conformed in all particulars' with those previously granted by the debentures (including the provision that the principal sum was repayable 'either in Brisbane, Sydney, Melbourne or London').

By 1 July 1944 the Australian Mutual Provident Society had transferred its inscribed 3½ per cent stock to new holders, including John Lavington Bonython, a South Australian newspaper editor, and their inscribed stock had been transferred from Brisbane to Adelaide. In December 1944 Mr Bonython et al wrote to the Deputy Registrar of Inscribed Stock at Adelaide, requesting that 'in accordance with the conditions on which the stock was issued the amount of the stock … be paid on maturity in London in sterling'. That request was refused, however, on the basis that they had not given the six months' notice required under the debentures and were therefore 'now precluded from exercising an option for payment in London'.

Whilst the Commonwealth of Australia was willing to repay the principal monies due on maturity of the inscribed 3½ per cent stock in Australian currency (equal, that is, to the amount inscribed) at Adelaide (or elsewhere in Australia, as required), Mr Bonython et al did not take up that offer. Instead, they commenced proceedings against the Commonwealth before the High Court of Australia, arguing that they were entitled to be repaid – rather more lucratively[7] – in pounds sterling in London. The judge, Chief Justice Latham, stated a case and referred it to the Full Court, which answered (by a majority) that the Commonwealth was not bound to repay the principal sums in either English currency in London or the equivalent of those principal sums in Australian currency. It followed, therefore,

[5] By way of the 1927 Financial Agreement, the constitutionality of which was confirmed via the approval, by referendum, of the Constitution Alteration (State Debts) Bill 1928 on 17 November 1928. The Bill then became law the following year.

[6] Pursuant to the Commonwealth Debt Conversion Act 1931 and the Financial Agreements (Commonwealth Liability) Act 1932.

[7] Had Mr Bonython et al been paid in pounds sterling in London, they would, owing to the rate of exchange, have received the equivalent of approximately 1,250 Australian pounds in respect of each £1,000 debenture.

that £1,000 of inscribed stock was worth just that – 1,000 Australian pounds – and was repayable in Australia. Chief Justice Latham gave judgment accordingly, in line with the majority.[8] Mr Bonython et al appealed to the Judicial Committee of the Privy Council (JCPC).

So goes the somewhat serpentine story of financial woe, fundraising, and federation – and ultimately of litigation – that paved the way for the JCPC's decision in *Bonython v Commonwealth of Australia*,[9] which, more than 70 years on, remains a leading case in the common law conflict of laws, still influencing the highest courts in the lands of England and other jurisdictions. It is this judgment with which this chapter is concerned.

Having already set out the background, the remainder of this chapter proceeds as follows. First, it sets out the reasoning of the JCPC. Second, it explores that reasoning, including from where the JCPC drew its inspiration. Third, it considers how the case has influenced the development of the common law conflict of laws, before offering some brief concluding remarks.

II. The JCPC's Reasoning in *Bonython v Commonwealth of Australia*

The primary question in *Bonython* was whether, under the debentures as issued in 1895, the appellants, Mr Bonython et al, ought to be repaid (as they contended) £1,000 sterling in respect of each £1,000 of inscribed 3½ per cent stock, which equated to around 1,250 Australian pounds; or whether they were only entitled to be repaid (as the respondent, the Commonwealth of Australia, argued) 1,000 Australian pounds in relation to each £1,000 debenture (or the equivalent of that sum in English currency).

Before deciding that central question, though, the JCPC first addressed two preliminary matters which are not particularly relevant, from a conflict of laws perspective, and can therefore be dealt with reasonably shortly.

First, it rightly declined to entertain the Commonwealth's submission that – whatever rights Mr Bonython et al had under the debentures – their present rights were to be determined solely by their status as holders of the inscribed 3½ per cent stock (the terms of which precluded payment of anything but its nominal amount in Australian currency), on the grounds that said submission had not previously been made and the High Court of Australia had thus proceeded on the footing that the appellants' rights concerning the currency in, and place at which, repayment should be made were unaltered by the switch from debentures to stock.[10] Second, the JCPC observed that the question of whether Mr Bonython et al had, in any

[8] *Bonython v The Commonwealth* [1948] HCA 2.
[9] [1951] AC 201 ('*Bonython*').
[10] *Bonython* 214–15.

event, lost their right to require payment in pounds sterling in London, by failing to give notice on or before 1 July 1944, was essentially academic: it was not fatal to the claim (given that the High Court of Australia's judgment did not prevent the appellants from obtaining repayment in Australia of the equivalent, in Australian currency, of the nominal amount of the inscribed stock), but nor would it assist them if they were only entitled to be repaid in English currency in London the equivalent of that nominal amount in Australian currency.[11]

Turning, then, to the key question of what obligation was created by the debentures, the JCPC began by considering whether, in 1895, the word 'sterling', taken together with the word 'pound', denoted English currency alone.[12] It quickly concluded, however, that it was impossible to infer from the same that English currency was intended. After all, in the late nineteenth century the 'pound' was the 'pound sterling' in both London and Queensland (and the latter term was often used in Australian commercial documents to refer to the unit of account in Australia); it was only subsequently, when the values of the two countries' currencies diverged, that the word 'sterling' was appropriated to the English pound, in particular.[13]

The JCPC's task, therefore, was to construe the debentures, according to their 'proper law', to ascertain what *was* envisaged by the expression 'pounds sterling'.[14] The JCPC determined that, in doing so, not too much emphasis was to be placed on the fact that the money of account in England and Queensland was the same at the material time, highlighting that by the late nineteenth century the latter was a self-governing colony able to make its own laws (including determining what was lawful money); and that the identity (or, more accurately, *similarity*) between the two monetary systems was itself 'over-stressed', in circumstances where the money *of payment* in each (distinct from the money *of account*) had undergone numerous changes and was substantially, but *not entirely*, the same.[15] The JCPC was categorical, also, that the obligation created by the debentures was the same whatever the place of repayment; it could not have been intended that holders should obtain a different measure of value, thereby creating a different liability, in accordance with the location chosen for repayment (the choice having been included in the debentures purely for their holders' convenience).[16]

Returning to their reference to the 'proper law', the JCPC rejected the contention that the *lex loci solutionis* – the law of the place where a contract is to be performed (or a debt is to be repaid) – governed the debentures and determined

[11] ibid 215.

[12] ibid 216.

[13] ibid 216–17.

[14] ibid 217. This was a question to be determined as at the date of issue of the debentures: see, *Mayor of Auckland Corporation v Alliance Assurance Co Ltd* [1937] AC 587, 603.

[15] ibid 217–19.

[16] ibid 219. As the JCPC put it: 'The position is wholly different from that which arises where the creditor is expressly given an option not only as to the place of payment but also as to the currency in which it shall be made'.

the *measure* of the obligation created by them.[17] The JCPC accepted that, if London was chosen as the place of repayment, the *mode of performance* of that obligation might (and probably would) be determined by English law as the *lex loci solutionis*,[18] but determined that the *substance* of the obligation fell to be determined by the 'proper law' of the contract, being 'the system of law by reference to which the contract was made or that with which the transaction has its closest and most real connexion';[19] and that, absent any *express reference* to that 'proper law', it was 'a matter of implication to be derived from all the circumstances of the transaction'.[20] The place of performance, the JCPC added, was but one factor to be taken into account when identifying the 'proper law' (and the substance of the obligation created by the contract), albeit 'sometimes a decisive one'.[21]

The advantages of such an approach to the 'proper law' were helpfully summarised in the eighth edition of *Dicey, Morris & Collins on the Conflict of Laws*, published shortly after the JCPC's judgment in *Bonython* was handed down.[22] First, the same law will apply (subject to certain exceptions) to all aspects of a contract, from its formation and validity to its interpretation and discharge. Second, the same law will, in principle, govern all obligations of all parties under a contract. Third, there is no place for *renvoi*: the 'proper law' applies because it is the law with which the contract is most closely connected (or that has been chosen by the parties), and it follows from this that it is the substantive legal principles of that 'proper law', and not its conflict of laws rules, with which the contract is associated (or that the parties have selected). Fourth, this method for determining the 'proper law' is flexible, allowing for a consideration of a variety of circumstances (including the nature of a contract, business custom and usage, and the place where a contract is made or to be performed).

Applying this 'proper law' rule in *Bonython*, the JCPC acknowledged the 'overwhelming evidence' that the 'proper law' was Queensland law.[23] It described the fact that the debentures were issued pursuant to Queensland legislation, which empowered the Governor of Queensland to raise loans of up to £2 million for public services in the colony, and the fact that those loans were secured against the revenue of Queensland, as indicators which were of 'great weight' (if not quite 'decisive').[24] Whilst it was not impossible that a self-governing colony's

[17] ibid 219.
[18] ibid.
[19] ibid.
[20] ibid 221.
[21] ibid 219–20.
[22] *Dicey and Morris on The Conflict of Laws*, 8th edn (Sweet & Maxwell 1967) 694–95.
[23] *Bonython* 221.
[24] ibid. The JCPC further drew a comparison between *R v International Trustee for the Protection of Bondholders AG* [1937] AC 500, in which the House of Lords held that the fact that the relevant loan notes had been issued in the US, were expressed to be in terms of US currency, and were payable, on one option, in New York by reference to US coins, all pointed to US law being the 'proper law'; and *Mount Albert Borough Council v Australasian Temperance and General Mutual Life Assurance Society* [1938] AC 224, in which the JCPC found that – despite the fact that the debentures in question had

legislature would authorise the raising of loans in a currency other than its own, the JCPC reasoned, where it had used terms which were apt to describe its own lawful money – as Queensland had – the 'strongest evidence to the contrary' was required to show that it intended some other currency.[25] In this instance, however, there were no countervailing factors, other than the fact that holders were given a choice of repayment in London and the fact that £1.25 million of the £2 million loan had been raised in London, and none of sufficient strength to displace that presumption.[26]

Consequently, the JCPC concluded that the obligation to repay would be satisfied by payment of whatever currency was, *as a matter of Queensland law*, valid tender for the discharge of the nominal amount of the debt.[27] Whether the parties thought that the money of account in England and Queensland might, despite still bearing the same name, diverge in value in the future, or whether such a divergence occurred, were irrelevant considerations; Queensland law governed the debentures and determined the meaning of the word 'pound'.[28] As a result, the Order of the High Court of Australia was affirmed and the JCPC advised that the appeal should be dismissed.

III. The JCPC's Decision in *Bonython*: The Reasons Behind the Reasoning

It is difficult to disagree with the JCPC's application of the 'proper law' analysis in *Bonython*. On the facts, all roads did lead to Queensland law. However, whether it automatically followed from the fact alone that the debentures were governed by Queensland law that the Australian pound was the money of account, as the JCPC apparently considered, is another matter.[29] In this respect, it has been said, also, that the 'main point' of *Bonython* was that a government is presumed to contract with reference to its own currency, 'a presumption quite different from that concerning the choice of law'.[30] For present purposes, though, the actual outcome

been issued by an Australian company and were repayable in Victoria in Australia (and bore interest payable biannually in that state) – the 'proper law' was New Zealand law, given that the debentures were issued under New Zealand legislation which fixed the debt and the security.

[25] ibid 222.

[26] ibid. Whilst the JCPC found the second factor 'more difficult to assess' than the first, in circumstances where no details of the transaction had been given and the history and fate of the debentures issued in London was unclear, it held that the 'safer course' was to examine the contract as between the appellants and the Queensland Government, and to disregard the question of whether the fact that similar debentures had been issued in London – 'a matter of mere speculation' – was a circumstance from which it could be implied that the debentures were to be repaid in anything but the lawful money of Queensland.

[27] ibid.

[28] ibid 222–23.

[29] See, for example, JHC Morris, 'The Eclipse of the Lex Loci Solutionis – A Fallacy Exploded' (1953) 6 *Vanderbilt Law Review* 505, 524.

[30] *Dicey and Morris on the Conflict of Laws*, 9th edn (Sweet & Maxwell, 1973) 740.

of the case was, and is, secondary. The point of primary importance is the JCPC's establishment (or, perhaps more accurately, *recognition*)[31] of the general rule, in the common law conflict of laws, for determining the law governing contractual obligations – still recognised today – which can be summarised as follows: *a contract is governed by the law chosen by the parties, or, in the absence of any such choice by the parties, by the law with which the contract has its closest and most real connection*. From where, though, did the JCPC draw its inspiration?

It is fair to say that, overall, the jurisprudence cited by the parties only took the JCPC so far. The appellants and the respondent relied heavily on earlier judgments – of both the Australian and English courts – which involved contractual constructions of 'sterling' and 'pound'. These included *Maudsley v Colonial Mutual Life Assurance Society Ltd*,[32] in which the Supreme Court of Victoria found that a life insurance policy for 'one thousand pounds sterling', issued in 1890, imposed an obligation to pay in Australian pounds only; and *Broken Hill Proprietary Co v Latham*,[33] a ruling from the English Court of Appeal reversing the decision below (in which it had been held, inter alia, that it was difficult to see why a debenture holder, demanding payment in London of £100, should be bound to accept something less than that sum in the absence of an explicit clause to that effect; and that such a holder was therefore entitled to receive payment in sterling without any deduction on account of the exchange value of the Australian pound). Notably, however, the JCPC's judgment did not even mention *Maudsley* or *Broken Hill Proprietary Co*.

Three such authorities invoked by the parties, though, had much more of an impact. The first was *Adelaide Electrical Supply Co Ltd v Prudential Assurance Co Ltd*,[34] in which the relevant contract used the term 'pound' (equally capable, at the material time, of describing English or Australian money) but the place of repayment had been changed from London to Australia. The House of Lords found that such an obligation was to be discharged in whatever currency was legal tender in the country in which the nominal amount of the debt was to be repaid (which, in that matter, was Australian currency). The JCPC commented upon the Law Lords' divergent views as to the identity, or similarity, of the English and Australian pounds throughout history – to which they attributed some of what they called the High Court of Australia's 'confusion' in *Bonython*[35] – before clarifying that the decision in *Adelaide Electrical Supply Co Ltd* was to be understood, too, by reference to the 'proper law' rule.[36] The fact that the contract in question had been altered so as to state that repayment was to be made *only* in Australia meant that it

[31] As to which, see further below.
[32] [1945] VLR 161. The life insurance policy in question had been issued by a New York company, via its Australian office, to a Melbourne resident; there were no English features to the dispute whatsoever.
[33] [1933] Ch 373.
[34] [1934] AC 122 ('*Adelaide Electrical Supply Co Ltd*').
[35] *Bonython* 216, 220. This was the same question of identity, or similarity, which the JCPC described, in *Bonython*, as 'over-stressed'.
[36] ibid.

was 'easy to conclude' that the place of performance was, on that occasion, *decisive* and determinative of not only the *mode of performance* of the obligation but also its *substance*.[37] Thus, had it been provided in *Bonython* that repayment would be made *only* in London, that would have been a similarly important factor in determining the substance of the obligation; repayment in the English capital, however, was one of four alternative modes of performance in *Bonython*, such that the fact that it *might* be chosen became 'a factor of little or no weight'.[38] If (as must be the case) the *substance* of the obligation is the same in every eventuality, the JCPC reasoned, 'how can it affect the rights of one debenture-holder who elects to be paid in Melbourne that another has elected to be paid in London?'.[39]

The second such case was *Mayor of Auckland Corporation v Alliance Assurance Co Ltd*,[40] in which the common unit of account used in the relevant contract was again the 'pound' (this time of England and New Zealand). In that matter, the JCPC held that the mode of performance of the contract was governed by the *lex loci solutionis*, such that the debt had to be discharged by repayment in the currency of the place of repayment; and that, if the holder exercised his option to be repaid in London, that debt was repayable in English currency (without any allowance for exchange).[41] At first blush this decision seems difficult to reconcile with *Bonython* and the JCPC's interpretation, along the way, of *Adelaide Electrical Supply Co Ltd*. In *Bonython*, however, it was identified that, whilst the JCPC's judgment in *Mayor of Auckland Corporation*[42] had twice 'correctly stated' the 'relevant principle' – that is, the 'proper law' rule – it had nonetheless held that, as a matter of construction, the *substance* of the obligation (like its *mode of performance*) was also to be determined by the place of performance.[43] Whilst the JCPC, unsurprisingly, did not express a view in *Bonython* as to whether it was right to do so in *Mayor of Auckland Corporation*, the JCPC's reference to its predecessors '[finding] it *possible*' to reach such a conclusion, in the light of 'the surrounding circumstances as the [JCPC] *found them to exist*',[44] hardly constituted the most ringing of endorsements.

The final such authority was *Goldsbrough, Mort & Co Ltd v Hall*,[45] another decision of the Supreme Court of Victoria (affirmed by the High Court of Australia).[46] Again, the question in that case was whether the obligation of the

[37] ibid 220. The JCPC further observed that this appeared, also, to have been the view of *Adelaide Electrical Supply Co Ltd* taken by the JCPC in *Payne v Deputy Federal Commissioner of Taxation* [1936] AC 497, 509.

[38] ibid 221.

[39] ibid.

[40] [1937] AC 587 ('*Mayor of Auckland Corporation*').

[41] ibid 606 and 609.

[42] ibid 604 and 606.

[43] *Bonython* 220–21.

[44] ibid 221.

[45] [1948] VLR 145.

[46] (1949) 78 CLR 1.

claimant company to redeem its debenture stock was to be calculated by reference to English or Australian money, in circumstances where the contract in question (originally made in 1895, but amended on several occasions before being finally consolidated in 1939) referred to 'pounds' (but not 'sterling') and the value of English and Australian currencies had diverged by the time of repayment in 1948. A distinction was once more drawn, at first instance, between the *discharging* of the obligation (ie, the money *of payment*) and the *measure* (or *substance*) of that obligation (ie, the money *of account*), the Supreme Court of Victoria holding that the latter was a matter of construction governed not by the *lex loci solutionis* but by the 'proper law' of the contract (and that the place(s) of payment was only one factor in determining that 'proper law', and not necessarily the most important).[47] The High Court of Australia – Starke J defining the 'proper law' of the contract as 'the system of law with reference to which the contract was made or the system with which the transaction has the closest and most real connection'[48] – upheld the Supreme Court of Victoria's conclusion that the claimant company was to repay the debenture holders in English pounds. The JCPC made clear, in *Bonython*, that the judgments of both courts in *Goldsbrough, Mort & Co Ltd* had been 'of the greatest assistance' in its consideration of the appeal, saluting its Australian colleagues for 'properly' applying the 'proper law' rule and identifying the governing law of the relevant contract by implication in the light of 'all the circumstances of the transaction'.[49]

Given its place in the common law conflict of laws pantheon, however, a striking characteristic of the JCPC's ruling in *Bonython* is its own relative lack of citation of private international law jurisprudence or literature. Indeed, the JCPC did not even use the term 'conflict of laws',[50] or resort (overtly, at least) to its copies of *Dicey and Morris* (as the 'prince of legal textbooks'[51] was then known). One or two exceptions aside,[52] the same is true, also, of *Adelaide Electrical Supply Co Ltd* and *Mayor of Auckland Corporation*, which might fairly be described, first and foremost, as 'currency cases'. It should not be assumed from this, though, that the JCPC was somehow breaking brand-new ground in *Bonython*. For not only was its articulation of the 'proper law' rule plucked from the High Court of Australia's judgment in *Goldsbrough, Mort & Co Ltd*; the origins of this rule, for which *Bonython* is so renowned, are in fact to be found in common law conflict of laws writings and decisions dating back to the nineteenth century.[53]

[47] *Goldsbrough, Mort & Co Ltd* (n 45) 148–53.

[48] *Goldsbrough, Mort & Co Ltd* (n 46) 27.

[49] *Bonython* 221.

[50] Albeit the appellants themselves did refer to the 'well known principle of the conflict of laws' that 'the mode of performance of a contract is to be governed by the law of the place of performance': see *Bonython* 209.

[51] *Dicey, Morris & Collins on the Conflict of Laws*, 15th edn (Sweet & Maxwell, 2012) xvii.

[52] See, *Adelaide Electrical Supply Co Ltd*, 151; *Mayor of Auckland Corporation* 606.

[53] *Dicey, Morris & Collins on the Conflict of Laws* (n 51) [32-007].

Amongst the earliest of such examples is John Westlake's seminal work, *A Treatise on Private International Law*, originally published in 1858.[54] The law 'by which to determine the intrinsic validity and effects of a contract', Westlake wrote, 'will be selected in England on substantial considerations, the preference being given *to the country with which the transaction has the most real connection*, and not to the law of the place of contract as such'.[55] Westlake's formulation was enthusiastically endorsed in 1899 in *South African Breweries Ltd v King*,[56] Mr Justice Kekewich describing it as a 'precise and accurate a statement as one can expect to find in any judgment or treatise, having regard to the necessarily infinite variety of facts which require consideration in cases of this character'.[57] It was adopted, also, by the Australian courts during the first half of the twentieth century,[58] some years before *Goldsbrough, Mort & Co Ltd* came to be decided. Geoffrey Cheshire took up the mantle after the Second World War,[59] and in *Boissevain v Weil*[60] the English Court of Appeal, invoking both Westlake and Cheshire, again referred to the 'proper law' of the contract as depending 'not so much on the place where it is made … or on the place where it is to be performed, but on *the place with which it has the most substantial connexion*'.[61]

Despite the lack of any explicit reference to such nineteenth and early twentieth century literature and case law in *Bonython*, its influence on the JCPC's decision (and the High Court of Australia's ruling in *Goldsbrough, Mort & Co Ltd* before it) is undeniable. Rather than *establish* the 'proper law' rule, then, what the JCPC really did, in *Bonython*, was *recognise* it. However, coming from the JCPC – led by Lord Simonds, who was appointed Lord Chancellor by Winston Churchill shortly after the determination of the appeal – this recognition was authoritative, which goes some way to explaining the weight that it continues to enjoy to this day. Moreover, the JCPC's articulation signalled the start of a welcome move away from the notion, still popular in the common law conflict of laws in 1951, of identifying the 'proper law' of a contract – in the absence of any express choice by the parties – by reference, instead, to their 'presumed' (or 'imputed') intention.

The beginnings of this test of 'presumed' intention date back even further than Westlake's 'most real connection' formulation. As early as 1760, in *Robinson v Bland*[62] – a case concerning a bill of exchange drawn in France but payable

[54] Westlake, *A Treatise on Private International Law, with Principal Reference to its Practice in England* (William Maxwell & Son, 1858).

[55] ibid 237 (emphasis added).

[56] [1899] 2 Ch 173.

[57] ibid 182.

[58] See, for example, *McLelland v Trustees Executors and Agency Co Ltd* (1936) 55 CLR 483; *Merwin Pastoral Co Pty Ltd v Moolpa Pastoral Co Pty Ltd* (1932) 48 CLR 565.

[59] See, for example, Cheshire, *International Contracts* (Jackson, Son & Company, 1948) 15.

[60] [1949] 1 KB 482.

[61] ibid 490 (emphasis added).

[62] [1558–1774] All ER Rep 177 ('*Robinson*').

in England – Lord Mansfield spoke of an exception being made (to the general rule, at that time, that the governing law was that of the place where a contract is concluded)[63] when the parties had, at the time of contracting, 'a view to a different kingdom'.[64] This was refined in 1865 in *Lloyd v Guibert*,[65] in which the Court of Exchequer Chamber referred to the law by which the parties 'intended that the transaction should be governed' or to which 'it is just *to presume that they have submitted themselves* in the matter'.[66] This test was widely applied in England throughout the nineteenth and early twentieth centuries, including in *Jacobs v Crédit Lyonnais*[67] and *Re Missouri Steamship Company*,[68] with the parties' 'presumed' intention identified by reference to factors such as 'the character of the contract and the nature of the transaction'[69] and 'the subject matter of [the] contract, the place where it was made, the contracting parties, and the things to be done'.[70]

The principle of party autonomy is, of course, one of the common law's fundamental and foundational values. Prima facie, therefore, one can see the attraction in focusing on the 'presumed' intention of the parties in instances where they have failed explicitly to choose the applicable law. The test, however, was open to criticism and was criticised, including by Westlake. Notwithstanding the decisions in *Jacobs* and *Re Missouri Steamship Company*, in which this notion of 'presumed' intention was preferred to his 'most real connection' articulation, Westlake remained wedded to the latter in subsequent (and successive) editions of *A Treatise on Private International Law*, refusing to incorporate any mention of the parties' intention.[71] Addressing *Jacobs* and *Re Missouri Steamship Company* head on, he conceded that 'in both cases a stress was laid by the learned judges on the intention of the parties, as the governing element in the choice of law', but added that he found this idea 'difficult to reconcile with the logical order to be followed'.[72] And he later remarked that 'even when the supposed intention of the parties has nominally been relied on, it has been in fact nothing more than a fictitious intention presumed from following this ['most real connection'] doctrine … and has been in itself no substantial guide to the choice of law'.[73]

[63] Briggs, *Private International Law in English Courts* (OUP, 2014) [7.09].

[64] *Robinson*, 179.

[65] (1865) LR 1 QB 115.

[66] ibid 120–121 (emphasis added).

[67] (1884) 12 QBD 589 ('*Jacobs*').

[68] (1889) 42 Ch D 321 ('*Re Missouri Steamship Company*').

[69] *Jacobs*, 601.

[70] *Re Missouri Steamship Company* 340–41.

[71] See, Falconbridge, 'Bills of Lading: Proper Law and Renvoi' (1940) 18 *Canadian Bar Review* 77, 87.

[72] Westlake, *A Treatise on Private International Law, with Principal Reference to its Practice in England*, 3rd edn (Sweet & Maxwell, 1890) 258.

[73] Westlake, *A Treatise on Private International Law, with Principal Reference to its Practice in England*, 6th edn (Sweet & Maxwell, 1922) 290.

Westlake was onto something. This 'presumed' intention test was employed only when the parties had not expressly selected the law that would govern their contract.[74] In those circumstances, though, such an intention was non-existent; the parties had most likely not given the matter a second thought, much less formed anything like a common intention.[75] What the courts were actually doing, then, was adopting the outlook of a reasonable person and asking themselves, *objectively*, what the 'proper law' was in the light of the facts and circumstances of each case (including the subject matter, the place of contracting, and the place of performance). That was a perfectly sensible way forward, entirely in line with Westlake's formulation. However, the attempt then to rebrand it as the 'presumed' intention of the parties – hinting at a subjective element which had no place in the analysis – was deeply artificial.[76] There is little to be gained from worshipping at the altar of party autonomy when parties have opted not to exercise it in respect of the law applicable to their contract. Choice and intention become irrelevant, and the answer to the 'proper law' enquiry must be found elsewhere.

Which is precisely where the purely objective 'proper law' rule, as articulated by the JCPC in *Bonython* (with more than a little help from the High Court of Australia in *Goldsbrough, Mort & Co*) came in. Over time, in a shift that would have warmed Westlake's heart, the idea of 'presumed' (or 'imputed') intention fell away, and the courts in England and other jurisdictions – in the absence of any explicit choice of law – turned straight to this 'closest and most real connection' test instead.

IV. The Influence of *Bonython v Commonwealth of Australia* on the Development of the Common Law Conflict of Laws

Bonython's impact was not immediate. For many years, in scenarios where there was no express choice of law, the English courts continued to consider, first, whether there were any indications of the parties' 'intention'; and it was only if the answer was 'no' that they would then apply the 'proper law' rule in *Bonython*, by considering with what system of law the contract in question had its 'closest and most real connection'. This was illustrated in 1953 in *The Metamorphosis*,[77] in which *Bonython* was not even cited, Mr Justice Karminski describing the 'legal principles … on the question of the proper law of a contract' as 'well settled'

[74] As at 1951, when *Bonython* was decided, such a selection would prevail provided that the foreign law was not contrary to public policy and the choice was 'bona fide and legal': see, for example, *Vita Food Products Inc v Unus Shipping Co Ltd* [1939] AC 277, 290 (and see, further, Helen Morton's contribution to this collection on the judgment in *Vita*).

[75] *The Assunzione (No 1)* [1954] P 150, 164.

[76] See, for example, Carter, 'The Proper Law of the Contract' (1950) 3 *International Law Quarterly* 255, 259.

[77] [1953] 1 WLR 543.

and stating: 'It is the law which the parties intended to apply … If no intention be expressed, the intention will be presumed by the court from the terms of the contract and the relevant surrounding circumstances'.[78] And in *James Miller & Partners Ltd v Whitworth Street Estates (Manchester) Ltd*,[79] Lord Hodson, despite having referred to *Bonython*, held that the House of Lords' task was to 'act on the evidence before it and fix the presumed intentions of the parties as best it can'.[80]

However, the line between the search for the 'presumed' intention and the application of the 'closest and most real connection' test was a very fine one,[81] and their results were often identical.[82] In *Armadora Occidental SA v Horace Mann Insurance Co*,[83] for example, Mr Justice Kerr held that the parties' intention, which 'determines the proper law of the contract', was 'to be inferred from the terms and nature of the contract';[84] and concluded (on account of the presence of a 'follow London' clause in the relevant contract) that the 'proper law' was English law.[85] The English Court of Appeal upheld his decision that English law applied,[86] but did so by employing the *Bonython* approach and asking itself 'with which country has this contract the closest and most real connection?'.[87] Similarly, in *Amin Rasheed Shipping Corp v Kuwait Insurance Co*,[88] the House of Lords was united in its finding that English law was the 'proper law'. However, whilst Lord Diplock (with whom Lords Roskill, Brandon of Oakbrook and Brightman agreed) reached that result on the grounds that the provisions of the contract in question, taken as a whole, 'by necessary implication point[ed] ineluctably to the conclusion that the intention of the parties was that their mutual rights and obligations … should be determined in accordance with … English law',[89] Lord Wilberforce came to the same conclusion on the basis that it was English law 'with which the contract ha[d] its closest and most real connection'.[90]

[78] ibid 547.

[79] [1970] AC 583 ('*James Miller*').

[80] ibid 605–06. It is worth noting, however, that in this case the respondents had argued that there was, in fact, 'a *real* intention'; that the House of Lords was divided (Lord Reid and Lord Wilberforce dissenting); and that Lord Wilberforce, at 614, criticised the English Court of Appeal's 'divergence' from the test in *Bonython* (amongst other authorities) and its 'reliance, in preference to surrounding circumstances, on subsequent conduct of the parties'.

[81] *Dicey, Morris & Collins* (n 51) [32-007]; *Lawlor v Sandvik Mining and Construction Mobile Crushers and Screens Limited* [2013] 2 Lloyd's Rep 98, 102 ('*Lawlor*').

[82] *Dicey, Morris & Collins* (n 51) [32-007]; *Lawlor*, 102.

[83] [1977] 1 WLR 520.

[84] ibid 524.

[85] ibid 525.

[86] *Armadora Occidental SA v Horace Mann Insurance Co* [1977] 1 WLR 1098 (CA).

[87] ibid 1100.

[88] [1984] AC 50 ('*Amin Rasheed Shipping Corp*').

[89] ibid 62.

[90] ibid 69. Lord Wilberforce observed thus: 'I regard this case as falling within the latter words [ie 'the system of law with which the contract has its closest and most real connection'] since I can find no basis for inferring, as between the parties to this contract, an intention that the contract should be governed either by English law or by the law of Kuwait … The court's task must be to have regard objectively to the various factors pointing one way or the other and to estimate, as best it can, where the preponderance lies'.

In practice, therefore, and as Lord Wilberforce also recognised in *Amin Rasheed Shipping Corp*,[91] the two tests were prone to merging into each other, and the English courts frequently found themselves skipping the 'presumed' intention enquiry and moving from the question of explicit choice of law straight to *Bonython*'s 'closest and most real connection' formulation.[92] This was attributable to the fact that (as noted above) the 'presumed' intention test was, in reality, an objective endeavour concerned not with eliciting any actual intention but with falsely imputing an intention that never existed,[93] based on the very same factors which arose for consideration when following the JCPC's lead in *Bonython*.[94] As a result, the notion of 'presumed' (or 'imputed') intention was rightly displaced in England, towards the end of the twentieth century, by the 'proper law' rule in *Bonython*. This change was reflected in the representation in *Dicey and Morris* of the general rule for determining the law governing contractual obligations. In the 7th edition,[95] for example – published in 1958 – the focus was still on 'the law … which the parties intended or may fairly be presumed to have intended to submit themselves'.[96] Fast forward to the 11th edition,[97] though – published in 1987 – and the 'proper law' of a contract was being defined as 'the system of law by which the parties intended the contract to be governed, or, where their intention is neither expressed nor to be inferred from the circumstances, the system of law with which the transaction has its closest and most real connection'.[98] More recently, the shift was succinctly summarised by the UK Supreme Court, quoting *Bonython*, in *Enka Insaat Ve Sanayi AS v OOO Insurance Company Chubb*:[99]

> Where a choice of law cannot be identified by interpreting the contract, the approach of the common law was at one time to presume that the parties must nevertheless have intended their contract to be governed by some particular system of national law and to impute a relevant intention to them … In the second half of the 20th century, however, the test of presumed intention came gradually to be superseded by an acknowledgement that at this stage of the analysis the court is no longer concerned with intention at all and is applying a positive rule of law, with the rule being that the contract is governed by the system of law with which it has its 'closest and most real connection'.[100]

[91] ibid 69.

[92] *Dicey, Morris & Collins* (n 51) [32-007].

[93] ibid; *Lawlor*, 102.

[94] Indeed, John Falconbridge argued that 'presumed' intention was 'merely a judicial mode of expressing the rule that the proper law is that of the country with which the transaction has the most real connection': see Falconbridge, *Essays on the Conflict of Laws* (Canada Law Book Company, 1947) 351. Similarly, Peter North has contended that the 'presumed' intention test was simply an example of the 'proper law' rule, where 'identification of the most closely connected law' is 'relatively easy': see North, *Private International Law Problems in Common Law Jurisdictions* (Martinus Nijhoff, 1993) 106.

[95] *Dicey and Morris on The Conflict of Laws*, 7th edn (Sweet & Maxwell, 1958).

[96] ibid 717.

[97] *Dicey and Morris on The Conflict of Laws*, 11th edn (Sweet & Maxwell, 1987).

[98] ibid 1161–62.

[99] [2020] 1 WLR 4117 ('*Enka Instaat VE Sanayi AS*').

[100] ibid 4129.

It might be queried – in circumstances where the application of the 'presumed' intention test and the 'closest and most real connection' enquiry so commonly delivered identical results – why any of this matters, and why the change set in motion by *Bonython* was to be welcomed. Four points might be made in response. First, the 'closest and most real connection' rule is less artificial and more intellectually honest. Second, in applying the 'presumed' intention test it was often said that, if the parties had agreed on the English courts' jurisdiction, their intention to have English law apply might also be presumed.[101] This, though, was wholly unconvincing; jurisdiction agreements are properly understood as ancillary to, or severable from, a contract, and there is no rational answer to the question why parties who intended both that the English courts should have jurisdiction *and* that English law should apply would explicitly record the first intention but stay silent on the second.[102] Third, the *Bonython* approach is (as was alluded to in *Enka Insaat Ve Sanayi AS*)[103] a *rule of law*, as opposed to an attempt at *contractual construction*,[104] applied 'not because it is the choice of the parties themselves but because they never intended to exercise their liberty to make a choice or, if they did, they … failed to make their choice clear'.[105] This is material, because – according to English law principles on contractual interpretation (which are constantly evolving) – it is the literal wording of a contract, construed as a whole in its context, which is king.[106] This is unlikely to assist, however, in situations where there is no express choice of law. By contrast, considerations which might well be legitimate in objectively identifying the law with which a contract is most closely connected – for example, negotiations between the parties and events after the contract was made (including mode of performance) – have been held to have little, or no, relevance to contractual construction.[107] Indeed, in *James Miller*, the House of Lords was understandably troubled by the English Court of Appeal's invocation of the subsequent conduct of the parties in order to infer their contractual 'intention' as to the governing law;[108] and in *Amin Rasheed Shipping Corp* Lord Wilberforce

[101] Briggs (n 63) [7.10], [7.310].

[102] Where the relevant jurisdiction agreement was not even expressed to be exclusive, such a proposition was less convincing still.

[103] *Enka Insaat Ve Sanayi AS* (n 99) 4129–30.

[104] *The Komninos S* [1991] 1 Lloyd's Rep 370, 374.

[105] *Compagnie d'Armement Maritime SA v Compagnie Tunisienne de Navigation SA* [1971] AC 572, 603–04.

[106] See, for example, *Nigeria v JP Morgan Chase Bank NA* [2019] 1 CLC 207, 224.

[107] See, for example, *Chartbrook Ltd v Persimmon Homes Ltd* [2009] 1 AC 1101 (negotiations between the parties); *Wasa International Insurance Co Ltd v Lexington Insurance Co* [2010] 1 AC 180 and *L Schuler AG v Wickman Machine Tool Sales* [1974] AC 235 (events after the contract was made).

[108] *James Miller*. Lord Hodson stated, at 606, that he could not 'assent to the view which seems to have found favour in the eyes of [the English Court of Appeal] that as a matter of construction the contract can be construed not only in its surrounding circumstances but also by reference to the subsequent conduct of the parties'. Similarly, Viscount Dilhorne observed, at 611, that he '[did] not consider that one can properly have regard to the parties' conduct after the contract has been entered into when considering whether an inference can be drawn as to their intention when they entered into the contract'. And Lord Wilberforce found, at 614–15, that 'subsequent conduct' could not be 'relevant' to the question of 'what intention ought to be imputed to [the parties] on the formation of the contract'.

emphasised that, if trying to infer such an 'intention', regard should not be had to 'conduct of the parties subsequent to the making of the contract'.[109] Fourth, although it is true that the flexibility of the 'closest and most real connection' rule may lead to disagreement,[110] it still offers greater certainty than the judicial wild goose chase that was the 'presumed' intention test.

The enduring influence of *Bonython* in England, then, is not in question. It was evident in *Armadora Occidental SA* and *Amin Rasheed Shipping Corp*, and underlined by the UK Supreme Court in *Enka Insaat Ve Sanayi AS*. Simply because the 'proper law' rule was a distinct improvement on what went before, however, does not mean that it was (or is) the best that could (or can) be hoped for. In this regard, the nature of the, not one but, two transformations which the English conflict of laws rules have undergone, since the judgments in *Armadora Occidental SA* and *Amin Rasheed Shipping Corp* were delivered, is revealing. First, the common law regime – 'proper law' test and all – was largely replaced, in civil and commercial matters, by European legislation, in the form of the Rome Convention[111] (for contracts concluded after 1 April 1991) and then the Rome I Regulation[112] (for contracts concluded after 17 December 2009).[113] Second, when the UK withdrew from the EU in January 2020, thereby cutting the legal strings which tied the Rome I Regulation – and its non-contractual obligations sibling, the Rome II Regulation[114] – into the British legal order, the UK opted to retain the provisions of both (with some minor amendments),[115] despite their innate 'Europeanness'. Accordingly, post-'Brexit', the rules in the Rome I Regulation continue to determine, by and large, the law governing contractual obligations in England. This was not exactly controversial. Whilst the Rome I Regulation is imperfect, and prone to imperfect interpretation, the common law regime has been heavily criticised, including for its blurring of the 'presumed' intention test and the 'closest and most real connection' rule and its approach to the (not infrequent) question of which law governs the determination of whether the parties actually formed a contract in the first place.[116] Certain matters, though – including the law applicable to agreements

[109] *Amin Rasheed Shipping Corp* 69.

[110] Briggs (n 63) [7.311].

[111] 1980 Rome Convention on the law applicable to contractual obligations (which was given effect, in English law, by the Contracts (Applicable Law) Act 1990).

[112] Regulation (EC) No 593/2008 of the European Parliament and of the Council of 17 June 2008 on the law applicable to contractual obligations (Rome I) [2008] OJ L177/6 ('Rome I Regulation') (which was given effect, in English law, by The Law Applicable to Contractual Obligations (England and Wales and Northern Ireland) Regulations 2009.

[113] ibid Art 28.

[114] Regulation (EC) No 864/2007 of the European Parliament and of the Council of 11 July 2007 on the law applicable to non-contractual obligations (Rome II) [2007] OJ L199/40.

[115] See, The Law Applicable to Contractual Obligations and Non-Contractual Obligations (Amendment etc) (EU Exit) Regulations 2019 (SI 2019 No 834).

[116] See, for example, Briggs, 'Secession from the European Union and Private International Law: The Cloud with a Silver Lining' Commercial Bar Association (24 January 2017), available at www.blackstonechambers.com/documents/Secession_from_the_European_Union_and_private_international_law.pdf. Professor Briggs went so far as to describe the common law regime as 'dreadful', stating

on arbitration and choice of court, as illustrated by *Enka Insaat Ve Sanayi AS* – are excluded from the Rome I Regulation's scope[117] and so remain, as ever, within the domain of the common law conflict of laws rules.[118] Although today such rules 'may be seen as confined to the margins of the law' in England,[119] therefore, those margins are by no means the barest of them all.

The impact of *Bonython* has not been limited, however, to this common law jurisdiction alone. The Canadian courts, for example, have followed in their English counterparts' footsteps, albeit they were somewhat quicker to disregard the 'presumed' intention test. In *Imperial Life Assurance Co of Canada v Colmenares*,[120] decided in 1967, the Supreme Court of Canada, citing *Bonython*, held that it had been

> accepted by the highest Courts in England that the problem of determining the proper law of a contract is to be solved by considering the contract as a whole in light of all the circumstances which surround it and applying the law with which it appears to have the closest and most substantial connection.[121]

In the US, too, the prevailing view – despite some initial resistance to party autonomy – has come to be that, in the absence of any choice of law by the parties, the governing law is that which has the 'most significant relationship' to the transaction and the parties, again to be determined by connecting factors (or 'contacts') such as the domicile of the parties.[122] The story is similar in Australia,[123] although there has been a greater reluctance to move straight from the question of express choice of law (or lack thereof) to the purely objective 'proper law' test. In *Akai Pty Ltd v The People's Insurance Company Ltd*,[124] the High Court of Australia acknowledged the complaints that 'presumed' intention is not 'intention' at all, and that there should only be two categories ('express choice' and 'no choice'), but reasoned that 'the better view' is that the first two categories (express choice and 'presumed' intention) are 'but species of the one genus, that concerned with

that it was 'hard to believe that there is a lawyer in full possession of his or her mind who would propose taking us back to these chapters of the common law'. His fiercest criticism, though, was reserved for the regime's rules on *non-contractual* obligations.

[117] Rome I Regulation, Arts 1(1), 1(2), 1(3), and 28.

[118] And the fact that the 'proper law' rule is 'capable of sensible application' outside the context of civil and commercial matters has been described as one of its strengths: Briggs (n 63) [7.308].

[119] ibid [7.06].

[120] *Imperial Life Assurance Co of Canada v Colmenares* [1967] SCR 443.

[121] ibid 448. The factors which will be taken into consideration include the domicile and residence of the parties; the place of contracting and the place of performance; and the nature and subject matter of the contract: see, for example, *Lilydale Cooperative Ltd v Meyn Canada Inc* 2015 ONCA 281 [10].

[122] *Dicey, Morris & Collins* (n 51) [32–005]. See, further, the American Law Institute's *Restatement (Second) of Conflict of Laws* (1969). At time of writing, preparatory work on a third such restatement is underway.

[123] And, indeed, in New Zealand.

[124] (1996) 188 CLR 148.

giving effect to the intention of the parties'.[125] There have also been calls for legislative change in Australia, modelled on the provisions of the Rome Convention and Rome I Regulation,[126] but to date those calls have gone unanswered, such that the common law conflict of laws continue to apply.[127]

Nor has the *Bonython* effect been felt only in common law countries. Where the 'presumed' intention test was once favoured in France and Germany, now those civil jurisdictions, too, have adopted a rule based on objective connections with a system of law,[128] although this is only relevant, of course, where the Rome I Regulation (applicable in all Member States of the EU, except Denmark) does not apply. Further, the influence of the 'proper law' rule can be seen in the Rome I Regulation itself (perhaps unsurprisingly, given the part that the UK played in its creation). Broadly speaking, under the Rome I Regulation there is either an express choice by the parties (Article 3(1)) or what Professor Adrian Briggs has characterised as a 'mechanised form' of a 'country of closest connection' rule (Article 4),[129] which identifies the applicable law in the absence of choice. And Article 4 contains both an 'escape clause' – providing that, where it is 'clear from all the circumstances of the case' that a contract is 'manifestly more closely connected' with a country other than that indicated (by Article 4), that other country's law will apply – and a fallback provision, echoing the 'proper law' rule in *Bonython*, which states that, where the applicable law cannot otherwise be determined by Article 4, a contract will be governed by the law of the country 'with which it is most closely connected'.

V. Concluding Remarks

So-called 'leading' cases are sometimes rooted more in myth than reality. That is not a fair charge, though, with *Bonython*. Yes, the 'proper law' rule for which it is famous dates back beyond 1951. However, the JCPC's judgment was not only authoritative but transformative, instigating a timely transition from the artificial

[125] ibid [67]. In so doing, though, the High Court of Australia also suggested, at [71], that a contractual submission to the exclusive jurisdiction of the tribunals of a particular country might 'be taken as an indication of the intention of the parties that the law of that country is to be the proper law of the contract'. This is highly unpersuasive, for the reasons already given.

[126] See, for example, Australian Law Reform Commission, 'Report No. 58: Choice of Law' (May 1992); see, also, Marshall, 'Reconsidering the Proper Law of the Contract' (2012) 13 *Melbourne Journal of International Law* 505.

[127] The position is the same in Singapore, despite similar considerations of possible reform. In 2003, the Singapore Academy of Law, referring to the fact that that there has not been any codification in Australia (despite the Australian Law Reform Commission's views), concluded that 'the common law has generally worked well'; that there was 'no compelling reason' for reform by codification; and that Singapore 'should not be sacrificing the flexibility of the common law': see, Singapore Academy of Law, Law Reform Sub-Committee, 'Report on Reform of the Law Concerning Choice of Law in Contract' (16 September 2003) [109]–[112].

[128] *Dicey, Morris & Collins* (n 51) [32-005].

[129] Briggs (n 116).

'presumed' intention test to the more satisfactory, and purely objective, 'closest and most real connection' enquiry. And yes, *Bonython*'s impact was not instantaneous (and has been greater in some common law jurisdictions than others). But that is the thing about stock: sometimes it takes a while to mature.

Whilst the 'proper law' rule was an undoubted improvement on the *status quo ante*, however, in England it has recently been relegated to the sidelines, with the provisions of the Rome I Regulation – an admittedly 'superior product',[130] albeit one that still finds a home for *Bonython's* 'closest and most real connection' enquiry[131] – preferred, notwithstanding the UK's departure from the EU. So far, such a demotion has not occurred in other common law countries, despite demands for reform, but it may yet come. For that is another thing about stock: one must also know when to sell it and move on.

[130] ibid.

[131] Rome I Regulation, Art 4(4).

5

M/S Bremen v Zapata Off-Shore Company: US Common Law Affirmation of Party Autonomy

RONALD A BRAND*

I. Introduction

The twentieth century brought issues of party autonomy to the forefront of the development of the conflict of laws. This was true both in new legal instruments, and in the cases that developed the common law.[1] In the US, this elevated status for party autonomy was experienced in both choice of law and choice of forum.[2] In choice of forum, the 1925 enactment of the Federal Arbitration Act ushered in a new respect and higher status for party choice of arbitration as the forum for dispute resolution.[3] A similar evolution occurred several decades later for party choice of court through common law development in the 1972 US Supreme Court decision in *M/S Bremen v Zapata Off-Shore Company*.[4]

* I thank Alexandra Smith and Emily Beeken for excellent research assistance, as well as for assistance in the writing of this chapter.

[1] The most prominent examples of legal instruments demonstrating respect for party autonomy are the Brussels Convention of 1968, which has become the Brussels I (Recast) Regulation (European Convention on Jurisdiction and Enforcement of Judgments in Civil and Commercial Matters, done at Brussels, 27 September 1968, 33 OJ Eur Comm (C189/1) 1 (28 July 1990) (consolidated and updated version of the 1968 Convention and the Protocol of 1971, following the 1989 accession of Spain and Portugal) ('Brussels Convention'), and the Rome I Convention, now in the form of the Rome I Regulation (Regulation (EC) No 593/2008 of the European Parliament and of the Council of 17 June 2008 on the law applicable to contractual obligations ('Rome I'), OJ Eur Union, L 177/6, 4 July 2008). Article 25 of the Brussels I (Recast) Regulation provides for honouring party choice of court, and Art 3 of the Rome I Regulation provides for honouring party choice of law. Regulation (EU) No 1215/2012 of the European Parliament and of the Council of 12 December 2012 on Jurisdiction and the Recognition and Enforcement of Judgments in Civil and Commercial Matters [2012] OJ L351/1, Art 25 ('Brussels I Recast Regulation').

[2] For a discussion of the evolution of US jurisprudence on party autonomy in choice of law, see Brand, *International Business Transaction Fundamentals*, 2nd edn (Wolters Kluwer, 2019) 413–20.

[3] Federal Arbitration Act, 9 USC §1.

[4] 407 US 1 (1972) (*The Bremen*).

The Bremen brought together the development of doctrines dealing with party autonomy in choice of court and *forum non conveniens*. The case also added to the development of US doctrines on applicable law when subject matter jurisdiction lies with federal courts in diversity cases – for which those courts normally apply state, not federal, law under the *Erie* doctrine.[5] When we add the comparison of developments in party choice of arbitration as a forum for dispute settlement with developments in party choice of court, it makes *The Bremen* a rich decision for conflicts scholars and practitioners alike, and an aid in understanding twentieth-century developments in conflict of laws jurisprudence generally in the US.

I begin this chapter with a discussion of fundamental elements of the development of party autonomy in US law and the historical context of the law prior to *The Bremen*. I follow with brief mention of how one prominent political family played a role in the facts that brought about *The Bremen* case. This leads into the facts of the case itself. After reviewing those facts, I discuss the legal analysis applied in the US Supreme Court and the case-specific results of that analysis. I follow with a discussion of how the decision contributed to the development of conflict of laws doctrines, and how those developments fit with the global evolution of related doctrines.

II. Party Autonomy Today: The Context for a Retrospective Look at Choice of Court

Completion of the Hague Convention on Choice of Court Agreements in 2005 has brought a global focus on party autonomy in the selection of national courts for the resolution of private disputes.[6] That Convention, through which contracting states commit to honour both party choice of court and the resulting judgments,[7] is in many ways a legislative representation of both civil law and common law developments regarding party autonomy over the course of the twentieth century.[8] These developments bring together choice of law,[9] choice of court and doctrines dealing

[5] nn 156–62 and accompanying text.

[6] Convention on Choice of Court Agreements (adopted 30 June 2005, entered into force 1 October 2015) 44 ILM 1294 (Hague Choice of Courts Convention).

[7] ibid Art 5 requires that a court chosen in an exclusive choice of court agreement take jurisdiction, and art 6 requires that a court not chosen decline jurisdiction, with limited exceptions. Article 8 obligates courts in contracting states to recognise and enforce judgments from the chosen court, with limited exceptions found in Art 9.

[8] Civil law developments are perhaps best exemplified in the 'Brussels process' that produced the Brussels I Convention of 1968, and successive iterations of the Brussels I Regulation in 2001 and 2012, respectively. Brussels Convention and Brussels I (Recast) Regulation (n 1) and by the 2015 Hague Principles on Choice of Law in International Commercial Contracts, available at www.hcch.net/en/instruments/conventions/specialised-sections/choice-of-law-principles.

[9] The 2005 Hague Convention on Choice of Court Agreements was the first instrument to have an autonomous choice of law rule providing that the law governing the validity of a choice of court agreement is to be the law of the state of the court chosen in that agreement. Hague Choice of Courts Convention (n 6) Arts 5, 6 and 9. While one may argue whether this truly promotes party autonomy

with how courts handle parallel proceedings when more than one court has jurisdiction to hear the same case. While they implicate all three of the traditional private international law pillars – jurisdiction, applicable law, and the recognition and enforcement of judgments – the discussion that follows focuses on the way in which private parties, through freedom of contract, may influence the exercise of jurisdiction by courts.

In the US, twentieth-century developments brought particular attention to the relationship between choice of court and the common law doctrine of *forum non conveniens*.[10] This relationship involves the intersection of rules that are not always consistent with one another and, in particular, the conflict a court must address when faced with both a party agreement on choice of court (and the respect for party autonomy that results in the enforcement of that agreement), and a request for the exercise of judicial discretion either to keep the case in contravention of a choice of court agreement or to send the case to a court not chosen, under the doctrine of *forum non conveniens*.

The evolution of doctrines of party autonomy in choice of court and the doctrine of *forum non conveniens* intersected in the Supreme Court's 1972 decision in *The Bremen*.[11] As happened in *The Bremen*, these doctrines come together when a motion is brought to stay or dismiss an action on grounds of *forum non conveniens* and there exists a choice of court clause in a contract between the parties. When the choice of court clause derogates from the forum court (as was the case in *The Bremen*), that clause may be a factor weighing in favour of dismissal on grounds of *forum non conveniens* so that the case is tried in the chosen court. When the clause involves prorogation in favour of the forum court, however, its enforcement runs counter to an argument in favour of litigation in another court on the grounds of *forum non conveniens*. In this latter category of cases, respect for the chosen forum may come into conflict with the application of the doctrine of *forum non conveniens* in a manner that allows courts to produce results that can be difficult to reconcile. While the Hague Convention on Choice of Court Agreements gives clear precedence to an exclusive choice of court agreement over the doctrine of *forum non conveniens*,[12] that same result does not always occur in the common law application of the doctrine, particularly in the US.

Following *The Bremen*, US courts have tended to honour choice of court clauses in freely negotiated contracts, even in the face of a *forum non conveniens* motion seeking litigation in a court not chosen by the parties in their contract.[13] In other

(it can have the opposite effect by favouring the stronger party that can impose terms on the weaker party, including the choice of court term) it was championed in the Hague Choice of Courts Convention as a bow to party autonomy generally.

[10] In civil law jurisdictions, this confluence was between choice of court and the doctrine of *lis alibi pendens*.

[11] *The Bremen* (n 4).

[12] Hague Choice of Courts Convention (n 6) Art 5(2).

[13] With the Supreme Court's 1991 decision in *Carnival Cruise Lines*, respect for choice of court clauses became, in the view of some commentators, almost unquestioning in allowing the imposition

cases, the existence of a choice of court agreement in favour of a foreign court can weigh in favour of a *forum non conveniens* motion to dismiss or stay proceedings in the forum not chosen.[14]

The US *forum non conveniens* doctrine – with its inclusion of public interest factors – allows courts broad discretion to decline to hear a case even when it is filed in a court with proper jurisdiction and venue.[15] Nonetheless, as in most countries, courts in the US now generally respect party autonomy in private commercial contracts and will uphold reasonable choice of forum clauses, including choice of court agreements.[16] This has not always been so, however. Prior to 1972, US courts were reluctant to enforce clauses that would choose to have litigation in a court other than the one in which proceedings were first brought.[17] This changed when the Supreme Court, in an admiralty case, ruled clearly in favour of upholding a business-to-business choice of court clause in a freely negotiated contract in *The Bremen*.[18]

III. Choice of Court Prior to *The Bremen*

An exclusive choice of court agreement typically has two functions: first, by party consent it confers the power to adjudicate on a court that, but for the clause, might not have had jurisdiction; and second, it may waive access to the jurisdiction of

of choice of court on weaker parties to a contractual relationship: *Carnival Cruise Lines Inc v Shute*, 499 US 972 (1991). See, eg, Borchers, 'Forum Selection Agreements in the Federal Courts After *Carnival Cruise*: A Proposal for Congressional Reform' (1992) 67 *Washington Law Review* 55; Heiser, 'Forum Selection Clauses in State Courts: Limitations on Enforcement After *Stewart* and *Carnival Cruise*' (1993) 45 *Florida Law Review* 361; Liesemer, 'Carnival's Got the Fun … and the Forum: A New Look at Choice-of-Forum Clauses and the Unconscionability Doctrine after *Carnival Cruise Lines Inc v Shute*' (1992) 53 *University of Pittsburgh Law Review* 1025.

[14] See n 143 and accompanying text.

[15] For a complete discussion of the US and other common law states' application of the doctrine of *forum non conveniens*, see Brand and Jablonski, Forum Non Conveniens: *History, Global Practice and Future Under the Hague Convention on Choice of Court Agreements* (OUP, 2007).

[16] There is a tendency to refer to choice of court agreements as 'forum selection clauses', setting up a comparison with arbitration agreements. See, eg, Born, *International Commercial Arbitration*, 3rd edn (Wolters Kluwer, 2021) 70 ('contractual dispute resolution provisions typically take one of two basic forms: (a) forum selection clauses; or (b) arbitration agreements'). 'Forum-selection clause' was the term used by the US Supreme Court for the choice of court agreement in *The Bremen* (n 4), 9: ('Forum-selection clauses have historically not been favored by American courts'). With the Convention on Choice of Court Agreements now in effect in more than 30 states, it makes sense for purposes of both consistency and clarity to distinguish between 'arbitration agreements' and 'choice of court agreements': www.hcch.net/en/instruments/conventions/status-table/?cid=98. As the US Supreme Court stated in *Scherk v Alberto-Culver Co* 417 US 506, 519 (1974), 'An agreement to arbitrate before a specified tribunal [as], in effect, a specialized kind of forum-selection clause that posits not only the situs of suit but also the procedure to be used in resolving the dispute'. Both are 'forum-selection clauses', and in this chapter I use 'choice of court agreement' and 'arbitration agreement' to designate these two principal kinds of 'forum-selection agreements'.

[17] nn 19–21 and accompanying text.

[18] *The Bremen* (n 4).

other courts.[19] The idea that parties may submit to jurisdiction by consent has long been recognised in the US.[20] It is the second function that US courts historically tended to question. Thus, prior to *The Bremen*, US courts hesitated to enforce choice of court clauses in international contracts when doing so would 'oust' the US forum court of jurisdiction.[21] This approach was largely inconsistent with the law in other nations, especially many civil law nations, which tended to respect party autonomy in forum selection from a much earlier date.[22]

A choice of court agreement cannot change sovereign rules of jurisdiction. Thus, it really is inappropriate to think of such an agreement as 'ousting' a court of jurisdiction. A court not chosen in a choice of court agreement still has jurisdiction to hear the case if its rules of jurisdiction allow it; it simply is subject to the contractual commitment of the parties that the case be heard in another court. Nonetheless, the ouster doctrine gathered multiple rationales in

[19] Juenger, 'Supreme Court Validation of Forum-Selection Clauses' (1972) 19 *Wayne Law Review* 49, 51.

[20] ibid 51.

[21] See, for example, *Carbon Black Export Inc v The Monrosa* 254 F2d 297, 300–01 (5th Cir 1958), *cert dismissed*, 359 US 180 (1959) ('agreements in advance of controversy whose object is to oust the jurisdiction of the courts are contrary to public policy and will not be enforced'). It has been said that this position rested on the rationale that '(1) the parties cannot by agreement in the contract alter the jurisdiction of the courts, and (2) such contractual stipulations are violative of public policy': Nanda, *The Law of Transnational Business Transactions* (Clark Boardman, 1986) §8.02(1)(a). Some commentators consider significant the distinction between conferring and ousting jurisdiction ('prorogation' versus 'derogation' in civil law terms). However, it has also been suggested that 'The real issue … is not whether the parties can by agreement "confer" or "oust" jurisdiction, but whether the selected or ousted court will exercise its own jurisdiction in such a way as to give effect to the intention of the parties': Delaume, *Transnational Contracts* (Oceana, 1986) §6.01. This latter approach is consistent with the language of the decision in *The Bremen* (n 4), 12 ('No one seriously contends in this case that the forum-selection clause "ousted" the District Court of jurisdiction over [the plaintiff's] action. The threshold question is whether that court should have exercised its jurisdiction to do more than give effect to the legitimate expectations of the parties, manifested in their freely negotiated agreement, by specifically enforcing the forum clause'). For a discussion of the pre-*Bremen* case law which often held choice of forum provisions void as against public policy, see Gruson, 'Forum-Selection Clauses in International and Interstate Commercial Agreements' (1982) *University of Illinois Law Review* 133, 138–47.

[22] See, for example, *Law v Garrett*, 8 Ch D 26 (CA 1878); *Glenor v Meyer* 2 H Bl 603 (CP 1796). See generally Mehren, 'International Commercial Arbitration: The Contribution of the French Jurisprudence' (1986) 46 *Louisiana Law Review* 1045 (discussing the civil law roots of party autonomy in forum selection); see also Aballi, 'Comparative Developments in the Law of Choice of Forum' (1986) 1 *New York University Journal of International Law and Politics* 178, 205 (mentioning that the civilian tradition of party autonomy allowed for enforcement of choice of court clauses); Cutler, 'Comparative Conflicts of Law: Effectiveness of Contractual Choice of Forum' (1985) 20 *Texas International Law Journal* 97, 113, 122 (discussing forum selection clauses acceptance in France and England); Lenhoff, 'The Parties' Choice of a Forum: "Prorogation Agreements"' (1960) 15 *Rutgers Law Review* 414 (noting civil law acceptance of forum selection clauses). But see Brand, *Transactions Fundamentals* (2019) 347 ('The traditional rule in Latin American nations was that the competence of a court to hear a case …, and a choice of forum or choice of law clause would not be taken to oust the court of its competency over a matter'); Mullenix, 'Another Choice of Forum, Another Choice of Law: Consensual Adjudicatory Procedure in Federal Court' (1988) 57 *Fordham Law Review* 291, 309 (noting that enforcement was not universal).

late-nineteenth- and early-twentieth-century decisions in US courts.[23] Some courts justified the ouster doctrine by claiming it protected the rights of the parties to have access to courts.[24] Others followed the doctrine based on concern for the restriction of remedies in a manner that could 'bring the administration of justice into disrepute'.[25]

The Massachusetts Supreme Judicial Court reasoned in 1856, that private parties should not be able to change rules of court, including jurisdictional rules, stating that 'The rules to determine in what courts and counties actions may be brought are fixed, upon considerations of general convenience and expediency, by general law'.[26] The most-quoted language supporting the ouster doctrine came in the US Supreme Court's 1874 decision in *Home Insurance Co v Morse*, where the Court stated that 'agreements in advance to oust the courts of the jurisdiction conferred by law are illegal and void'.[27] The ouster doctrine persisted even though other courts, and commentators, criticised it as baseless, thus preventing private agreements from influencing the exercise of jurisdiction by courts.[28]

Two developments helped set the stage for ending the ouster doctrine. The Federal Arbitration Act of 1925 required that courts both honour private agreements to arbitrate and honour the resulting arbitral awards, thus providing legislative foundation for party autonomy in choosing a forum for dispute resolution.[29] The ability to choose arbitration, and thus remove a case from

[23] See Marcus, 'The Perils of Contract Procedure: A Revised History of Forum Selection Clauses in the Federal Courts' (2008) 82 *Tulane Law Review* 973, 994–95 ('the ouster doctrine required a court that had jurisdiction over a case to adjudicate, notwithstanding the parties' agreement to litigate elsewhere'); Gruson, 'Forum-Selection Clauses' (1982) 138–47.

[24] *Home Ins Co v Morse*, 87 US 445 (1874) ('every citizen is entitled to resort to all the courts of the country, and to invoke the protection which all the laws or all those courts may afford him. A man may not barter away his life or his freedom, or his substantial rights'.). See also *Healey v Eastern Building and Loan Assoc*, 17 Pa Super 385, 392 (Pa Super 1901) ('The general jurisdiction of the several courts of the commonwealth is established by law, not only for the security of private rights, but, by securing these, for the promotion of the good order and peace of society. It is against public policy, therefore, that parties should, by the terms of a private agreement, in advance oust their jurisdiction') (*quoting* Rea's Appeal, 13 WNC 546).

[25] *Nute v Hamilton Mut Ins Co* 72 Mass 174 (1856) is the first reported case of the ouster doctrine, in which the Massachusetts Supreme Court rejected a choice of court provision in an insurance policy as an inappropriate attempt to alter a court's procedural rules: at 184. In 1916, the same court interpreted its *Nute* decision to contain a general prohibition on 'ousting' the jurisdiction of a court: *River Paper Co v Hammermill Paper Co* 223 Mass 8, 15–16, 111 NE 678, 680 (1916).

[26] *Nute* (ibid) 184.

[27] *Home Ins Co v Morse* (n 24) 451. See Juenger, 'Supreme Court Validation' (1972).

[28] See, for example, *Kulukundis Shipping Co v Amtorg Trading Corp* 126 F2d 978, 983–84, 1942 AMC 364, 371–72 (2d Cir 1942) (describing the history of hostility to the ouster doctrine); *US Asphalt Ref Co v Trinidad Lake Petroleum Co* 222 F 1006, 1007 (SDNY 1915) ('a more unworthy genesis cannot be imagined'); Professor Leflar criticised the ouster doctrine as a 'traditional thought precluding set[] of senseless words', noting that it may have been helpful when judges were paid per case and thus did not want to find cases outside of their jurisdiction: Leflar, '*The Bremen* and the Model Choice of Forum Act' (1973) 6 *Vanderbilt Journal of Transnational Law* 375, 376, 384.

[29] Federal Arbitration Act (n 3) §§1–14. See Juenger (n 19). ('If a court would yield to a private agreement requiring the parties to seek justice before the U.S.S.R. Chamber of Commerce Foreign Trade Arbitration Commission … why not defer to the courts of a sister state?'); Borchers,

consideration by courts that otherwise have jurisdiction, weakened the arguments behind the ouster doctrine. The second development was the willingness of federal courts exercising admiralty subject matter jurisdiction to embrace party choice, particularly in international cases.[30]

The Second Circuit Federal Court of Appeals began to carve away at the ouster doctrine in 1949, in *Krenger v Pennsylvania Railroad Co*,[31] when it honoured a choice of court agreement it found to be reasonable, while continuing to claim allegiance to the ouster doctrine. In his concurring opinion, Learned Hand J found there to be no 'absolute taboo against [choice of court] contracts at all',[32] insisting that choice of court clauses are only invalid when they are unreasonable.[33] The same Court followed in 1955, in *Wm H Muller & Co v Swedish American Line Ltd*,[34] enforcing a choice of court clause in admiralty, holding that such clauses are enforceable as long as they are 'not unreasonable'.[35] The *Muller* court echoed Hand J's concurrence in *Krenger*, which had been a case of diversity jurisdiction. In *Muller*, the Court applied a *forum non conveniens* test, weighing the choice of court agreement selecting Swedish courts against other *forum non conveniens* factors in determining the reasonableness of the agreement.[36] Noting the many contacts with Sweden, and the likelihood of a just outcome in Swedish courts, the Court found that the agreement was reasonable and should be enforced.[37]

Despite the Second Circuit's decision in *Muller*, the Fifth Circuit held fast to the ouster doctrine in its 1958 decision in *Carbon Black Export v The Monrosa*,[38] providing a blanket refusal to enforce a choice of court agreement.[39] The *Carbon Black* decision provided a new anchor for the ouster doctrine, supporting the view that a US court with jurisdiction to adjudicate had the absolute responsibility to

'Forum Selection Agreements in the Federal Courts After *Carnival Cruise*' (1992) 61–62 (describing the Federal Arbitration Act as a 'crack' in the 'crumbling ouster doctrine').

[30] This was likely due to admiralty jurisdiction's broad inclusion of all things relating to the sea, including suits between foreigners for acts done in foreign waters: 28 USC §1333. See Marcus, 'The Perils of Contract Procedure' (2008) 997. In the early twentieth century, a number of admiralty courts followed the Ouster Doctrine and declared choice of forum clauses void per se. See, for example, *Kuhnhold v Compagnie Generale Transatlantique* 251 F 387, 388 (SDNY 1918); *Gough v Hamburg Amerikanische Packetfahrt Aktiengesellschaft* 158 F 174, 175 (SDNY 1907); *Prince Steam-Shipping Co v Lehman* 39 F 704, 704 (SDNY 1889). However, dismissal of jurisdiction in admiralty courts often relied on the doctrine of *forum non conveniens*: Marcus (n 23) 996. The doctrine originated in admiralty courts as early as the eighteenth century but did not move into mainstream courts until the mid-nineteenth century. In admiralty, the doctrine was meant to limit the adjudicatory power US Courts had over aliens to avoid insulting foreign powers.

[31] *Krenger v Pennsylvania RR* 174 F2d 556, 560–61 (2d Cir), *cert denied*, 338 US 866 (1949).

[32] ibid 560–61 (Hand J, concurring).

[33] ibid.

[34] 224 F2d 806 (2d Cir 1955).

[35] ibid 808.

[36] ibid.

[37] ibid.

[38] 254 F2d 297 (5th Cir 1958).

[39] The Supreme Court originally granted certiorari in the *Carbon Black* case, setting up a resolution of the conflict with the Second Circuit, but then dismissed the writ because the clause at issue in *Carbon Black* was not drafted broadly enough to cover an *in rem* action. *Carbon Black* (n 21).

exercise that jurisdiction.[40] This remained particularly troubling for courts exercising admiralty jurisdiction, who took the doctrine as preventing them from declining jurisdiction even when it might be reasonable to do so.[41]

Commentators tended to reject the harshness of the ouster doctrine and the *Carbon Black* decision, instead embracing the Second Circuit's 'reasonableness' doctrine set forth by *Muller*.[42] By 1964, the Supreme Court signalled a possible shift, recognising the validity of a non-exclusive choice of court agreement in a purely domestic contract.[43] Nonetheless, the ambivalent state of US law on choice of court was reflected in the black letter of the Restatement (Second) Conflict of Laws, completed in 1971, where section 80 stated: 'The parties' agreement as to the place of the action cannot oust a state of judicial jurisdiction, but such an agreement will be given effect unless it is unfair or unreasonable'.[44]

The cases demonstrate that the development of US law on choice of court agreements must be considered along with the doctrine of *forum non conveniens*, and many courts simply deal with a choice of court agreement as one factor in a *forum non conveniens* analysis.[45] This was clearly the case in the Second Circuit's *Muller* decision, which balanced the choice of court agreement there with other traditional *forum non conveniens* factors.[46] While the *forum non conveniens* doctrine was not a firm part of US law until it became widely accepted through the Supreme Court's 1947 decision in *Gulf Oil v Gilbert*,[47] the *Gilbert* list of private interest factors generally is applied to include the extent to which the parties have agreed on a court or otherwise waived jurisdiction in other courts.[48]

In 1948, Congress effectively pre-empted common law *forum non conveniens* in the context of the transfer of a case from one Federal District Court to another by enacting 28 USC §1404(a). That provision states:

> For the convenience of parties and witnesses, in the interest of justice, a district court may transfer any civil action to any other district or division where it might have been brought or to any district or division to which all parties have consented.[49]

[40] Marcus (n 23) 994–95.

[41] See, for example, *Can Malting Co v Paterson SS Ltd* 285 US 413, 422 (1932) ('the proposition that a court having jurisdiction must exercise it is not universally true; else the admiralty court could never decline jurisdiction on the ground that the litigation is between foreigners').

[42] See, for example, Juenger (n 19) 55.

[43] *National Equipment Rental Ltd v Szukhent* 375 US 311, 315–16 (1964).

[44] Restatement (Second) Conflict of Laws §80 (1971). In 1988, this provision was amended to read: 'The parties' agreement as to the place of the action will be given effect unless it is unfair or unreasonable'.

[45] nn 138–143 and accompanying text.

[46] *Muller* (n 34) (weighing the *forum non conveniens* factors against the choice of court agreement in order to measure reasonableness).

[47] *Gulf Oil Corp v Gilbert* 330 US 501, 504 (1947). For a more detailed discussion of the development and application of the *forum non conveniens* doctrine in the US, see Brand and Jablonski, Forum Non Conveniens (1007) 37–74.

[48] See Brand and Jablonski (n 15) 46.

[49] 28 USC §1404(a).

IV. Zapata Off-Shore Drilling Company: Of Oil Rigs and Presidents

The Bremen is most interesting for its legal impact. Its ties to US political history, however, add a gloss to the context of the case. The Zapata Off-Shore Company was founded by George HW Bush, who later became the 41st President of the United States.

The path to George HW Bush's ownership of Zapata Off-Shore began with the involvement of both of his grandfathers in the early development of the US oil industry. His paternal grandfather, Samuel Bush, was President of Buckeye Steel Casings, a company in which the Rockefeller family's Standard Oil held a large minority interest.[50] George HW Bush's maternal grandfather, George Herbert Walker, was a Director of Petroleum Bond and Share, and the Barnsdall Corporation, both involved in the oil industry.[51] He was also president of Georgian Manganese, a mineral enterprise in the Soviet Caucasus owned by Averell Harriman, who also acquired Dresser Manufacturing, which provided oil field services.[52]

George HW Bush's father, Prescott Bush, was on the board of directors of Dresser Manufacturing, which became heavily involved in defence contracting in World War II.[53] Soon after his 1945 marriage to Barbara Pierce, George HW Bush moved to Odessa, Texas, to work at a subsidiary of Dresser and learn the oil business.[54] After a number of associations with others to develop both land-based and off-shore drilling operations, Bush focused on off-shore drilling, with global operations in the Persian Gulf, Trinidad and Borneo.[55] His efforts were supported by his uncle, Herbert Walker, who helped finance the Zapata Off-Shore Company.[56] Bush and the company moved to Houston, where the oil rig business grew, concluding contracts with Gulf Oil, Standard Oil of California and Royal Dutch Shell, in the Persian Gulf.[57]

After an unsuccessful 1964 run for a US Senate seat from Texas, George HW Bush won a seat in the US House of Representatives, taking that office in January 1967. He sold his Zapata Off-Shore Company stock for approximately $1 million, and his uncle, Herbert Walker Jr, continued to be the primary investor in the company.[58]

[50] Phillips, *American Dynasty: Aristocracy, Fortune, and the Politics of Deceit in the House of Bush* (Penguin Books, 2005) 151.

[51] ibid 151.

[52] ibid 152.

[53] ibid 152–53.

[54] Schweizer and Schweizer, *The Bushes: Portrait of a Dynasty*, 1st edn (Anchor Books, 2005) 95.

[55] ibid 140.

[56] The name of the company came earlier when Bush and his then business partner, George John Overby, saw a movie poster for the Marlon Brando film, *Viva Zapata*, and decided to name their company at that time Zapata Petroleum: Schweizer and Schweizer (n 55) 104.

[57] Schweizer and Schweizer, *The Bushes* (2005) 140.

[58] ibid.

V. *The Bremen v Zapata Off-Shore Company*[59]

A. The Facts

Also in 1967, Zapata Off-Shore Company entered a contract to drill wells in the Adriatic Sea. To do so, they needed a tug to tow their rig, the *Chapparal*, from Louisiana to a point just off the Italian coast near Ravenna, Italy.[60] Zapata solicited and received bids from several companies, including Unterweser Reederei, a German firm.[61] When Unterweser submitted the low bid for the job, it was asked by Zapata to provide a contract for approval.[62] Unterweser submitted its contract, which contained the details of the towage, as well as a choice of court clause and two clauses that would exculpate Unterweser from liability to the drilling rig, even for damage resulting from the negligence of Unterweser or its employees.[63] The choice of court clause stated: 'Any dispute arising must be treated before the London Court of Justice'.[64]

A Zapata vice president reviewed the contract submitted by Unterweser, and made several changes, but did not alter the choice of court clause or the exculpatory clauses.[65] The Zapata vice president then signed the contract with those changes and forwarded it to Unterweser in Germany. Unterweser accepted the changes in November 1967.

Unterweser selected the deep-sea tug, the *Bremen*, to tow the *Chapparal*. The Bremen departed Venice, Louisiana, with the *Chaparral* oil rig in tow on 5 January 1968.[66] On 9 January, while still in the Gulf of Mexico, a storm caused the elevator legs attached the *Chapparal* to break off and fall into the sea, and also caused serious damage to the rig's platform.[67] Zapata instructed the *Bremen* to tow the rig to port in Tampa, Florida.[68]

B. The Legal Development of the Case

With the tug and platform in Florida, on 12 January 1968, Zapata brought suit in admiralty in the US District Court in Tampa,[69] claiming *in personam* jurisdiction

[59] *The Bremen* (n 4).
[60] ibid 2.
[61] ibid.
[62] ibid.
[63] The exculpatory clauses stated: '1. … [Unterweser and its] masters and crews are not responsible for defaults and/or errors in the navigation of the tow. 2 … b) Damages suffered by the towed object are in any case for the account of its owners'. *The Bremen* (n 4) 3, fn 2.
[64] *The Bremen* (n 4) 2.
[65] ibid 3. The contract also provided that any insurance for the *Chapparal* was to be 'for account of Zapata', and Zapata chose to be self-insured on all its rigs.
[66] ibid.
[67] ibid.
[68] ibid.
[69] US district courts have subject matter jurisdiction for admiralty and maritime matters under Art III, S 2 of the United States Constitution and 28 USC §1333.

over Unterweser for damages and *in rem* jurisdiction over the *Bremen*, alleging breach of contract and negligent towing.[70] Unterweser moved to dismiss the action for either lack of jurisdiction or on *forum non conveniens* grounds or, in the alternative, to stay the action pending the submission of the dispute to the 'London Court of Justice' pursuant to the choice of court clause in the contract.[71]

Unterweser also commenced an action against Zapata in the High Court of Justice in London, seeking damages for breach of the towage contract.[72] Zapata's challenge to jurisdiction in London (by motion to set aside service outside the jurisdiction) was rejected, leaving the parties with parallel proceedings in the US and England.[73] Lord Willmer, in the English Court of Appeal, noted that 'The law on the subject … is not open to doubt …. It is always open to parties to stipulate that a particular Court shall have jurisdiction over any dispute arising out of their contract'.[74] While he also stated that this 'is not an inflexible rule', and that the English court has discretion, he did not find 'sufficient circumstances … to make it desirable, on the grounds of balance of convenience, that proceedings should not take place in' England.[75]

The District Court in Tampa denied Unterweser's motion to dismiss or stay Zapata's action there, relying on the Fifth Circuit's statement in the *Carbon Black* decision that 'agreements in advance of controversy whose object is to oust the jurisdiction of the courts are contrary to public policy and will not be enforced'.[76] That Court also issued an anti-suit injunction, enjoining Unterweser from pursuing its action in the UK.[77]

The Fifth Circuit Court of Appeals upheld the District Court's application of the *forum non conveniens* doctrine as applied by the District Court, also giving little weight to the choice of court clause. It instead gave significant weight in the *forum non conveniens* analysis to preserving the choice by a US plaintiff of a US court.[78] The Appeals Court also expressed concern about the exculpatory clauses in the towing contract, which it found to be 'apparently contrary to public policy

[70] The relatively quick filing of the case allowed Zapata to claim *in rem* jurisdiction over the Bremen through arrest by the US marshal while the vessel was still in port. The tug was then released. Unterweser provided security in the amount of $3,500,000, the amount of damages Zapata was claiming in the suit: *The Bremen* (n 4) 4.

[71] *The Bremen* (n 4) 4. Note that there is (and was) no 'London Court of Justice'. Willmer LJ interpreted these words to mean the High Court of Justice in the UK: *Unterweser Reederei GmbH v Zapata Off-Shore Co* ('*The Chaparral*') [1968] 2 Lloyd's Rep 158, 162–63 (CA).

[72] *The Bremen* (n 4) 4.

[73] *The Chaparral.*

[74] ibid 162–63.

[75] ibid 162–63.

[76] *The Bremen* (n 4) 6, quoting *Carbon Black* (n 21) 300–01. See also *Re Unterweser Reederei GmbH* 428 F2d 888, 893 (5th Cir 1970) (using the same language).

[77] *Re Unterweser Reederei GmbH* 296 FSupp 733 (MD Fla 1969).

[78] This element relies heavily on the language in *Gulf Oil Corp v Gilbert* (n 47) 508 that 'unless the balance is strongly in favour of the defendant, the plaintiff's choice of forum should rarely be disturbed': *The Bremen* (n 4) 6.

and unenforceable in American courts', stating that such clauses 'would be held prima facie valid and enforceable by an English court'.[79] Thus,

> The district court was entitled to consider that remanding Zapata to a foreign forum, with no practical contact with the controversy, could raise a bar to recovery by a United States citizen which its own convenient courts would not countenance.[80]

The decision of the original Court of Appeals panel of three judges, which included a dissent by one of them, was taken up by the Fifth Circuit *en banc*. The result was a *per curium* adoption of the original Court of Appeals majority opinion, with six of the 14 judges participating then joining a dissent written by Wisdom J, who had written the dissent in the original panel.[81] The principal focus of the earlier majority opinion was on the doctrine of *forum non conveniens*, with the choice of court clause being one factor considered by the Court. The decision found that factor to be outweighed by other factors, including the plaintiff's choice of forum to begin litigation, and the fact that the exculpatory clauses, considered to be in violation of US public policy, would be upheld in a UK court.[82]

In the Supreme Court, the majority opinion, written by Burger CJ, held the choice of court clause in the towing contract to be enforceable. Burger's analysis began with language focused more on practical matters of international trade than on prior common law:

> Here we see an American company with special expertise contracting with a foreign company to tow a complex machine thousands of miles across seas and oceans. The expansion of American business and industry will hardly be encouraged if, notwithstanding solemn contracts, we insist on a parochial concept that all disputes must be resolved under our laws and in our courts. Absent a contract forum, the considerations relied on by the Court of Appeals would be persuasive reasons for holding an American forum convenient in the traditional sense, but in an era of expanding world trade and commerce, the absolute aspects of the doctrine of the *Carbon Black* case have little place and would be a heavy hand indeed on the future development of international commercial dealings by Americans. We cannot have trade and commerce in world markets and international waters exclusively on our terms, governed by our laws, and resolved in our courts.[83]

Burger acknowledged that the decision he authored went against existing US common law, stating that 'Forum-selection clauses have historically not been

[79] *Re Unterweser Reederei, GmbH* (n 7), 895.

[80] ibid.

[81] *Re Unterweser Reederei GmbH* 446 F2d 907 (1971).

[82] The Supreme Court listed the following factors considered by the Court of Appeals in the balancing test required by the *forum non conveniens* doctrine: (1) the flotilla never 'escaped the Fifth Circuit's mare nostrum, and the casualty occurred in close proximity to the district court'; (2) a considerable number of potential witnesses, including Zapata crewmen, resided in the Gulf Coast area; (3) preparation for the voyage and inspection and repair work had been performed in the Gulf area; (4) the testimony of the Bremen crew was available by way of deposition; (5) England had no interest in or contact with the controversy other than the forum-selection clause. *The Bremen* (n 4) 7.

[83] *The Bremen* (n 4) 8–9.

favored by American courts'.[84] Noting that the case was one in admiralty jurisdiction, he went on to state that the 'correct doctrine to be followed' in such cases is that choice of court clauses 'are prima facie valid and should be enforced unless enforcement is shown by the resisting party to be "unreasonable" under the circumstances'.[85] He then reasoned that, if, as the Court had held in *National Equipment Rental Ltd v Szukhent*,[86] parties may validly consent to be found for service of process through contractual agents in jurisdictions in which they have no other presence, then it was logical to uphold an agreement to suit in a specific court as well.[87] He also found support in comparative common law analysis, acknowledging that the approach he was now championing 'is substantially that followed in other common-law countries including England'.[88]

Burger's opinion seemed to cut away at the application of *forum non conveniens* balancing of factors in cases involving choice of court clauses. Thus, the fact that the damage occurred in the Gulf of Mexico, which is closer to the US than to the UK, was merely fortuitous, and 'The elimination of all such uncertainties by agreeing in advance on a forum acceptable to both parties is an indispensable element in international trade, commerce, and contracting'.[89] Moreover, after noting that both the District Court and the Court of Appeals had 'placed the burden on Unterweser to show that London would be a more convenient forum than Tampa', he clearly states that 'the contract expressly resolved that issue'.[90] He then seems to distance the appropriate analysis for choice of court further from the doctrine of *forum non conveniens*, stating, 'The correct approach would have been to enforce the forum clause specifically unless Zapata could clearly show that enforcement would be unreasonable and unjust, or that the clause was invalid for such reasons as fraud or overreaching'.[91]

Burger CJ's opinion returns to a discussion of *forum non conveniens*, however, when he notes that a choice of court clause in a 'freely negotiated private international agreement' itself rebuts any claim of inconvenience for either party in a *forum non conveniens* analysis.[92] In doing so, he reverts to language used in a *forum non conveniens* analysis, stating that, on the convenience scale,

> Whatever 'inconvenience' Zapata would suffer by being forced to litigate in the contractual forum as it agreed to do was clearly foreseeable at the time of contracting. In such circumstances it should be incumbent on the party seeking to escape his contract to show that trial in the contractual forum will be so gravely difficult and inconvenient that he will for all practical purposes be deprived of his day in court. Absent that, there

[84] ibid 9.
[85] ibid 10, citing cases including the *Muller* decision of the Second Circuit.
[86] 375 US 311 (1964).
[87] *The Bremen* (n 4) 11.
[88] ibid.
[89] ibid 13–14.
[90] ibid 15.
[91] ibid.
[92] ibid 16.

is no basis for concluding that it would be unfair, unjust, or unreasonable to hold that party to his bargain.[93]

While the Court of Appeals had relied on the US/English difference in treatment of exculpatory clauses as a matter of public policy in refusing to enforce the choice of London courts, Burger CJ quotes at length from Wisdom J's dissent in that Court in support of being extremely careful in exercising any reliance on domestic public policy grounds for upending party agreements, especially where 'the conduct in question is that of a foreign party occurring in international waters outside our jurisdiction'.[94]

Ultimately, in any common law balancing test, one of the most important factors is the burden of proving which side the balance of factors favours. On this matter, Burger CJ found that the District Court 'erroneously placed the burden of proof on Unterweser to show that the balance of convenience was strongly in its favor'.[95] In a footnote, he states that the London Court had applied 'the proper burden of proof', when it noted that 'There is probably a balance of numbers in favour of the Americans, but not, as I am inclined to think, a very heavy balance'.[96] Providing guidance for the trial court on remand, he noted that Zapata (as the party asking that the choice of court agreement *not* be honoured) would have the 'opportunity to carry *its heavy burden* of showing not only that the balance of convenience is strongly in favour of trial in Tampa (that is, that it will be far more inconvenient for Zapata to litigate in London than it will be for Unterweser to litigate in Tampa), but also that a London trial will be so manifestly and gravely inconvenient to Zapata that it will be effectively deprived of a meaningful day in court'.[97]

One of the clear results of the decision in *The Bremen* was to put to rest the ouster doctrine that had provided the foundation for denying effect to party choice of court, with the result being that choice of court clauses are thus seen as having nothing to do with the existence or non-existence of jurisdiction. Rather:

The argument that such clauses are improper because they tend to 'oust' a court of jurisdiction is hardly more than a vestigial legal fiction. It appears to rest at core on historical judicial resistance to any attempt to reduce the power and business of a particular court and has little place in an era when all courts are overloaded and when businesses once essentially local now operate in world markets. It reflects something of a provincial attitude regarding the fairness of other tribunals. No one seriously contends in this case that the forum selection clause 'ousted' the District Court of jurisdiction over Zapata's action. The threshold question is whether that court should have exercised its jurisdiction to do more than give effect to the legitimate expectations of the parties, manifested in their freely negotiated agreement, by specifically enforcing the forum clause.[98]

[93] ibid 18.
[94] ibid, quoting *Re Unterweser Reederei, GmbH* (n 76) 907–08 (Wisdom J, dissenting).
[95] ibid.
[96] ibid fn 19.
[97] ibid 19 (emphasis added).
[98] ibid 12.

What Burger CJ's opinion did not do was use the opportunity presented to clearly separate the analysis of choice of court agreements from the doctrine of *forum non conveniens*. This was unfortunate. By not providing for a clear separation, the Supreme Court left open the continued confusion raised by the question of just how the presence of a freely negotiated choice of court agreement affects a motion for dismissal on the grounds of *forum non conveniens*. This stands in stark contrast to the position taken, for example, in the EU under the Brussels I (Recast) Regulation, where a choice of court agreement naming the court of a Member State gives that court jurisdiction that is explicitly stated to be exclusive.[99] In the EU system, there is no balancing to be done. The existence of a valid choice of court agreement both starts and ends the analysis.

VI. *The Bremen* and the Continued Development of US Common Law on Choice of Court Agreements[100]

A. General Development of Choice of Court Doctrine

While *The Bremen* was a case in admiralty, it did not take long for both lower federal courts[101] and state courts[102] to extend its rationale to non-admiralty cases. Subsequent courts,[103] and the Restatement,[104] have interpreted *The Bremen* to provide a presumption of validity for a choice of court agreement, with the party contesting the agreement carrying the burden of proving grounds for an exception.

[99] Brussels I (Recast) Regulation (n 1) Art 25.

[100] This section of the current chapter is developed largely from Brand and Jablonski (n 15) 187–210.

[101] See, for example, *Coastal Steel Corp v Tilgham Wheelabrator Ltd* 709 F2d 190 (3d Cir), *cert denied*, 464 US 938, 104 S Ct 349 (1983); *Crown Beverage Co v Cerveceria Moctezuma SA* 663 F2d 886, 888 (9th Cir 1981); *Staco Energy Prod Co v Driver-Haris Co* 509 F Supp 1226, 1227 (SD Ohio 1981) (dictum); *Republic Int'l Corp v Amco Eng'rs Inc* 516 F2d 161, 168 (9th Cir 1975); *Shepard Niles Crane & Hoist Corp v Fiat SpA* 84 FRD 299, 305 (WDNY 1979) (dictum); *Hoes of Am Inc v Hoes* 493 F Supp 1205, 1209 (CD Ill 1979); *Cruise v Castleton Inc* 449 F Supp 564 (SDNY 1978); *Gaskin v Stumm Handel GmbH* 390 F Supp 361 (SDNY 1975).

[102] See, for example, *Abadou v Trad* 624 P2d 287 (Alaska 1981); *Volkswagenwerk AG v Klippan GmbH* 611 P2d 498 (Alaska), *cert. denied*, 449 US 974 (1980); *Societe Jean Nicolas et Fils JB v Mousseux* 123 Ariz 59, 597 P2d 541 (1979); *Smith, Valentino & Smith Inc v Superior Court* 17 Cal 3d 491, 551 P2d 1206, 131 Cal Rptr 374 (1976); *Elia Corp v Paul N Howard Co* 391 A2d 214 (Del Super Ct 1978); *Green v Clinic Mawsters Inc* 272 NW2d 813 (SD 1978); *Hi Fashion Wigs Profit Sharing Trust v Hamilton Inv Trust* 579 SW2d 300 (Tex Civ App 1979).

[103] See, for example, *Santamauro v Taito do Brasil Industria E Comercia* 587 F Supp 1312, 1314 (ED La 1984) ('The burden is on the party resisting enforcement of the clause to prove that the choice was unreasonable, unfair or unjust, or to show that the clause is invalid by reason of fraud or overreaching or that enforcement would contravene a strong public policy of this forum'); *City of New York v Pullman Inc*, 477 F Supp 438, 441 fn 10 (SDNY 1979), *aff'd*, 662 F2d 919 (2d Cir 1981), *reh'g denied*, 28 September 1981, *cert denied*, 454 US 1038, 102 S Ct 1038 (1982) ('Agreements entered into by knowledgeable parties in an arm's-length transaction that contain a forum selection provision are enforceable absent a showing of fraud, overreaching, unreasonableness or unfairness').

[104] Restatement (Second) of the Conflict of Laws §80 (1971).

While Burger CJ indicated that choice of court agreements would be enforced, he noted qualification to this rule by limiting it to agreements 'unaffected by fraud, undue influence, or overweening bargaining power'.[105] His *Bremen* analysis ultimately provided three exceptions to the enforcement of a choice of court clause: (1) where enforcement of the provision would result in substantial inconvenience, or denial of an effective remedy;[106] (2) where there has been fraud, overreaching, or unconscionable conduct in contract relations;[107] and (3) where enforcement would result in a violation of public policy or the transaction is otherwise unfair, unjust or unreasonable.[108] Success in the application of these exceptions is relatively rare.[109] The first – dealing with inconvenience or denial of an effective remedy – is worth further comment, however, since it can be seen as a modified *forum non conveniens* analysis. In the language of *The Bremen* decision:

> [W]here it can be said with reasonable assurance that at the time they entered the contract, the parties to a freely negotiated private international commercial agreement contemplated the claimed inconvenience, it is difficult to see why any such claim of inconvenience should be heard to render the forum clause unenforceable.[110]

The continued validity of some form of *forum non conveniens* analysis in the face of an otherwise valid choice of court agreement clearly is inconsistent with full respect for party autonomy in choosing a forum. Cases have most clearly faced this limitation on party choice when dealing with the related issues of transfer between

[105] *The Bremen* (n 4) 12.

[106] ibid 18.

[107] ibid 15. The Supreme Court further developed the fraud exception in *Scherk v Alberto-Culver Co* (n 16) when it stated: 'This qualification does not mean that any time a dispute arising out of a transaction is based upon an allegation of fraud … the clause is unenforceable. Rather, it means that [a] … forum-selection clause in a contract is not enforceable if the *inclusion of that clause in the contract* was the product of fraud or coercion'. *Scherk v Alberto-Culver Co* (n 16) 519 fn 14 (emphasis in original).

[108] *The Bremen* (n 4) 15. The Court rejected Zapata's argument that the exculpatory clause contained in the agreement violated US public policy.

[109] Commentators have divided these exceptions in different ways. See, for example, Covey and Morris, 'The Enforceability of Agreements Providing for Forum and Choice of Law Selection' (1984) 61 *Denver Law Journal* 837, 842 ('The primary limitations … are fraud, public policy, adhesion, statutory restrictions and inconvenience of the contractual forum'); Gruson (n 21) 163–85 (dividing the exceptions into the categories of (1) fraud, (2) bargaining relationship between the parties, (3) nature of the selected forum, (4) public policy of the forum, (5) statutory restrictions on forum-selection clauses, (6) inconvenience of the contractual forum and (7) other instances of unreasonableness). See also The Model Choice of Forum Act, §3, which lists the following exceptions to enforcement of choice of forum clauses: '(1) the court is required by statute to entertain the action; (2) the plaintiff cannot secure effective relief in the other state, for reasons other than delay in bringing the action; (3) the other state would be a substantially less convenient place for the trial of the action than this state; (4) the agreement as to the place of the action was obtained by misrepresentation, duress, the abuse of economic power, or other unconscionable means; or (5) it would for some other reason be unfair or unreasonable to enforce the agreement. Reese, 'The Model Choice of Forum Act' (1969) 17 *American Journal of Comparative Law* 292, 294.

[110] *The Bremen* (n 4) 16.

federal courts under 28 USC §1404(a). A year after *The Bremen*, in *Plum Tree Inc v Stockment*,[111] the Third Circuit US Court of Appeals stated:

> Congress set down in § 1404(a) the factors it thought should be decisive on a motion for transfer. Only one of these – the convenience of the parties – is properly within the power of the parties themselves to affect by a forum-selection clause. The other factors – the convenience of witnesses and the interest of justice – are third party or public interests that must be weighed by the district court; they cannot be automatically outweighed by the existence of a purely private agreement between the parties. Such an agreement does not obviate the need for an analysis of the factors set forth in § 1404(a) and does not necessarily preclude the granting of the motion to transfer.[112]

While the interpretation of a statute is a different matter than the application of a common law doctrine, the §1404(a) analysis is very similar to that applied under the common law doctrine of for a *forum non conveniens*,[113] and the Third Circuit in *Stockment*, clearly applied the balancing of both private interest and public interest factors to the §1404(a) analysis.

As noted earlier,[114] in the EU, Article 25 of the Brussels I (Recast) Regulation allows a useful comparison with US case law on business-to-business choice of court issues.[115] Article 25 provides that where parties have agreed 'that a court or the courts of a Member State are to have jurisdiction to settle any disputes which have arisen or which may arise in connection with a particular legal relationship, that court or those courts shall have jurisdiction'.[116] The same article goes on to provide that '[s]uch jurisdiction shall be exclusive unless the parties have agreed otherwise'.[117] Because the Brussels Regulation does not allow for declining such exclusive jurisdiction, Article 25 ends the analysis when the alternative forum is another EU Member State, and no *forum non conveniens* claim may be asserted.[118]

There exist at least two important differences between the Brussels scheme for choice of court clauses and that existing under the common law in the US. First,

[111] 488 F2d 754 (3d Cir 1973).

[112] *Plum Tree Inc* (n 111) 757–58.

[113] The State of New York has taken a clear position on the intersection between choice of court and *forum non conveniens*, but in a rule that only applies in limited circumstances. When New York recodified its doctrine of *forum non conveniens* in 1984, the legislature specifically provided that its courts cannot stay or dismiss an action on *forum non conveniens* grounds where the contract contains both a New York choice of forum clause and a New York choice of law clause and the transaction involved exceeds $1,000,000 in value. NY CPLR §327 (McKinney, 2001) (1984 NY Laws, Ch 421, §2). This provision assures that New York courts will accept jurisdiction in accordance with the parties' choice in large transnational contracts, and that a *forum non conveniens* challenge cannot be used to frustrate the agreement of the parties. It does not, however, provide a similar rule when the choice of court agreement leads away from New York courts.

[114] n 99 and accompanying text.

[115] Brussels I Recast Regulation (n 1), Art 25.

[116] ibid.

[117] ibid.

[118] But see *Erich Gasser GmbH v MISAT Srl* Case C-116/02 [2003] ECR I-14693 (holding that Brussels I (Recast) Regulation, Art 29 *lis pendens* (first seised) rule trumps Art 25 exclusive choice of court rule). For more general discussion of the *Italian torpedo* problem this creates, see Brand, 'Transaction Planning Using Rules on Jurisdiction and the Recognition and Enforcement of Judgments' (2014) 358 *Recueil des cours de l'Académie de La Haye* 212–47.

unlike the Brussels rule, US courts have not been willing to consider the allocation of authority to the chosen court to be either absolute[119] or exclusive.[120] Thus, the existence of a choice of court clause does not guarantee that the dispute may be resolved only in that forum, unless the clause expressly creates such exclusivity.[121] In this respect, under the Brussels system, European courts go further in their respect for the chosen court.

The other difference works the other way. US courts will uphold choice of court clauses in consumer contracts where European courts will not do so. The Brussels rule honours a choice of court clause in a consumer contract only if the agreement: (1) is entered into after the dispute has arisen; (2) allows the consumer to bring proceedings in courts other than those otherwise available; or (3) provides for jurisdiction in the courts of the state that is the habitual residence of both the consumer and the other party.[122] Similar limitations are included for insurance contracts and individual contracts of employment.[123]

US law provides no such limitation on the enforcement of choice of court clauses for consumer, insurance, and employment contracts. In *Carnival Cruise Lines Inc v Shute*,[124] the Supreme Court upheld enforcement of a clause requiring that disputes be brought in the state courts of Florida. A Washington State consumer purchased a cruise ticket from a local travel agent for a trip off the coast of Mexico.[125] The choice of court clause in fine print was on a cruise ticket that was not received until after the consumer had arranged and paid for the cruise.[126] Blackmun J relied in part on an economic rationale to enforce the clause, stating that 'passengers who purchase tickets containing a forum clause like that at issue in this case benefit in the form of reduced fares reflecting the savings that the cruise line enjoys by limiting the fora in which it may be sued'.[127] Thus, the Supreme Court made clear the wide breadth of the *Bremen* policy favouring enforcement of choice of court clauses, encompassing even consumer contracts that contain no element of true negotiation.[128]

[119] See, for example, *Sudduth v Occidental Peruana Inc*, 70 F Supp 2d 691 (ED Tex 1999) (denying defendant's motion to dismiss on *forum non conveniens* grounds in favour of the chosen court, holding that the mandatory choice of court clause was invalid under *Bremen*); *Dentsply International Inc v Benton*, 965 F Supp 574 (MD Pa 1997) (refusing to enforce the mandatory choice of court clause in an employment contract holding that it was the result of unequal bargaining power).

[120] See, for example, *Steve Weiss & Co Inc v INALCO*, 1999 WL 386653 (SDNY 1999) (not reported in F Supp 2d) (stating that 'where parties only specify in a contract clause where jurisdiction is proper' the clause generally will not be enforced unless other language clearly identifies 'the parties intent to make jurisdiction exclusive'); *Hull 753 Corp v Flugzeugwerke* 58 F Supp 2d 925 (ND Ill 1999) (holding that a clause granting jurisdiction to German courts was not exclusive absent clear language that only German courts shall have jurisdiction).

[121] nn 136–47 and accompanying text.

[122] Brussels I (Recast) Regulation (n 1), Art 19.

[123] ibid Arts 15 and 23.

[124] 499 US 585 (1991).

[125] ibid 587.

[126] ibid.

[127] ibid 594.

[128] For a discussion of the application of the unconscionability doctrine to invalidate such clauses, see Mullenix, 'Gaming the System: Protecting Consumers from Unconscionable Contractual Forum-Selection and Arbitration Clauses' (2015) 66 *Hastings Law Journal* 719.

B. The Convergence of Choice of Court Clauses and the *Forum Non Conveniens* Doctrine

The US common law doctrines on enforcement of choice of court clauses and *forum non conveniens* have had an uncomfortable evolutionary relationship, necessitating a clear understanding of the manner in which the two doctrines intersect. *The Bremen* does provide some guidance on the intersection of the doctrines of choice of court and *forum non conveniens*, but its language has not always been consistently considered in subsequent lower court decisions. The Court of Appeals, in its treatment of the case, concluded that 'a forum-selection clause "will not be enforced unless the selected state would provide a more convenient forum than the state in which suit is brought"'.[129] It determined that 'the District Court did not abuse its discretion in refusing to decline jurisdiction on the basis of *forum non conveniens*'.[130] While the Supreme Court decided the case with a primary focus on the choice of court agreement, and not on a *forum non conveniens* analysis, it specifically remanded the case to the trial court in a manner that would seem to mix the choice of court and *forum non conveniens* analyses:

> [T]o allow Zapata opportunity to carry its heavy burden of showing not only that the balance of convenience is strongly in favor of trial in Tampa (that is, that it will be far more inconvenient for Zapata to litigate in London than it will be for Unterweser to litigate in Tampa), but also that a London trial will be so manifestly and gravely inconvenient to Zapata that it will be effectively deprived of a meaningful day in court, we remand for further proceedings.[131]

This language can be interpreted to require a modified version of *forum non conveniens* analysis, in which the burden is on the party seeking to avoid the chosen court to prove that court to be 'manifestly and gravely inconvenient'.[132] Subsequent courts have neither followed this balancing of conveniences approach, nor have they applied the same allocation of the burden of proof in all regards.

The categorisation of choice of court agreements in US jurisprudence creates special issues in the application of *The Bremen* principles in the context of a *forum non conveniens* analysis. In most US courts, there exists a presumption that a choice of court agreement is persuasive and not mandatory (ie, non-exclusive, not exclusive). An exclusive ('mandatory') choice of court clause[133] may lead honouring that clause if, under *The Bremen* analysis, there is no substantial inconvenience, fraud or public policy reason for a contrary result, but a majority presumption of non-exclusivity may prevent enforcement at the outset.[134] Moreover, courts have interpreted certain choice of court clauses to be non-exclusive, but accompanied

[129] *The Bremen* (n 4) 7 (quoting from the Court of Appeals).
[130] ibid.
[131] ibid 19.
[132] ibid.
[133] Courts often use the term 'mandatory' clause to refer to an exclusive clause in US courts.
[134] nn 136–137 and accompanying text.

by a waiver of the right to challenge jurisdiction and venue when an action is brought in the chosen court.[135] In these situations, the application of the clause may depend upon which party gets to the court first, and the court in which it files the case.

The combination of the choice of court and *forum non conveniens* doctrines creates the possibility of at least six different basic factual relationships with conceivable further variations on each of them. This can be demonstrated in the following table:

Table 5.1 *Forum non conveniens* status

Choice of court clause	Chosen court	Court not chosen
Exclusive clause	1	2
Non-exclusive clause (with waiver of right to contest)	3	4
Non-exclusive clause	5	6

This table demonstrates the possibilities at the intersection between choice of court and *forum non conveniens*, and the complexity that remains despite what might seem like reasonable clarity in the majority opinion in *The Bremen*.

The majority US rule is that all choice of court clauses are non-exclusive unless clearly stated otherwise.[136] The rationale for this position has been stated as follows:

> To be mandatory, a forum selection clause must contain language that clearly designates a forum as the exclusive one.
>
> A permissive clause merely grants jurisdiction to the named forum, and does not preclude a cause of action from being brought elsewhere. If the court determines that a forum selection clause is not mandatory, that does not mean that the clause is effectively written out of the contract. It simply means that the clause does not preclude a party from bringing suit in any jurisdiction where venue is proper.
>
> For a forum selection clause to be mandatory, the clause must clearly display the intent of the contracting parties to choose a particular forum to the exclusion of all other fora. Despite containing forceful words like 'shall,' the clause will not be deemed mandatory unless it is clear that the clause mandates the exclusive use of a particular forum.[137]

This strong preference for interpreting choice of court clauses as non-exclusive provides some guidance, but is not always conclusive in all courts. At least one court would appear to find all choice of court clauses to be exclusive.[138]

[135] See Brand and Jablonski (n 15) 201–02.

[136] See, for example, *Steve Weiss & Co Inc v INALCO SpA* 1999 WL 386653 (SDNY 1999) (not reported in F Supp 2d) ('In the absence of specific exclusionary language, this court will not assume an intent to confer exclusive jurisdiction on Italian courts').

[137] *Arguss Communications Group Inc v Teletron Inc* 2000 WL 36936 *6–7 (DNH 1999) (not reported in F Supp 2d) (citations omitted).

[138] *Florida Polk County v Prison Health Servs Inc* 170 F3d 1081, 1083–84 (11th Cir 1999) ('It is a venerable principle of contract law that the provisions of a contract should be construed so as to give every

A split in Federal Circuit Courts demonstrates the lack of clarity on the interplay of an exclusive choice of court clause with the doctrine of *forum non conveniens*. The Second Circuit has indicated that a federal district court should begin by applying *The Bremen* test to determine the enforceability of a choice of court clause, and that a defendant's motion to dismiss on *forum non conveniens* grounds should be considered only if the court first finds that the parties did *not* form a contract with a valid choice of court clause.[139] The Fifth Circuit has taken a similar approach, rejecting a *forum non conveniens* challenge to an exclusive choice of court clause on the grounds that 'increased cost and inconvenience are insufficient reasons to invalidate foreign forum-selection or arbitration clauses'.[140] The Seventh Circuit has interpreted *The Bremen* to mean that a choice of court clause is to be enforced unless the

> party challenging its enforcement can 'clearly show that enforcement would be unreasonable and unjust, or that the clause was invalid for such reasons as fraud or overreaching,' or that 'trial in the [chosen] forum will be so gravely difficult and inconvenient that he will for all practical purposes be deprived of his day in court.'[141]

Thus, the Seventh Circuit finds an exclusive choice of court clause presumptively valid and enforceable.[142] The First Circuit, on the other hand, has ruled that a choice of court clause does not control the decision on a *forum non conveniens* motion to dismiss, but is 'simply one of the factors that should be considered and balanced' by the court in its *forum non conveniens* analysis.[143]

Despite this split in the Circuits (and recognising that not all courts give clear consideration to whether the clause in question is exclusive or non-exclusive), the general approach to exclusive choice of court clauses is to enforce them, either under *The Bremen* test or under a *forum non conveniens* analysis.[144] Chosen courts

provision meaning,' and 'To read the forum-selection clause as permissive would render it surplusage, [but to] read the clause as mandatory – thus requiring all litigation arising out of the contract to take place in the [selected court] – gives the provision meaning').

[139] *Evolution Online Sys Inc v Koninklijke PTT Nederland NV* 145 F3d 505, 509–10 (2d Cir 1998). See also *Sudduth v Occidental Peruana Inc* (n 119), where the district court denied the defendant's motion to dismiss on *forum non conveniens* grounds only after determining that a mandatory choice of court clause was invalid under the *Bremen* standards.

[140] *Mitsui & Co (USA) Inc v Mira M/V* 111 F3d 33, 37 (5th Cir 1997).

[141] *AAR International Inc v Nimelias Enterprises SA*, 250 F3d 510, 525 (7th Cir 2001), quoting from *The Bremen* (n 4) 15, 17. See also *Northwestern Nat'l Ins Co v Donovan* 916 F2d 372, 378 (7th Cir 1990) (holding that agreement to an exclusive choice of court clause waives objections to venue on the basis of cost or inconvenience to the party).

[142] *AAR International* (ibid) 525, quoting from *Bonny v Society of Lloyd's* 3 F3d 156, 160 (7th Cir 1993).

[143] *Royal Bed & Spring Co Inc v Famossul Industria e Comercio de Moveis Ltda* 906 F2d 45, 51 (1st Cir 1990).

[144] See, for example, *Mercier v Sheraton International Inc* 981 F2d 1345 (1st Cir 1992) (applying *forum non conveniens* analysis despite apparent exclusive choice of court clause but dismissing in favour of the Turkish court named in the clause). When New York recodified its doctrine of *forum non conveniens* in 1984, it specifically provided that its courts cannot stay or dismiss an action on *forum non conveniens* grounds where the contract contains both a New York choice of forum clause and a New York choice of law clause and the transaction involved exceeds $1,000,000. NY CPLR §327 (McKinney's 2001) (1984 NY Laws, Ch 421, §2).

have kept cases when faced with a *forum non conveniens* motion to dismiss,[145] and courts not chosen have dismissed cases in favour of the court selected in the clause.[146] Nonetheless, some courts have refused to enforce clauses choosing another court when considered in the context of a motion to dismiss based on *forum non conveniens*.[147]

While the Second Circuit relies strictly on a *Bremen* analysis when the choice of court clause is exclusive,[148] it applies a *forum non conveniens* analysis when addressing a non-exclusive choice of court clause. This is demonstrated in the case of *John Boutari & Son, Wines & Spirits SA v Attiki Importers & Distribs*,[149] where the Second Circuit held that dismissal of an action on a distributorship contract

[145] See, for example, *Heller Financial Inc v Midwhey Powder Co* 883 F3d 1286 (7th Cir 1989) (denying motion for dismissal or transfer under 28 USC §1404(a)); *Poddar v State Bank of India*, 79 F Supp 2d 391, 393 (SDNY 2000) (denying dismissal where clause created mandatory jurisdiction in courts in both India and the US); *Cambridge Nutrition AG v Fotheringham*, 840 F Supp 299 (SDNY 1994) (enforcing New York choice of court clause despite motion to dismiss brought by Spanish defendant for whom trial in New York was inconvenient).

[146] See, for example, *Royal Bed & Spring Co v Famoussul Industria E Comercio de Moveis Ltda* (n 143) (enforcing Brazilian choice of court clause in distributorship agreement under a *Bremen* analysis); *Caribe BMW Inc v Bayerische Motoren Werke Aktiengesellschaft* 821 F Supp 802, *set aside, vacated and remanded on other grounds*, 19 F2d 745 (1st Cir 1994) (finding German choice of court clause valid and enforceable on a multi-factor analysis); *Bonny v Society of Lloyd's* (n 142) (honouring English choice of court clause under *Bremen* analysis by dismissal of action under securities underwriting contract); *General Elec Co v G Siempelkamp GmbH & Co*, 29 F3d 1095 (6th Cir 1994) (dismissing case on *forum non conveniens* challenge in favour of German courts in accordance with choice of court clause in the sales contract); *Omron Healthcare v Maclaren Exports*, 28 F2d 600 (7th Cir 1994) (applying *forum non conveniens* analysis to enforce English choice of court clause in distributorship contract); *Aceequip Ltd v Am Eng'g Corp* 153 F Supp 2d 138 (DC Conn 2001) (denying motion to dismiss in favour of Japanese court when mandatory clause selected Connecticut forum); *Lawler v Schumacher Filgters Am* 832 F Supp 1044 (ED Va 1993) (enforcing choice of court clause in consultancy agreement naming German courts as the chosen forum); *Hunter Distrib Co v Pure Beverage Partners* 820 F Supp 284 (ND Miss 1993) (granting motion to dismiss for improper venue when faced with choice of court clause naming Arizona courts); *TUC Electronics Inc v Eagle Telephonics Inc* 698 F Supp 35 (D Conn 1988) (dismissing case brought in Connecticut in face of New York state court choice of court clause, applying combination of *Bremen* and *forum non conveniens* factors); *Santamauro v Taito do Brasil Industria E Comercia Ltda* 587 F Supp 1312 (ED La 1984) (applying *Bremen* analysis to dismiss action on sales contract brought in Louisiana despite Brazilian choice of court clause); *Skyline Steel Corp v RDI/ Caesars Riverboat Casino LLC* 44 F Supp 2d 1337, 1338 (ND Ala 1999) (sending case to chosen forum under 28 USC §1404(a) transfer statute, but stating, 'the law of the Eleventh Circuit is that forum selection clauses are virtually impossible to overcome by an application of the general principles of forum non conveniens').

[147] See, for example, *Sudduth v Occidental Peruana Inc* (n 119) (refusing enforcement of clause requiring disputes to be brought in Peruvian courts where both parties were in the US); *Pearcy Marine v Seacor Marine* 847 F Supp 57 (SD Tex 1993) (finding London choice of court clause to be unenforceable as a result of unequal bargaining power). Similarly, courts have found that the existence of a valid choice of court clause does not prevent a transfer for *forum non conveniens* purposes under 28 USC §1404(a). *Plum Tree Inc* (n 111) 757–58 (3d Cir 1973) ('Such an agreement does not obviate the need for an analysis of the factors set forth in §1404(a) and does not necessarily preclude the granting of the motion to transfer').

[148] *Evolution Online Sys Inc v Koninklijke PTT Nederland NV* (n 139) 509–10.

[149] 22 F3d 51 (2d Cir 1994). See also *Blanco v Banco Industrial de Venequela SA* 997 F2d 974 (2d Cir 1993) (affirming a dismissal on *forum non conveniens* grounds even though New York was one of three jurisdictions named in a non-exclusive choice of court clause).

on *forum non conveniens* grounds was erroneous, and that the case should be tried in a US Federal District Court despite a choice of court clause choosing a Greek court. The result was based in part on a finding that the clause was permissive and not mandatory. The Ninth Circuit applied a similar analysis to a case involving a clause selecting the Hong Kong courts but affirmed a dismissal on grounds of *forum non conveniens.*[150]

At least one commentator has stated that, in cases dealing with the convergence between choice of court clauses and the *forum non conveniens* doctrine, it makes 'little difference' whether the *Bremen* factors are applied, or the case is analysed under the *forum non conveniens* analysis.[151] This does not seem to hold true in all circumstances, however. In US courts, the designation of the type of choice of court clause helps determine whether the court will focus on a *Bremen* or a *forum non conveniens* analysis. This determination, in turn, has a substantial impact on the burden placed on each of the parties and the opportunity to challenge the trial court's decision on appeal.

Even if one can carefully catalogue each case to fit within the chart set forth above, that will not explain some US cases, or the opinions of some commentators. It has been suggested that 'Using *forum non conveniens* terminology, the parties lack the authority to contractually reallocate the various public interest factors, or those private ones of third parties not related to the contract'.[152] The same author suggests that, at a minimum, 'the existence of a forum selection clause should remove the individual parties' convenience or inconvenience from the court's consideration of the various private and public interest factors'.[153] The US is alone in requiring a balance of public interest factors among those countries in the common law world that have adopted the *forum non conveniens* doctrine. All other jurisdictions weigh only private interest factors in their *forum non conveniens* analysis.[154] The idea that *any* choice of court agreement, no matter what the type, may decide the private interest balance in favour of the chosen forum but will still subject the parties to a *forum non conveniens* analysis on the public interest factors would mean that no court could stop with the *Bremen* factors, and that the balancing required under traditional *forum non conveniens* analysis would always be necessary, even in the face of a valid, exclusive choice of court agreement. Even the cases that take this approach, however, often end up enforcing the choice of court agreement.[155]

[150] *FIL Leveraged US Government Bond Fund Ltd v TCW Funds Management Inc* 156 F3d 1236 (9th Cir 1998).

[151] McLemore, 'Forum-Selection Clauses and Seaman Personal Injury' (2000) 25 *Tulane Maritime Law Journal* 327, 350 ('The issue is essentially one of fairness and justice').

[152] Heiser, 'Forum Selection Clauses in State Courts' (1993) 396.

[153] ibid 397. See *Arthur Young & Co v Leong* 383 NYS2d 618, 619 (App Div), *appeal dismissed*, 390 NY2d 927 (1976) (stating that the existence of a choice of court clause 'obviated considerations of inconvenience to a party or a witness').

[154] See Brand and Jablonski (n 15) 111–13.

[155] See, for example, *Smith, Valentino & Smith Inc v Superior Court* 131 *Cal Rptr* 374, 551 P2d 1206, 1209–10 (Cal 1976) (enforcing Pennsylvania choice of court clause despite residence of plaintiff's

The US Supreme Court in *Erie v Tompkins* held that, in cases brought in Federal District Court under diversity subject matter jurisdiction (ie, cases not involving a question related to the Constitution, a federal statute, or a treaty), the court must apply state substantive statutory and common law.[156] Thus, while the federal court applies its own procedural rules, it generally must apply state substantive law in determining the issues before it. While there are some very limited areas of federal common law, when common law is applied in federal district courts exercising diversity subject matter jurisdiction, it most often is state common law that is being applied. This raises the question of whether the decision in *The Bremen* is either a rule on a procedural matter (in which case federal law applies) or created a rule of federal common law. The US Supreme Court has yet to address these questions.

Three cases in the US Supreme Court have addressed the question of enforceability of choice of court clauses.[157] Many thought the *Erie* question was going to be addressed in *Stewart Organization v Ricoh Corp*,[158] but the Court applied the 28 USC §1404(a) transfer statute, avoiding the question of whether there is federal common law on either choice of court or *forum non conveniens*. Because the Court has yet to comment on the *Erie* question in the wake of the *Bremen* decision, the applicable law has remained relatively unguided. The Circuits remain split on the *Erie* question for the enforceability of choice of court clauses in the context of diversity jurisdiction. Seven circuits have held that the enforceability of a choice of court clause implicates federal procedure.[159] The Seventh and Tenth Circuits have held that the law governing the contract as a whole also governs the enforceability of the choice of court agreement.[160] The First Circuit has not affirmatively decided the issue.[161] The Fourth Circuit has had different panels reach different conclusions, the first applied *Erie* and the second applied federal law.[162]

witnesses in California); *Prudential Resources Corp v Plunkett*, 583 SW2d 97, 99–100 (Ky Ct App 1979) (enforcing choice of court clause even where one party's witnesses would have to be presented by deposition since they would be unable to appear in person); *Hauenstein & Bermeister Inc v Met-Fab Indus* 320 NW2d 886, 890 (Minn 1982) (enforcing choice of court clause where inconvenienced witnesses could submit testimony by deposition).

[156] *Erie RR Co v Tompkins* 304 US 64 (1938).

[157] See *Stewart Org Inc v Ricoh Corp* 487 US 22, 33–41 (1988); *Scherk v Alberto-Culver Co* (n 16); *The Bremen* (n 4).

[158] *Stewart Org Inc v Ricoh Corp* (n 157) 33–41.

[159] *Phillips v Audio Active Ltd* 494 F3d 378 (2d Cir 2007); *Jumara v State Farm Ins Co* 55 F3d 873 (3d Cir 1995); *Ginter ex rel Ballard v Belcher, Prendergast & Laporte* 536 F3d 439 (5th Cir 2008); *Wong v PartyGaming Ltd* 589 F3d 821 (6th Cir 2009); *Fru-Con Const. Corp v Controlled Air Inc* 574 F3d 527 (8th Cir 2009); *Doe 1 v AOL LLC* 552 F3d 1077 (9th Cir 2009); *Manetti-Farrow Inc v Gucci America Inc* 858 F2d 509 (9th Cir 1988); *P & S Business Machines Inc v Canon US A Inc* 331 F3d 804 (11th Cir 2003).

[160] *Abbott Laboratories v Takeda Pharmaceutical Co Ltd* 476 F3d 421 (7th Cir 2007); *Yavuz v 61 MM Ltd*, 465 F3d 418 (10th Cir 2006).

[161] *Rivera v Centro Medico de Turabo Inc* 575 F3d 10 (1st Cir 2009).

[162] *Nutter v New Rents Inc* 945 F2d 398 (4th Cir 1991) (applying *Erie*); *Bryant Elec Co v City of Fredericksburg* 762 F2d 1192 (4th Cir 1985) (applying federal law).

VII. Conclusion

The case of *The Bremen* provides both a turning point toward greater respect for party autonomy and an incomplete resolution of issues involving proper treatment of choice of court agreements in international contracts. By clearly rejecting the ouster doctrine that had gained hold in US jurisprudence during the first half of the twentieth century, it brought choice of court analysis more closely in line with the treatment of arbitration agreements under the New York Convention. By not clearly separating choice of court analysis from the *forum non conveniens* doctrine, the case failed adequately to bring choice of court clauses clearly in line with arbitration clauses. It thus left arbitration in a preferred position in international contracts when compared to choice of court, frustrating both contract drafters and dispute resolution advocates. US ratification and implementation of the 2005 Hague Convention on Choice of Court Agreements could go a long way to solve the concerns left hanging by *The Bremen*.

6

Lucy's Argument: The *Spycatcher* Case in Australia

REID MORTENSEN

I. A Style More Appropriate to *Boys Own* or *Biggles*

At the conclusion of his memoir *Spycatcher: The Candid Autobiography of a Senior Intelligence Officer*,[1] Peter Wright, an MI5 agent discouraged with the British secret service, pondered retiring to Australia.[2] He did so. Accordingly, when Margaret Thatcher's Government tried to ban the publication of *Spycatcher*, it began in September 1985 by litigating in Australia. It was compelled to supplement that with proceedings in the UK, Hong Kong and New Zealand, but it meant that the Australian litigation was bound to receive disproportionate media attention. It did; but that attention arguably owed even more to the heightened sense of nationalism in Australia in the 1980s and to Wright's nationalistic lawyer.

It is still debatable whether *Spycatcher* deserved the attention that the British Government gave to it. Wright retired from MI5 in early 1976, so anything to be banned in the proceedings in the Supreme Court of New South Wales could not have happened within the previous decade. The book dealt with Wright's whole career as a counter-intelligence spy. The earlier pages were dominated by accounts of MI5's methods of surveillance and intelligence gathering,[3] with Wright's own expertise in electronic surveillance receiving most attention.[4] It recounted an assassination attempt and abduction,[5] relations with the CIA and FBI over many years,[6] Wright's view of MI5's relations with the French secret service,[7] and his

[1] Wright with Greengrass, *Spycatcher: The Candid Autobiography of a Senior Intelligence Officer* (William Heinemann Australia, 1987).

[2] ibid 381–82.

[3] ibid 45–47, 49–53, 131–32, 141–42, 171–72, 311–12.

[4] ibid 18–21, 32–34, 47–48, 56–67, 70–73, 81–88, 92–95, 99–100, 105–12, 118–20, 131–36, 140, 156, 167–68, 179–87, 195–97, 238–39, 358–59.

[5] ibid 154–58.

[6] ibid 100–05, 146–54, 302–07, 345–48, 364.

[7] ibid 239–40.

unsuccessful attempt to conduct surveillance of the Irish Government during The Troubles.[8] The latter part of *Spycatcher* dealt with Wright's Soviet spy-catching work.[9] This included his interrogation of Sir Anthony Blunt,[10] and his belief that MI5 Director-General Sir Roger Hollis was a Soviet 'mole'.[11] It ended with Wright's period as an adviser to a later Director-General, Sir Michael Hanley, whom Wright regarded as ill-experienced.[12] The book was readable, and written like a spy novel. One judge was to describe *Spycatcher* as being 'in a style … more appropriate to *The Boys Own Paper* or *Biggles' Flying Omnibus*'.[13]

Similar works in this genre had been published in the years before *Spycatcher*. Chapman Pincher's *Their Trade is Treachery*[14] had relied significantly on Wright as a source, and first revealed the official investigations into the suspicions that Hollis was a Soviet mole. Nigel West, the pen name for British MP Rupert Allason, had from 1980 published a series of books,[15] including *A Matter of Trust: MI5 1945–72*,[16] in which Allason denied that Hollis was working for the Soviets. The British Government took no action against Pincher. It had obtained an ex parte injunction against Allason in 1982 but, after he agreed to deletions, publication of *A Matter of Trust* was permitted.[17] In 1984, interviews with Wright, in which he continued to express his suspicions about Hollis, were published in *The Times* and broadcast in a Granada television documentary, and no action was taken.[18] The Government's inconsistent approach to these disclosures would be prominent in the Australian *Spycatcher* proceedings, as Wright's lawyer tried to secure an explanation as to why this book, specifically, was the subject of multinational litigation.

However, the legal significance of the Australian *Spycatcher* case – *Attorney-General (United Kingdom) v Heinemann Publishers Australia Pty Ltd*[19] – lies elsewhere. It certainly created an international media circus and notoriety for Wright's Australian lawyer. Specifically for Australia, the adjudication also gave rise to more serious judicial consideration of the implications of its recently granted legal independence and of the nation's place within the Commonwealth. However, for

[8] ibid 160–62.

[9] ibid 42–43, 95–96, 120–43, 164–78, 187–88, 193–98, 204–12, 221, 235–38, 241–97, 320–35.

[10] ibid 164, 213–32.

[11] ibid 76–78, 89–92, 96–97, 143–44, 177–78, 189, 190–94, 199–204, 213, 232–34, 279, 282, 289–91, 321, 336–42, 372, 376, 379–81.

[12] ibid 298–302, 332–34, 349, 357–61, 376.

[13] See *Attorney-General (United Kingdom) v Heinemann Publishers Australia Pty Ltd* (1987) 8 NSWLR 341, 373–74 ('*Spycatcher* NSWSC').

[14] Pincher, *Their Trade is Treachery: The Full Unexpurgated Truth About the Penetration of the Free World's Secret Defences* (Sidgwick & Jackson, 1981).

[15] West, *MI5: British Security Service Operations, 1909–1945* (Stein and Day, 1981); West, *MI6: British Secret Intelligence Service Operations: 1909–45* (Weidenfeld and Nicolson, 1983).

[16] West, *A Matter of Trust: MI5 1945–72* (Weidenfeld and Nicolson, 1982).

[17] See the account referred to in *Attorney-General v Guardian Newspapers Ltd (No 2)* [1990] 1 AC 109, 131–32 ('*Spycatcher* UK').

[18] See ibid 132.

[19] (1988) 165 CLR 30 ('*Spycatcher* HCA'). See also *Spycatcher* NSWSC (n 13) and *Attorney-General (United Kingdom) v Heinemann Publishers Australia Pty Ltd* (1987) 10 NSWLR 86 ('*Spycatcher* NSWCA').

private international law, *Spycatcher*'s importance lies in its giving a simple, coherent and certain doctrine for prohibiting foreign governments' attempts at exercising their sovereignty outside their borders. And, although the doctrine was described by the High Court of Australia with restraint and discipline, it actually originates in the back-room research of a rising law graduate. This chapter is an account of the Australian *Spycatcher* litigation, from the *cause célèbre* trial in Sydney to the High Court's consolidation of disparate precedents into a single doctrine that reconciled private and public international law. An appreciation of the context of Australian nationalism in the 1980s helps to understand how this was achieved.

II. Australian Legal Nationalism … and a Nationalist

The High Court of Australia decided the *Spycatcher* case in the year of Australia's bicentennial celebrations. It was not entirely a coincidence that the shape of the decision was a clearer expression of nationalism in private international law doctrine. In anticipation of the Australian bicentennial but, in truth, compatibly with decolonisation processes that the UK had pursued since the end of the Second World War, the last stage of Australian legal independence had been reached only two years beforehand. It had been a slow evolutionary process,[20] beginning with the grant of responsible government to New South Wales in 1842[21] – being replicated in the other Australian colonies[22] – the federation of the Australian colonies into the Commonwealth of Australia in 1901,[23] the recognition of Australia as a 'freely associated' dominion within the British Commonwealth of Nations in the Balfour Declaration of 1926, and the adoption of the Statute of Westminster in 1942.[24] The Australian federal Parliament had terminated appeals to the Privy Council in federal matters in 1968.[25] However, while the Commonwealth – the Australian national polity – enjoyed its independence by the 1970s, the states still effectively related to the UK as colonies: state governors were appointed by the Queen on the recommendation of the British Government; matters of state law could still, as an alternative to the High Court, be taken on appeal to the Privy Council; and the British Parliament could still legislate for Australia. All of that ceased with the passage in both the British and Australian federal Parliaments of the Australia Acts in 1986,[26] with the Queen's personal status as sovereign of each

[20] McKibbin, Connors and Harmes, *A Legal History for Australia* (Hart Publishing, 2021) 193–206, 243–62, 268–98.

[21] Australian Constitutions Act 1842.

[22] Australian Constitutions Act 1850.

[23] Commonwealth of Australia Constitution Act 1900.

[24] Statute of Westminster 1931; Statute of Westminster Adoption Act 1942.

[25] Privy Council (Limitation of Appeals) Act 1968; see also Privy Council (Appeals from the High Court) Act 1975.

[26] Australia Act 1986 (UK); Australia Act 1986 (Cth).

of the states reinforced.[27] It did not take long for the High Court of Australia, from then the sole final court of appeal in all matters of federal, state and territory law, to become aware that it was no longer shadowed by the Privy Council.[28]

Even before Sir Anthony Mason was appointed Chief Justice of Australia in 1987, the High Court had signalled that, while decisions of the House of Lords and its alter ego, the Privy Council, would be persuasive, they would no longer bind any Australian court.[29] However, it was the Mason court – the only High Court bench to be colloquially tagged with the Chief Justice's name – which gave effect to that position.[30] It was the Mason court that in 1992 would overrule the Privy Council's refusal to recognise prior Aboriginal and Torres Strait Islander claims to land,[31] and which elevated the pre-British settlement of the continent above what had been emphasised in the bicentennial celebrations. The Mason court was a bench of judges who mostly shared a mildly reformist outlook.[32] Although there is a legitimate argument that it was politicised,[33] it would be more accurate to describe the court's private law jurisprudence as 'distinctive' rather than 'activist' – even if some argue it to be 'distinctly Australian'.[34] The Mason court was not known for delivering joint judgments,[35] and Sir Anthony claimed that this had much to do with the deeply controversial nature of the cases before it.[36] Putting *Spycatcher* to one side, in private international law appeals the Mason court began with what was certainly a 'distinctly Australian' approach to applicable law in interstate litigation that came close to constitutionalising the whole field.[37] Entrenched positions, which have been considered rare in the Mason court,[38] nevertheless led to a retreat from there to extremely conservative, but uncertain, positions in questions of applicable law in tort.[39] These had to wait for two more Chief Justices before being corrected.[40] And, in *forum non conveniens*, the Mason court was markedly less reformist than other Commonwealth courts

[27] Australia Act 1986 (Cth), s 7.

[28] Gageler, 'The Coming of Age of Australian Law' in McDonald, Chen and Gordon (eds), *Dynamic and Principled: The Influence of Sir Anthony Mason* (Federation Press, 2022) 13–16.

[29] *Cook v Cook* (1986) 162 CLR 376, 390.

[30] McKibbin, Connors and Harmes (n 20) 296–97.

[31] *Mabo v Queensland (No 2)* (1992) 175 CLR 1, departing from *Cooper v Stuart* (1889) 14 App Cas 286. See McKibbin, Connors and Harmes (n 20) 314, 329–31.

[32] Gageler (n 28) 28–9.

[33] See Pierce, *Inside the Mason Court Revolution: The High Court of Australia Transformed* (Carolina Academic Press, 2006) 248–57.

[34] Lindell, 'Judge & Co: Judicial Law-Making and the Mason Court' (1998) 5 *Agenda* 83, 86.

[35] Gageler (n 28) 30; Mason, 'The High Court of Australia – Reflections on Judges and Judgments' (2013) 16 *Southern Cross University Law Review* 3, 10.

[36] Mason (ibid) 10.

[37] *Breavington v Godleman* (1988) 169 CLR 41.

[38] Gageler (n 28) 29.

[39] *McKain v RW Miller (South Australia) Pty Ltd* (1988) 174 CLR 1; *Stevens v Head* (1993) 176 CLR 433. See also Davies 'Exactly What is the Australian Choice of Law Rule in Torts Cases?' (1996) 70 *Australian Law Journal* 711.

[40] *John Pfeiffer Pty Ltd v Rogerson* (2000) 203 CLR 503 ('*Pfeiffer*').

of final appeal[41] although, at the very least, in *Voth v Manildra Flour Mills Pty Ltd*[42] it did give some certainty to Australian law by producing a joint judgment of four judges. Its record in private international law cases makes its approach and decision in *Spycatcher* all the more significant.[43]

Spycatcher also introduced the nation and the world to the Australian nationalist Malcom Bligh Turnbull. Intelligent, supremely self-confident, stubborn, arrogant and articulate – for his political oratory he was later known as 'the great communicator'[44] – in 2015 Turnbull would become the 29th Prime Minister of Australia. While studying law at Sydney University, Turnbull had worked as a journalist with the *Nation Review*, Radio 2SM and media baron Kerry Packer's Channel 9 television network.[45] At Oxford as Rhodes Scholar for New South Wales, he had also worked with the *Sunday Times*.[46] Turnbull was a 31-year-old solicitor when, in 1986, Wright and his publisher, Heinemann Australia, approached him to represent them against the British Government's efforts at stopping the publication of *Spycatcher* in Australia.[47] Turnbull had already practised at the Sydney Bar,[48] but squabbled with other barristers who were offended by his pincer movements of hard-ball litigation and of the print and broadcast media against Packer's opponents. He therefore left the Bar to work as in-house counsel for Packer (and while doing so suffered a Supreme Court decision that he had abused court process on Packer's behalf).[49] Turnbull and Packer's other in-house lawyer, Bruce McWilliam, left after a year, and established their own solicitors' practice with a general retainer for Packer's media business.[50] Soon afterwards, having received a recommendation from London solicitor David Hooper and another media-savvy Australian lawyer, London barrister Geoffrey Robertson, Heinemann and Wright gave instructions to Turnbull McWilliam

[41] cf *Oceanic Sun Line Special Shipping Company Inc v Fay* (1988) 165 CLR 197 with *Spiliada Maritime Corp v Cansulex Ltd* [1987] AC 460; *McConnell Dowell v Lloyd's Syndicate 396* [1988] 2 NZLR 257; *Brinkerhoff Maritime Drilling Corp v PT Airfast Services Indonesia* [1992] 2 SLR 776; *Amchem Products Inc v British Columbia (Workers Compensation Board)* [1993] 1 SCR 897.

[42] (1990) 171 CLR 538.

[43] For a similar assessment of the Mason court's approach in private international law, see Lindell (n 34) 86.

[44] Murphy, 'Malcolm's Back in the Middle' *Sydney Morning Herald* (18 September 2010), available at www.smh.com.au/national/malcolms-back-in-the-middle-20100917-15gdu.html; Blair, 'The Great Communicator' *The Daily Telegraph* (10 October 2015), available at www.dailytelegraph.com.au/blogs/tim-blair/the-great-communicator/news-story; Kenny, 'Election 2016: Malcolm Turnbull's Q&A Appearance His Best Campaign Performance' *The Australian* (21 June 2016), available at www.theaustralian.com.au/commentary/opinion/election-2016-malcolm-turnbulls-qa-appearance-his-best-campaign-performance/news-story.

[45] Turnbull, *A Bigger Picture* (Hardie Grant Books, 2020) 23–32.

[46] ibid 34–41.

[47] ibid 57.

[48] ibid 41–44.

[49] ibid 47–55.

[50] ibid 55–56.

to defend the *Spycatcher* claims in New South Wales.[51] They took on the entire matter for a paltry flat fee of A$20,000.[52]

Before *Spycatcher* was even finalised in the High Court, Turnbull had been a partner in establishing an investment bank: Whitlam Turnbull.[53] Through the 1990s he pursued banking and business interests, including a large stake in Internet service provider OzEmail, which he sold for A$57 million before the tech bubble burst.[54] He became a partner of Goldman Sachs Australia in 1998.[55] When Turnbull entered federal Parliament for the (centre-right) Liberal Party in 2004,[56] he was the wealthiest parliamentarian in Australia. However, through the 1990s he was best known for leading the campaign for Australia to become a republic. Turnbull cofounded the Australian Republican Movement (ARM) in 1993, and was the most prominent advocate in the 1999 referendum campaign to amend the Australian Constitution to replace the Queen as Head of State with a parliamentary-appointed President.[57] The referendum failed overall, and in all states.[58] He left the leadership of the ARM in 2000, and did not pursue the republican cause at all after he entered Parliament.

Turnbull's distinctive republican nationalism is important in the *Spycatcher* litigation. Apart from his powerful drive to win at all costs, it explains Turnbull's doggedness throughout the trial and appeals, and the tone of the media and political circus that he created in Australia and the UK. The fee cannot have been a motivation.[59] He did gain something in addition to his fees by publishing his own account of the *Spycatcher* proceedings,[60] and it also reveals that Australian independence – often negatively expressed as anti-British sentiment – impelled Turnbull throughout the proceedings. He wrote admirably of former Labor Prime Minister Gough Whitlam's assertion of Australian independence, and compared it unfavourably with Whitlam's Liberal Party predecessors in Government who were 'British to the bootstraps'.[61] At trial in *Spycatcher*, the British Government's efforts

[51] Turnbull, *The Spycatcher Trial* (Hardie Grant Publishing, 2020), republishing Turnbull, *The Spycatcher Trial* (William Heinemann, Melbourne,1988) 6, 8, 10, 12, 57.

[52] ibid 58.

[53] ibid 70–73.

[54] ibid 74–93.

[55] ibid 91–93, 105.

[56] ibid 118–20.

[57] ibid 94–104; Australia, Republic Advisory Committee and Turnbull, 'An Australian Republic: The Options' (Australian Government Publishing Service, Canberra,1993); Turnbull, *The Reluctant Republic* (William Heinemann Australia, Melbourne,1993). See Constitution Alteration (Establishment of a Republic) Bill 1999.

[58] To amend the Australian Constitution, a bill passed by the federal Parliament must be supported by a majority of voters and a majority of voters in a majority of the states: Constitution, s 128. See Australian Electoral Commission, '1999 Referendum Report and Statistics' (19 January 2011), available at www.aec.gov.au/Elections/referendums/1999_Referendum_Reports_Statistics/summary_republic.htm.

[59] n 52 and the text thereto.

[60] Turnbull (n 51).

[61] ibid 112.

at stopping Turnbull's cross-examination of Sir Robert Armstrong, the British Cabinet Secretary, led him to admit that 'these British … I hated with a passion'.[62] The optics in the trial in Sydney reinforced his wild colonial boy persona: Turnbull, alone, a business-suited solicitor-advocate, against teams of Queen's Counsel in the inherited English trappings of wigs and silk gowns. And also, a solicitor was cross-examining the British Cabinet Secretary.[63] He played to the gallery,[64] and got the media attention he wanted.[65] And while Turnbull denied it,[66] he did descend to an uglier side of Australian nationalism – 'pommy bashing'. The best thing he could say about Armstrong was that he 'had none of the mannered effeminacy that is so common with Englishman of his background'.[67] The wild colonial boy of the 1980s was a marked contrast to the suave, charming but still pugnacious federal politician of the 2010s.

Turnbull is the most important figure in the *Spycatcher* litigation and in presenting the principle of private international law that it developed. However, he was not himself responsible for developing the argument that was eventually accepted by the High Court in *Spycatcher*. In 1980, Turnbull had married Lucinda Mary Hughes, then a law student at Sydney University. Lucy is daughter of Tom Hughes KC, Attorney-General of Australia from 1969 to 1971 in John Gorton's Liberal Government. She is also a great-granddaughter of Sir Thomas Hughes, first Lord Mayor of Sydney in 1903. A formidable lawyer and politician herself, Lucy Turnbull would become Lord Mayor of Sydney in 2003, a century after her great-grandfather.[68] She was admitted to practise as a solicitor in New South Wales only in 1988,[69] but was engaged in the Turnbull McWilliam *Spycatcher* team from its initial preparations for trial in 1986. Peter Wright saw that Lucy Turnbull had had a critical role in winning his case,[70] and Malcolm Turnbull has consistently credited Lucy with the development of (what he called) 'the public international law' submission that a foreign government could not enforce its governmental interests in Australian courts.[71] Indeed, a surprising aspect of the *Spycatcher* litigation is that, throughout, the defence was a family affair: Malcolm Turnbull handling almost all of the advocacy, Lucy Turnbull undertaking the research and developing the ultimately decisive argument, and her father Tom Hughes appearing at the first hearing in the High Court.[72]

[62] ibid 70.
[63] Turnbull (n 45) 61.
[64] Norton-Taylor, 'From Spycatcher to Prime Minister: the Malcolm Turnbull I Knew' *The Guardian* (15 September 2015). available at www.theguardian.com/australia-news/2015/sep/14/malcolm-turnbull-spycatcher-lawyer-prime-minister.
[65] Turnbull (n 51) 121–26.
[66] ibid 121.
[67] ibid 48.
[68] Turnbull (n 45) 71, 114–15.
[69] Turnbull (n 51) 158.
[70] Wright (n 1) Acknowledgments.
[71] Turnbull (n 51) 159; Turnbull (n 45) 59, 66.
[72] Turnbull (n 51) 153.

III. The Law before *Spycatcher*

The private international law dimension to *Spycatcher* grew as the case proceeded through the appeal courts. Hardly mentioned, and treated by the judge as an afterthought, at trial, the private international law issues monopolised the submissions to the High Court of Australia. However, there was a need to refashion the presentation of private international law doctrine in the High Court as, otherwise, it gave the Turnbulls only two tools with which to work. Neither was closely fit for purpose.

The first was the common law's denial of jurisdiction to hear and determine proceedings that involved the enforcement of a foreign penal law. Although often expressed as a restraint on the court's jurisdiction,[73] the doctrine is one that leads a court to dismiss a claim on its merits. As explained by Lord Watson in the Privy Council's decision in *Huntington v Attrill*:[74]

> The rule has its foundation in the well-recognised principle that crimes, including in that term all breaches of public law punishable by pecuniary mulct or otherwise, at the instance of the State Government, or of some one representing the public, are local in this sense, that they are only cognizable and punishable in the country in which they were committed.

More would be made of that explanation, but the consequence was that even if proceedings were 'in the shape of a civil suit', they 'ought not to be admitted' if the purpose for bringing them was, in effect, to punish for breach of a penal law of that kind.[75] Lord Watson recognised that the line between penal laws that were within the ban, and laws that remained enforceable, was not easily drawn,[76] and conceded that penalties might be recoverable at common law when pursued 'by private persons in their own interest'.[77] At the time the *Spycatcher* trial began, the *Huntington v Attrill* doctrine had led courts to conclude that foreign government efforts to enforce confiscatory laws,[78] or to take control of funds to prevent the commission of foreign crimes,[79] had to be dismissed. The doctrine had, in obiter, been considered applicable to forfeiture laws.[80] It is also invariably coupled with a similar, and much older, denial of jurisdiction to enforce foreign revenue laws.[81]

[73] eg, *Huntington v Attrill* [1893] AC 150 (*Huntington*) at 155; *Government of India v Taylor* [1955] AC 491 (*Taylor*) at 507; *Attorney-General (New Zealand) v Ortiz* [1984] AC 1 (*Ortiz*) at 20; *Williams & Humbert Ltd v W&H Trade Marks (Jersey) Ltd* [1986] AC 387 at 437.

[74] *Huntington* (n 73) 156.

[75] ibid.

[76] ibid 156–61.

[77] ibid 157.

[78] eg, *Banco de Vizcaya v Don Alfonso de Bourbon y Austria* [1935] 1 KB 140; *Ortiz* (n 73).

[79] *Schemmer v Property Resources Ltd* [1975] Ch 273, 288.

[80] *R v Cuthbertson* [1981] AC 470, 476.

[81] *Holman v Johnson* (1775) 1 Cowp 341, 343; 98 ER 1120, 1121; *Attorney-General (Canada) v Schulze* (1901) 9 SLT 4; *Municipal Council of Sydney v Bull* [1909] 1 KB 7, 12; *Cotton v R* [1914] AC 176, 195; *Indian and General Investment Trust Co Ltd v Borax Consolidated Ltd* [1920] 1 KB 539, 550; *Re Visser*

A second, but more questionable, tool that was available to the Turnbulls was the emergent idea that the common law would deny the enforcement of a public law of a foreign country. There is a hint of this category in Lord Watson's advice in *Huntington v Attrill*,[82] and *Dicey & Morris* had advocated its existence.[83] However, 'the public law exclusion' was only stated as recently as 1982 in the English Court of Appeal's decision in *Attorney-General (New Zealand) v Ortiz*.[84] This was an attempt by the New Zealand Government to recover a Maori carving that had, after its sale to an English art dealer, eventually come to auction at Sotheby's in London. The proceedings were based on the Historic Articles Act 1962 (NZ), by which historical artefacts in New Zealand were forfeited to the Crown (in right of New Zealand). The House of Lords, speaking through Lord Brightman, dismissed the proceedings on the ground that the conditions for forfeiture under the New Zealand statute itself were not satisfied.[85] The Court of Appeal had reached the same conclusion, but gave additional obiter reasons on which Lord Brightman thought best not to comment.[86] Although there had been an earlier concession in extradition proceedings that a foreign public law might not be enforced in English courts,[87] at first instance in *Ortiz* Justice Staughton could find nothing in the common law to support it.[88] Lord Denning was the first to introduce the possibility that 'other public laws' of a foreign country – and Lord Denning apologised to his 'New Zealand friends' for calling them 'foreign'[89] – should not be enforced in civil litigation. Recognising that the term 'other public laws' is 'uncertain', Lord Denning nevertheless thought that uncertainty could not stop the court from holding that a rule prohibiting their enforcement should not be adopted.[90] The example of the ban on enforcing 'penal' and 'revenue' laws was given, and these too were uncertain terms.[91]

For Lord Denning in *Ortiz* the term 'other public laws' was *eiusdem generis* with penal and revenue laws.[92] He nevertheless did better than that, and landed on the idea that the courts should not assist a foreign government to exercise its sovereign authority beyond its own borders by enforcing 'any of its laws which purport to exercise sovereignty beyond the limits of its authority'.[93] As difficult as it might be to characterise proceedings under this test, Lord Denning suggested a three

[1928] 1 Ch 877, 884; *Taylor* (n 73) 514; *Regazzoni v KC Sethia Ltd* [1958] AC 301, 330; *United States of America v Harden* [1963] SCR 366, 369–73; *Bath v British and Malayan Trustees Ltd* [1969] 2 NSWR 114; *Re Dwelle Estate* (1969) 69 WWR 212; *Re Lord Cable, Deceased* [1977] 1 WLR 7, 13.

82 n 74 and the text thereto.

83 Morris, *Dicey and Morris on the Conflict of Laws*, 9 edn (Stevens & Sons, 1973) 79–80.

84 *Ortiz* (n 73).

85 ibid 49.

86 ibid 46.

87 *R v Governor of Pentonville Prison; Ex part Budlong* [1980] 1 WLR 1110, 1125.

88 *Attorney-General (New Zealand) v Ortiz* [1982] QB 349, 367–71.

89 *Ortiz* (n 73) 20.

90 ibid.

91 ibid.

92 ibid.

93 ibid 21.

step analysis: (1) 'determine the relevant act' to characterise; (2) 'decide whether it is of a sovereign character'; and (3) if so, 'ask whether it was exercised [beyond] the territory of the sovereign state … which is illegitimate'.[94] Precedent would help this characterisation.[95] He concluded that the Historic Articles Act was a New Zealand public law that should not be enforced.[96]

Lord Denning's was a lone voice in *Ortiz*. Lord Justice Ackner doubted that the 'other public law' category existed in law,[97] and Lord Justice O'Connor thought it unnecessary to deal with the question.[98] As would be expected, *Dicey & Morris* thought that Lord Denning was correct,[99] but before Turnbull brought it to the New South Wales courts in *Spycatcher* there was no judicial support for denying enforcement of 'other public laws' of a foreign country other than in the slightest nod from Lord Justice Kerr in 1986.[100]

IV. The *Spycatcher* Proceedings in Australia

A. In the Supreme Court of New South Wales, Equity Division

In September 1985, the British Government began proceedings in the Equity Division of the Supreme Court of New South Wales permanently to restrain the publication of Wright's *Spycatcher*.[101] It also sought an account of profits from any sales of the book. Further, the Government secured ex parte injunctions, so Wright and Heinemann gave undertakings not to publish *Spycatcher* or extracts from the book anywhere in the world. The trial began in November 1986, and lasted 22 days – and it was this that made the *Spycatcher* case a *cause célèbre* that attracted unusual media attention in Australia and the UK, and which made Malcolm Turnbull a national figure. Turnbull's nationalism also made the trial more than a claim for breach of confidentiality. It was a David and Goliath story. The British Government had engaged leading commercial firm Stephen Jaques Stone James – now King & Wood Mallesons – which briefed Theo Simos QC, Bill Caldwell QC and a promising junior and future Supreme Court judge, Rowan

[94] ibid.

[95] In *Ortiz* (n 73) 21–24, Lord Denning cited *Don Alonso v Cornero* (1792) Hob 212, 80 ER 359 (incorrectly cited in the judgment and in *Dicey & Morris*); *King of Italy v Marquis Cosimo de Medici Tornaquinci* (1918) 34 TLR 623; *Princess Paley Olga v Weisz* [1929] 1 KB 718; and *Brokaw v Seatrain UK Ltd* [1971] 2 QB 476.

[96] *Ortiz* (n 73) 24.

[97] ibid.

[98] ibid.

[99] Collins (ed), *Dicey and Morris on the Conflict of Laws*, 11th edn (Steven & Sons, 1987) I 108.

[100] *Re State of Norway's Application* [1987] QB 433, 475.

[101] An injunction granted in New South Wales could be immediately enforceable in other Australian states and territories by registration under the Service and Execution of Process Act 1901 (Cth), s 21.

Darke. Bill Gummow QC, a future justice of the High Court of Australia whom Turnbull dismissed as 'a first-class academic lawyer rather than an advocate',[102] brought considerable expertise in equity,[103] although his role at trial seems to have been limited to reading out affidavits.[104] Australian Prime Minister Bob Hawke had been contacted by Margaret Thatcher to support the British Government's claim, and so Turnbull was also opposite the Commonwealth Solicitor-General, Dr Gavan Griffith QC, and another talented junior and future Federal Court judge, Alan Robertson. The Australian Government lawyers, though, advised the court that they would only intervene on questions of Crown privilege,[105] and withdrew after hearing the evidence.[106] The Australian Government nevertheless gave express support for the British Government's claims throughout the trial and appeals.

The trial judge was Justice Philip Powell. As was inevitable for anyone who had practised successfully at Sydney's equity Bar, Powell was a traditionalist – known for his devotion to legal antiquities in civil procedure.[107] However, as the trial progressed, Turnbull sensed in Powell a sympathetic judge who was taking a 'dim view' of the British Government's witnesses.[108] He was also annoyed at the 'tricky' pleading in which the British Government's lawyers had engaged.[109] The course of the trial, though, shows Turnbull using it as a public showcase. Former Prime Minister Gough Whitlam QC who, as the Prime Minister dismissed by a Governor-General was Australia's most potent symbol of republicanism, gave evidence for Heinemann and Wright that the UK's importance to Australia was 'smaller and diminishing'.[110] He believed that it would be in Australia's interest to show that it did not condone 'such illicit and undercover activities by a country with which it has been so closely associated as the UK'.[111] Whitlam plainly enjoyed himself in the witness box,[112] but his evidence helped no one and, given the ultimate outcome in the High Court, was entirely irrelevant. However, the evidence of Sir Robert Armstrong, Thatcher's Cabinet Secretary, was relevant at trial and in the Court of Appeal, and represented the most spectacular collapse on the Government's side. Armstrong himself had been mentioned briefly in Wright's *Spycatcher*,[113] but his first-hand knowledge of minor events in the book did not help. Turnbull demolished him in cross-examination. Armstrong had

[102] Turnbull (n 51) 47.
[103] See Meagher, Gummow and Lehane, *Equity: Doctrine and Remedies*, 2nd edn (Butterworths, 1984).
[104] Turnbull (n 51) 47–48.
[105] ibid 46.
[106] *Spycatcher* NSWSC (n 13) 355.
[107] Hallen, Hoff and Tang, 'Obituary – The Honourable Philip Ernest Powell AM QC (1930–2016)' [2016] (Spring) *Bar News: The Journal of the New South Wales Bar Association* 70.
[108] ibid 71.
[109] *Spycatcher* NSWSC (n 13) 376.
[110] Turnbull (n 51) 113.
[111] ibid 114.
[112] ibid.
[113] Wright (n 1) 351–52.

given evidence admitting that he had given 'a misleading impression', but that that did not 'contain a lie'.[114] Rather, he said, 'it is perhaps being economical with the truth'[115] – a phrase that has passed into the English language. After Armstrong's convoluted explanation as to why the British Attorney-General was not involved in a decision not to seek an injunction to restrain the publication of Pincher's *Their Trade is Treachery*,[116] Turnbull described it as 'Sir Humphrey Appleby at his best'.[117] Justice Powell joined in Turnbull's playing to the gallery when, after Simos failed in the Court of Appeal to overturn discovery orders that the judge had ordered, he deadpanned: 'There goes my peerage'.[118] The tortuous cross-examination of Sir Robert Armstrong then resumed. In his judgment, Justice Powell eventually concluded:[119]

> Sir Robert Armstrong has been revealed as having rather less expertise in relation to security and intelligence matters than a cursory reading of his affidavits would otherwise have led one to believe; to which might be added that Sir Robert Armstrong's knowledge of operational matters and matters relating to the technology of intelligence gathering appears to be virtually non-existent.

The cross-examination is also what created the media storm in the UK and saw questions about Armstrong's performance asked in the House of Commons.[120]

Michael Codd, the Australian Cabinet Secretary, also gave evidence of the Australian Government's support for the British Government's claim, and suggested that if *Spycatcher* was published the Australian security service would lose confidence in MI5.[121] The judge called this 'complete and utter moonshine'.[122]

Justice Powell refused the British Government its injunction and, with a period to wait, allowed *Spycatcher* to be published.[123] Any private international law arguments received short shrift. Turnbull saw their significance and understood that if they had succeeded then the British Government's claim was completely misconceived, 'regardless of the contents of the book'.[124] Lucy Turnbull had framed the private international law arguments, but her husband later claimed that their technicalities were such that different views could easily be taken of them.[125] That is exactly what happened in the Supreme Court and in the Court of Appeal. As a

[114] Turnbull (n 51) 59.
[115] ibid.
[116] Armstrong answered: 'I don't think it was really correct to describe it as a decision. As I, again, tried to suggest on Friday, I think it was a kind of – it was a conclusion to which all those who were consulted came, that there was no basis for proceeding to try to restrain publication, and that being the general view and general conclusion, there was no proposition to put to the Attorney-General, there was no suggestion that he should take action': ibid 115.
[117] ibid.
[118] ibid 71.
[119] *Spycatcher* NSWSC (n 13) 377.
[120] Turnbull (n 45) 61–64.
[121] Turnbull (n 51) 109–12.
[122] ibid 112.
[123] *Spycatcher* NSWSC (n 13) 385.
[124] Turnbull (n 51) 24.
[125] ibid.

result, Heinemann and Wright had to succeed on the merits of the book.[126] Hence the 22-day trial, and Justice Powell's focus on the questions of confidentiality that were addressed in accordance with New South Wales law.

The judge concluded that Wright's employment in MI5 was within the British Crown's prerogative.[127] There was no doubt that this employment relationship was subject to an obligation of confidentiality, an obligation that stemmed from the nature of a security service and not specifically from the UK statute which imposed penalties for security leaks – the Official Secrets Act 1939.[128] That obligation could continue even after the employment ceased, but not indefinitely: information that had been subject to confidentiality could cease to be confidential.[129] The age of the material in Wright's *Spycatcher* was certainly a hurdle for the British Government. As we have seen, it was at best 10 years old, and some material dealing with the technologies used was at least 20 years old.[130] The *Boys Own* or *Biggles* style of the book meant that much of the material was not discussed in the detail that it had been in other published materials.[131] Justice Powell thought that it was difficult to see that the UK's national security would be detrimentally affected by publication.[132]

Of significance for the doctrine to be developed later in the High Court, the judge considered that he had to assess the British Government's claim that publication would affect its national security, even if that would not be given the deference that similar claims by the Australian or New South Wales Government might make about security questions.[133] It is here that Armstrong's performance under cross-examination had its effect.[134] The British Government's inconsistent response to the publication of *Their Trade is Treachery* and *A Matter of Trust*, and the broadcasting of material on television, had long removed the quality of confidentiality from material in *Spycatcher*.[135] Publication could not cause the Government any detriment.[136]

In finding that the British Government had no enforceable claim for preserving confidentiality, no need arose to consider the private international law questions. As mentioned before, Turnbull had thought his case was not strongest with arguments based on *Huntington v Attrill*[137] and *Ortiz*[138] – although Justice Powell did not consider the latter in the context of the enforcement of an

[126] ibid.
[127] *Spycatcher* NSWSC (n 13) 365.
[128] ibid 369.
[129] ibid 370.
[130] ibid 372–73.
[131] ibid 373.
[132] ibid.
[133] ibid 377.
[134] ibid.
[135] ibid 378.
[136] ibid 379.
[137] *Huntington* (n 73) 377.
[138] *Ortiz* (n 73) 377.

'other public law'.[139] The only issue was the enforcement of a foreign penal law, and the British Government's claim did not have this quality.[140] Critical to this conclusion was that any obligation of confidentiality did not depend on the operation of the Official Secrets Act.[141] If there was an obligation of confidentiality, 'whether it be contractual, equitable, or arising out of a fiduciary relationship', the implication is that it was a private legal relationship and not inherently penal.[142] Again, the *kind of law* being enforced rather than of the *purpose* of enforcement was an important distinction that would be emphasised on appeal.

Wright, Heinemann and Turnbull had their first win. Justice Powell dismissed the proceedings. However, he also made orders to protect the parties' positions in the event of an appeal, and so held Wright and Heinemann to their undertakings for four weeks or a later date set by the Court of Appeal.[143] *Spycatcher* still could not be published.

B. In the New South Wales Court of Appeal

The British Government appealed but, before the appeal was heard in July 1987, a version of *Spycatcher* was published in the US. That could have given rise to a question whether Wright and Heinemann were in breach of the undertakings not to publish – which they had given to the Supreme Court in 1985 – but was not seriously pursued. Newspapers in the UK and New Zealand also tried to publish extracts. An application to restrain newspaper publication was successful in the English courts,[144] but failed in New Zealand.[145] In the New South Wales Court of Appeal, Theo Simos still led for the Government, with support from Bill Caldwell. Bill Gummow and Rowan Darke had dropped out, but British Treasury counsel, John Laws, had joined the team as a junior. Turnbull thought that the future Sir John Laws, who would become a distinguished English appeal judge, was frustrated in having Simos monopolise the argument.[146] The Australian Government did not appear. Turnbull again sat alone.

It was a strong Court of Appeal: the Chief Justice of New South Wales, Sir Laurence Street; the President of the Court of Appeal, Justice Michael Kirby; and Justice Michael McHugh. Kirby and McHugh would later serve as Justices of the High Court of Australia. Kirby – possibly the best-known judge in Australian history – has a reputation for judicial activism and even radicalism, but has

[139] (nn 82–100 and the text thereto).
[140] *Spycatcher* NSWSC (n 13) 384.
[141] ibid 385.
[142] ibid.
[143] ibid.
[144] *Spycatcher* UK (n 17).
[145] *Attorney-General (United Kingdom) v Wellington Newspapers Ltd* [1988] 1 NZLR 129 (*Spycatcher* NZ); *Attorney-General (United Kingdom) v Wellington Newspapers Ltd (No 2)* [1988] 1 NZLR 180.
[146] Turnbull (n 51) 151.

been a consistent and committed constitutional monarchist and devoted to the Commonwealth.[147] Indeed, in the *Spycatcher* appeal, Justice Kirby observed that 'it might seem strange to the uninstructed eye to see the United Kingdom in this judgment declared to be a "foreign state"'.[148] He said: 'As Australia approaches the bicentenary of the establishment of an English colony, our association with the United Kingdom is underlined and renewed'.[149] Justice Kirby then reprised Lord Denning's apology in *Ortiz* to New Zealanders,[150] and hoped that 'our British friends will forgive me calling them a "foreign state"'.[151] He then asserted an Australian independence that, unlike Turnbull's pommy-bashing, was a deep implication of the Balfour Declaration and which saw Australia, in essence, as a realm within the Commonwealth:[152]

> So the United Kingdom is a foreign State. But is there any difference … in the fact that it is a friendly foreign power, that it is a member of the Commonwealth of Nations, as Australia is, and that the present claim is brought to enforce a duty owed to the Crown, which by our Constitution is also the Crown in Australia? … Britain is relevantly a foreign State. To say otherwise is to deny the self respect and independence of the members of the Commonwealth of Nations, including those which still acknowledge the Queen as their Head of State.

Expecting perhaps that a lay audience would read his judgment, Justice Kirby also explained that Australian independence and sovereignty were not undermined by the fact that Australian laws were similar to those in the UK[153] – and indeed, all of the private international law precedents cited before the Court of Appeal were English. Further, he – with Lord Denning – was plainly embarrassed that the private international law had abandoned the diplomatic convention that Commonwealth countries are not foreign to each other. These two considerations would ultimately direct the outcome for the British Government.

Tensions would arise between Kirby and Turnbull during Turnbull's campaigns for an Australian republic in the 1990s,[154] but throughout the *Spycatcher* proceedings he was expecting that, with Justice McHugh, Justice Kirby would lend a sympathetic ear to the respondent's case.[155] Sir Laurence Street was dismissed as

[147] Kirby was instrumental in establishing Australians for a Constitutional Monarchy (ACM) in 1992, partly to counter the influence of Turnbull's Australian Republican Movement. He only resigned from ACM on his appointment to the High Court in 1996, but has not abandoned his monarchist commitments. In 2010 he was appointed to the Eminent Persons Group that reviewed the future of the Commonwealth of Nations: Brown, *Michael Kirby: Paradoxes and Principles* (Federation Press, 2011) 240–45, 270, 411.

[148] *Spycatcher* NSWCA (n 19) 137.

[149] ibid.

[150] n 89 and the text thereto.

[151] *Spycatcher* NSWCA (n 19) 137.

[152] ibid 138.

[153] ibid 141.

[154] Brown (n 147) 257.

[155] Turnbull (n 51) 69.

'an Anglophile',[156] which Turnbull meant to be understood as a reproach. And that is how the judges lined up.

Justices Kirby and McHugh found for Wright and Heinemann; Chief Justice Street dissented. All three addressed the question of the enforcement of penal or public laws, although this is positioned ambiguously in Justice McHugh's judgment. Justice McHugh suggested that it was unnecessary to decide the private international law questions.[157] For him, they would only be relevant if the British Government had a substantive claim and, as a result, the justiciability of that claim would have to be considered.[158] Still, he concluded that there was no foreign public or penal law to enforce in New South Wales.[159] He reached this point by characterising the laws on which the Government's claim was based, and these were the equitable principles of confidence. They were neither penal nor public.[160] Even if the particular equitable obligation in this case paralleled duties under the Official Secrets Act, the Act was not being enforced.[161] It was also not an attempt to enforce the prerogative in right of the UK.[162] And Justice McHugh expressly rejected Lucy's argument which, by this time, had taken its final form. He refused to extend the ban on enforcing foreign penal or revenue laws to 'the concept of the manifestation of foreign sovereignty to cover actions by foreign governments to restrain breaches of confidential information',[163] (though he allowed that claims of that kind were possible).[164]

Ultimately, though, Justice McHugh thought that there was no enforceable obligation of confidence. There was no employment agreement.[165] Any fiduciary duty would parallel the obligation of confidence.[166] And any equitable obligation of confidence in relation to 'government information' could ground an injunction where, amongst other things, disclosure would be 'inimical to the public interest because national security, relations with foreign countries or the ordinary business of government will be prejudiced'.[167] Whether the scope of the equitable obligation was defined by the *lex fori* or English law was not decided, though Justice McHugh tilted towards New South Wales law.[168] The equitable obligation would nevertheless, in New South Wales, not be pitched higher than it could have been in England.[169] As a result, an enforceable obligation of confidentiality in

[156] ibid.
[157] *Spycatcher* NSWCA (n 19) 188.
[158] ibid.
[159] ibid 194.
[160] ibid.
[161] ibid 194–95.
[162] ibid 195.
[163] ibid.
[164] ibid.
[165] ibid 189.
[166] ibid 193.
[167] ibid (n 19) 191, quoting Justice Mason in *Commonwealth of Australia v John Fairfax & Sons Ltd* (1980) 147 CLR 39, 52.
[168] ibid 192.
[169] ibid.

the New South Wales courts still required the British Government to prove that the public interest of the UK would be detrimentally affected by publication.[170] However, he thought that this was not a question the courts could consider.[171] The diplomatic entanglements that could arise if an Australian court decided that publications were not in the public interest of another country were potentially embarrassing.[172] They could possibly be adverse to the interests of third countries.[173] And if it were possible to allow that foreign countries could bring claims to enforce their public interests, but the courts denied one in any given case, it could give rise to the foreign country being aggrieved.[174] It was better just to refuse all claims by foreign governments to enforce their public interests.[175] But this analysis all took place within the context of the foreign government having brought a claim to enforce an equity.

Chief Justice Street's is, uncharacteristically, the most adventurous judgment. The British Government's claim for an injunction also rested on Wright's obligation of confidence,[176] but this arose by his appointment to MI5 by the Government in the exercise of the prerogative.[177] For the Chief Justice, this was the public law basis of the claim.[178] There was no employment agreement to enforce.[179] Like Justice McHugh, Chief Justice Street thought that it was the nature of the law being enforced that should be characterised;[180] it was just that he thought that the claim was based on something other than an equitable obligation. As a result, he also accepted that *Huntington v Attrill* was applicable, and the claim was properly treated as one that would be indirectly enforcing a penal law.[181] The Chief Justice thought that, to be a foreign penal law, the proceedings need not be for the enforcement of a monetary penalty.[182] Apparently rejecting Simos' argument that the Official Secrets Act had no place in the proceedings, he concluded that the obligation of confidence was 'underwritten' by the Act and this gave the proceedings a penal quality.[183] Still, the whole analysis blended *Huntington* with Lord Denning's 'other public law' category from *Ortiz*.[184] Despite recognising the shaky position of that category when the Lords' speeches in *Ortiz* were considered,[185] Chief Justice Street assumed that the position stated

[170] ibid.
[171] ibid 196.
[172] ibid.
[173] ibid.
[174] ibid 197.
[175] ibid.
[176] ibid 99.
[177] ibid.
[178] ibid 99–100.
[179] ibid 98.
[180] ibid 113.
[181] ibid 111.
[182] ibid 112.
[183] ibid 115–16.
[184] ibid 113.
[185] ibid 114.

in Lord Denning's judgment and in *Dicey & Morris* about the unenforceability of foreign public laws was law in New South Wales.[186] Even if the claim was not penal, it 'also lies within the broader category of enforcement of a public law of a foreign state'.[187] In general, the claim should be unenforceable.[188]

This was not what Turnbull was expecting of the Chief Justice, but his account of *Huntington* and *Ortiz* then took an unusual turn. Michael Codd's evidence that the Australian Government supported the British Government's claim dislodged the application of *Huntington* and *Ortiz* in this case. There was no precedent for it, but Chief Justice Street held:[189]

> I do not accept the principle enunciated by Dicey and Morris as absolute in the sense of denying to the local sovereign the right, and hence the courts of the local country the capacity, to open those doors to the foreign sovereign in a case such as this, that is to say where the local sovereign … is not just acquiescent, not just requesting, but positively supportive in the protection of its own national interest, in the courts of this country entertaining and enforcing the claim of the foreign sovereign.

Admitting that the executive government's power could be exercised ad hoc, the Chief Justice nevertheless concluded that it could give a foreign government assistance 'by lifting the jurisdictional fetter on the local courts'.[190] The British Government's claim should therefore succeed.[191]

The President's approach to *Huntington* and *Ortiz* foreshadowed how they would be read by the High Court; Justice Kirby seems to have adopted much of Lucy's argument. Where Justice McHugh treated the 'justiciability' question as secondary to the substantive claim, Justice Kirby – like the Chief Justice – treated it as logically the principal question to answer.[192] It is here that his understanding of Australian independence had some influence, because Justice Kirby treated the House of Lords' approach in *Ortiz* as one an Australian court could disregard when he stated a preference for Lord Denning's judgment.[193] In his assessment of *Huntington* and the ban on the enforcement of foreign revenue laws, he considered them to be species of a broader genus of 'those public laws which represent the public power and authority of the foreign sovereign state'.[194] Further, he avoided the question of which law was to be characterised when assessing whether the ban on enforcing foreign public laws was applicable. Rather than considering whether the court was to characterise the nature of the Official Secrets Act, any employment agreement, the equitable duty of confidence or any fiduciary duties – the task that the Chief Justice and Justice McHugh had approached differently – Justice

[186] ibid 116.
[187] ibid.
[188] ibid.
[189] ibid 121.
[190] ibid 122.
[191] ibid 126.
[192] ibid 136.
[193] ibid 137.
[194] ibid.

Kirby held that it was 'the nature of the action' that had to be characterised.[195] In truth, it was the purpose of the action that he characterised because he asked what was the action for:[196]

> I have no doubt that the action is one, directly or indirectly, for the enforcement of the public law of secrecy imposed by the statutes, common law and prerogative in the United Kingdom upon officers and former officers of the security services of that country, including MI5.

The causes of action that had been pleaded were simply 'the vehicles' by which that purpose would be achieved.[197] This effectively bypassed Simos' submissions that the British Government was merely trying to enforce the same kind of private obligations that any ordinary employer would be entitled to enforce.[198]

Justice Kirby reinforced the principle that one sovereign should not use the courts of another 'to enforce beyond its jurisdiction' its 'high public policy' that gives expression to its sovereignty.[199] To illustrate the problems of Simos' arguments, what if that that support was sought by (apartheid) South Africa, Libya or the Soviet Union?[200] What if New Zealand courts were asked by France to stop its agents answering questions about the bombing of the Rainbow Warrior in Auckland Harbour?[201] Justice McHugh regarded the President's comments in this respect as unhelpful,[202] but the point was that the UK was probably the easiest country for which Australia could give friendly support. In practice, Margaret Thatcher just had to telephone Bob Hawke to get it. Litigation of this kind brought by other countries could be much more fraught. Justice Kirby also dismissed the appeal.[203]

C. In the High Court of Australia

The political dimension to the *Spycatcher* case meant it was always destined for the High Court of Australia, but the decision in the New South Wales Court of Appeal guaranteed the conditions for special leave to appeal. The Court of Appeal gave no *ratio decidendi*. In the majority, Justice McHugh dismissed the appeal because there was no obligation of confidence to enforce. Justice Kirby dismissed it on private international law grounds. The conditions for an appeal to the High Court were therefore satisfied.[204] Although Chief Justice Street had upheld the appeal,

[195] ibid 140.
[196] ibid.
[197] ibid.
[198] ibid.
[199] ibid 142.
[200] ibid 141.
[201] ibid.
[202] ibid 195.
[203] ibid 145.
[204] The Judiciary Act 1903 (Cth), s 35A(a)(ii), allows a grant of special leave to appeal to the High Court where there are differences of opinion within the one court as to the state of the law.

the importance of a response to Lucy's argument in his judgment at least clarified that, in the High Court, the only question would be one of private international law.

For the British Government, the critical constraint on Wright and Heinemann was the undertaking given in September 1985 not to publish *Spycatcher* or extracts. A version of *Spycatcher* had been published in the US before the Court of Appeal's hearing, and Justice Kirby seems to have had suspicions that, much of *Spycatcher* already being in the public domain, this may have been an attempt 'to force the hand of the court' to refuse the injunction restraining further publication.[205] However, the British Government had not complained of any breach of undertaking.[206] The Government having lost the appeal on 24 September 1987, the Court of Appeal ordered that the undertakings only continue into that afternoon. The Court then agreed to extend the undertakings for four days until an appeal on that question could be heard by the High Court. Simos and Caldwell then took an urgent appeal to a judge of the High Court. Turnbull sent his father-in-law, Tom Hughes QC, to respond to the appeal. It came before Sir William Deane, but he refused to continue the undertakings.[207] Justice Deane thought that publication in the US – with further distribution in large numbers in Canada and elsewhere by airport sales – meant that any confidentiality around *Spycatcher* had already been long lost, and it would not be preserved even if there were a successful appeal.[208] Heinemann could now publish, and *Spycatcher* was available in Australian bookshops on 8 March 1988, months before the High Court began to hear the appeal against the Court of Appeal's decision.

Simos and Caldwell were still representing the British Government in the High Court. John Laws had returned to England, and Mark Robinson from the Sydney Bar replaced him. Malcolm Turnbull appeared for Wright and Heinemann, with Lucy Turnbull, now a solicitor, instructing at the Bar table for the first time.[209] Turnbull was disappointed that the judges wanted to hear submissions only on the questions of law, and only on the private international law point at that.[210] From the outset, the Mason court seemed likely to dismiss the appeal. Simos spent more time answering the judges' questions than Turnbull did re-presenting Lucy's argument.[211] He did, nevertheless, reinforce that, in the Court of Appeal, Sir Laurence Street had been wrong in his qualification to *Ortiz* when holding that the executive government could suspend the jurisdictional ban on the enforcement of foreign public laws. Turnbull argued that 'The Executive cannot change the rights of individuals'.[212]

[205] *Spycatcher* NSWCA (n 19) 184.
[206] ibid.
[207] *Attorney-General (United Kingdom) v Heinemann Publishers Australia Pty Ltd* (1987) 75 ALR 461.
[208] ibid 465–66.
[209] Turnbull (n 51) 158.
[210] ibid.
[211] ibid 159.
[212] *Spycatcher* HCA (n 19) 33.

For the Mason court, the *Spycatcher* case was the most unified it ever would be on a question of private international law. The Chief Justice was joined by Justices Wilson, Deane, Dawson, Toohey and Gaudron in delivering a joint judgment. These included the most activist and the most conservative judges on the High Court. Sir Gerard Brennan gave a concurring judgment. He was, however, the only judge in the High Court to allude to Australian independence, and again cast it in mild tones:[213]

> In describing the United Kingdom Government as 'foreign', I do not depreciate the historical, institutional and ethnic ties between this country and the United Kingdom. The description of the United Kingdom Government as 'foreign' merely makes the point that Australia and the United Kingdom are independent in their internal government and in the conduct of their foreign affairs.

In the joint opinion, the shift in the approach to *Ortiz* that Justice Kirby had taken in the Court of Appeal was consolidated, but given greater precision. The ban on courts hearing claims that involved the enforcement of a penal law,[214] a revenue law[215] or a law of confiscation[216] was described as a 'rule' – singular.[217] Accordingly, while the judges did not conclusively opt for Lord Denning's judgment in *Ortiz*,[218] they did treat the 'jurisdictional bar' as a unified rule with a number of species of application. It was clear, though, that it was not a ban on the enforcement of foreign public laws. They said: 'The expression "public laws" has no accepted meaning in our law'.[219] And, of course, Lord Denning's detailing of his 'other public laws' category in *Ortiz* had showed that it had a more limited application than the term 'public law' would suggest.[220] The judges settled on the term 'governmental interests' as the best descriptor of claims that would be subject to the ban – 'the rule applies to claims enforcing the interests of a foreign sovereign which arise from the exercise of certain powers peculiar to government'.[221] As stated in these terms, the rule would not carry the uncertainty that Lord Denning had admitted that the 'other public laws' category bore.[222]

In the joint opinion, the judges also emphasised that the rule did not concentrate on the characterisation of the *kind of law* that was being enforced, but the *purpose* of the proceedings. As the judges put it, 'the action is to be characterized by reference to the substance of the interest to be enforced, rather than the form of the action'.[223] It did not matter, then, that the British Government brought

[213] *Spycatcher* NSWCA (n 19) 48.
[214] *Spycatcher* HCA (n 19) 40–41.
[215] ibid 40, 42.
[216] ibid 41.
[217] ibid 40–44.
[218] ibid 42.
[219] ibid.
[220] nn 89–96 and the text thereto.
[221] *Spycatcher* HCA (n 19) 42.
[222] ibid 43; see *Ortiz* (n 73) 20.
[223] ibid 46.

actions based on private law claims.[224] That was not the 'central interest' behind the Government's reasons for bringing the proceedings.[225]

> It is in truth an action in which the United Kingdom Government seeks to protect the efficiency of its Security Service as 'part of the Defence Forces of the country'. The claim for relief made by the appellant in the present proceedings arises out of, and is secured by, an exercise of a prerogative of the Crown, that exercise being the maintenance of national security. Therefore the right or interest asserted in the proceedings is to be classified as a governmental interest. As such, the action falls within the rule of international law which renders the claim unenforceable.

That being the case, the judges then only had to address Sir Laurence Street's qualification that the support of the Australian Government could require the courts to lift the 'jurisdictional bar' that made foreign governmental interests unenforceable. Not only had this been a surprisingly novel suggestion, but the judges also identified two additional problems with it. The first, agreeing with Turnbull's submission, was a constitutional point. To allow application of a legal principle to depend on the exercise of an executive discretion would offend the exclusive constitutional role of the courts for determining legal entitlements.[226] Accordingly, without spelling it out explicitly, the judges were intimating that Chief Justice Street's qualification could not have a constitutionally valid place in a common law rule. The second was the risk of embarrassing the Australian Government and compromising its foreign policy if *any* role were permitted to it. The availability of an executive power to suspend the ban on court's enforcing foreign governmental interests would require it to compare one foreign state with another,[227] and to signal its hostility to a foreign state if it were to refuse to certify that the proceedings should not be subject to the ban.[228] The courts were in an even worse position to make that assessment without executive assistance.[229] All previous authorities conceded no qualification of Chief Justice Street's kind:[230] 'the friendliness or hostility of the foreign State seeking to enforce its claim in the court of the forum has no relevant connexion with the principle'.[231]

In his concurring judgment, Justice Brennan reinforced the wisdom of denying claims of these kind by foreign governments altogether. *Huntington* and *Ortiz* were ignored – the only question was whether to allow the claim was contrary to the public policy of New South Wales.[232] It was an unusual tack, especially given how resistant Australian courts have been to denying application of a foreign law

[224] ibid.
[225] ibid 46–47.
[226] ibid 47.
[227] ibid.
[228] ibid.
[229] ibid.
[230] ibid.
[231] ibid.
[232] ibid 50.

on the ground of public policy.[233] However, Justice Brennan took it as Australian public policy that Australian courts should not enforce claims that would injure 'Australian security and foreign relations'.[234] Again, the courts had no capacity for assessing whether Australian security would be affected by either prohibiting or permitting the disclosure of the secrets of foreign intelligence services. And, as with the judges in the joint opinion, allowing the courts to take the Australian Government's opinion on whether the foreign government's claim should be allowed would, itself, be putting the Government in an embarrassing position.[235]

The appeal was unanimously dismissed and the *Spycatcher* litigation was over.

V. The Significance of *Spycatcher*

Commentators, with one exception, have tended to misunderstand the breadth of the High Court's decision in *Spycatcher.* In general, the jurisdictional bar on a foreign government enforcing its governmental interest in a civil court has been treated as a separate ground for denying a claim beside the other bans on enforcing penal, revenue, public, expropriation and confiscatory laws.[236] Some even claim that the High Court accepted the 'other public laws' exclusion.[237] However, the authors of the Australian text *Nygh* rightly understand *Spycatcher* as providing an overarching principle that embraces the different jurisdictional bars to enforcement.[238] That, of course, was the central point of Lucy Turnbull's argument. As Malcolm Turnbull is recorded as submitting to the High Court, 'The principle behind the unenforceability of foreign penal and revenue laws is that they are manifestations of a foreign sovereign's power'.[239]

Spycatcher showed the Mason court at its best in private international law adjudication. The contributors to the joint opinion included the most radical and conservative of the judges on the early Mason bench, Sir William Deane and Sir Daryl Dawson. As a result, the decision demonstrated both respect for the weight of English precedents in the field and a creative systemisation of those precedents

[233] Apart from Justice Brennan's judgment in *Spycatcher*, an Australian court has only once resorted to public policy to deny effect to a foreign law – specifically by refusing to recognise an Islamic divorce secured in Lebanon: *In the Marriage of El Oueik* (1977) 29 FLR 171.

[234] *Spycatcher* HCA (n 19) 50.

[235] ibid 50.

[236] I myself make this mistake. Australia: Mortensen, Garnett and Keyes, *Private International Law in Australia*, 4th edn (LexisNexis Butterworths, 2019) 232–40; New Zealand: Hook and Wass, *The Conflict of Laws in New Zealand* (LexisNexis New Zealand, 2020) 143–44. UK: Beaumont and McEleavy, *Anton's Private International Law*, 3rd edn (W Green, 2011) 122–25; Lord Collins of Mapesbury, *Dicey, Morris and Collins on the Conflict of Laws*, 15th edn (Sweet & Maxwell, 2012) I 107–21; Torremans (ed), *Cheshire, North and Fawcett's Private International Law*, 15th edn (OUP, 2017) 15–25.

[237] *Cheshire, North and Fawcett* (ibid) 123.

[238] Davies, Bell, Brereton and Douglas, *Nygh's Conflict of Laws in Australia*, 10th edn (LexisNexis Butterworths, 2020) 441.

[239] *Spycatcher* HCA (n 19) 32.

into, what Beaumont and McEleavy recognised was, a 'more focused'[240] approach to the whole question of unenforceable claims in litigation initiated by foreign governments. An aspect of that more focused approach was the alignment of public and private international law doctrine in the High Court's judgment.[241] Turnbull himself always described it as a public international law argument.[242] The High Court seemed to regard it as both public and private international law.[243] In both fields, it was a ban on one sovereign enforcing interests peculiar to its sovereignty within the borders of another sovereign,[244] whether that was treated as a jurisdictional bar or an inherent limitation of sovereignty.[245] And, while in *Ortiz* Lord Denning had admitted the uncertainty of the 'other public laws' category and yet enforced it,[246] the Mason court's approach made that irrelevant. Properly sceptical of a clear line between public and private law,[247] it did not matter whether the claim was to enforce the Official Secrets Act or the equitable obligation of confidence. What mattered was whether the foreign government was attempting to exercise 'certain powers peculiar to government'.[248] And while these claims have not been common – in no small part because of the spectacular failure of the British Government's efforts at banning Wright's memoir – the clarity of that thinking has seen the High Court's *Spycatcher* decision regarded as 'a helpful and practical test' in England,[249] as well as being applied in Australia.[250]

The discipline of the joint opinion also means that there was no overt claim of Australian independence underlying the judges' doctrine, as there had been in Turnbull's advocacy or in the more tempered tones of Justice Kirby's judgment in the Court of Appeal.[251] However, the *Spycatcher* doctrine is inherently a claim of a nation's independent sovereignty. There is also a hint of the Mason court's 'distinctly Australian' approach to its jurisprudence in the contours of its common law doctrine that foreign governmental interests could not be enforced in an Australian court. Rejecting Chief Justice Street's decision in the Court of Appeal that the executive government's certificate could suspend the jurisdictional bar

[240] Beaumont and McEleavy, *Anton* (2011) 125.

[241] Mills, *The Confluence of Public and Private International Law: Justice, Pluralism and Subsidiarity in the International Constitutional Ordering of Private Law* (CUP, 2009) 228.

[242] Turnbull (n 51) 159, 160.

[243] *Spycatcher* HCA (n 19) 40.

[244] ibid 42.

[245] ibid 41.

[246] ibid 40.

[247] ibid 42.

[248] ibid.

[249] *Government of the Islamic Republic of Iran v The Barakat Galleries Ltd* [2009] QB 22, 57–58. See also *United States Securities and Exchange Commission v Manterfield* [2010] 1 WLR 172, 178–79; but *cf Mbasogo v Logo Ltd* [2007] QB 846, 874.

[250] *Petrotimor Companhia de Petroleos SARL v Commonwealth of Australia* (2003) 126 FCR 354, 415–16, 436–38; *Robb Evans & Associates v European Bank Ltd* (2004) 61 NSWLR 75, 79, 85–88, 90–91, 95; *Surgibit IP Holdings Pty Limited v Ellis (No 2)* [2017] NSWSC 1379, [19].

[251] nn 148–56 and the text thereto.

to these claims,[252] the joint opinion appealed, in part, to a constitutional limitation. Always vigilant towards executive and legislative encroachments on judicial power, the judges thought that allowing executive suspension of the jurisdictional bar 'would be subversive of the role of the courts and of the constitutionally entrenched position of the judicature in this country'.[253] It is a hint of the High Court's later explicit recognition that the common law of Australia must conform to the requirements of the Australian *Constitution* as the nation's basic law.[254] In the majority opinion and in Justice Brennan's view, only legislation passed by the federal Parliament could open Australian courts to foreign governments wishing to protect their national security.[255] To this, Turnbull had no objection. He hoped that the Five Eyes countries (Australia, Canada, New Zealand, the UK and the US) could pass 'complementary legislation' to prevent the publication of information that was 'both secret and of current operational significance'.[256] However, his argument all along was that *Spycatcher* was neither. In the meantime, he celebrated the fact that 'Lucy's public international law had won the day!'[257]

Ultimately, litigation is conducted for the litigants, and Peter Wright had won the day. Turnbull, though, secured more for him than a legal entitlement to publish. Wright had left MI5 with no pension,[258] and had been living in Tasmania in poverty.[259] Turnbull also thought that Wright did not have good prospects, guessing that, without more, *Spycatcher* might have sold 50,000 copies.[260] And, whatever the Englishman Wright thought about it, the pommy-bashing had helped him. Together, Turnbull and the British Government had made *Spycatcher* famous and infamous, and it sold two million copies. Peter Wright died in 1995 a wealthy man. Malcolm Turnbull was underpaid for his efforts in the *Spycatcher* case in Australia,[261] but it is possible to see that, like *Spycatcher* itself, his appearances throughout the proceedings also took on something of the style of a *Boys Own* adventure.

[252] nn 189–191 and the text thereto.

[253] *Spycatcher* HCA (n 19) 47. The opposite approach was taken in New Zealand, where in the Court of Appeal Sir Robin Cooke held that 'the New Zealand Government can unlock the door to New Zealand Courts for a foreign Government by appropriate evidence of its support': *Spycatcher* NZ (n 145) 174.

[254] *Lange v Australian Broadcasting Corporation* (1997) 189 CLR 520, 556, 565–66, 572; *Pfeiffer* (n 40) 534, 567.

[255] *Spycatcher* HCA (n 19) 48, 51, 53.

[256] Turnbull (n 51) 160.

[257] ibid.

[258] Wright (n 1) 367.

[259] Turnbull (n 45) 58.

[260] Turnbull (n 51) 16, 30.

[261] Turnbull (n 45) 62.

7

Conflicts and Public Law Concerns

A New Way of Conceiving the Conflict of Laws: Morguard Investments Ltd v De Savoye

ANGELA SWAN OC[1]

I. Introduction

It is not an exaggeration to say that the decision of the Supreme Court of Canada in *Morguard Investments Ltd v De Savoye*[2] dramatically changed the law on the recognition and enforcement of foreign judgments in Canada. It also changed the approach of Canadian law to the taking of jurisdiction after service *ex juris* or in dealing with issues of *forum non conveniens*. I take some credit for that change as La Forest J, the judge who gave the reasons of the Court, found support for the result he came to in an article I had published some five years before.[3] La Forest J substantially adopted the arguments I had made for reforming the old common law rules on the enforcement of foreign judgments.

My argument was that the old common law rules no longer made sense. They treated a judgment of a Canadian province,[4] brought for enforcement in another province, like a truly foreign judgment from outside Canada. In particular, the old

[1] This chapter should be read with Swan, 'Freedom From the Conflict of Laws is in Your Grasp' (2020) 51 *Advocates' Quarterly* 21, and probably many others, some of which can be found in the footnotes to this chapter.

[2] [1990] 3 SCR 1077, 76 DLR (4th) 256.

[3] Swan, 'The Canadian Constitution, Federalism and the Conflict of Laws' (1985) 63 *Canadian Bar Review* 272.

[4] Canada is made up of 10 provinces and three territories; they are Yukon, the Northwest Territories and Nunavut. For the sake of brevity, I shall treat the territories as if they were provinces. The principal difference between the provinces and the territories is that, while the former get their legislative power and constitutional position from the Constitution Act, 1867, the act of the UK Parliament that created Canada, the latter get their power from Parliament. Some of the arguments I shall make about provincial power under the Canadian Constitution do not then, strictly speaking, apply to a territory. I shall ignore that fact.

rules ignored the implicit connection between a restrained or responsible assertion of jurisdiction, often involving service *ex juris*, and the concomitant expectation that any resulting judgment would be enforced, at least with respect to judgments from or within the component parts of a federation.

Canada does not have, as the US[5] and Australia[6] have, any constitutional or federal legislation dealing with the taking of jurisdiction by their component states and any consequential issues of recognition or enforcement. After *Morguard*, the Canadian position more closely resembled the situation in those federal states, but still shows important differences.

II. What did *Morguard* do?

My argument, one that I have made more than once,[7] is that *Morguard* fundamentally changed how Canadian courts approach problems with geographically complex facts, ie, the problems that are the diet of the Conflict of Laws. While *Morguard* dealt with the enforcement in British Columbia of a money judgment given by a court in Alberta, it offers the basis for an argument that one can conceive of cases with geographically complex facts in quite different ways than the traditional approach to conflicts suggests. This consequence of *Morguard* is enhanced when a case that I regard as its companion, *Moran v Pyle National (Canada) Ltd*,[8] is considered. The lesson one can draw from these two cases – *Moran* dealing with jurisdiction and choice of law, *Morguard* with enforcement – is that one can argue that a basis for a revolution in how Conflicts is conceived has been laid.

I shall limit my analysis and arguments to private law, ie, principally, but not exclusively, the problems of contracts and torts. I am prepared to argue that other private law problems of, for example, corporations and shareholders, property, estates and families, are amenable to the same analysis and arguments, but those problems emerge much less frequently as conflicts cases.

We do not have laws because they are nice things to have; we have them because they let us do things that could not be done without them. The principal feature of what I can call the traditional approach to conflicts problems was that it ignored the goals of private law and, coming back to the importance of *Morguard*, what has to be the central feature of a federation, viz, the legislative power of its component parts, in Canada, the provinces, and their ability to do things differently from other provinces. Rules were applied with no thought for the values or goals that

[5] Constitution of the United States, XIV Amendment and Art IV, s 1.
[6] Service and Execution of Process Act 1992 (Cth).
[7] See, for example, Swan, 'The Future of the Conflict of Laws: Can *Morguard* (1990) Point the Way?' in O'Dell (ed), *Leading Cases of the Twentieth Century* (Round Hall, 2000) 405; Swan, 'How Should a Court Approach the Recognition or Enforcement of a Foreign Judgment?' 29 *Dublin University Law Journal* 443; Swan and Black, 'Concurrent Judicial Jurisdiction: A Race to the Court House or to Judgment? *Lloyd's Underwriters v Cominco Ltd*' (2008), 46 *Canadian Business Law Journal* 252.
[8] [1975] 1 SCR 393, 43 DLR (3d) 239.

underlie or, depending on the image you prefer, support the law; they were often brutally applied with no thought for any goal that might be relevant. I shall return to this point later.

What *Morguard* did was to anchor the approach it took in the values inherent in a federation like Canada. The Constitution of Canada confers on each province various powers – the 'Division of Powers' is among the principal topics discussed in law school classes on the Constitutional Law of Canada. The Constitution Act 1867[9] provides:

> 92 In each Province the Legislature may exclusively make Laws in relation to Matters coming within the Classes of Subjects next hereinafter enumerated; that is to say,
>
> …
>
> 13. Property and Civil Rights in the Province.
> 14. The Administration of Justice in the Province, including the Constitution, Maintenance, and Organization of Provincial Courts, both of Civil and of Criminal Jurisdiction, and including Procedure in Civil Matters in those Courts.

It is accepted that a province has no power to legislate extra-territorially.[10]

I shall explore the contribution of *Morguard* by looking at two central features of the traditional approach to conflicts. I shall look first what is understood in both Canada and Australia to be an important goal of conflicts, viz, the desire that decisions on cases with geographically complex facts be uniform, ie, be the same, regardless of where the action may be brought. I shall then describe how I believe a court in Canada or Australia should approach cases with relevant geographically complex facts.[11]

III. The Claim that Results should be Uniform[12]

The argument that I want to explore is forcefully put in the Australian High Court in *Breavington v Godleman*:

> The operation of the choice of law rules of private international law, whether by their own force in matters not involving the exercise of federal jurisdiction, or by force of

[9] 30 & 31 Vict, c 3.

[10] See, for example, *Hunt v T & N plc*, [1993] 4 SCR 289, 109 DLR (4th) 16; *Tolofson v Jensen*, [1994] 3 SCR 1022, 120 DLR (4th) 289 [71]. It is conceded that the Canadian Parliament may legislate extra-territoriality and it has done so in a very small number of instances. See, *inter alia*: s 6(2) and s 290 of the Criminal Code, RSO 1985, c C-46 and the Foreign Extraterritorial Measures Act, RSC 1985, c F-29 (though, in the case of the latter, the legislation is conscious of the general reluctance to legislate extra-territorially).

[11] 'Conflicts' problems can only be identified as those in which there are relevant foreign facts. The determination of what facts, foreign or not, are *relevant* to the court's decision is of course at the heart of the judicial process.

[12] See, most recently: Swan, 'Freedom From the Conflict of Laws' (2020). See also: Swan, 'Federalism and the Conflict of Laws: The Curious Position of the Supreme Court of Canada' (1995) 46 *University of South Carolina Law Review* 923.

> s. 79 [of the Judiciary Act, 1903] in matters of federal jurisdiction, allows for the possibility that tortious liability (or the extent thereof) in respect of actions occurring in Australia may be determined by reference to different substantive laws depending upon the location or venue of the court in which action is brought. The undesirability of that possibility is obvious, not only in terms of its potential as an inducement to forum shopping, but in terms of perception of the law itself. It is not only undesirable, but manifestly absurd that the one set of facts occurring in the one country may give rise to different legal consequences depending upon the location or venue of the court in which action is brought.[13]

La Forest J in *Tolofson v Jensen*,[14] adopted these statements from the High Court and said:

> The nature of our constitutional arrangements – a single country with different provinces exercising territorial legislative jurisdiction – would seem to me to support a rule that is certain and that ensures that an act committed in one part of this country will be given the same legal effect throughout the country.

La Forest J went on to use this argument to justify the imposition of the choice of law rule that torts should be governed by the *lex loci delicti*.[15]

The facts of one case before the Ontario Court of Appeal, *Québec (Sa Majesté du Chef) v Ontario Securities Commission*,[16] illustrate the problem. The facts, as set out in the headnote, were:

> In August 1988, the Ontario Securities Commission (OSC) decided that it had jurisdiction to adjudicate about a transaction by which the Quebec Government had implemented its public policy over the asbestos industry in Quebec. On a combined appeal and judicial review application, the Divisional Court upheld the OSC's decision. The Quebec Government appealed.
>
> By its August 1988 decision, the OSC had decided it could review the transaction by which Société Nationale de l'Amiante (SNA), a Quebec Crown corporation, had purchased from General Dynamics Corporation in two stages, the first stage in 1981 and the second in 1986, the shares of its subsidiary, General Dynamics (Canada) Ltd., which subsidiary owned a control block of 54.64% of the shares of Asbestos Corporation Ltd. (ACL), a public company whose shares were traded on the Montreal and Toronto stock exchanges. In the transaction, SNA had paid the equivalent of $80 per ACL share, whose average trade price was $5.55 in December 1986. OSC staff asserted that SNA should offer to purchase the 500,000 ACL shares held by minority shareholders residing in Ontario and elsewhere. The issues for the OSC, which were set out in a notice of hearing dated April 13, 1988, were: whether SNA had failed to comply with the follow-up offer provisions of s. 91(1) of the *Securities Act*; whether the OSC ought to apply under s. 122(1) of the Act to the court for an order that SNA comply with the follow-up offer

[13] [1988] HCA 40, 169 CLR 41, per Wilson and Gaudron JJ [15].

[14] n 10. For analysis of the judgment in *Tolofson*, see Professor Blom's contribution to this collection.

[15] For a brutal and pointless application of it, see *Castillo v Castillo*, 2005 SCC 83, [2005] 3 SCR 870. For criticism, see Swan, 'Federalism and the Conflict of Laws' (1995).

[16] (1992) 10 OR (3d) 577, 97 DLR (4th) 144 (*sub nom Re The Queen in right of Quebec and Ontario Securities Commission*). Leave to appeal refused, 19930527.

> provisions; and, whether the OSC ought to order that the exemptions in ss. 34, 71, 72 and 92 of the Act not apply to SNA nor to the Quebec Government.

McKinlay JA stated the issue:

> As stated above, the simple legislative objective involved in this appeal is regulation of the operation of capital markets in Ontario for the protection of all who use them. This includes the protection of persons and corporations dealing in Ontario markets whether or not they are resident in Ontario. Thus, the Province of Québec, when using Ontario markets, is afforded the same protection as all other users. The success of such an objective is vital to the health and growth of commerce in Ontario.
>
> The objective of the Province of Québec in carrying out the transactions involved was announced in 1977 by the Québec Government. Its intent was to create an asbestos manufacturing industry in Québec to complement the asbestos mining industry, thereby creating substantial new employment in regions of Québec where the rate of unemployment exceeded 20%.
>
> There can be no doubt that both objectives represent 'compelling governmental interests'. The question posed by the appellant's argument is, 'Which is the more compelling?' For Québec to comply with the provisions of the Ontario Act, the cost to it, we are told, would be approximately $100,000,000. But that $100,000,000 is saved at the expense of persons who have invested in shares trading on Ontario markets, trusting that all who use those markets will trade in accordance with the rules. I see no way the courts can assist in advancing interprovincial harmony in a situation such as this, since there is no objective way of choosing which governmental interest is more compelling. *However, I see no reason why residents of one province should suffer financial loss for the purpose of benefiting another province in advancing its legitimate interests.*[17]

McKinlay JA clearly sees the case as a 'conflicts' case. In the result, the Ontario Court of Appeal dismissed the appeal and upheld the decision of the Ontario Securities Commission.[18]

The shareholders' claim to a follow-up offer was based on the Ontario Securities Act. Let us suppose that the National Assembly passes legislation to immunise the Québec Government from liability for failing to make a follow-up offer. The Québec Court of Appeal is asked by the Province to dismiss a proceeding by the shareholders under the Ontario Securities Act. The Court of Appeal accedes to the Government's request. Assume that, contrary to the facts, both appeals are brought before the Supreme Court. What should that Court do?

[17] (1992) 10 OR (3d) 577, 590–91 (emphasis added). McKinlay JA, as the quotation above makes clear, referred to an important and then current American approach to Conflicts, 'Interest Analysis', and to three Conflicts scholars, including me.

[18] In the end the minority shareholders did not share in the $100 million fund as they might have hoped. The Ontario Securities Commission subsequently declined to make an order against the Québec Government to punish it for what it had done. That decision was ultimately upheld by the Supreme Court; *Committee for the Equal Treatment of Asbestos Minority Shareholders v Ontario (Securities Commission)* 2001 SCC 37, [2001] 2 SCR 132. The end of the minority shareholders' long and unsuccessful fight may have come with *Hurst v Société Nationale de l'Amiante* (2008), 93 OR (3d) 338, 53 BLR (4th) 10 (CA).

There are a few things to keep in mind. Under the Canadian Constitution the provinces have *exclusive* jurisdiction over Canadian stock exchanges and the trading of securities. First, there is no federal Securities Act; there are only provincial acts.[19] Second, there is no common law principle governing follow-up offers; any remedy is wholly statutory. Even if there were a common law principle, Québec is not a common law jurisdiction; it is civilian jurisdiction so that a 'common law' principle would not provide a criterion for decision.[20]

I argue that the Supreme Court can properly dismiss both appeals; there is nothing in the law of follow-up offers that gives the Court a basis for allowing one and dismissing the other. The Supreme Court could, of course, say that either court of appeal had got its own provincial law wrong; what it cannot say is that there a correct *Canadian* approach to follow-up offers that would justify a single solution being imposed on each province.

It is, of course, obvious from what McKinlay JA said that there is no choice of law rule for follow-up offers. Those rules were developed long before there was any concern for takeover bids and follow-up offers. The absence of a choice of law rule makes the arguments of the Australian High Court in *Breavington* and those of the Supreme Court of Canada in *Tolofson v Jensen* very hard if not impossible to sustain. But would a choice of law rule change anything? As McKinlay JA explains, Ontario has excellent reasons for requiring Québec to make a follow-up offer; *Moran* would clearly support such a solution. It could easily adopt the choice of law rule that the law to govern takeover bids is that of the exchange where the bid was made. Québec could equally have very good reasons – $100 million is a large amount for the province to have to pay – for rejecting that rule and adopting some other, eg, the domicile or residence of the bidder or simply the assertion of some kind of governmental immunity.

In the terms used by American conflicts scholars some decades ago, what McKinlay JA described was a 'true conflict'.[21] Currie suggested that in such a case, the court seized of the matter would apply the *lex fori*.[22]

[19] In *Reference re Securities Act* 2011 SCC 66, [2011] 3 SCR 837, the Supreme Court held, on a Reference from the Governor-in-Council, that a proposed Canadian Securities Act, was invalid, as exceeding the powers assigned by the Constitution Act, 1867 to Canada. In the result, the only Securities Acts in Canada are provincial, though there is a Canada Business Corporations Act, RSC 1985, c. C-44, which has provisions dealing with corporate finance and shareholders' rights. It only applies to corporations incorporated under it. There are provincial and territorial Business Corporation Acts.

[20] I shall deal later with my argument that, consistently with the division of powers under the Constitution Act, 1867, there can be no such thing as a *Canadian* common law, even if Québec is left out. In other words, the Supreme Court has no power to impose a uniform common law on the provinces. It is, of course, a fact that the common law and, indeed, the whole of Canadian law, is largely uniform across the country but that is no more than a coincidence. This aspect of the role of the Supreme Court has not, at least to my knowledge, been explored in Canada by anyone other than me. See: Swan (n 12).

[21] See, for example, Currie, *Selected Essays on the Conflict of Laws* (Duke University Press, 1963). See also Hill, 'Resolving a True Conflict between State Laws: A Minimalist Approach' (2005) 29 *Melbourne University Law Review* 39.

[22] Currie (ibid). I shall not engage with the very many articles and books dealing with, inter alia, choice of law in the US and other jurisdictions like the EU. The principal reason for my reluctance is

The Australian and Canadian Constitutions also strongly militate against the idea that results should be independent of the place where litigation occurs. The essence of federations like those of Australia and Canada is that the component parts, the states or provinces, can differ with respect to those matters that in Canada come within the heading of 'Property and Civil Rights *in the Province*'; these matters are within the *exclusive* power of the provinces. Ontario can, for example, have its own rule for unmarried but cohabiting couples; Québec can have another.[23] It is, as I have said, a fact that the law in both Australia and Canada is very similar across each country and that fact is, of course, something to be expected. It is true that Québec has the *Civil Code of Quebec* but, while the way in which the law is stated differs significantly from the common law, there are very few points where the actual operation of the law leads to different results.

It may well be that both courts could agree on a common principle. Such a principle may be seen in the decision of Dickson J, as he then was, in *Moran v Pyle National (Canada) Ltd.*[24] He said:

> Cheshire, [*Private International Law*] 8th ed. (1970), p. 281, has suggested a test very similar to this; the author says that it would not be inappropriate to regard a tort as having occurred in any country substantially affected by the defendant's activities or its consequences and the law of which is likely to have been in the reasonable contemplation of the parties. Applying this test to a case of careless manufacture, the following rule can be formulated: *where a foreign defendant carelessly manufactures a product in a foreign jurisdiction which enters into the normal channels of trade and he knows or ought to know both that as a result of his carelessness a consumer may well be injured and it is reasonably foreseeable that the product would be used or consumed where the plaintiff used or consumed it, then the forum in which the plaintiff suffered damage is entitled to exercise judicial jurisdiction over that foreign defendant.* This rule recognizes that the purpose of negligence as a tort is to protect against carelessly inflicted injury and thus that the predominating element is damage suffered. By tendering his products in the market place directly or through normal distributive channels, *a manufacturer ought to assume the burden of defending those products wherever they cause harm as long as the forum into which the manufacturer is taken is one that he reasonably ought to have had in his contemplation when he so tendered his goods.* This is particularly true of dangerously defective goods placed in the interprovincial flow of commerce.[25]

It is not hard to imagine that an Ontario court could come to the same conclusion; Dickson J identifies important principles of the *law of torts*; he does not just

that they all, in a great variety of ways, accept the structure of the Conflicts of Law as requiring a choice of law rule and, principally, the selection of a jurisdiction to 'govern' the matter. I shall only deal very briefly with the Canadian position. Suffice it to say, I reject completely all choice of law rules and all that goes with them, characterisation, *renvoi*, the 'incidental question' and other exotica.

[23] See, for example., *Québec (Attorney General) v A*, 2013 SCC 5, [2013] 1 SCR 61 [280]. The Supreme Court was deeply divided. The ability of Québec to have its Civil Code of Québec is, of course, and was a very important reason for giving the province power to go its own way, starting with the Quebec Act, the British North America (Quebec) Act 1774 (14 Geo III c 83).

[24] *Moran* (n 8).

[25] *Moran* (n 8) (emphasis added); [1975] 1 SCR 393, 408–09.

talk 'Conflicts'. Notice, however, the problem that arises if, instead of talking, as Dickson J did, pure common sense, he had adopted as a choice of law rule, the *lex loci delicti*. What is the place of the tort in a product liability case? Is it where the product causes harm (Saskatchewan), or where it was negligently manufactured or assembled (Ontario), or some other place outside Canada, perhaps, where its components were manufactured? The choice between those provinces *on that basis* cannot be made by any principle because there is not one.[26] I suppose the Supreme Court could dictate that one of Saskatchewan, Ontario or the place outside Canada shall be deemed to be the *lex loci delicti* but it's not hard to imagine situations where that rule might cause serious problems.[27] We have then the result that, while ignoring or not talking Conflicts, we will almost certainly achieve uniformity, actually talking Conflicts and choice of law rules, is very likely to have the opposite result.

We can, of course, play around with choice of law rules but at what cost? The fundamental problem of all choice of law rules is that they are and have to be unprincipled. This consequence can be illustrated by a decision the Alberta Court of Appeal.

In *Greenshields Inc v Johnston*,[28] the plaintiff, an investment dealer and stockbroker, sued the defendant, RH Johnston, and his corporation, RH Johnston & Associates Ltd, for an amount due on the cancellation by the defendants of a contract for the purchase and sale of bonds, sold by the plaintiff to the corporate defendant. The individual defendant had guaranteed the debt of the corporation to the plaintiff. When the guarantee was given, the defendant lived in Alberta, where the plaintiff also had an office; the transactions were effected in Edmonton, in Alberta. The guarantee that the defendant executed had a choice of law clause which provided that the guarantee was to be 'construed in accordance with' the law of Ontario. The defendant claimed that the guarantee was void as a result of non-compliance with the Alberta Guarantees Acknowledgment Act.[29] That act then required the guarantor appear before a notary to acknowledge the guarantee. If this step was not taken, the guarantee was unenforceable in Alberta.

[26] The problems of choice of law rules in defamation illustrate the point: see, for example, *Breeden v Black* 2012 SCC 19, [2012] 1 SCR 666 and *Éditions Écosociété Inc. v Banro Corp* 2012 SCC 18, [2012] 1 SCR 636. These cases were two of a quadrilogy. The principal reasons were given in *Club Resorts Ltd v Van Breda* 2012 SCC 17, [2012] 1 SCR 572; the other was *Club Resorts Ltd v Charron*. But now see *Haaretz.com v Goldhar* 2018 SCC 28, [2018] 2 SCR 3, where some restraint has been imposed on the extravagant taking of jurisdiction previously favoured by the Supreme Court.

[27] See, for example, the dreadful, pointless and very unfair decision in *Castillo v Castillo* 2005 SCC 83, [2005] 3 SCR 870. For criticism: see Swan (n 1).

[28] (1981) 119 DLR (3d) 714, [1981] 3 WWR 313, (Alta SC); aff'd (1981) 131 DLR (3d) 234, [1982] 2 WWR 97 (Alta CA). For comment, see: Swan (n 1).

[29] RSA 1970, c 163. That version of the Act provided: '3. No guarantee has any effect unless the person entering into the obligation, (a) appears before a notary public, (b) acknowledges to the notary public that he executed the guarantee, and (c) in the presence of the notary public signs a statement, at the foot of the certificate of the notary public in the form set out in the Schedule. The legislation appears to have been first enacted in 1942. There is a long history of opposition to banks, principally based, originally in Montreal, now in Toronto, on the part of prairie legislatures, ie, Alberta, Saskatchewan and Manitoba.

The trial judge held that the law to 'govern' the contract was the law of Ontario by virtue of the choice of law clause in the guarantee and that, the requirements for the recognition of a choice of law clause being met, notwithstanding the failure of the creditor or guarantor to comply with the Act, the guarantee was enforceable against the guarantor. The Court of Appeal dismissed the appeal.

Now imagine that a Canadian bank, based in Toronto, doing business in Alberta and tired of the risks to the enforcement of guarantees posed by the Alberta legislation, redrafted its standard guarantee to provide: 'The parties agree that the Guarantees Acknowledgment Act does not apply to this guarantee'. The debtor does not, of course, read the guarantee agreement and, if she or he had, would not have understood the significance of the provision. Can there be any doubt – the Act is silent on the point – that the clause would be unenforceable? If the parties cannot, by an express clause, exclude the effect of the Act, how is it possible that a mere choice of law clause can exclude it? The same problem would be raised if a creditor added a clause to a loan agreement providing: 'The Criminal Code and, in particular s 347 (criminal interest), do not apply to this loan'. What general counsel to a bank would advise the bank to use such language?[30]

It would be one thing for an Ontario court, dealing with a claim against an Alberta guarantor by an Ontario creditor, perhaps caught unawares by the existence of the Guarantees Acknowledgment Act, to refuse to enforce the guarantee because, unlike the Alberta courts, the Ontario court is not committed to forwarding the purposes of Alberta legislation. An Alberta court *has to forward the purposes of Alberta law*, which, on the facts, was to protect an Alberta resident from the claims of a creditor under a guarantee. It may well be that the Guarantees Acknowledgment Act is unusual legislation but, while it stands unrepealed, an Alberta court is bound to apply it, at least where there is an Alberta guarantor and a creditor doing business in Alberta.[31]

With respect to an argument that the result should be the same in both Alberta and Ontario, it is easy to pose the question: what kinds of guarantors is the Act intended to protect? On the facts of *Greenshields Inc v Johnston*, the guarantor lived in Alberta and entered into the guarantee there; the creditor, based in Toronto, happened to use an Ontario form of guarantee. What about the owner of an Ontario corporation, based in Toronto where the owner also lives, who, to secure funding for her corporation, goes, actually or virtually, to Edmonton and executes a guarantee? Is she the kind of person the Act was intended to protect? Remember that a province cannot legislate extra-territorially and the courts of a province are

[30] The fact that the answer to this rhetorical question may be obvious does not mean that Canadian banks do not draft extraordinary provisions in the agreements they impose on their customers. See Swan, 'Have We Lawyers Gone Mad? Three Examples of Terrible Drafting and a Proposed Solution' *Lexology*, 20210107.

[31] The Guarantees Acknowledgment Act causes problems because it is both unusual and is seen by courts as catching creditors by unfair surprise, particularly where the guarantor may not need protection. The guarantor in *Greenshields* admitted that he understood the guarantee, so might not have been entitled to much sympathy. For a discussion of other idiosyncratic legislation that has caused problems in the conflict of laws, see Swan (n 12) fn 112.

similarly limited. It is reasonable to assume that across the spectrum of guarantors, ranging from those living all their lives in Alberta and those who go there for a brief moment to execute a guarantee or who don't even go there at all, an Alberta court could draw the line at a different point than an Ontario court; one court might apply the Act, the other might refuse to do so. On what basis could anyone say that both courts should or must draw the line at the same point? Can there be any reasonable expectation that a choice of law rule would lead to uniformity? Absent a choice of law clause, the proper law of the contract could easily differ, depending on the relative extent of the Alberta and Ontario connections. In other words, the search for uniform solutions is a chimera.

This case and the general problem of the application of the Guarantees Acknowledgment Act in the circumstances has elicited a very curious and illuminating response from Professors Pitel and Rafferty. They say:

> Note that the approach in *Greenshields Inc.* uses the traditional multilateral approach to choice of law. The Alberta statute does not invalidate the contract since it is not governed by Alberta law. The court starts with the choice of law rule, finds Ontario to be the proper law, and applies it. Vaughan Black has argued that a different, unilateral approach should apply.[32] Under such an approach, the Alberta court would start with the Alberta statute and interpret its provisions. If the contract in question fell within them, and there was no appearance before a notary public, the statute would invalidate the contract. Ontario law would not enter into the analysis. *One concern with this approach, however, is that starts with the law of the forum without explaining why. This has the potential to undercut the whole notion of choice of law rules.*[33]

The italicised sentences are very surprising. Both Vaughan Black and I make our arguments precisely to challenge the whole Conflicts structure: choice of law rules are *never* the appropriate solution to any legal problem. In their last sentence Pitel and Rafferty offer no reason for hanging on to choice of law rules; they do not argue that their application would offer a preferable solution; they just think we should hang onto them because we have always done so.

The more interesting argument is the penultimate sentence. This question it raises is where I have to go now.

IV. How, then, should a Court Decide a Conflicts Case?

An excellent illustration of where to start thinking about a legal problem with geographically complex facts is provided by the Law of Admiralty.[34] In Canada, the

[32] Black, 'The Strange Cases of Alberta's Guarantees Acknowledgement Act: A Study in Choice-of-Law Method' (1987) 11 Dalhousie Law *Journal* 208. This article deals with more cases and offers a very comprehensive and useful analysis of not only cases under the Guarantees Acknowledgment Act, but choice of law more generally.

[33] Pitel and Rafferty, *Conflict of Laws*, 2nd edn (Irwin Law, 2016) 297 (emphasis added).

[34] See, for example, Ehrenzweig, *Private International Law: A Comparative Treatise on American International Conflicts Law, Including the Law of Admiralty* (Oceana Publications, Inc, 1967). Ehrenzweig

Federal Court has jurisdiction in Admiralty matters. Some cases in the Supreme Court illustrate the approach.

In *Todd Shipyards Corp v Altema Compania Maritima SA*[35] the question was the relative priority of a maritime lien, arising under the law of the US, against a ship and a mortgage on the ship. Under US law, the law of the place where repairs to the ship were made, the shipyard would have priority over the mortgage; Canadian maritime law would prefer the mortgagee. The reasons for judgment in the Supreme Court do not refer to conflicts or choice of law rules at all. Ritchie J, giving the judgment of the Court, said:

> I do not find it necessary to go further than the decision in *The Strandhill* [*v Walter W Hodder Company* [1926] SCR 680, [1926] 4 DLR 801], to find authority for holding that the necessary repairs furnished by Todd Shipyards Corporation in New York gave rise to a maritime lien against the defendant ship which is enforceable in this country, but the further question to be determined in this case is whether that lien takes precedence over the respondent's mortgage claim, and in my view this question must be determined according to the law of Canada (*ie*, the *lex fori*).[36]

In the result he held that because the repairs were done in New York and, because under American law a maritime lien attached at that point, the lien would be recognised in Canada and the shipyard would have priority over the mortgagee. In other words, Ritchie J applied the *lex fori* but, in doing so, was not so insular or arrogant as to imagine that the foreign law was irrelevant.

Similarly, in *Holt Cargo Systems Inc v ABC Containerline NV (Trustees of)*,[37] Binnie J dealt with the validity of the plaintiff's maritime lien wholly in the context of Canadian law, making relevant the fact that the lien had arisen in the US. There was no discussion of a choice of law rule. The Supreme Court applied Canadian law as the *lex fori* and considered carefully the reasons that would justify the recognition of a maritime lien in the circumstances and giving it priority over the mortgagee.[38] The other issue in the case, viz, the effect to be given in an Admiralty

explores the contribution of the Law of Admiralty to the development of an approach to Conflicts on which I have based mine. See Swan, 'Book Review, AA Ehrenzweig, *Private International Law: A Comparative Treatise on American International Conflicts Law, Including the Law of Admiralty*' (1969) 19 *University of Toronto Law Journal* 479.

[35] [1974] SCR 1248, 32 DLR (3d) 571.

[36] [1974] SCR 1248. Ritchie J referred to *Cheshire's Private International Law*, 8th edn at 676. Cheshire said: 'Where, for instance, two or more persons prosecute claims against a ship that has been arrested in England, the order in which they are entitled to be paid is governed exclusively by English law. In the case of a right *in rem* such as a lien, however, this principle must not be allowed to obscure the rule that the substantive right of the creditor depends upon its proper law. The validity and nature of the right must be distinguished from the order in which it ranks in relation to other claims. Before it can determine the order of payment, the court must examine the proper law of the transaction upon which the claimant relies in order to verify the validity of the right and to establish its precise nature. When the nature of the right is thus ascertained the principle of procedure then comes into play and ordains that the order of payment prescribed by English law for a right of that particular kind shall govern'. Cheshire feels compelled to talk 'Conflicts' when all he is saying is that each creditor must have a valid claim.

[37] [2001] 3 SCR 907, 207 DLR (4th) 577.

[38] There can be no arguments based on competing expectations. Lien-holders know that ships are usually mortgaged and that some jurisdictions give the mortgagee priority over a lien-holder;

case to foreign (Belgian) bankruptcy proceedings and a fight between the Federal Court and the Quebec Superior Court was similarly dealt with without any reference to an analysis that could be described as based on choice of law rules or the Conflict of Laws.[39]

A court before which a dispute has been brought has no choice but to start its analysis from where it is. As babies, we can only be solipsistic; we have to look at the world from where we sit or lie. As an individual matures, she understands that the points of view of others must be considered; so too a court may find the criteria for decision in some law other than its own.[40] I shall return to this point later.

So it is with a court. It must look at the world from where it is; it has no choice. This fact is the reason that the concern Pitel and Rafferty express in the penultimate sentence in the quotation above is misplaced. That said, it does not follow, as the Admiralty cases I have mentioned illustrate, that the court's analysis of a case stops with the *lex fori*. A court can properly take foreign law into account if the foreign facts show that the *lex fori* is not the appropriate basis for decision.

It would be in this way that the Ontario court, on the facts of *Moran*, would consider Saskatchewan law to be a preferable basis for the decision, even if all choice of law rules were abandoned and the court started from Ontario law. And, of course, in the facts of *Greenshields Inc v Johnston*, an Alberta court has no reason to consider Ontario law, just as it would not allow a creditor to provide that the Guarantees Acknowledgement Act should not apply to a guarantee properly caught by that Act.

To answer the concern of Pitel and Rafferty,[41] we can ask, 'Where else would or could a court start than from its position in a local, ie, territorial, legal system, the *lex fori*?' Once the structure that is Conflicts analysis is removed there is, so to speak, nothing between the judge and the real issue in the case. The starting place the judge can now adopt is the recognition that a court can only look at the world from where it is. It is, as I have said, a kind of solipsism, just as we, as individuals, have to look at the world from where we are, though we can, as we must, accept

mortgagees know that ships have to incur repairs or buy fuel at places where the lien-holder may have priority.

[39] The approach applied in *Todd Shipyards* and *Holt Cargo* was ignored by the Federal Court of Appeal in *JPMorgan Chase Bank v Lanner (The)*, 2008 FCA 399, 305 DLR (4th) 442 (*sub nom JP Morgan Chase Bank v Mystras Maritime Corp*), a case where the law to decide the controversy was clearly Canadian maritime law. Richard CJ, approached the case as a conflicts case and applied the law chosen in a choice of law clause in the contract between the debtor ship and one creditor to determine the priority between two creditors. The idea that the choice of law clause in the contract that one creditor had with the debtor could control questions of priority between two creditors to the assets of the debtor is very odd and has to be wrong. See Swan, Case Comment, 'The Perils of a Conflicts Analysis: Look Before You Leap', *Kent Trade and Finance Inc v JP Morgan Chase Bank*' (2010) 8 *Canadian International Lawyer* 15.

[40] See, for example, *Gillespie Management Corp v Terrace Properties* (1989) 62 DLR (4th) 221 (BCCA), where the fact that a contract was illegal under the law of Washington state was a defence to an action for breach of contract brought in British Columbia. The proper law was conceded to be that of British Columbia.

[41] Pitel and Rafferty, *Conflict of Laws* (2016).

that others' points of view are valid. This observation does not mean, as I have shown, that a court or we can only see the world from one point of view; so too a court may find the criteria for decision in some law other than its own.[42]

V. Conclusion

The edifice of the Conflict of Laws is a monstrous structure. It is, as I have told generations of students, wholly idiosyncratic or special to Conflicts. Its structure requires those who accept its role in deciding cases to abandon everything they accept in dealing with ordinary cases in private law. Where a court gets guidance in a contracts case from remembering that the purpose of the Law of Contracts is the protection of the reasonable expectations of those who rely on promises,[43] a court dealing with a conflicts case has to abandon that goal and talk only about irrelevant things like the place where the contract was made or where the parties did business, etc.[44]

Case after case is decided without reference to any goals of the law of contracts or the law of torts. The Supreme Court has declared that limitation periods are matters of 'substantive' law and therefore determined by the *lex causae*.[45]

An argument that is often made is that choice of law rules provide certainty and simplicity.[46] This argument is often made with respect to liability for motor vehicle accidents; cars and those driving them often cross internal and international boundaries. What would those who argue for simplicity say to a suggestion that

[42] See, eg, *Gillespie Management Corp v Terrace Properties* (1989) 62 DLR (4th) 221 (BCCA), where the fact that a contract was illegal under the law of Washington state was a defence to an action for breach of contract brought in British Colombia. The proper law was conceded to be that of British Columbia.

[43] See, eg, Swan, Adamski and Na, *Canadian Contract Law*, 4th edn (LexisNexis, 2018) 3. This goal is often associated with the great American contract scholar, Arthur Corbin. In his contract treatise, *Corbin on Contracts* Vol 1 (West Publishing Co, 1963) 2, § 1, he said: 'That portion of the field of law that is classified and described as the law of contracts attempts the realization of reasonable expectations that have been induced by the making of a promise'. Canadian courts frequently refer to and accept the validity and utility of the goal.

[44] See, for example, *The Assunzione* [1954] P 150 (CA). The judgments in the Court of Appeal deal exhaustively with the various 'connecting factors' the contract in question had with France and Italy in an attempt to discover the proper law but never discussed the actual problem between the parties to discover if the result might differ under either possibly applicable law. We have to assume the parties were fighting about something; it would have been nice to know what it was and what a solution – a sensible solution – might have looked like.

[45] See *Tolofson* (n 10). See also *Castillo* (n 15) [37] and the reasons for judgment of Bastarache J for an extraordinary view of the relation of the Supreme Court and provincial legislatures. Bastarache J relied on the 'vested rights' theory of conflicts, a theoretical basis for conflicts rejected about a century ago. Section 23 of Sch B to the Ontario Limitations Act, SO 2002, c 24 reflects this characterisation of limitation periods, providing that they are substantive. This required characterisation makes no sense; limitation periods have a purpose and their application should reflect that fact. See Swan (n 1) Part 2, where the problems of limitation periods are considered.

[46] This goal is behind the adoption of the *lex loci delicti* in *Tolofson* (n 10).

any case involving a multi-state traffic accident be dealt with by flipping a coin? If the choice of law rule being propounded, as in *Castillo v Castillo*,[47] is brutally pointless, why not cut out all the costs of litigation and flip a coin?[48]

One cannot simultaneously have a commitment to the rational elaboration of the law and at the same time support choice of law rules of the traditional jurisdiction-selecting type because those rules cannot be a more rational solution than flipping a coin.[49]

What *Morguard* and *Moran* show is that one can approach conflicts problems with values and constitutional structures central to one's reasoning. That approach will provide uniformity and will satisfy and desire that results reached in the judicial process reflect the values that have to be respected.

[47] *Castillo* (n 15).
[48] One flip at trial, the best of three on appeal, best of five on further appeal; the variations are endless?
[49] Consider again the process of reasoning in *The Assunzione* (n 44).

8

Tolofson v Jensen: Reframing the Canadian Common Law Choice of Law Rule for Torts

JOOST BLOM

I. *Tolofson v Jensen* and Common Law Reasoning in Private International Law

Tolofson v Jensen[1] is a good case to include in a study of common law reasoning in private international law, because the reasoning is in some ways untypical of Canadian common law decisions in the area. Some aspects of the reasoning have had, and continue to have, important consequences for the development of the law. *Tolofson* is also a useful example of how the impact of a common law decision can lie as much in the style of the reasoning as in the principles it articulates. Perhaps this is truer in private international law than in many other areas. Here, decisions of courts of final appeal on a particular point are often scarce, which means that the decisions that exist may acquire an oracular aura because they stand so alone.

II. The Canadian Common Law before *Tolofson*

In *Tolofson*, the Supreme Court of Canada consolidated the appeals of two motor vehicle negligence cases, *Tolofson v Jensen* from the British Columbia Court of Appeal[2] and *Lucas v Gagnon* from the Ontario Court of Appeal.[3] Both called into question the existing Canadian common law on choice of law in tort claims. That law was notoriously unsatisfactory. It rested on the English common law embodied in *Phillips v Eyre*,[4] including the gloss put upon that case by *Machado v Fontes*.[5]

[1] *Tolofson v Jensen* [1994] 3 SCR 1022.
[2] *Tolofson v Jensen* 1992 CanLII 931 (BCCA), 89 DLR (4th) 129.
[3] *Lucas v Gagnon* (1992) 11 OR (3d) 422, Ont CA.
[4] *Phillips v Eyre* (1870) LR 6 QB 1, Ex Ch.
[5] *Machado v Fontes* [1897] 2 QB 231, CA.

That this was the law of Canada had been confirmed by the Supreme Court in *McLean v Pettigrew*.[6] The plaintiff in that case had been injured in an automobile accident in Ontario, when she and the defendant driver and his wife, all of whom lived in Quebec, were visiting Ottawa, Ontario in the defendant's car. The plaintiff brought her action for damages in Quebec.

The choice of law issue was that the plaintiff had a quasi-delictual (negligence) claim under Quebec law but no tort action under Ontario law, because, at the time, a non-commercial passenger could not claim any loss or damage for injuries received in a car accident.[7] The court followed the English authorities already referred to, and held that the plaintiff was entitled to recover damages because her claim was valid under the *lex fori*, Quebec law, and the act done by the defendant was wrongful, in the sense of non-justifiable, by the *lex loci delicti*, the law of Ontario, because it was punishable as a provincial driving offence.

Because provincial tort laws differed considerably as to liability arising out of motor vehicle accidents, *McLean* produced a situation in which the *lex fori* determined the existence of a tort cause of action, but the *lex loci delicti*'s only role was to preclude liability if the defendant broke no law at all, penal or civil, in that jurisdiction. This was, among other things, a blatant invitation to forum-shop if the accident happened in a province under whose law a civil claim was unavailable but damages could be recovered under the law of the province in which the claim was brought. *McLean* was nearly 50 years old, and ripe for reassessment, when *Tolofson v Jensen* and *Lucas v Gagnon* came before the Supreme Court.

The rule in *Phillips v Eyre* was on its way out elsewhere. In the UK the courts had modified it to make it more flexible,[8] and Parliament eventually replaced it altogether with a basic rule applying the *lex loci delicti*, with a flexible exception based on a 'substantially more appropriate' criterion.[9] The Australian High Court, in *Breavington v Godleman*,[10] had also begun the abandonment of the rule.[11]

Canadian lower courts had been chipping away at *McLean v Pettigrew* when they could. The most important such case up to *Tolofson* was the Ontario Court of Appeal's decision in *Grimes v Cloutier*.[12] That case confined *McLean* to cases where

[6] *McLean v Pettigrew* [1945] SCR 62. Quebec courts considering private international law did not have to follow English common law principles. n 114 sets out the current Quebec choice of law rule.

[7] The bar was in the Highway Traffic Act, RSO 1937, c 288, s 47. It has long since been removed.

[8] *Chaplin v Boys* [1971] AC 356, HL; *Red Sea Insurance Co Ltd v Bouygues SA* [1995] 1 AC 190, PC (HK).

[9] The Law Commission had recommended the statutory change in 'Private International Law: Choice of Law in Tort and Delict' Law Com No 193 (1990). The recommendations were implemented by the Private International Law (Miscellaneous Provisions) Act 1995, c 42 (UK), Pt III.

[10] [1988] HCA 40, 169 CLR 41.

[11] The seven judges agreed that the law of the state in which an accident occurred determined what heads of damage were recoverable. Three judges, Wilson and Gaudron JJ (joint judgment), and Deane J, based this on the full faith and credit provision in s 118 of the Australian Constitution. Three judges, Brennan, Dawson and Toohey JJ, modified the *Phillips v Eyre* rule to give the dominant role to the *lex loci delicti*. The remaining judge, Mason CJ, held that the common law rule was the *lex loci delicti* alone.

[12] *Grimes v Cloutier* (1989) 61 DLR (4th) 505, Ont CA. The accident took place in Quebec and the issue was whether to apply its no-fault scheme, which excluded civil liability.

both the plaintiff and the defendant were from the forum province. Only in such a case did the *lex fori* have the most significant relationship with the action.[13]

III. The Cases Appealed in *Tolofson v Jensen*

A. *Tolofson v Jensen*

Kim Tolofson was 12 when, in July 1979, he was injured in a collision in Saskatchewan. He was riding in a car in which he and his father had travelled from British Columbia. The Tolofsons' car collided with a car driven by Jensen, a Saskatchewan resident. Kim Tolofson's action was brought in 1987 in British Columbia against his father, Roger Tolofson, and against Jensen. The father applied for a declaration that two provisions of Saskatchewan law that were in effect in July 1979 applied to the action. One was a one-year limitation period that had expired and the other was a rule that a gratuitous passenger could not recover against a driver except in the case of wilful or wanton misconduct. (Both rules had been abolished by the time the action was commenced.)

The BC Court of Appeal, affirming the chambers judge, held that *McLean v Pettigrew* applied.[14] BC law applied to the issue of limitations (irrespective of whether that was characterised as procedural or substantive law) and the need to prove wilful and wanton misconduct, and neither was a defence under BC law. The second limb of *McLean* was met because Roger Tolofson's conduct was not justifiable by Saskatchewan law, as it constituted a motor vehicle offence. The court added that this result accorded with the reasonable expectations of the parties; the trip began and was intended to end in British Columbia.[15] That a second defendant was a resident of Saskatchewan was insufficient reason to distinguish *McLean*.[16]

B. *Lucas v Gagnon*

Heather Gagnon brought an action in Ontario for injuries she received in a two-vehicle accident in Quebec, and as litigation guardian she claimed for the injuries suffered by her two children. The action was brought against her husband, Rejean Gagnon, the driver of the car in which he and the plaintiffs were riding. The plaintiffs' claims were originally also made against the driver of the other car, Lavoie,

[13] ibid 524–25.
[14] *Tolofson v Jensen* (n 2).
[15] ibid 144.
[16] *Tolofson v Jensen* (n 2). The court distinguished *Grimes v Cloutier* (1989) 61 DLR (4th) 505, Ont CA on the basis that, in that case, no defendant was from the forum province. Also, in *Grimes*, the plaintiff had the right to receive some compensation under Quebec law, whereas Kim Tolofson would receive no compensation if Saskatchewan tort law were applied.

a resident of Quebec. The plaintiffs' actions against him were discontinued but Rejean Gagnon crossclaimed against him for contribution and indemnity in the event that he (Gagnon) was held liable. The choice of law issue, as in *Grimes*, was that Ontario law had retained common law tort liability, whereas Quebec law had replaced ordinary civil liability with a mandatory no-fault compensation scheme. Heather Gagnon had received the maximum benefits under that scheme from her husband's Ontario insurer, under an arrangement between the Ontario and Quebec insurance authorities.

The Ontario Court of Appeal held that the plaintiffs' claims against Gagnon were governed by Ontario law.[17] *Grimes* was distinguished, and *McLean* held to apply, on the basis that the only defendant in *Lucas* was an Ontario resident. The Quebec resident driver, Lavoie, was a defendant to the husband's crossclaim, but that was not a basis on which *McLean* could be displaced. It was displaced, however, so far as Gagnon's crossclaim against Lavoie was concerned. As in *Grimes*, Lavoie's being a resident of Quebec meant that Quebec law applied and Lavoie was not liable to Heather Gagnon.

IV. The Judgment

The Supreme Court of Canada reversed both decisions. The plaintiffs' claims were, in each case, defeated by the rules of the *lex loci delicti*. The law of the province where the action was brought no longer had any application in tort choice of law. The judgment was for a unanimous court on all points except one, in relation to which two judges gave short separate judgments.

The essential components of the court's decision are set out here. Certain aspects of the reasoning are then taken up in more detail in the next part.

The Anglo-Canadian choice of law rules, as embodied in *McLean v Pettigrew*, showed 'insufficient reference to the underlying reality in which they operate and to general principles that should apply in responding to that reality'.[18] As a matter of principle, the law that determined tort liability should be the law of the place where the tort was committed. The reference to the law of the forum, which stemmed from *Phillips v Eyre*,[19] was illogical. It commingled the concepts of jurisdiction and choice of law.[20] *McLean* was therefore declared no longer to be law. The *lex loci delicti* rule was subject to no exceptions, at least in an interprovincial case. It was on this point that two judges gave separate judgments. They preferred to keep open the possibility of such an exception in intra-Canadian cases as well as international ones.[21]

[17] *Lucas v Gagnon* (n 3).
[18] *Tolofson v Jensen* (n 1) 1046.
[19] *Phillips v Eyre* (n 4).
[20] *Tolofson v Jensen* (n 1) 1054.
[21] ibid 1078 (Sopinka and Major JJ).

Having decided that the law of Saskatchewan governed all substantive issues in the *Tolofson* action, the court had to characterise the limitations rule in Saskatchewan as procedural or substantive. The court decided that henceforth, all limitation rules, no matter whether they were framed in terms of right or remedy, should be regarded in Canadian private international law as substantive. A procedural characterisation should be confined to rules that 'make the machinery of the forum court run smoothy as distinguished from those determinative of the rights of *both* parties'.[22]

Kim Tolofson's claim was therefore barred both by the Saskatchewan limitation period and by the rule that a gratuitous passenger must show wilful or wanton misconduct by the driver. The plaintiffs' claims in *Lucas* were barred by the Quebec no-fault compensation scheme. None of the plaintiffs could have recourse to the *lex fori*.

V. The Reasoning

A. Relationship to Contemporaneous Supreme Court of Canada Decisions

The principal judgment was given by Justice Gerard La Forest, who sat on the court from 1985 to 1997. In the 12 years that La Forest J was on the Supreme Court, that court heard five private international law cases. He gave the sole or principal judgment in four of them,[23] all decided between 1990 and 1994. All of them were ground-breaking treatments of their subjects, and all were either completely or nearly unanimous decisions. They were, chronologically: *Morguard Investments Ltd v De Savoye*,[24] on foreign judgments and the substantive limits on the jurisdiction of domestic courts; *Hunt v T&N plc*,[25] on the constitutional ability of a province to enact laws that blocked the enforcement of other provinces' court orders; *Thomson v Thomson*,[26] the first interpretation by the court of the Hague Child Abduction Convention;[27] and *Tolofson v Jensen*.[28] In the field of private international law, the Supreme Court has never had a string of foundational decisions like these, either before or after. In retrospect, *Tolofson* was a culmination.

[22] ibid 1072 (emphasis in the original).

[23] The only private international law case to which he was a party in which he did not write the principal judgment was *Amchem Product Inc v British Columbia (Workers' Compensation Board)* [1993] 1 SCR 897.

[24] *Morguard Investments Ltd v De Savoye* [1990] 3 SCR 1077 (panel of seven, unanimous).

[25] *Hunt v T&N PLC* [1993] 4 SCR 289 (panel of seven, unanimous).

[26] *Thomson v Thomson* [1994] 3 SCR 551 (panel of nine, two concurring judgments disagreeing with his judgment on one or other of two issues).

[27] Hague Convention on the Civil Aspects of International Child Abduction, 25 October 1980, Can TS 1983 No 35 (entered into force 1 December 1983).

[28] *Tolofson v Jensen* (n 1) (panel of seven, two concurring judgments disagreeing with his judgment on one issue).

Three features of the reasoning in *Tolofson* deserve special attention in this paper. First, the interplay between Canadian constitutional law, public international law, and private international law. Second, the approach taken to non-Canadian authorities. Third, the subsequent evolution of the principles established by the case.

B. Interplay of Canadian Constitutional Law, Public International Law, and Private International Law

i. The Lines of Reasoning on Choice of Law

In its judgments in *Morguard*[29] and *Hunt*[30] the Supreme Court of Canada, for the first time, established the principle that the constitution imposed territorial limits on the jurisdiction of a province's courts. 'Properly restrained jurisdiction'[31] was defined by a requirement that the defendant or the subject matter of the action have a 'real and substantial connection'[32] with the forum jurisdiction. At the same time, the court placed a 'full faith and credit' obligation, seen as implicit in the federal structure of the country, on the courts of each province to enforce judgments from other provinces that met the constitutional standard of 'properly restrained' jurisdiction. These requirements were rooted in two principles. One was an implied obligation of comity between the legal systems of provinces, and the other was the long-recognised (but poorly defined) incapacity of a province to give its laws extraterritorial effect. The standard of judicial jurisdiction and the correlative obligation to recognise other provinces' judgments were an expression both of the relationship between provincial legal systems and of the maximum territorial ambit of provincial legal authority.

In *Tolofson*, after reviewing the common law on tort choice of law, La Forest J described the authorities as deficient because 'in none of these cases was the [choice of law] rule approached on the basis of Canadian constitutional imperatives'.[33] The judgment's response is to add a theory of choice of law to the constitutional framework already in place. However, the analysis begins with public international law: 'On the international plane, the relevant underlying reality is the territorial limits of law under the international legal order'.[34] Respect for those limits is seen as implicit in comity between jurisdictions, not only within the federation but also internationally:[35]

> From the general principle that a state has exclusive jurisdiction within its own territories and that other states must under principles of comity respect the exercise of its

[29] *Morguard Investments Ltd v De Savoye* (n 24).
[30] *Hunt v T&N PLC* (n 25).
[31] *Morguard Investments Ltd v De Savoye* (n 24) 1103.
[32] ibid 1108.
[33] *Tolofson v Jensen* (n 1) 1044–45.
[34] ibid 1047.
[35] ibid 1047.

> jurisdiction within its own territory, it seems axiomatic to me that, at least as a general rule, the law to be applied in torts is the law of the place where the activity occurred, i.e., the *lex loci delicti*.[36]

'Sound practical considerations' also supported such a rule. It was certain, easy to apply and predictable, and seemed to meet normal expectations. 'Ordinarily people expect their activities to be governed by the law of the place where they happen to be.'[37] '[C]haotic situations would often result if the principle of territorial jurisdiction were not, at least generally, respected.'[38]

La Forest J goes on to consider whether there might be exceptions to the 'axiomatic' general rule. He does not dismiss the theoretical possibility but says that any exception would need to be very carefully defined.[39] He considers a number of exceptions, drawn from the authorities, and does not accept any of them. To apply the *lex fori* to an accident that took place elsewhere, as *McLean v Pettigrew* did,[40] was to 'fly against the territorial principle' and invite forum shopping.[41] Moreover, the requirement of actionability by the *lex fori* was related more to jurisdiction than to choice of law. Such a jurisdictional safeguard was arguably unnecessary within Canada, since jurisdiction had to satisfy the real and substantial connection requirement and the *forum non conveniens* discretion was available.[42]

Nor was an exception based on the interest of a state other than the *locus delicti* consistent with the territorial principle. Any rule that displaces the *lex loci delicti* must:

> [B]e capable of escaping the spectre that a multiplicity of jurisdictions may become capable of exercising jurisdiction over the same activity in accordance with their own laws. This would not only encourage forum shopping but have the underlying effect of inhibiting mobility.[43]

The judgment discusses *Babcock v Jackson*,[44] which applied New York law as between New Yorkers who had an accident in Ontario. The choice of law issue, as in the *Tolofson* claim and *McLean v Pettigrew*, was an Ontario statute exempting the driver from liability to a gratuitous passenger for ordinary negligence. The approach in *Babcock* was given short shrift, citing its uncertainty[45] and the likelihood that it would create or prolong litigation.[46] The 'flexible exception' that Lords Wilberforce and Hodson had favoured in *Boys v Chaplin*,[47] based on the

[36] ibid 1050.
[37] ibid 1050.
[38] ibid 1051.
[39] ibid 1052.
[40] *McLean v Pettigrew* [1945] SCR 62.
[41] *Tolofson v Jensen* (n 1) 1052.
[42] ibid 1054–55 and 1064.
[43] ibid 1055.
[44] *Babcock v Jackson* 191 NE 2d 279 (1963), NY Ct Apps.
[45] *Tolofson v Jensen* (n 1) 1056.
[46] ibid 1057.
[47] *Chaplin v Boys* (n 8) 380 and 391–92, respectively.

tort issue having its most significant relationship with a law other than the *lex loci delicti*, was rejected for the same reason.[48]

An exception in favour of the *lex fori*, limited to cases where the parties are nationals or residents of the forum, was also unacceptable, at least in interprovincial cases. Cases like *McLean* and *Babcock* had rejected the *lex loci delicti* essentially because they considered the 'foreign' rules in question to be contrary to the public policy of the forum.[49] These were laws that 'the legislature having power to enact it within its territory has chosen to adopt', and for the forum to refuse to apply them, and prefer the *lex fori*, was to overlook that 'such differences are a concomitant of the territoriality principle'.[50] And such 'public policy' problems, especially between provinces, tended, La Forest J said, to disappear over time.[51] (In fact, since *Tolofson*, differences between provincial laws have increased rather than decreased as far as accident compensation schemes are concerned, although it is probably true that limitation laws, and common law liability for negligence where it is still used, have become more uniform.)

The judgment also examines arguments of convenience for applying forum law rather than the law of another jurisdiction, but finds them unpersuasive. The fact that compensation may implicate local healthcare systems and insurers, when all parties are from the forum, did not point to any solid advantage to the forum province from applying its liability rules.[52] The difficulty of proving and applying foreign law, when all parties are from the forum, did mean that there was 'some merit' to allowing judges in such cases to apply their own law, but it was of less concern within Canada.[53] Any rule geared to the non-involvement of foreign residents could create a problem that parties would be added to or kept out of a proceeding for tactical reasons.[54]

The upshot: 'there is little to gain and much to lose in creating an exception to the *lex loci delicti* in relation to domestic litigation'.[55] In international cases such an exception might not be 'indefensible',[56] particularly if it was part of a reciprocal choice of law agreement like the *Hague Convention on Traffic Accidents*, which allows for an exception where all parties are from the forum.[57]

[48] *Tolofson v Jensen* (n 1) 1057.
[49] ibid.
[50] ibid 1058.
[51] ibid 1059.
[52] ibid 1059.
[53] ibid 1060.
[54] ibid 1061.
[55] ibid 1062.
[56] ibid.
[57] Hague Conference on Private International Law, Convention on the Law Applicable to Traffic Accidents (1971). Article 4(b) displaces the *lex loci delicti* in favour of the state of registration if all vehicles involved in the accident are registered in the same state. Canada is not one of the 21 parties to the convention, but the Uniform Law Conference of Canada promulgated a Uniform Conflict of Laws (Traffic Accidents) Act in 1970 based on the convention. The state-of-registration rule is in s 4. The Act has been adopted in Yukon, Conflict of Laws (Traffic Accidents) Act, RSY 2002, c 38.

In the passages just described, the reasoning, more than common law cases usually do, propounds a thesis. It is that the territorial principle favours, even demands, the adoption of a choice of law rule directed at the *lex loci delicti*. Arguments are marshalled in support of the thesis. Arguments for making exceptions to the *lex loci* rule in particular cases are discounted partly because the exceptions would run counter to the thesis.

Then, in an even more striking passage, the judgment turns to constitutional considerations. This discussion follows two tracks. One, for which several of the judgments in *Breavington v Godleman*[58] are cited as strong support,[59] is that a federal system, like Australia's and Canada's, ought to have 'a rule that is certain and that ensures that an act committed in one part of this country will be given the same legal effect throughout the country'.[60] The desirability of a uniform approach to choice of law throughout the country 'militates strongly in favour of the *lex loci delicti* rule'.[61] Having made this very suggestive constitutional point, however, La Forest J undercuts it with a disclaimer. He said he did 'not wish to enter largely into this or to come to any final, and indeed in many situations, tentative view'.[62] The cases were not argued in constitutional terms in the courts below, and the constitutional elements were 'largely dealt with in this Court as a mere backdrop to other issues'.[63]

He then takes up the other track in his constitutional discussion, which is that choice of law is connected to the constitutional concept of extraterritoriality. The permissible content of a choice of law rule – private international law being a matter of provincial law – is seen as connected to the territorial limits on provincial legislative authority. 'Unless the courts' power to create law in this area exists independently of provincial power, the courts would appear to be limited in exercising their powers to the same extent as the provincial legislatures.'[64] The passage is not entirely clear but seems to consider that the forum court's decision to apply forum law must respect the limits on the forum *legislature*'s authority to prescribe rules for the particular case. Conversely, the forum court's decision to apply the law of another province is apparently regarded as equivalent to accepting the other province's *legislative* authority to prescribe rules for the case.

Given the earlier disclaimer, it is hard to know how seriously the reader of the judgment is meant to take this linkage with territorial limits on provincial legislative power, or the observation that a choice of law system in which either of two provinces' rules might apply to the same incident would amount to an 'arguably impermissible' overlapping of legislative authority.[65] The only guidance given is

[58] *Breavington v Godleman* (n 10).
[59] *Tolofson v Jensen* (n 1) 1063–64.
[60] ibid 1064.
[61] ibid.
[62] ibid 1065.
[63] ibid.
[64] ibid.
[65] ibid 1066.

that 'the wiser course would appear to be for the Court to avoid devising a rule that may possibly raise intractable constitutional problems'.[66]

ii. Comments on the Reasoning on Choice of Law

It has to be said that, looking back on it after three decades have passed, the theoretical scaffolding that La Forest J erects around his choice of law analysis is not fully watertight.

One issue is the connection the judgment makes between the choice of law problem and the territorial principle in public international law. Two criticisms can be made. One is that it conflates the concepts of prescriptive jurisdiction, a state's authority to law down legal norms, and of enforcement jurisdiction, the authority to ensure compliance with the state's laws. International law has quite strict territorial rules about enforcement jurisdiction, but hardly any around prescriptive jurisdiction. It is prescriptive jurisdiction that is at issue when choice of law decisions are made. The forum court – whose enforcement powers are exercised within the territory of the forum – decides whether or not to give effect to one or other state's law.[67] Here the guidance of public international law is anything but clear.[68] Of particular relevance to the use of territorial theory in *Tolofson* is the statement in one international law treatise, when introducing the subject of jurisdictional competence: 'There is no assumption (even in criminal cases) that individuals or corporations will be regulated only once, and situations of multiple jurisdictional competence occur frequently'.[69]

The other criticism is that this emphasis on territoriality in public international law cannot be of general application in choice of law theory. It has (some) plausibility only in the areas of tort and property, because they generally have strong physical elements that can be localised within a territory. Contracts, personal status and other choice of law areas cannot be convincingly analysed in terms of a territoriality principle. Even with respect to physically localised issues, it can be argued that the territorial 'principle' relied on in *Tolofson* should not be seen as a logical principle derived from state sovereignty, but as an approach to achieving justice in private legal matters. The methods of private law are more relevant than those of international law.[70]

[66] ibid.

[67] *Tolofson* was cited in the Supreme Court of Canada in an international law context by two dissenting judges, to support their view that Canadian courts should abstain from adjudicating wrongs committed outside Canada on the basis of new common law torts drawn from customary international human rights law: *Nevsun Resources Ltd v Araya* 2020 SCC 5 [252]–[256] (Brown and Rowe JJ).

[68] Crawford, *Brownlie's Principles of International Law*, 8th edn (OUP, 2012) 471–72.

[69] ibid 457.

[70] Kincaid, '*Jensen v Tolofson* and the Revolution in Tort Choice of Law' (1995) 74 *Canadian Bar Review* 539 and J Walker, 'Are We There Yet – Towards a New Rule for Choice of Law in Tort' (2000) 38 *Osgoode Hall Law Journal* 331 argue that La Forest J's reliance on comity is misplaced, and that private law values, including the parties' expectations, should guide choice of law decisions. Banu, 'Assuming Regulatory authority for Transnational Torts: An Interstate Affair? A Historical Perspective

Another aspect that deserves comment is the assertion that the application of the law of the place of the accident is consistent with ordinary people's expectations. Such remarks are true enough if one is speaking of rules of conduct, but by and large choice of law in tort is not about what conduct was expected of the wrongdoer, but about what right to compensation the victim could expect to have from them. None of the three choice of law questions before the court was about the standard of conduct. Limitations (in the *Tolofson* action) and no-fault compensation schemes (in *Lucas*) have nothing to do with conduct. The Saskatchewan gratuitous passenger rule in the *Tolofson* action took the form of a 'wilful and wanton misconduct' requirement, but that was a rule, not about setting the standard for drivers' behaviour, but about protecting them (and their insurers) from ordinary negligence claims by gratuitous passengers. The lower courts in both the *Tolofson* and the *Lucas* claims had observed that, as between the passengers and the drivers, who in both cases were members of one family travelling together, expectations as to rights to compensation were probably directed to their home jurisdiction's law rather than the law of the place where the accident happened. The only comment made on that line of thinking is when La Forest J refers at one point to the view of 'some commentators' that parties who travel together from their home jurisdiction reasonably expect their home law to apply to them; he simply says he disagrees with that assumption.[71]

A third aspect, the difficulties with which have become more evident since *Tolofson*, as Canadian constitutional law has evolved, is the suggestion that a choice of law rule ought to respect the territorial limits on provincial legislative authority. A serious problem with this line of reasoning is that the territorial limits on provincial legislative authority were unclear at the time and are, if anything, less clear now. Deducing a choice of law rule from those limits is all but hopeless.[72] A case that illustrates the difficulty is *Unifund Insurance Co v Insurance Corp of British Columbia*.[73] The case concerned a particular rule in Ontario insurance legislation about indemnification as between insurers, which an arbitrator had applied as between insurers in relation to a motor vehicle accident that took place in British Columbia. One party's insurer was from Ontario, the other parties' insurers were from British Columbia. The Supreme Court of Canada decided that whether Ontario legislation could constitutionally apply to the case depended on whether the matter being regulated had a 'sufficient connection' with Ontario.[74] (In this case, the court held, it did not.) How can one possibly construct a choice of

on the Canadian Private International Law Tort Rules' (2013) 31 *Windsor Yearbook of Access to Justice* 197 examines *Tolofson*'s linkage of private international law with public international concepts of state sovereignty.

[71] *Tolofson v Jensen* (n 1) 1057.

[72] *cf* the argument made in *British Columbia v Imperial Tobacco Canada Ltd* 2004 BCCA 269, aff'd 2005 SCC 49, [2005] 2 SCR 473, going the other way, that the choice of law rule, after *Tolofson*, has become the definition of a province's territorial legislative reach (rejected by Rowles JA, [169]–[171]).

[73] *Unifund Insurance Co v Insurance Corpn of BC* 2003 SCC 40, [2003] 2 SCR 63.

[74] Analysed in E Edinger and V Black, 'A New Approach to Extraterritoriality: *Unifund Assurance Co v ICBC*' (2004) 40 *Canadian Business Law Journal* 161.

law rule based on what facts would constitute a 'sufficient connection' with which jurisdiction?

To be fair, as noted earlier, La Forest J acknowledged that his views on the constitutional questions were tentative and that the constitutional dimensions of choice of law had not been squarely addressed in argument. The problem is that the constitutional suggestions appear to dovetail with a rigorous insistence that the *lex loci delicti* principle should have zero exceptions in interprovincial cases and very few exceptions in international ones. The combined effect is to convey that choice of law is set in a matrix that is both logically and constitutionally constructed, and that forbids rules that would allow inconsistent outcomes in different courts. This is enough to discourage almost any attempt to loosen *Tolofson* by introducing qualifications or more flexible criteria.[75]

C. Approach to Non-Canadian Authorities

A striking feature of the *Tolofson* decision is that the rule the court adopts – a strict *lex loci delicti* rule – is one that the courts in both England and the US, two of the most powerful influences on Canadian common law, were conspicuously moving away from because of its rigidity.[76] The judgment openly prefers the state of the law before these developments, as where it says that the 'practice of most states until recently favoured exclusive reference to the *lex loci*',[77] and goes on to adopt the latter principle in preference to the more recent developments. The newer American approaches, in particular, get cursory treatment. *Babcock v Jackson*[78] is said not to have been accepted yet in the 'vast majority' of the American states,[79] and is criticised for its 'extreme uncertainty'.[80] No assessment is made of its merits.

[75] The criticism of over-constitutionalisation was made by Castel, 'Back to the Future – Is the New Rigid Choice of Law Rule for Interprovincial Torts Constitutionally Mandated' (1995) 33 *Osgoode Hall Law Journal* 35; Junger, 'Case Comment: *Tolofson v Jensen*' (1995) 23 *Manitoba Law Journal* 689. Nationally uniform, constitutionally mandated choice of law rules are supported by Herbert, 'The Conflict of Laws and Judicial Perspectives on Federalism: A Principled Defence of *Tolofson v Jensen*' (1998) 56 *University of Toronto Law Journal* 3. The tangle between choice of law and the constitutional notion of extraterritoriality that *Tolofson* encourages is shown by the strained reasoning in *Castillo v Castillo* 2005 SCC 83, [2005] 3 SCR 870, especially the separate judgment of Bastarache J. The case concerned the interpretation – and, according Bastarache J, the constitutional validity – of Alberta legislation that purported to make Alberta limitations law applicable even to claims governed by the substantive law of another jurisdiction.

[76] The most important decisions, up to 1994, were *Chaplin v Boys* (n 8) and *Babcock v Jackson* (n 44).

[77] *Tolofson v Jensen* (n 1) 1051.

[78] *Babcock v Jackson* (n 44).

[79] The only case cited in support of this statement is a pre-*Babcock* case, *Richards v United States*, 369 US 1 (1962) at 11–14. A categorisation of the current choice of law approaches of the states is given in Symeonides, 'Choice of Law in the American Courts in 2020' (2021) 69 *American Journal of Comparative Law* 177, 195. About half the states follow the 'most significant relationship' methodology.

[80] *Tolofson v Jensen* (n 1) 1056.

The foreign authority most prominently cited in *Tolofson* is the Australian High Court's decision in *Breavington v Godleman*,[81] the only recent non-Canadian decision that supported a strict *lex loci delicti* rule. Even that case is selectively used, because the importance of the constitutional underpinnings of the strict rule, for the judges that adopted it, is referred to only obliquely as a 'technical basis' that 'cannot be directly transported to our situation'.[82] Yet support for the strict rule is what is drawn from the decision.

On the characterisation of limitation periods, the judgment refers to the 'position in most civil law countries'[83] to treat limitations rules as substantive, and finds that the 'continental approach' is persuasive,[84] but undertakes no detailed analysis of the foreign law.

Especially in relation to the *lex loci delicti* rule, it has to be said that the reasoning in *Tolofson* uses non-Canadian jurisprudence more to bolster the court's conclusions than to survey and to weigh the alternative approaches on offer. That is related to the deductive approach the court takes to the tort choice of law problem, seeing the problem more strongly in terms of first principles than policy choices.

D. Subsequent Evolution of the Canadian Private International Law Principles Established in *Tolofson*

Two developments are noteworthy. They are both attempts, largely unsuccessful, to introduce some flexibility into the *lex loci delicti* principle that *Tolofson* laid down.

i. The 'Injustice Exception'

The only slight opening that *Tolofson* left for flexibility in *interprovincial* cases is a vague observation that difficulties may arise 'where the wrong arises out of some transnational or interprovincial activity' and 'territorial considerations become muted or conflict'.[85] There is an acknowledgement that the rule might be more flexible in *international* cases, but these hints are kept faint: 'I am not averse to retaining a discretion in the court to apply our own law [rather than the *lex loci delicti*]' if a rigid *lex loci delicti* rule 'could give rise to an injustice,' but 'I can … imagine few cases where this would be necessary'.[86] Elsewhere, La Forest J says that

[81] *Breavington v Godleman* (n 10).
[82] *Tolofson v Jensen* (n 1) 1063.
[83] ibid 1069.
[84] ibid 1070.
[85] ibid 1050.
[86] ibid 1054.

an exception might be 'defensible' in international cases, especially if it is done on a reciprocating basis between states, but he leaves the comment at that.[87]

Litigants in international cases have repeatedly tried to take advantage of these dicta but have generally failed. The problem is that the judgment in *Tolofson* gave little indication of what might make it 'unjust' to apply the law of the place of the accident. The pivotal case, from 2002,[88] involved an Ontario resident's claim for the injuries he had suffered as passenger in a car owned and driven by Ontario residents, in an accident in the state of New York. Here it was the defendant that argued for application of the *lex fori*, Ontario law, on the basis that it would be 'unjust' to award the victim the more generous damages available under New York law. Other cases had applied the *lex fori* in similar situations.[89]

The Ontario Court of Appeal said that the tendency of these previous decisions was to misapply *Tolofson* by holding, in effect, that it is unjust to apply the *lex loci delicti* if none of the parties is connected with the jurisdiction where the accident takes place. La Forest J had explicitly rejected an exception based on the parties' common residence in the forum jurisdiction. 'It is not mere differences in public policy that can ground the exception to the general rule of *lex loci delicti*'.[90] The motion judge had applied Ontario law, citing in support the rule in the *Hague Convention on Traffic Accidents*, which would allow application of the law of the state of registration. But to do so was contrary to La Forest J's dictum pointing out that the rules in the convention applied by way of reciprocity, which was not the case here. In sum, the thicket of dicta in *Tolofson*, about exceptions that should *not* be made to the rule, proved impenetrable in *Wong v Lee*.

And so it has remained. No case since *Wong v Lee* has given effect to the 'injustice exception' in an international case.[91]

ii. Geographically Distributed Torts

La Forest J seemed to contemplate that future courts might develop a rule other than *lex loci delicti* for torts that could not readily be localised. After describing the application of the law of the place where the activity occurred as 'axiomatic',[92] he added:

> There are situations, of course, notably where an act occurs in one place but the consequences are directly felt elsewhere, when the issue of where the tort takes place itself raises thorny issues. In such a case, it may well be that the consequences would be held

[87] ibid 1062.

[88] *Wong v Lee* 2002 CanLII 44916, 58 OR (3d) 398, Ont CA.

[89] *Hanlan v Sernesky* (1998) 38 OR (3d) 479, Ont CA (distinguished in *Wong v Lee* (n 88) [16]); *Wong v Wei* 1999 CanLII 6635 (BCSC).

[90] *Wong v Lee* (n 88) [16].

[91] See *Somers v Fournier* 2002 CanLII 45001 (ONCA), 214 DLR (4th) 611 [32]–[47]; *Das v George Weston Ltd* 2018 ONCA 1053, leave to appeal to SCC refused, 38529 (8 August 2019); *Long v Dundee Resort* 2013 ONSC 4238.

[92] n 36 and accompanying text.

> to constitute the wrong. Difficulties may also arise where the wrong directly arises out of some transnational or interprovincial activity. There territorial considerations may become muted; they may conflict and other considerations may play a determining role.

The first part of this passage describes a situation in which the *locus delicti* can plausibly be found to exist in one or other of two (or possibly more) jurisdictions. The second part, referring to a wrong that 'directly arises out of some transnational or interprovincial activity', suggests a somewhat different problem: that the inter-jurisdictional nature of the wrongdoer's activity may make the *lex loci delicti* a less than optimal rule, and that considerations other than territorial ones may then be allowed to 'play a determining role'.

Several cases have dealt with the first problem. Mostly it arose in the jurisdictional context, where the question is whether the court has jurisdiction against a non-resident defendant based on the defendant's having committed a tort within the province.[93] Here, unlike in choice of law, it is theoretically acceptable for a tort to have more than one *situs*, with each one being a potential basis for jurisdiction. Nevertheless, the courts have consistently taken the view that the geographically distributed tort in question had only one *situs* even for jurisdictional purposes. Usually it was because the initial impact on the plaintiff was in that place. The tort was not located in a second jurisdiction merely because the defendant acted, or the plaintiff suffered additional harm, in that other place.[94]

Cases that were actually choice of law cases, where only one jurisdiction's law can apply to one wrong, have taken a similar line. In determining the *locus delicti* they have given primary importance to the place of initial impact on the victim and rejected the place where the wrongdoer's acts or omissions occurred or the plaintiff suffered follow-on damage. Thus a negligence claim against a Canadian company, for allegedly failing to exercise reasonable care for the safety of a supplier's workers at a factory in Bangladesh, which had collapsed, was held governed by the law of Bangladesh even if corporate policy was set in Ontario; 'it was the injury in Bangladesh', said the Ontario Court of Appeal, 'that crystallised the alleged wrong'.[95]

[93] A proceeding that concerns a tort committed in the province is presumed to have a real and substantial connection with the province, which is the constitutional requirement for jurisdiction *simpliciter* (the term often used in Canada to distinguish the authority to take jurisdiction, which is a question of law, from the discretion to exercise that jurisdiction). At common law this presumption takes the form of a judge-made 'presumptive connecting factor;' see *Club Resorts Ltd v Van Breda* 2012 SCC 17, [2012] 1 SCR 572 [88]. In the uniform Court Jurisdiction and Proceedings Transfer Act, which has been adopted in British Columbia, Saskatchewan, Nova Scotia and Yukon, the presumption is a statutory one; see, for example, Court Jurisdiction and Proceedings Transfer Act, SBC 2003, c 28, s 10(g).

[94] *Gulevich v Miller* 2015 ABCA 411 (negligent report by radiologist prepared in Ontario but relied upon by medical professionals in Alberta, tort committed in Alberta); *Greta Inc v Robert De Lange* 2013 ONSC 3086 (conspiracy by foreigners to financially injure an Ontario corporation, tort committed in Ontario).

[95] *Das v George Weston Ltd* (n 91), leave to appeal to SCC refused, 38529 (8 August 2019) [90]. For a case on follow-on injury subsequent to the initial impact, see *Brill v Korpach Estate* 1997 ABCA 205.

Claims based on negligent misrepresentations by a manufacturer that led to errors in maintaining an aircraft based in Ontario were held to be claims for torts committed in Ontario, where the misrepresentations were received and acted upon, not in Pennsylvania, where the manufacturer was based, nor New York, where the aircraft crashed.[96] The courts have had to use a different approach when dealing with other claims based on purely economic harm that could not be tied to a particular event. One case assigned a *locus* to the torts of inducing breach of contract and conspiracy by identifying the place where the 'defining activity' took place, which was the negotiation and execution of an agreement allegedly aimed at causing the economic harm to the plaintiff.[97]

As for the 'transnational or interprovincial activity' dictum, the only cases that so far have taken their cue from that idea are three decisions of the Supreme Court of Canada.[98] These cases, all from Ontario, concerned defamation. Jurisdiction *simpliciter*[99] in a defamation action, the court confirmed in all three, can be based on the commission of the tort in the province through a publication of the allegedly defamatory material there.[100] That being so, and assuming the *locus delicti* is the same for jurisdictional as for choice of law purposes, the *lex loci delicti* rule from *Tolofson* would mean that the defamation was governed by the law of Ontario to the extent that it was published there.

The cases were fought mainly on the basis of a *forum non conveniens* application, and the party seeking to have the action stayed argued in each case that the defamation claim was governed, not by Ontario law, but by the law of the jurisdiction where the most substantial harm took place, which they argued was outside Ontario. La Forest J's dictum, quoted at the start of this section, was cited. The court saw some virtues in this departure from *lex loci delicti* in the first two of these cases, but did not need to decide on the question because in each of them Ontario was found to be the place of most substantial harm.[101] In the third case, which involved Internet defamation, two judges firmly adopted the new rule,[102] three just as firmly rejected it,[103] and the other four opted to express no opinion.[104] The result so far is therefore inconclusive.

See also Walsh, 'Territoriality and Choice of Law in the Supreme Court of Canada: Applications in Product Liability Claims' (1997) 76 *Canadian Bar Review* 91.

[96] *Thorne v Hudson* 2016 ONSC 5507. The court applied the *locus delicti* analysis in a jurisdiction case, *Central Sun Mining Inc v Vector Engineering Inc* 2013 ONCA 605.

[97] *Barrick Gold Corp v Goldcorp Inc* 2011 ONSC 3725 [645]–[655].

[98] Another departure from the *lex loci delicti* rule has been made in relation to statutory claims for misrepresentations relating to securities: *Pearson v Boliden Ltd* 2002 BCCA 624, 222 DLR (4th) 453, leave to appeal to SCC refused, 29578 (18 September 2003).

[99] n 91.

[100] *Éditions Écosociété Inc v Banro Corp* 2012 SCC 18, [2012] 1 SCR 636; *Breeden v Black* 2012 SCC 19, [2012] 1 SCR 667; *Haaretz.com v Goldhar* 2018 SCC 28, [2018] 2 SCR 3.

[101] *Éditions Écosociété Inc v Banro Corp* (ibid) [56]–[62]; *Breeden v Black* (ibid) [33].

[102] *Haaretz.com v Goldhar* (n 100) [109]–[119] (Abella J), [144]–[150] (Wagner J).

[103] ibid [196]–[204] (McLachlin CJ, Moldaver and Gascon JJ).

[104] ibid [91]–[94] (Côté J, with whom Brown, Rowe and Karakatsanis JJ agreed).

VI. The Legacy of *Tolofson*

The legacy of *Tolofson v Jensen* is profound, but its impact has been felt within a fairly narrow area. In this respect it contrasts with *Morguard*[105] and *Hunt*,[106] whose influence has reached into practically every nook and cranny of Canadian private international law. Despite the array of suggestive, even speculative, obiter dicta in La Forest J's judgment, the decision's impact has been confined to its two strict *rationes decidendi*, which are the tort choice of law rule and the characterisation of limitation statutes as substantive, not procedural, in nature. The reasoning has not generated principles of broader application. Even when it comes to localising the tort for the purposes of jurisdiction, courts have been more inclined to refer to the earlier authority of *Moran v Pyle*[107] than to *Tolofson*.[108]

The decision that limitation statutes are to be characterised as substantive has, on the whole, been absorbed smoothly into the law. One reason is that the change affected only limitation rules framed in terms of loss of a remedy; ones that were framed in terms of extinction of the right were already substantive. Also, the law in other jurisdictions had already been evolving in this direction.[109] The emphasis on confining a procedural characterisation to rules truly tied to the smooth functioning of the court system has been useful.

The impact of the decision on choice of law, though more radical, has been circumscribed by virtue of the fact that the territorial principle at the heart of the decision is ill-suited for general application. No other area of choice of law has received the kind of recasting that *Tolofson* gave to tort, because no other area can – or should – be made to conform to the underlying premise of strict territoriality. The Supreme Court of Canada itself, in the nearly 30 years since *Tolofson*, has used it only as a handy authority for generalities like 'courts should be cautious in carving out exceptions to conflicts rules'[110] and 'Certainty [is] one of the key purposes being pursued in framing a conflicts rule'.[111]

But within the scope of what the case touches, the legacy of *Tolofson* can be described as profound. It was the first attempt by the Supreme Court of Canada to derive a choice of law rule from first principles. This is both the strength of the case and its shortcoming. It is a strength because it is always sound to ask whether a rule makes sense in terms of the fundamental premises of the area of law to which it relates. It is a shortcoming, because two of the first principles upon which La Forest J constructs his thesis are, as already suggested, drawn from doctrines in

[105] *Morguard Investments Ltd v De Savoye* (n 24).
[106] *Hunt v T&N PLC* (n 25).
[107] *Moran v Pyle National (Canada) Ltd* [1975] 1 SCR 393.
[108] See, for example, *SSAB Alabama Inc v Canadian National Ralway Co*, 2020 SKCA 74.
[109] *Tolofson v Jensen* (n 1) 1071, referring to the Foreign Limitation Periods Act 1984 (UK).
[110] *Haaretz.com v Goldhar* (n 100) [37].
[111] *Club Resorts Ltd v Van Breda* (n 93) [38]. See also *Lapointe Rosenstein Marchand Melançon LLP v Cassels Brock & Blackwell LLP* 2016 SCC 30, [2016] 1 SCR 851 [128]; *Spar Aerospace Ltd v American Mobile Satellite Corp* 2002 SCC 78, [2002] 4 SCR 205 [20].

international law (territoriality principle in exercising jurisdiction) and constitutional law (inability of a province to legislate extra-territorially) that are complex, even murky, in and of themselves, and doubtfully apposite to framing choice of law principles.

The justice of the actual results in the *Tolfson* and *Lucas* cases, while not beyond debate, is entirely defensible. However, the reasoning essentially pre-empts any future development of the law it lays down. The judgment goes out of its way to anticipate how future courts may want to modify the *lex loci delicti* rule and more or less tells them not to do it. This is a very unusual, possibly unique, use of obiter dicta to create a kind of defensive zone against any attempt to encroach on the *ratio decidendi*. The consistency with which lower courts have aligned themselves against making any exception to the *lex loci delicti* principle[112] is testimony to how effective the defensive zone has been. This is where the depth of *Tolofson*'s legacy lies.

It is to be hoped that the Supreme Court of Canada will eventually revisit the question whether an 'axiomatic' *lex loci delicti* rule serves the law consistently well.[113] The mere fact that common law Canada has a tort choice of law rule more rigid than any other major common law country, and more rigid than Quebec,[114] should be enough to prompt such a reconsideration. It is true that the High Court of Australia also adheres to the view that the *lex loci delicti* rule should operate without exception,[115] and, going even further than *Tolofson*, has extended the 'no exceptions' rule to international as well as intra-Australian cases.[116] But, unlike *Tolofson*, it has uncoupled the choice of law question from the Australian constitution,[117] treating it as a question of common law,[118] which at least in theory leaves the law free to develop.[119]

In its earlier decision in *Morguard*,[120] the court performed the signal service of liberating Canadian private international law from its traditional constraints by

[112] nn 88–91 and accompanying text.

[113] The chances that change will come from a provincial legislature are vanishingly small. There is little political incentive to lay down a more flexible choice of law rule. For one thing, if only one province did so, it would disturb the uniformity of approach among Canadian common law jurisdictions. For another, even lawyers who understand the problem are probably inclined to view such a task as better left to courts than to legislative drafters.

[114] The Civil Code of Quebec, CQLR c CCQ-199,1 Art 3126, requires application of the law of the state where the wrongdoer's act or omission occurred, but if the injury appeared in another state, the law of that state applies if the wrongdoer should have foreseen that the injury would manifest itself there. Moreover, if both the wrongdoer and the victim are domiciled or resident in the same state, the law of that state applies. It is quoted in *Tolofson v Jensen* (n 1) 1076, in relation to the issue whether the Quebec no-fault scheme was intended to apply to cases such as Heather Gagnon's, where both parties were non-residents. The scheme was held to override the general choice of law rule.

[115] *John Pfeiffer Pty Ltd v Rogerson* [2000] HCA 36, 203 CLR 503.

[116] *Régie National des Usines Renaut SA v Zhang* [2002] HCA 10, 210 CLR 491 [75]–[76]; *Neilson v Overseas Projects Corp of Victoria Ltd* [2005] HCA 54, 223 CLR 331.

[117] On the previous coupling: see (n 11) and accompanying text.

[118] *John Pfeiffer Pty Ltd v Rogerson* (n 115) [66]–[70] and [138]–[143].

[119] Gray, 'Flexibility in Conflict of Laws Multistate Tort Cases: The Way Forward in Australia' (2004) 23 *University of Queensland Law Journal* 435.

[120] *Morguard Investments Ltd v De Savoye* (n 24).

invoking the Canadian federal system as demanding a more open and purposeful approach to common law private international law. In *Tolofson*, by contrast, it invokes the federal system in order to suggest, if not actually impose, constraints from which the common law had been free. The emphasis is still on 'order and fairness' but the 'order' now looms larger than the 'fairness'.[121]

If the occasion to do so arises, the Supreme Court of Canada should remove the shadow cast on Canadian common law by La Forest J's warnings that any departure from a strictly territorial application of the law of a province would 'give rise to serious constitutional concerns', and that it is 'arguable that it is not constitutionally permissible' for different courts to apply different provinces' laws so as to apply 'conflicting rules in respect of the same incident'.[122]

This vision of a constitutionally mandated choice of law system, in which variations among provinces' choice of law rules are impermissible, is undesirable in tort choice of law and is actually unachievable outside that field. It is also inconsistent with fundamental features of the choice of law system. Every province has laws that regulate certain types of contracts, overriding the proper law of the contract, so that litigating in one province may have one result in the province whose regulations apply, and another in a different province.[123] It is also inconsistent with the Supreme Court of Canada's recognition, more recently, that variations in provincial private international law are not contrary to the federal system, but are the very thing the federal system is supposed to make possible.[124]

If the constitutional constraint is removed as ill-founded, courts can start asking whether logic really does demand that every substantive issue relating to a tort claim ought to be relegated, without exception, to the *lex loci delicti*. The issues that have the most to do with the law of the place where the accident occurs are ones of duty of care and standard of care. Even in motor vehicle cases, these are in fact seldom the reason why choice of law is argued. Most of the cases on tort choice of law in road accident cases concern guest statutes (now largely obsolete), mandatory no-fault compensation schemes that replace ordinary civil claims, and limitation periods. The link between those issues and the territory where the accident takes place is less compelling, as courts – including the lower courts in both actions in *Tolofson* – have often noted. Links with the personal circumstances of the parties become more relevant.

Whether a rigid adherence to *lex loci delicti* is under any and all circumstances the optimal choice of law for determining the limitation period for a tort claim is something that should be open to argument. The same goes for rules that mandatorily relegate accident victims to no-fault compensation. Once one moves beyond motor vehicle accidents, flexibility becomes still more strongly arguable. An area

[121] *Tolofson v Jensen* (n 1) 1058. See also J Swan, 'The New Choice of Law Rule in Torts: The Aftermath of *Tolofson v Jensen; Lucas v Gagnon*' (1999) 12 *Revue québécoise de droit international* 47.

[122] *Tolofson v Jensen* (n 1) 1066.

[123] That is the basis for *forum non conveniens* decisions like *Avenue Properties Ltd v First City Development Corp Ltd* (1986) 32 DLR (4th) 40, BCCA.

[124] *Club Resorts Ltd v Van Breda* (n 93) [34].

like products liability, where the locus of the tort must be arbitrary to some extent, may particularly lend itself to a choice of law approach that is not solely driven by the place of the tort.[125]

Given how few choice of law cases reach the courts to begin with, and how seldom any of them reaches the Supreme Court, a reassessment of *Tolofson* may be far off. Still, the issue of choice of law in defamation has made it to the Supreme Court not once, but several times in the last few years.[126] An opportunity to relax *Tolofson*'s grip, whether it presents itself in this or some other area of tort, may – who knows? – come sooner rather than later.

[125] Walsh (n 95); see also Pitel and Rafferty, *Conflict of Laws*, 2nd edn (Irwin Law, 2016) 269–70. Damages may be another example; see Porretta, 'Assessing Tort Damages in the Conflict of Laws: Loci, Fori, Illogical' (2012) 91 *Canadian Bar Review* 97.

[126] nn 98–104 and accompanying text.

9

The Limits of Our Tolerance for Acts of Foreign States

The Legacy of Kuwait Airways (Nos 4 and 5)

MICHAEL DOUGLAS

I. Introduction

'Those who fail to learn from history are condemned to repeat it', said Winston Churchill in a 1948 speech to the House of Commons.[1] Churchill spoke in the wake of a World War that was preceded by Western appeasement of fascist aggression in Europe. At the time of writing this chapter, the West is once again grappling with how to deal with aggression in Europe; this time, amidst Russia's invasion of Ukraine. How can nations that value democracy, liberty and human rights tolerate war crimes committed by invading forces of Putin's Russia? What role can those values play in crystallising real action in our domestic institutions to address global threats, and assist the people of Ukraine?

Twenty years ago, the House of Lords contended with related issues posed by the Iraqi invasion of Kuwait. It considered: to what extent should a common law court have regard to the content of public international law in resolving conflict of laws issues? How can action taken in accordance with Iraqi domestic law but in violation of international law be consistent with English public policy enforceable by an English court? *Kuwait Airways Corporation v Iraqi Airways Co (Nos 4 and 5)*[2] was a critical case in the development of common law conflict of laws reasoning. Like the decisions that preceded it, the House of Lords judgment traversed complex issues of tort and private international law. This account

[1] Apparently – although ironically, this quotation itself may be of a misunderstanding of history according to: America's National Churchill Museum, 'Those Who Fail to Learn from History …' 16 November 2012, available at www.nationalchurchillmuseum.org/blog.html. In 1935, Churchill said that 'want of foresight' and 'unwillingness to act' were 'the features which constitute the endless repetition of history': *Hansard*, HC (series 5) Vol 301, col 602 (2 May 1935) (Winston Churchill).

[2] *Kuwait Airways Corporation v Iraqi Airways Co (Nos 4 and 5)* [2002] 2 AC 883, HL.

focuses on the latter. The case has been the subject of quality commentary many times in the last two decades.[3] Like other chapters of this book, this account focuses on how the case has contributed to the development of the common law and the modes of reasoning in conflict of laws cases.

This chapter sets out the case's background, procedural history, and key holdings of the House of Lords. It then addresses three key aspects of the case's contribution to the conflict of laws: public policy, act of state and non-justiciability, and the interaction between public and private international law.

II. Background

On 2 August 1990, Iraq invaded Kuwait.[4] Within 12 hours, it had seized the airport.[5] Within three days, Iraq occupied Kuwait. A few days later, on 8 and 9 August, the Revolutionary Command Council of Iraq (RCC) purported to legitimise its invasion by passing resolutions to integrate Kuwait into Iraq.[6]

In the course of its invasion, Iraq removed 10 aircraft belonging to Kuwait Airways Corporation (KAC) – two Boeing 767s and eight airbuses – from Kuwait to Iraq. The Iraqi Government then purported to make such action lawful; the RCC passed a resolution, Resolution 369, which would dissolve KAC and transfer KAC's property throughout the world to Iraqi Airways Co (IAC), including the 10 seized aircraft. Resolution 369 came into effect on 17 September. IAC maintained the aircraft, repainted some of them, but could make limited use of them. The response of the international community to Iraq's aggression meant that international flights had ceased.

The United Nations responded swiftly to the invasion. On 6 August 1990, the Security Council passed Resolution 660, which condemned the invasion, demanded Iraq's withdrawal of all its forces, and determined that the invasion

[3] Including, eg, Briggs, 'Public Policy in the Conflict of Laws: A Sword and a Shield? A Note on *Kuwait Airways Corp v Iraq Airways Co (Nos 4 and 5)*' (2002) 6 *Singapore Journal of International and Comparative Law* 953; O'Keefe, 'English Public Policy Internationalised – and Conversion Clarified Too' (2002) 61 *CLJ* 499; Carruthers and Crawford, '*Kuwait Airways Corporation v Iraqi Airways Company*' (2003) 52 *ICLQ* 761; Peel, 'The Scope of Double Actionability and Public Policy' (2003) 119(Jan) *LQR* 1; Rogerson, '*Kuwait Airways Corp v Iraqi Airways Corp*: The Territoriality Principle in Private International Law – Vice or Virtue?' (2003) 56 *CLP* 265.

[4] The facts underlying this case were summarised by Lord Goff in *Kuwait Airways Corporation v Iraqi Airways Co (No 1)* [1995] 1 WLR 1147, HL 1150–51, and recounted by Brooke LJ for the Court of Appeal throughout the judgment reported at *Kuwait Airways Corporation v Iraqi Airways Co (Nos 4 and 5)* [2002] 2 AC 883, CA and *Kuwait Airways Corporation v Iraqi Airways Co (Nos 4 and 5)* [2001] 3 WLR 1117, CA. See also Warbrick, 'III. The Invasion of Kuwait by Iraq' (1991) 40 *ICLQ* 482. For a comparison of motivations underlying the Iraqi invasion, see Lawson, 'Rethinking the Iraqi Invasion of Kuwait' (2001) 1 *Review of International Affairs* 1.

[5] Nanda, 'The Iraqi Invasion of Kuwait: The UN Response' (1991) 15 *Southern Illinois University Law Journal* 431, 432.

[6] Resolutions 312 and 313.

amounted to a breach of international peace and security.[7] A few days later the Security Council passed Resolution 662, which reiterated its position and decided that the 'annexation of Kuwait by Iraq under any form and whatever pretext [had] no legal validity, and [was] considered null and void'.[8] Between those sat Resolution 661, which imposed severe sanctions on Iraq.[9]

While the United Nations pontificated, members of the international community took their own steps in response to the invasion. On 8 August 1990, the US and UK announced they would send forces into the Gulf to defend ally states.[10] On 19 November 1990, the United Nations Security Council passed Resolution 678, which authorised Member States 'to use all necessary means to uphold and implement resolution 660 (1990) and all subsequent relevant resolutions and to restore international peace and security in the area'.[11] This provided legal cover for coalition forces to take military action against Iraq, in what became Operation Desert Storm of the First Gulf War. Coalition airstrikes on Iraq began on 17 January 1991. The coalition succeeded in liberating Kuwait;[12] by 28 February 1991, the First Gulf War was won. Iraq's defeat still echoes today.

Shortly before the commencement of Operation Desert Storm, six of the 10 aircraft were flown to Iran on the instruction of Iraqi authorities. The remaining aircraft were destroyed in the coalition's aerial campaign. The surviving six were returned to KAC in 1992, in varying condition. Iraq had eventually acknowledged its liability for losses caused by its invasion of Kuwait. On 5 March 1991, the RCC passed Resolution 55, under which all decisions made by the RCC relating to Kuwait were rescinded.

III. Procedural History

KAC commenced proceedings against both IAC and Iraq in England's Commercial Court on 11 January 1991, arguing that the defendants wrongfully interfered with the aircraft.[13] It sought delivery up of all 10 aircraft (at a time when that was still possible), together with consequential damages; or alternatively, payment of the value of the aircraft. KAC obtained default judgment on 11 and 24 May 1991, obtaining damages in excess of US$500 million.

[7] SC Res 660, UN Doc S/RES/660 (6 August 1990).
[8] SC Res 662, UN Doc S/RES/662 (9 August 1990).
[9] SC Res 661, UN Doc S/RES/661 (6 August 1990).
[10] Warbrick, 'The Invasion of Kuwait' (1991) 483–84. This was called Operation Desert Shield.
[11] SC Res 678, UN Doc S/RES/678 (19 November 1990).
[12] The conflict was explained in Freedman and Karsh, *The Gulf Conflict, 1990–1991: Diplomacy and War in the New World Order* (Faber, 1994).
[13] For a case analysis focusing on the tort of conversion, see Douglas, 'Kuwait Airways Corporation v Iraqi Airways Company [2002]' in Douglas, Hickey and Waring (eds), *Landmark Cases in Property Law* (Bloomsbury Publishing, 2015) 205.

Iraq and IAC purported to set aside default judgment; they also challenged service of the writ. They asserted state immunity;[14] claimed that the matter was not justiciable; relied on the double actionability rule;[15] and argued *forum non conveniens*, among other things. The execution of the default judgment was stayed, and later set aside. Evans J held that IAC did not enjoy state immunity with respect to KAC's claim, and that the writ had not been validly served on Iraq.[16] Appeals and cross-appeals made their way to the House of Lords,[17] which held that IAC was entitled to immunity for acts done prior to Resolution 369 coming into force, but that subsequent acts were not done in the exercise of sovereign authority and therefore not covered by state immunity.[18] The matter was remitted to the Commercial Court.

Mance J considered IAC's liability,[19] which involved application of the choice of law rule for tort: the double actionability rule. KAC's success depended on actionability under both Iraqi law of usurpation and English law of conversion.[20] Further, it depended on showing that it was owner of the aircraft. But under Iraqi law, title had been vested in IAC by Resolution 369. The subsequent repeal of Resolution 369 by Resolution 55 did not give KAC title retrospectively.[21] Mance J refused to recognise Resolution 369 as a matter of public policy.[22] His Honour held that IAC's alleged conversion was actionable in both England and Iraq,[23] but that a further trial would be necessary for KAC to prove that it had incurred losses under heads of damage compensable under both English and Iraqi law.

In a subsequent trial on damages and certain other issues, Aitkens J held that KAC's claim failed on causation. The situation for KAC would have been the same in the absence of IAC's conversion.[24] From these decisions, IAC and KAC each appealed. The result of the Court of Appeal's complex decision[25] was that IAC was liable to pay damages for the six aircraft flown to Iran, but not the four aircraft that were destroyed in Iraq during Operation Desert Storm.[26] IAC appealed, and KAC cross-appealed, to the House of Lords.

[14] State Immunity Act 1978.

[15] As expressed in *Phillips v Eyre* (1870) LR 6 QB 1, then modified by *Boys v Chaplin* [1971] AC 356, HL.

[16] See *Kuwait Airways Corporation v Iraqi Airways Co* [1992] EWHC 67 (Comm).

[17] The Court of Appeal judgment is reported at: *Kuwait Airways Corporation v Iraqi Airways Co (No 1)* [1994] 1 Lloyd's Rep 276, CA.

[18] *Kuwait Airways (No 1)* (n 4). Noted at: Fox, 'The Commerciality of the Spoils of War' (1996) 112(Apr) *LQR* 186; Evans, 'When the State Taketh and the State Giveth' (1996) 45 *ICLQ* 401.

[19] *Kuwait Airways Corporation v Iraqi Airways Co (No 5)* [1999] CLC 31.

[20] See *Kuwait Airways (Nos 4 and 5)* (HL) (n 2) [111].

[21] *Kuwait Airways (Nos 4 and 5) (HL)* (n 2) [13].

[22] *Kuwait Airways (No 5)* (n 19) 75.

[23] In Iraq through 'usurpation'.

[24] *Kuwait Airways Corporation v Iraqi Airways Co* [2000] 2 All ER (Comm) 360.

[25] *Kuwait Airways (Nos 4 and 5)* (CA) (n 4).

[26] The Court of Appeal decision was analysed in Davies, '*Kuwait Airways Corp v Iraqi Airways Co*: The Effect in Private International Law of a Breach of Public International Law by a State Actor' (2001) 2 *Melbourne Journal of International Law* 523.

IV. In the House of Lords – Again

The majority of the House of Lords dismissed IAC's appeal, with Lord Scott of Foscote dissenting.[27] Their Lordships considered many interconnected issues of private international law. First, they considered the choice of law rule for conversion committed in a foreign jurisdiction, which, at the time, was the double actionability rule.[28] Second, they considered that, as the tort of conversion depends on the claimant having title to property at the time of the conversion,[29] the choice of law rule for transfer of title to moveable property: the *lex situs* rule.[30] (According to Iraqi law at the relevant time, the *situs* was Iraq.) Third, they considered the act of state doctrine,[31] which provided that English courts will not adjudicate upon, or call into question, legislative or other governmental acts of a foreign state within its own territory.[32] Fourth, they considered justiciability – or rather, the principle of non-justiciability. Fifth, and most importantly, they considered the public policy exception to the application of foreign law, and in relation to the act of state doctrine. The latter three issues are the focus of the parts below.

Lord Nicholls of Birkenhead, with whom Lord Hoffmann relevantly agreed,[33] considered that the applicable law for the issue of status to the aircraft was Iraqi law. Iraqi law provided, via Resolution 369, that KAC lacked the title necessary for its conversion claim.[34] His Lordship held that enforcement or recognition of Resolution 369 in circumstances where it was contrary to public international law would be manifestly contrary to English public policy, and so it was not given effect.[35] The non-justiciability principle did not require a court to not adjudicate on acts of foreign states in violation of international law.[36] The double actionability rule would require application of the Iraqi law, but it was applied on the footing that Resolution 369 was ineffective.[37]

[27] KAC's cross-appeal was also dismissed in application of torts principles that are not the focus of this chapter.

[28] See (n 15).

[29] Possession or immediate right to possession: see Tettenborn (ed), 'Wrongful Interference with Goods' in Jones (ed), *Clerk & Lindsell on Torts*, 23rd edn (Sweet & Maxwell, 2020) [16-43]ff.

[30] Peel recognised that the case therefore involved an incidental question: Peel, 'The Scope of Double Actionability' (2003) 5–6. On the incidental question, see Davies, Bell, Brereton and Douglas, *Nygh's Conflict of Laws in Australia*, 10th edn (LexisNexis Butterworths, 2020) 398–401. As to the *lex situs* rule: *Cammell v Sewell* (1860) 5 H & N 728; *Castrique v Imrie* (1870) LR 4 HL 414; *Inglis v Roberston* [1898] AC 616, HL.

[31] Which affirms the second issue, as regards acts of a foreign state regarding property within its jurisdiction at the time of the act: *Luther v Sagor* [1921] 3 KB 532, CA. The distinction between the *lex situs* rule and the application of act of state to property issues may be 'more apparent than real': Rogerson, '*Kuwait Airways Corp v Iraqi Airways Corp*' (2003) 266.

[32] *Kuwait Airways (Nos 4 and 5)* (HL) (n 2) [135].

[33] ibid [125].

[34] ibid [13].

[35] ibid [29].

[36] ibid [24]–[25].

[37] ibid [45].

Lord Steyn agreed that Iraq's gross breaches of international law were justiciable,[38] recognising that the Court of Appeal 'broke new ground' as the first case to recognise that acts of a foreign state within its own territory may be refused recognition on the basis of international law.[39] The Court of Appeal therefore extended the public policy exception from its previous grounding in gross violations of human rights to flagrant breaches of international law.[40] His Lordship added that not every violation of international law would justify invocation of public policy. This violation did justify the exclusionary doctrine, and so he agreed that double actionability required application of Iraqi law without Resolution 369.

Lord Hope of Craighead agreed with both Lord Nicholls and Steyn[41] and added further reasons. His Lordship started with the act of state doctrine,[42] then considered the scope of a public policy exception to justiciability of foreign acts of state. Like the rest of the majority, he appealed to *Oppenheimer v Cattermole*,[43] where the House of Lords invoked public policy to refuse to give effect to a Nazi decree depriving a German Jew of citizenship.[44] Like Lord Steyn, his Lordship emphasised that courts should take care with public policy exceptions in transnational litigation, but added that 'there is no need for restraint on grounds of public policy where it is plain beyond dispute that a clearly established norm of international law has been violated'.[45] In the circumstances of the case, where the UK supported the Security Council resolutions founding Iraq's breaches of international law, there could be no embarrassment to the UK's diplomatic relationships by refusing to give effect to Resolution 369 as part of the *lex situs*.[46]

In dissent, Lord Scott of Foscote emphasised that the action 'had nothing whatever to do with England' except as the forum of the litigation.[47] Among other things, his Lordship took a different approach to the structure of the choice of law issues and, specifically, to characterisation – the issue of selecting the subject to which a choice of law rule would apply.[48] He said the action was 'not an action in rem to recover property [but] an action in personam for tort'.[49] The policy of the dissent was expressed as follows: 'It is not a function ever claimed for English law to provide tortious causes of actions to citizens of foreign countries who are injured by acts in those countries committed by other citizens of foreign countries'.[50] Lord Scott held, in application of the double actionability rule, that

[38] ibid [113].
[39] ibid [114].
[40] ibid.
[41] ibid [170].
[42] ibid [135].
[43] *Oppenheimer v Cattermole* [1976] AC 249, HL.
[44] *Kuwait Airways (Nos 4 and 5)* (HL) (n 2) [137]; see also [18], [28], [114], [117].
[45] ibid [140].
[46] ibid [146]–[148].
[47] ibid [174].
[48] On different approaches to 'what is characterised', see Forsyth, 'Characterisation Revisited: An Essay in the Theory and Practice of the English Conflict of Laws' (1998) 114 *LQR* 141.
[49] *Kuwait Airways (Nos 4 and 5)* (HL) (n 2) [193]; see also [161].
[50] ibid [198].

KAC's claim was not actionable in Iraq and therefore not in England. The dissent thus provokes consideration of the difficult question of the interaction between the double actionability rule, its 'flexible exception',[51] and the broader role of public policy as an exclusionary doctrine to the application of foreign law.[52] The majority used public policy to engage with a version of the *lex loci delicti* that was consistent with English policy, while Lord Scott refused, holding that any flexible exception was not justified where the action had little connection to England.[53]

While the double actionability rule has fallen into disfavour in England[54] and elsewhere,[55] the many other private international law issues canvassed in the case remain important subjects of conflicts of laws in common law legal systems.

V. Public Policy

Public policy featured prominently in the reasons of the majority of the House of Lords, and it is in respect of this issue that the case made its greatest contribution to common law conflict of laws reasoning. It did so in several respects.

First, it reaffirmed the common law orthodoxy that public policy should be rarely invoked as an 'escape route'[56] to exclude the recognition or enforcement of otherwise applicable foreign law.[57] Mere difference between the *lex fori* and foreign *lex causae* is insufficient to engage public policy. The court was influenced by decades of authority to that effect, including *Oppenheimer v Cattermole*,[58] where Lord Cross said that a court should 'be very slow to refuse to give effect to the legislation of a foreign state in any sphere in which, according to accepted principles of international law, the foreign state has jurisdiction'.[59] Lord Hope warned that, 'where there is any room for doubt [as to whether the public policy exception should be applied], judicial restraint must be exercised'.[60] Lord Nicholls said that 'Exceptionally and rarely, a provision of foreign law will be disregarded when it would lead to a result wholly alien to fundamental requirements of justice

[51] *Boys v Chaplin* (n 15).

[52] See Peel (n 3) 4–8; Carruthers and Crawford, '*Kuwait Airways Corporation v Iraqi Airways Company*' (2003) 766.

[53] *Kuwait Airways (Nos 4 and 5)* (HL) (n 2) [187]–[188].

[54] Collins et al, *Dicey, Morris & Collins on the Conflict of Laws*, 15th edn (Sweet & Maxwell, 2012) vol 2, ch 35.

[55] See, eg, Australia: *John Pfeiffer Pty Ltd v Rogerson* [2000] HCA 36, (2000) 203 CLR 503; *Regie Nationale des Usines Renault v Zhang* [2002] HCA 10, (2002) 210 CLR 491. See the comparative review of jurisdictions that have codified a form of the double actionability rule in Symeonides, *Codifying Choice of Law Around the World: An International Comparative Analysis* (OUP, 2014) 83.

[56] Carter, 'The Role of Public Policy in English Private International Law' (1993) 42 *ICLQ* 1, 1.

[57] *cf* doctrines in France and Germany: *Dicey, Morris & Collins* (n 54) vol 1 [5-004]; Carter (ibid) 3. See also Kahn-Freund, 'Reflections on Public Policy in the English Conflict of Laws' in *Selected Writings* (Stevens & Sons, 1978) 233ff.

[58] Cited by Lord Hope of Craighead: *Kuwait Airways (Nos 4 and 5)* (HL) (n 2) [138].

[59] *Oppenheimer v Cattermole* (n 43) 277.

[60] *Kuwait Airways (Nos 4 and 5)* (HL) (n 2) [140].

as administered by an English court'.[61] This approach continues today; in 2022, the Court of Appeal described the test for engaging public policy as 'demanding', and that public policy should not become 'a backdoor route to the application of English law'.[62] The narrow role for public policy is seen in other common law approaches to the conflict of laws,[63] including, for example, Australia,[64] Canada[65] and Hong Kong.[66]

Second, the case elaborates on what may satisfy the high threshold for the invocation of public policy in the conflict of laws. Lord Nicholls quoted Cardozo J, who famously held in *Loucks v Standard Oil Co of New York* that a foreign decree will only be excluded where it 'would violate some fundamental principle of justice, some prevalent conception of good morals, some deep-rooted tradition of the common weal'.[67] With appeal to *Oppenheimer v Cattermole*, IAC had argued that the *Loucks* threshold could only be engaged in the case of gross infringement of human rights permissible under the foreign applicable law.[68] The majority rejected that argument, holding that enforcement or recognition of Resolution 369 would be manifestly contrary to public policy because it was a gross breach of established rules of international law – albeit not international law directly concerning human rights.

They did so for slightly different reasons. Lord Steyn said that not every violation of international law would justify invocation of public policy.[69] Lord Nicholls said that the particular law in issue, Resolution 369, was 'simply not acceptable' and 'a gross violation of established rules of international law of fundamental importance',[70] but did not make the broader point about whether certain violations of international law could be consistent with English policy. Lord Hope favoured a broader role for public policy with respect to acts of state: 'It would seem therefore to be contrary to principle for our courts to give effect to legislative and other acts of foreign states which are in violation of international law as declared under the Charter of the United Nations'.[71]

This aspect of the case goes to a broader issue: the role of public international law in a domestic legal system and its relationship to the conflict of laws, ie private international law. That issue is addressed further below. The present point is that

[61] ibid [16].
[62] *Husayn v Foreign and Commonwealth Office* [2022] EWCA Civ 334 [57].
[63] See Garnett, *Substance and Procedure in Private International Law* (OUP, 2012) [3.16]–[3.21].
[64] See, for example, *Attorney-General (United Kingdom) v Heinemann Publishers Australia Pty Ltd* (1988) 165 CLR 30, HCA 49–50 (Brennan CJ); *Kok v Resorts World at Sentosa Pte Ltd* [2017] WASCA 150, (2017) 323 FLR 95 [18] (Martin CJ) (a case concerning foreign judgments).
[65] See *Sangi v Sangi* [2011] BCSC 523 [273]ff.
[66] *Chen Li Hung v Ting Lei Miao* [2000] 1 HKC 461, [2000] 1 HKLRD 252, CFA; Wolff, 'Hong Kong's Conflict of Contract Laws: Quo Vadis?' (2010) 6 *Journal of Private International Law* 465.
[67] *Loucks v Standard Oil Co of New York*, 120 NE 198 (1918), 202.
[68] *Kuwait Airways (Nos 4 and 5)* (HL) (n 2) [24].
[69] ibid [114].
[70] ibid [28]–[29].
[71] ibid [145].

a violation of international law may justify invocation of a public policy exception to the application of foreign law in a domestic legal system. In *Yukos Capital Sarl v OJSC Rosneft Oil Co (No 2)*, Hamblen J elaborated that whether the doctrine should be applied in a case of violation of international law depends upon 'the clarity of the breach, the gravity of the breach and whether manageable standards exist to determine the allegation'.[72] In *Belhaj v Straw*, members of the Supreme Court interpreted the requisite standard to demand a 'serious' violation of international law.[73] Yet this begs the question: which violations of international law are not serious?

Third, and related to the second point, the case may be authority for recognition of 'transnational',[74] 'truly international'[75] or 'cross-border'[76] public policy. Lord Steyn said that 'Local values ought not lightly to be elevated into public policy on the international level';[77] but the values in play here were not merely local, but essentially universal. This formulation of the doctrine depends on 'public policy considerations that transcend state boundaries' and has relevance to international arbitration.[78] In that context, 'transnational public policy' has been used to described aspects of the *lex mercatoria* that enjoy widespread, even almost universal consensus.[79] Such ideas were invoked by Edelman J when discussing the role of proportionality in Australian constitutional law: 'Foreign doctrines can become part of the local jurisprudence, consciously or unconsciously, where they have a force that transcends jurisdictional boundaries'.[80] A comparative law technique has justified the importation of 'structured proportionality' as a prominent fixture of Australia's current constitutional landscape;[81] the High Court has recognised that proportionality has been adopted by 'virtually every effective system of constitutional justice in the world, with the partial exception of

[72] *Yukos Capital Sarl v OJSC Rosneft Oil Co (No 2)* [2011] EWHC 1461 (Comm), [2011] 2 Lloyd's Rep 443, [139], also considering *JSC BTA Bank v Ablyazov* [2011] EWHC 202 (Comm), [2011] 2 All ER (Comm) 10, [59]–[76] (Teare J).

[73] *Belhaj v Straw* [2017] UKSC 3, [2017] AC 964 [257] (Lord Neuberger of Abbotsbury PSC); [255] (Lord Sumption JSC); *cf* [107] (Lord Mance JSC).

[74] See Mills, 'The Dimensions of Public Policy in Private International Law' (2008) 4 *Journal of Private International Law* 201, 215; Chong, 'Transnational Public Policy in Civil and Commercial Matters' (2012) 128(Jan) *LQR* 88.

[75] Lalive, 'Transnational (or Truly International) Public Policy and International Arbitration' in Sanders (ed), *Comparative Arbitration Practice and Public Policy in Arbitration* (Kluwer, 1986).

[76] See McKibbin, 'Substantive Public Policy in Cross-Border Litigation: A Common Law Study' (PhD thesis, University of Southern Queensland, 2019) 170ff.

[77] *Kuwait Airways (Nos 4 and 5)* (HL) (n 2) [114].

[78] Pryles, 'Reflections on Transnational Public Policy' (2007) 24 *Journal of International Arbitration* 1, 3; Renner, 'Towards a Hierarchy of Norms in Transnational Law?' (2009) 64 *Journal of Arbitration* 533.

[79] Lalive, 'Transnational (or Truly International) Public Policy and International Arbitration' in Sanders (ed), *Comparative Arbitration Practice and Public Policy in Arbitration* (Kluwer, 1986) [109].

[80] *Clubb v Edwards* [2019] HCA 11, (2019) 267 CLR 171 [466]. See also *Applicant S v Minister for Immigration and Multicultural Affairs* [2004] HCA 25, (2005) 217 CLR 387, an immigration case that considered conduct of the Taliban in Afghanistan, which cited Kuwait Airways in referring to 'the standards of civil societies which seek to meet the calls of common humanity': [46].

[81] See generally Chordia, *Proportionality in Australian Constitutional Law* (Federation Press, 2020).

the United States'.[82] In the conflict of laws, international norms certainly play an important role in shaping the content of the public policy exception applied by common law courts.[83]

Fourth, the majority considered public policy to be a dynamic doctrine that should 'move with the times'.[84] Contemporary standards should determine the acceptability of a common law court applying foreign law.[85] As globalisation continues, common law courts may thus take cognisance of 'the need for a concerted, international response to … threats to the rule of law in a democratic society'.[86] Courts may thus adapt public policy to unique circumstances, albeit cautiously. Winfield once said, in a passage quoted by Bokhary PJ of the Hong Kong Court of Final Appeal, 'variability of public policy is a stone in the edifice of the doctrine, and not a missile to be flung at it'.[87] While famously denigrated as an 'unruly horse',[88] flexibility in the doctrine is also its virtue.[89]

Fifth, the case conceived of public policy as a sword, rather than merely as a shield.[90] That is to say, the exclusionary doctrine was not used as a defence (ie, a shield) to guard against a claim with foreign elements; it was used by KAC, the claimant, in order to render its claim enforceable in circumstances where Iraqi law would not otherwise recognise a cause of action.[91] This role runs contrary to historical authority, which conceived of public policy only so as to 'disable', not to 'enable' recognition of foreign law.[92] (This 'sword role' remains 'an inchoate area of the common law'.)[93] In this respect, the case is representative of a broader trend in common law conflict of laws reasoning: the occasional manipulation of escape devices, like *renvoi*,[94] to avoid application of unpalatable *lex causae* to do justice in a particular case.[95] Public policy is the most honest[96] of these safety nets, which

[82] *Clubb v Edwards* [2019] HCA 11, (2019) 267 CLR 171, [466], quoted in *Palmer v Western Australia* [2021] HCA 5, (2019) 95 ALJR 229 [264].

[83] See *Belhaj v Straw* (n 73) [257]; McLachlan, *Foreign Relations Law* (CUP, 2014) [12.157].

[84] *Kuwait Airways (Nos 4 and 5)* (HL) (n 2) [145], citing *Blathwayt v Baron Cawley* [1976] AC 397, HL 426.

[85] *Kuwait Airways (Nos 4 and 5)* (HL) (n 2) [28] (Lord Nicholls of Birkenhead).

[86] *Kuwait Airways (Nos 4 and 5)* (HL) (n 2) [145] (Lord Hope of Craighead).

[87] *Chen Li Hung v Ting Lei Miao* [2000] 1 HKC 461, [2000] 1 HKLRD 252, 262, quoting Winfield, 'Public Policy in the English Common Law' (1928) 42 *Harvard Law Review* 76, 95.

[88] *Richardson v Mellish* (1824) 2 Bing 229, 252; 130 ER 294, 303 (Burrough J).

[89] *cf* arguments for the value of the distinct nature of equity: Gummow, 'Equity: Too Successful?' (2003) 77 *Australian Law Journal* 30, 33.

[90] Briggs, 'Public Policy in the Conflict of Laws' (2002).

[91] See Lindsay, 'The Exclusion of Foreign Law in International Private Law' (PhD thesis, University of Glasgow, 2017) [6-66].

[92] *Rodriguez v Speyer Brothers* [1919] AC 59, 125, HL. See further McKibbin, 'Substantive Public Policy in Cross-Border Litigation' (2019) 177–80.

[93] Yeo, *Choice of Law for Equitable Obligations* (OUP, 2004) [1.81].

[94] See *Neilson v Overseas Projects Corporation of Victoria* [2005] HCA 54, (2005) 223 CLR 331.

[95] See generally Symeonides, *Choice of Law* (OUP, 2016) 64; Garnett, 'The Dominance of Uniformity of Outcome in Australian Choice of Law: Is It Time to Relax the Grip?' (2013) 37 *Australian Bar Review* 192.

[96] Or 'transparent': Garnett, *Substance and Procedure* (2012) [11.37].

define the outer limits of the 'tolerance of difference' in common law systems of conflict of laws.[97]

Sixth, the case affirmed the application of a public policy exception to the act of state doctrine. That proposition has been reaffirmed by the highest authority,[98] discussed below.

VI. Act of State and Non-Justiciability

Arguably, *Kuwait Airways* is not about public policy in the abstract but only in relation to act of state doctrine. The act of state doctrine is a creature of the common law, not shared by systems of other traditions,[99] which operates even where a state would lack foreign state immunity under the widely accepted principles in force in a given domestic jurisdiction. The doctrine, or 'rule',[100] provides that courts will not adjudicate upon, or call into question, legislative or other governmental acts of a foreign state within its own territory.[101] Older authority frames act of state in terms that a court 'cannot' adjudicate such acts;[102] that is, that courts lack jurisdiction to determine questions that turn on these acts of state.[103] Arguably, the better view is that it is deployed as a principle of non-exercise of jurisdiction in discrete circumstances.[104] Different aspects of the rule are explored below.

'Act of state' is often deployed together with the term 'justiciability'.[105] In general, 'justiciability' denotes that a matter is capable of judicial determination,[106] or 'capable of being tried according to law'.[107] The conflict of laws is just one area in which justiciability is deployed. Another is where a common law court of an adversarial tradition is called upon to make a purely advisory opinion.[108]

[97] Mills, 'The Dimensions of Public Policy' (2008) 202.

[98] *Belhaj v Straw* (n 73) [11] (Lord Mance JSC), [153], [156] (Lord Neuberger of Abbotsbury PSC), [201] (Lord Sumption JSC).

[99] '[T]he doctrine is peculiar to Anglo-American law': Mann, *Foreign Affairs in English Courts* (Clarendon Press, 1986) 164.

[100] *Dicey, Morris & Collins* (n 54), [5R-019]. For Mann, defenders of the act of state doctrine rely on maxims rather than legal principles: Mann (ibid) 164.

[101] *Kuwait Airways (Nos 4 and 5)* (HL) (n 2) [135]; *Attorney-General (United Kingdom)* (n 64) 40 (Mason CJ, Wilson, Deane, Dawson, Toohey and Gaudron JJ).

[102] *Salaman v Secretary of State for India* [1906] 1 KB, CA 639.

[103] *Belhaj v Straw* (n 73), [232] (Lord Sumption JSC).

[104] Garnett has argued that the act of state doctrine may be replaced with principles of non-exercise of jurisdiction: Garnett, 'Foreign States in Australian Courts' (2005) 29 *Melbourne University Law Review* 704.

[105] See Davies et al, *Nygh's Conflict of Laws* (2020) 273–81.

[106] *CGU Insurance Ltd v Blakeley* [2016] HCA 2, (2016) 259 CLR 339, 350 [26] (French CJ, Kiefel, Bell and Keane JJ); see also *Shergill v Khaira* [2014] UKSC 33, [2015] AC 359 [38]–[41] (Lord Neuberger of Abbotsbury PSC, Lord Sumption and Lord Hodge JJSC).

[107] Mann, *Foreign Affairs* (1986), 63.

[108] See, eg, *Hobart International Airport Pty Ltd v Clarence City Council* [2022] HCA 5 [29]–[41] (Kiefel CJ, Keane and Gordon JJ). On the differences between Australia and the US regarding 'hypothetical jurisdiction', see Leeming, *Authority to Decide: The Law of Jurisdiction in Australia*, 2nd edn (Federation Press, 2020) 40–41.

As regards matters with a foreign element, it has been said that a claim may be non-justiciable if it involves issues arising out of transactions between sovereign states,[109] such that the court would be in a 'judicial no-man's land', with 'no judicial or manageable standards' by which to judge.[110] Arguably, 'justiciability is neither a concept nor a principle', but a 'category of argument', or a 'doctrine'.[111] Confusion over what it is parallels confusion over its scope in the conflict of laws. In 2017 Lord Sumption JSC remarked, '"Non-justiciability" is a treacherous word, partly because of its lack of definition, and partly because it is commonly used as a portmanteau term encompassing a number of different legal principles with different incidents'.[112]

In *Kuwait Airways*, the House of Lords referred to both 'act of state'[113] and 'justiciability' or 'non-justiciability'.[114] However, they did not make a clear distinction between these concepts.[115] O'Keefe noted that the concepts appear one in the same from their Lordships' speeches, but in *Buttes Gas and Oil Co v Hammer (No 3)*,[116] Lord Wilberforce made it clear that they are distinct, and that 'non-justiciability' is broader than act of state.[117] FA Mann was highly critical of *Buttes Gas*;[118] he wrote extensively on these doctrines[119] in works quoted in *Kuwait Airways* by the Court of Appeal[120] and Lord Hope.[121] Lord Mance is also a critic. Extrajudicially, he has written that 'courts can and should adjudicate upon civil claims and public law claims, without it being necessary or appropriate to resort to a doctrine of non-justiciability'.[122]

Years after *Kuwait Airways*, the distinction between these concepts remains difficult to comprehend. The difficulty is compounded by their public law character.[123] Non-justiciability may be demanded by the separation of powers achieved by a constitution of a certain common law system, while another common law system may approach the issue with a different conceptual footing.[124]

[109] Davies et al (n 30) 277.
[110] *Buttes Gas and Oil Co v Hammer (No 3)* [1982] AC 888, HL, 931, 938 (Lord Wilberforce).
[111] McGoldrick, 'The Boundaries of Justiciability' (2010) 59 *ICLQ* 981, 983–84.
[112] *Mohammed v Secretary of State for Defence* [2017] UKSC 1, [2017] AC 821 [79].
[113] See section IV above.
[114] *Kuwait Airways (Nos 4 and 5)* (HL) (n 2) [26], [113] and [133]ff.
[115] O'Keefe, 'Decisions of British Courts During 2002 Involving Questions of Public or Private International Law: A Public International Law: Act of State Doctrine – Public Policy Exception – Justiciability of Sovereign Acts of Foreign State' (2002) 73 *British Yearbook of International Law* 400, 404.
[116] *Buttes Gas and Oil Co v Hammer (No 3)* [1982] AC 888, HL 931 (Lord Wilberforce).
[117] O'Keefe, 'Decisions of British Courts During 2002' (2002) 404.
[118] See the account in Lord Mance, 'Justiciability' (2018) 67 *ICLQ* 739.
[119] Including in Mann (n 99); Mann, 'International Delinquencies before Municipal Courts' (1954) 70 *LQR* 181.
[120] See *Kuwait Airways (Nos 4 and 5)* (HL) (n 2) [311]–[312].
[121] *Kuwait Airways (Nos 4 and 5)* (HL) (n 2) [144]–[145], [148].
[122] Lord Mance, 'Justiciability' (2018) 756.
[123] See Dickinson, 'Acts of State and the Frontiers of Private (International) Law' (2018) 14 *Journal of Private International Law* 1.
[124] As regards the doctrine in the US, see *Maduro Board of the Central Bank of Venezuela v Guaido Board of the Central Bank of Venezuela* [2021] UKSC 57, [2022] 2 WLR 167 [131], [160]. On the historical differences between the UK, the US, Canada and Australia, see Sim, 'Non-Justiciability in Australian

In Australia, non-justiciability is 'said to rest partly on international comity and expediency',[125] and also on the basis that certain issues 'can only be resolved on a state to state level'.[126] In the UK, Lord Sumption JSC has explained: 'the act of state doctrine is influenced by the constitutional separation of powers, which assigns conduct of foreign affairs to the executive'.[127] Even if the separation of powers rationale is accepted, common law systems may differ in their approaches to 'separation of powers'.[128] Lord Neuberger has warned that English courts should exercise great caution in relying on reasoning of foreign courts, especially those with a 'coherent written constitution'.[129] In Canada, for example, a majority of the Supreme Court recently held that the act of state doctrine has 'played no role in Canadian law' and is not part of Canadian common law.[130]

With respect to English law, the UK Supreme Court clarified these doctrines, at least to some extent, in *Belhaj v Straw*.[131] In a judgment on two cases, the Court considered claims by foreign nationals alleging wrongs attributable to manifestations of the UK Government caused by mistreatment in various foreign states and aboard US aircraft. In holding that the claims could proceed, a divided Court articulated different strains of the act of state doctrine, 'disaggregating'[132] it into three rules.[133] Lord Neuberger articulated them in a judgment with which the majority (4:3) agreed:[134]

> The first rule is that the courts of this country will recognise, and will not question, the effect of a foreign state's legislation or other laws in relation to any acts which take place or take effect within the territory of that state.
>
> The second rule is that the courts of this country will recognise, and will not question, the effect of an act of a foreign state's executive in relation to any acts which take place or take effect within the territory of that state.
>
> The third rule has more than one component, but each component involves issues which are inappropriate for the courts of the United Kingdom to resolve because they involve a challenge to the lawfulness of the act of a foreign state which is of such a nature that a municipal judge cannot or ought not rule on it. Thus, the courts of this country

Private International Law: A Lack of "Judicial Restraint"?' (2009) 10 *Melbourne Journal of International Law* 102; see also Cohn, 'Form, Formula and Constitutional Ethos: The Political Question/Justiciability Doctrine in Three Common Law Systems' (2011) 59 *American Journal of Comparative Law* 675.

[125] *Petrotimor Companhia De Petroleos SARL v Commonwealth* [2003] FCAFC 3, (2003) 126 FCR 354 [50] (Black CJ and Hill J).

[126] *Victoria Aircraft Leasing v United States* [2005] VSCA 76, (2005) 12 VR 340 [35].

[127] *Belhaj v Straw* (n 73) [225]; see also Mann (n 99) 63.

[128] See Stellios, *The Federal Judicature: Chapter III of the Constitution*, 2nd edn (LexisNexis, 2020) [3.29]; Beck, *Australian Constitutional Law: Concepts and Cases* (CUP, 2020) 371–72; Lindell, Cowan and Zines's *Federal Jurisdiction in Australia*, 4th edn (Federation Press, 2016) 162–63.

[129] *Belhaj v Straw* (n 73), [133].

[130] *Nevsun Resources Ltd v Araya*, 2020 SCC 5, [2020] SCJ No 5 [28] (Abella J).

[131] *Belhaj v Straw* (n 73) [257].

[132] ibid [11].

[133] Teo, 'Narrowing foreign affairs non-justiciability' (2021) 70 *ICLQ* 505, 509–10.

[134] Just understanding how their Lordships agreed or disagreed with one another is difficult and could justify an Excel spreadsheet. See Dickinson, 'Acts of State' (2018) 15; Teo (ibid) 512–13.

> will not interpret or question dealings between sovereign states … Similarly, the courts of this country will not, as a matter of judicial policy, determine the legality of acts of a foreign government in the conduct of foreign affairs. It is also part of this third rule that international treaties and conventions, which have not become incorporated into domestic law by the legislature, cannot be the source of domestic rights or duties and will not be interpreted by our courts.[135]

In application of the third rule, courts will determine whether a matter with foreign elements is non-justiciable on a 'case-by-case basis'.[136] Yet all aspects of act of state involve some sort of non-justiciability. The Supreme Court recently held that 'Where it applies, the foreign act of state doctrine holds national courts incompetent to adjudicate upon the lawfulness or validity of the sovereign acts of a foreign state'.[137]

The majority position from *Belhaj* maintains the proposition from *Kuwait Airways* that the act of state doctrine is (generally) subject to a public policy exception.[138] The claimants alleged they were tortured; torture was a sufficiently grave violation of international human rights law to engage the exception. The result was their claims were justiciable through an exception to the act of state doctrine.[139] Dicta differed on what other sorts of violations of international law would engage the doctrine. Lord Neuberger and Lord Sumption considered[140] that state aggression and annexation could engage the public policy exception, relying on *Nissan v Attorney General*.[141] Lord Sumption considered *Kuwait Airways*, and stated that:

> Recognition of the influence of international law does not mean that every rule of international law must be adopted as a principle of English public policy, even if it is acknowledged as a peremptory norm (*jus cogens*) at an international level.[142]

Despite these developments,[143] the legacy of *Kuwait Airways* as regards act of state and justiciability is not entirely satisfactory. The act of state doctrine remains a difficult area of law, in which it may be impossible to identify a single 'common law' position.[144] A common theme between jurisdictions is that this is a pragmatic

[135] *Belhaj v Straw* (n 73) [121]–[123], recounted in *Maduro Board* (n 124) [113].
[136] ibid [107].
[137] *Maduro Board* (n 124) [155].
[138] Certain acts with respect to foreign property may be an exception to the exception (ie, not subject to a public policy exception), echoing the *Moçambique* rule; further, there may be an exception to the exception where acts of a foreign government occur outside of that state's territory: see *Belhaj v Straw* (n 73) [156]–[165]. See *British South Africa Co v Companhia de Moçambique* [1893] AC 602, HL; *Habib v Commonwealth of Australia* [2010] FCAFC 12, (2010) 183 FCR 62, [41].
[139] *Belhaj v Straw* (n 73) [153]; Smith, 'Acts of State in Belhaj and Rahmatullah' (2018) 134(Jan) *LQR* 20, 22–23.
[140] *Belhaj v Straw* (n 73) [123], [237].
[141] *Nissan v Attorney General* [1970] AC 179, HL 237.
[142] *Belhaj v Straw* (n 73) [257].
[143] For subsequent consideration, see *Reliance Industries Ltd v Union of India* [2018] EWHC 822 (Comm), [2018] 1 Lloyd's Rep 562 [104]–[106] (applying *Belhaj* act of state to arbitration); see generally Teo (n 133).
[144] But in New Zealand, Simon France J followed *Belhaj* in *X v Attorney-General* [2017] NZHC 768, [2017] 3 NZLR 115.

doctrine deployed in political contexts, with embedded exceptions deployed for countervailing pragmatic ends. In my view, the admonition of Mann still holds some truth today:

> Public policy dominates one of the most difficult and perplexing topics which, in the field of foreign affairs, may face the municipal judge in England: the doctrine of the foreign act of State displays in every respect such uncertainty and confusion and rests on so slippery a basis that its application becomes a matter of speculation.[145]

VII. The Interaction between Public and Private International Law in Common Law Systems

Another major contribution of *Kuwait Airways* was the use of public international law sources as the premises from which the majority reasoning proceeded to resolve conflict of laws problems. Lord Nicholls expressly recognised that, in appropriate circumstances, 'it is legitimate for an English court to have regard to the content of international law in deciding whether to recognise a foreign law'.[146] Lord Steyn referred to the Security Council resolutions as 'proof' of Iraq's annexation of Kuwait,[147] while Lord Hope said that 'The arguments for giving effect to international law as declared by the resolutions of the Security Council could hardly be more compelling'.[148]

The interaction between private international law and public international law has long been a subject of interest to those engrossed in the former discipline.[149] For example, in his course at the Hague Academy, Mann compared two approaches to the role of public international law in relation to act of state:

> The foreign State, under its own law, may allow overriding effect to public international law so as to invalidate a statute or an executive act which is contrary to the law of nations. In such circumstances the case is the same as that in which the issue relates to the invalidity of the foreign act of State under its own constitutional law … Or in the foreign country the violation of public international law cannot be considered by the courts, whether for legal or factual reasons. Yet the issue may be raised in the courts, and under the law, of the forum. Here the law of the forum should prevail. It has frequently been suggested that this follows from *ordre public*: all rules of public international law are of necessity so fundamental and essential an element of the legal order that they are part of public order. On the other hand it has been suggested that public international law should be applied directly without the interposition of public policy.[150]

[145] Mann (n 99) 164, quoted in *Maduro Board* (n 124) [112], and quoted indirectly in *Scarffe & Obannon* [2020] FamCA 77 [47].

[146] *Kuwait Airways (Nos 4 and 5)* (HL) (n 2) [26].

[147] ibid [113].

[148] *Kuwait Airways (Nos 4 and 5)* (HL) (n 2) [147].

[149] See generally Lipstein, 'The General Principals of Private International Law' (1973-II) 135 *Recueil des Cours* 97, II; Kahn-Freund, *General Problems of Private International Law* (AW Sijthoff, 1976) ch 2.

[150] Mann, 'Conflict of Laws and Public Law' (1971-I) 132 *Recueil des Cours* 107, IV, quoted in Mills (n 74) 214 fn 67.

Mann preferred the latter view, as it left less room for discretion. Writing on *Kuwait Airways*, Rogerson, commented: 'The late Dr Mann would be delighted that in *Kuwait Airways Corp v Iraqi Airways Corp* the English court has finally taken public international law into its heart'.[151]

However, even the majority in *Kuwait Airways* did not directly apply public international law in the sense that Mann may have preferred. Rather, they identified the content of public international law as a reason why the House of Lords could engage the public policy doctrine of English law. The decision is thus consistent with the dualist model of international law, which also requires legislatures to implement international treaties with domestic legislation.[152] So, for example, in the Australian context, the argument that the Parliament of a State of the Federation is limited by obligations of the ICCPR,[153] in circumstances where the Executive has committed to the covenant but it has not been given force via Commonwealth legislation, was rejected by the High Court as 'incompatible with the long accepted dualism of international law and Australian domestic law'.[154] Common law courts apply the policy of their own law, even in matters with a foreign element.[155] In *Belhaj*, Lord Mance described *Kuwait Airways* as authority for the principle that 'recognition will, exceptionally, be refused, when recognition would conflict with a fundamental principle of *domestic* public policy'.[156] Similarly, Lord Neuberger said that 'The circumstances in which this exception to the [act of state doctrine] should apply appear to me to depend ultimately on domestic law considerations, although generally accepted norms of international law are plainly capable of playing a decisive role'.[157] Lord Sumption described the *Kuwait Airways* public policy exception in terms of '*English* public policy … informed by any relevant norms of international law binding on the United Kingdom'.[158]

The correct view is that public international law is not a part of the common law but is a source of common law reasoning.[159] Common law courts might use international law as a persuasive source, but they are not bound to do so. For example, in *Al-Kateb v Godwin*, the High Court of Australia was held that the Australian Constitution could not be construed with reference to international

[151] Rogerson (n 3), 271.

[152] See *Kazemi Estate v Islamic Republic of Iran*, 2014 SCC 62, [2014] 2 SCR 173 [150]–[151]; Chong, 'Transnational Public Policy' (2012) 90.

[153] International Covenant on Civil and Political Rights, adopted 16 December 1966, General Assembly resolution 2200A (XXI).

[154] *Tajjour v New South Wales* [2014] HCA 35, (2014) 254 CLR 508 [48] (French CJ).

[155] See generally Davies et al (n 30) 325.

[156] *Belhaj v Straw* (n 73) [37] (emphasis added).

[157] ibid [154].

[158] ibid [257] (emphasis original).

[159] ibid [252], citing *R v Jones (Margaret)* [2007] 1 AC 136, HL [11] (Lord Bingham), who in turn cited Brierly, 'International Law in England' (1935) 51 *LQR* 24, 31; cf Kirby, 'The Growing Impact of International Law on the Common Law' (2012) 33 *Adelaide Law Review* 7.

law sources created after the creation of the Constitution.[160] Yet in relation to construction of ordinary domestic statutes, Australian courts will presume that legislation is intended to be consistent with international law,[161] including customary international law.[162] The point was made by Brennan J in the classic native title case, *Mabo*: 'The common law does not necessarily conform with international law, but international law is a legitimate and important influence on the development of the common law, especially when international law declares the existence of universal human rights'.[163]

Not all principles of public international law, even *jus cogens*, will be given effect by a common law court. Lord Neuberger made the point plainly: 'international treaties and conventions, which have not become incorporated into domestic law by the legislature, cannot be the source of domestic rights or duties and will not be interpreted by our courts'.[164] So, for example, in application of the act of state doctrine, common law courts may refrain from adjudicating matters that seemingly involve violations of international law that are less than clear, as the following case illustrates.

The Law Debenture Trust Corporation plc v Ukraine[165] is sadly relevant to the environment in which this chapter has been written. In short, the case concerned obligations of Ukraine with respect to bonds, which it sought to avoid on the basis, among other bases, that relevant contractual arrangements had been procured by duress applied by Russia, in the form of Russia's military aggression in Crimea and interference with Ukraine's eastern provinces. The claimant retorted that Russia's threats and violence were non-justiciable, while Ukraine argued that Russia's acts were beyond the scope of act of state, relying on *Kuwait Airways*.[166] In the absence of violations of the UN Charter or resolutions of the Security Council, the situation was distinguished, and therefore Ukraine's argument failed through application of the principle of non-justiciability articulated in *Belhaj*.[167] Blair J's judgment quotes from, and is consistent with, the point expressed by Lord Mance in *Belhaj*. Although the prohibition of use of armed force and aggression are key examples of *jus cogens*, they are also paradigmatic of the issues upon which domestic courts should not adjudicate under the act of state doctrine.[168] Fortunately, the Court of Appeal took a different view and partially upheld Ukraine's appeal.[169]

[160] *Al-Kateb v Godwin* [2004] HCA 37, (2004) 219 CLR 562, 589 [62].

[161] *Jumbunna Coal Mine NL v Victorian Coal Miners' Association* (1908) 6 CLR 309. See Herzfeld and Prince, *Interpretation*, 2nd edn (Lawbook, 2020) [9.350].

[162] eg, *Firebird Global Master Fund II Ltd v Republic of Nauru* [2015] HCA 43, (2015) 258 CLR 31.

[163] *Mabo v Queensland (No 2)* [1992] HCA 23; (1992) 175 CLR 1, 42.

[164] *Belhaj v Straw* (n 73) [123].

[165] *The Law Debenture Trust Corporation plc v Ukraine* [2017] EWHC 655 (Comm), [2017] QB 1249.

[166] ibid [308].

[167] ibid [374] and [377].

[168] *Belhaj v Straw* (n 73) [107].

[169] *The Law Debenture Trust Corporation plc v Ukraine* [2018] EWCA Civ 2026, [2019] QB 1121. When this chapter was being finalised, judgment was pending from a further appeal to the Supreme Court, which was heard in November 2021.

Although the third rule of non-justiciability from *Belhaj* was prima facie applicable, the public policy exception was engaged.[170] Among other reasons, the Court held that:

> [T]here is an especially strong public policy in this country that no country should be able to take advantage of its own violation of norms of ius cogens … domestic public policy here is informed by public policy inherent in international law when it identifies norms as peremptory norms with the character of ius cogens. Identification of norms as having that character indicates the strong international public policy which exists to ensure that they are respected and given effect.[171]

Kuwait Airways provokes consideration of another issue related to the role of public international law in conflict of laws: whether the conflict of laws is 'international' law, in the sense that common principles are shared between nation states. An orthodox 'English' view of the conflict of laws is that it is domestic law.[172] I share this view: the very existence of the Hague Conference on Private International Law, an organisation dedicated to the harmonisation of private international law rules between legal systems, and the prospect of 'conflicts of conflicts rules' through the doctrine of *renvoi*,[173] suggest that private international law is not as 'international' as its public cousin. However, many distinguished minds might disagree.[174] Apart from scholars who take a more theoretical approach to the discipline, common lawyers like Mills have challenged 'the myth that private international law is not actually international'.[175] This very book may be representative of the truth of that view: that common lawyers should pay attention to 'global' private international law. Certainly, if ever there was a legal discipline in which it would be acceptable to rely upon 'foreign' sources, it is the conflict of laws.

VIII. Conclusion

Kuwait Airways is a rich contribution to the conflict of laws. It developed the common law on several fronts, especially as regards the proper role of a domestic court in adjudicating complex issues on the international stage. As a case delivered at the beginning of the twenty-first century, it engages with a question that has unfortunately become more important than ever: to what extent should members of the international community continue to give effect to the Westphalian value

[170] *The Law Debenture Trust Corporation plc v Ukraine* (ibid) [173]–[180].
[171] ibid [180].
[172] *Dicey, Morris & Collins* (n 54) [1-001].
[173] See *Neilson v Overseas Projects Corporation of Victoria* (n 94).
[174] See, eg, Ruiz Abou-Nigm, McCall-Smith and French, *Linkages and Boundaries in Private and Public International Law* (Hart, 2018).
[175] Mills, 'The Private History of International Law' (2006) 55 *ICLQ* 1, 1. See also Mills, *The Confluence of Public and Private International Law: Justice, Pluralism and Subsidiarity in the Constitutional Ordering of Private Law* (CUP, 2009).

underlying the act of state doctrine that '[e]very sovereign state is bound to respect the independence of every other sovereign state'?[176] In the same way that state immunity shifted from an absolute to a restrictive theory,[177] through this case, the House of Lords moved act of state away from an absolutist position towards one that pays greater attention to international norms that may hold nation states accountable. Given the malleability of public policy in the conflict of laws, the line may continue to shift – and so it should.

It should not be the case that a UN Security Council resolution is needed for Russia's (ongoing) aggression to engage a public policy exception to the act of state doctrine.[178] With autocratic states holding permanent membership of the Security Council, common law courts of nations that value democracy and liberty should rethink the status of resolutions of that organ as sources of domestic law. Apart from General Assembly resolutions, formal condemnation of actions by nation states and their proxies, from allied nations of shared values, should also influence the development of the common law. In the same way that a Nazi decree is not a law at all,[179] a judiciary that sends Aleksei Navalny to prison for nine years for daring to challenge a tyrant[180] is not a judiciary at all. Russian judgments should be treated by common law courts accordingly.[181] As the fallout of Russia's invasion makes its way through common law courts,[182] public policy should feature prominently. It should do so not merely for doctrinal reasons, but with an eye to material justice. The conflict of laws must adapt to meet the demands of history, as it sadly repeats itself in the wars of the twenty-first century.

[176] *Underhill v Hernandez*, 186 US 250 (1897) 250 (Fuller CJ).

[177] *The Philippine Admiral* (1976) 2 WLR 214, HL 228A (Lord Cross); Australian Law Reform Commission, 'Foreign State Immunity' Report No 24 (1984) 9–14, [11]–[16].

[178] *cf* Teo (n 133) 512.

[179] *Oppenheimer v Cattermole* (n 43).

[180] See Troianovski and Safronova, 'Aleksei Navalny, Fiery Putin Critic, Is Handed a New, 9-Year Prison Sentence' *New York Times* (22 March 2022).

[181] Russia is a signatory to the HCCH Convention of 2 July 2019 on the Recognition and Enforcement of Foreign Judgments in Civil or Commercial Matters (the Judgments Convention).

[182] It has already begun, as lawyers apply to get off the record for Russian entities in common law courts, on the basis of Russia's crimes: *JSC VTB Bank v Katunin* (Eastern Caribbean High Court, British Virgin Islands, 22 March 2022, unreported) [4].

10

Bid Industrial Holdings (Pty) Ltd v Strang and Another (Minister of Justice and Constitutional Development, Third Party)

An Analysis

ELSABE SCHOEMAN

I. Introduction

South African law may be classified as a mixed or a hybrid legal system, drawing upon Roman–Dutch law, English law and African customary or indigenous law to constitute its body of 'common law'.[1] Having been colonised and governed during different periods of its history by The Netherlands (1652–1795 and 1803–06) and Britain (1795–1803 and 1806–1910) until it became the Union of South Africa in 1910, South Africa became an independent republic in 1961. In 1996, the country adopted its final constitution, the Constitution of the Republic of South Africa, 1996, after having become a constitutional democracy following the abolition of apartheid in 1994. As a result, modern-day South African law presents as a rich tapestry of different legal traditions woven together through legislation and case law against the backdrop of the unwritten common law, with the Constitution as the supreme law of the land and the Constitutional Court as the final court of appeal. The role of the Constitution and the courts vis-à-vis the common law is clear:

> **Interpretation of Bill of Rights**
>
> 39. (1) When interpreting the Bill of Rights, a court, tribunal or forum—
>
> (a) must promote the values that underlie an open and democratic society based on human dignity, equality and freedom;

[1] Hosten, Edwards, Bosman and Church, *Introduction to South African Law and Legal Theory*, 2nd edn (1995, Reprint, Butterworths, 1997) 337ff. 'Common law' is used here in the sense of the unwritten body of law that forms the backbone of a legal system. Common law rules may be written

> (b) must consider international law; and
> (c) may consider foreign law.
>
> (2) When interpreting any legislation, and when developing the common law or customary law, every court, tribunal or forum must promote the spirit, purport and objects of the Bill of Rights.
>
> (3) The Bill of Rights does not deny the existence of any other rights or freedoms that are recognised or conferred by common law, customary law or legislation, to the extent that they are consistent with the Bill.
>
> ...
>
> **Inherent power**
>
> 173. The Constitutional Court, the Supreme Court of Appeal and the High Court of South Africa each has the inherent power to protect and regulate their own process, and to develop the common law, taking into account the interests of justice.

As one of the sources of its common law, the influence of English law is clearly to be seen in certain areas of South African law, such as the law of civil procedure, the law of evidence and commercial law, as well as in private international law, where significant reliance was placed on English law conceptions of private international law by legal practitioners and judges throughout the twentieth century.[2] It is, therefore, no coincidence that one of the landmark cases of the early twenty-first century, *Bid Industrial Holdings (Pty) Ltd v Strang and Another (Minister of Justice and Constitutional Development, Third Party)*,[3] is a case that invokes the sanction of the Constitution (striking down jurisdictional arrest as unconstitutional) and then proceeds to employ an Anglo-common law doctrine (*forum (non) conveniens*) to fill the resulting gap in the law. But, in an interesting twist, the common law rule, struck down by the Constitution, had its origins in Roman-Dutch law,[4] one of the other constituents of South Africa's hybrid common law. Furthermore, the Anglo-common law doctrine introduced to fill the gap had been applied in South African admiralty cases,[5] yet only entered the mainstream

into statutes, and the common law is also supplemented by other sources of law, such as international conventions. Importantly, the common law is not static – it is a living law, constantly developing, often through comparative reference to foreign legal systems.

[2] ibid 1347. Many South African lawyers, including judges, had trained in England and English language sources were more readily accessible. Although English law was the dominant influence, reference was also made to the laws of other foreign countries, notably those of Canada, Australia, the US and the European continent: see, for example, *Ex parte Spinazze* 1985 (3) SA 650 (A), 662G-665A.

[3] 2008 (3) SA 355 (SCA) ('*Bid Industrial Holdings*').

[4] *Bid Industrial Holdings* [26].

[5] See *Cargo Laden and Lately Laden on Board the MV Thalassini Avgi v MV Dimitris* 1989 3 SA 820 (A); *Dias Compania Naviera SA v MV AL Kaziemah and others* 1994 3 All SA 4 (D); *M T Tigr Bouygues Offshore SA v Owners of The M T Tigr* 1998 4 SA 740 (C). Berman J (*Great River Shipping Inc v Sunnyface Marine Ltd* 1992 4 SA 313 (C) 316D-F) described s 7(1)(a) of the Admiralty Jurisdiction Regulation Act 105 of 1983 as 'the *forum non conveniens* principle expressed in statutory form'. The section provides as follows: 'A court may decline to exercise its Admiralty jurisdiction in any proceedings instituted or to be instituted, if it is of the opinion that any other court in the Republic or any other court or any arbitrator, tribunal or body elsewhere will exercise jurisdiction in respect of the said

cross-border jurisdictional arena through the case of *Bid Industrial Holdings*. This illustrates, par excellence, the intricate interplay between different legal traditions and influences in South African private international law.

II. *Bid Industrial Holdings (Pty) Ltd v Strang*

There were two legal issues in *Bid Industrial Holdings*: (1) whether a prima facie case had been made out on the merits for the claim brought in delict; and (2) whether the arrest of a foreign defendant to found or confirm jurisdiction,[6] a common law rule embodied in legislation,[7] was unconstitutional.

A. Facts

The facts were simple: the plaintiff (appellant in the Supreme Court of Appeal) wanted to bring proceedings in the Johannesburg High Court (Witwatersrand Local Division) against the defendants (respondents in the Supreme Court of Appeal) for damages in delict. The plaintiff was a South African company and the defendants were Australian citizens, domiciled and resident in Australia (it was not clear from the case report in which Australian state(s) they resided or were domiciled). They were directors of two Australian companies with extensive interests in southern Africa. In order to establish jurisdiction in a South African court, the plaintiff applied for the arrest of the defendants to found or confirm jurisdiction in terms of the statutory provision referred to above.[8] It would also have been possible to attach an asset to found or confirm jurisdiction but, although this had been an option at some stage, it was no longer possible. The defendants had also

proceedings and that it is more appropriate that the proceedings be adjudicated upon by any such other court or by such arbitrator, tribunal or body.'

[6] *Bid Industrial Holdings* [61]: arrest could be ordered if the defendant was present anywhere in the country. For academic comment on *Bid Industrial Holdings*, see, eg, Eiselen, 'Goodbye Arrest *ad fundandam*, Hello *forum non conveniens*?' (2008) 2008 *Journal of South African Law* 794; Theophilopoulos, 'Arresting a Foreign Peregrinus: *Bid Industrial Holdings (Pty) Ltd and a New Jurisdictional Lacuna*' (2010) 21 *Stellenbosch Law Review* 132.

[7] Section 19(1) of the Supreme Court Act 59 of 1959, since repealed by the Superior Courts Act 10 of 2013, which read as follows: '(a) A provincial or local division shall have jurisdiction over all persons residing or being in and in relation to all causes arising … within its area of jurisdiction and all other matters of which it may according to law take cognizance … (b) … (c) Subject to the provisions of section 28 … any High Court may – (i) issue an order for attachment of property or arrest of a person J to confirm jurisdiction … also where the property or person concerned is outside its area of jurisdiction but within the A Republic: Provided that the cause of action arose within its area of jurisdiction; and (ii) where the plaintiff is resident or domiciled within its area of jurisdiction, but the cause of action arose outside its area of jurisdiction and the property or person concerned is outside its area of jurisdiction, issue an order for attachment of B property or arrest of a person to found jurisdiction regardless of where in the Republic the property or person is situated.' Section 28 prohibited the arrest of a South African resident.

[8] See (n 7).

refused to submit to the jurisdiction of the court.[9] As a result, the plaintiff had no other option but to resort to the arrest of the defendants.[10]

B. Reasoning

The Supreme Court of Appeal chose not to address the issue regarding the merits of the claim, leaving it undecided on appeal;[11] it need not be considered further here. It is the second issue, namely the constitutionality of the arrest of the person to establish jurisdiction, that sparked reform of the law relating to jurisdiction in cross-border litigation. As pointed out above, the empowering statutory provision was derived from the common law (having its origins in Roman–Dutch law)[12] and therefore 'the common law had to be developed so as to abolish the rule'.[13] However, exactly what this reform entails beyond the pronouncement of the unconstitutionality of the relevant statutory provision is not completely clear, and this will be addressed in more detail later.

There was little, if any, doubt that the arrest of the person to establish jurisdiction could not pass constitutional muster. This was despite counsel for the plaintiff arguing that jurisdictional arrest was merely symbolic and that it would not lead to detention in custody – instead, it would amount to no more than a 'tap on the shoulder'.[14] It was further argued that such an 'arrested' defendant could almost immediately secure release by consenting to jurisdiction, offering security or effecting payment.[15] Howie P dismissed these arguments in no uncertain terms:[16]

> [T]he process of arrest is always to engage the relevant agencies of the State to effect the arrest and then to restrict the arrestee's freedom pending attainment of some lawful purpose. If, for example, that purpose is not attained on the day of the arrest, the arrestee must necessarily remain in detention by the State until it is attained. Such detention can ordinarily only be in a prison. Jurisdictional arrest, therefore, unquestionably aims to limit the arrestee's liberty.

[9] *Bid Industrial Holdings* [18].

[10] It was not clear where the alleged cause of action had arisen; however, there were factual connections with the jurisdictional area of the Johannesburg High Court: [20]. Although the defendants were often in South Africa on business, they were not in the country at the time of the court application: [5].

[11] *Bid Industrial Holdings* [17]. The claim in delict was based on the wrongful and intentional interference by the defendants with the plaintiff's contractual rights under a joint-venture partnership agreement (with southern African interests) between the plaintiff and the defendants. However, since the delict of interference with contractual relations is committed by a stranger or outsider to a contract, the issue arose as to whether the defendants, as parties to the contract, could have done so. Moreover, if they had breached the contract, that would form the basis for a contractual claim and there would be no need for a claim in delict: [8]–[13].

[12] ibid [26].

[13] As argued by the respondents: ibid [4].

[14] ibid [21].

[15] ibid [33].

[16] ibid [36].

Therefore, jurisdictional arrest amounted to a breach of the defendant's right to freedom and security of the person,[17] as well as the defendant's concomitant rights to equality, human dignity and freedom of movement.[18] Even the defendant's right to a fair trial might be compromised. In any event, it was abundantly clear that jurisdictional arrest infringed a host of constitutionally entrenched rights, the limitation of which could not be justified in terms of section 36 of the Constitution.[19]

Having declared jurisdictional arrest unconstitutional, Howie P proceeded to consider what he called a 'substitute practice'[20] in cases where arrest was the only way to establish jurisdiction over a foreign defendant. He referred to the adequacy of mere physical presence in a foreign jurisdiction as a ground of international competence for the recognition and/or enforcement of foreign judgments according to South African private international law, as well as the practice in England (and other Anglo-common law jurisdictions) where a defendant may be served with process on the basis of mere temporary presence within the jurisdiction.[21] Although Howie P averred that this was subject to the case having a connection with the country, that is not, strictly speaking, correct – it is possible to serve a defendant even if there is no connection with England.[22] However, it would make no sense to serve someone and establish jurisdiction in the court of a country that has no connection with the case – one reason would be difficulty in enforcing the ensuing judgment. In addition, such a defendant would be able to plead *forum non conveniens* (that there is another competent and more appropriate forum to hear the case) in England (as well as in other Anglo-common law jurisdictions).[23]

Throughout his judgment, Howie P remained concerned about effectiveness,[24] although he conceded that this was no longer an overriding consideration for the assumption of jurisdiction by a court,[25] as well as that it was the responsibility

[17] Section 12 of the Constitution of the Republic of South Africa, 1996.

[18] Sections 9,10 and 21 of the Constitution of the Republic of South Africa, 1996.

[19] *Bid Industrial Holdings* [59]. Section 36 provides as follows: '(1) The rights in the Bill of Rights may be limited only in terms of law of general application to the extent that the limitation is reasonable and justifiable in an open and democratic society based on human dignity, equality and freedom, taking into account all relevant factors, including – (a) the nature of the right; (b) the importance of the purpose of the limitation; (c) the nature and extent of the limitation; (d) the relation between the limitation and its purpose; and (e) less restrictive means to achieve the purpose. (2) Except as provided in subsection (1) or in any other provision of the Constitution, no law may limit any right entrenched in the Bill of Rights.'

[20] *Bid Industrial Holdings* [52].

[21] ibid.

[22] Torremans (ed), *Cheshire, North and Fawcett: Private International Law*, 15th edn (OUP, 2017) 324. However, a defendant cannot be enticed into a jurisdiction in order to serve proceedings and establish jurisdiction: Collins (gen ed), *Dicey, Morris and Collins on The Conflict of Laws*, 15th edn (Sweet & Maxwell, 2012) vol I [11-108] fn 296.

[23] Collins (ibid) [11-102] and [11-108] read with [12R-001]. On *forum non conveniens*, see *Spiliada Maritime Corp v Cansulex Ltd*, which is discussed in section III of this chapter.

[24] See, for example, *Veneta Mineraria Spa v Carolina Collieries (Pty) Ltd (In Liquidation)* 1987 (4) SA 883 (A), 893E, per Viljoen JA: 'A Court can only be said to have jurisdiction in a matter if it has the power not only of taking cognisance of the suit but also of giving effect to its judgment.'

[25] *Bid Industrial Holdings* [57]: 'As to the principle of effectiveness, despite its having been described as "the basic principle of jurisdiction in our law" it is clear that the importance and significance of

of the plaintiff to make sure that it selected a jurisdiction that could render an effective judgment.[26] However, Howie P continued to search for a more solid foundation than mere physical presence in which to ground jurisdiction. Finding that section 19(1)(a) of the Supreme Court Act[27] required 'nothing short of residence and the defendant's residence within the jurisdiction is one situation in which a "cause arises", the defendant then being amenable to that court',[28] he continued:[29]

> I nevertheless consider that jurisdiction in the present case will fall within the terms of s19(1)(a) if the matter can be said to involve a 'cause arising' or be a matter of which the court may according to law take cognizance'. A 'cause arising' is not to be confused with a cause of action, and to determine what a 'cause arising' is, as also to determine of what matter a court may take cognizance, one is driven back to the common-law jurisdictional principles. If those principles can be developed to accommodate a situation like the present there will be conformity with s 19(1*)(a)*. Which is not to say that the common law must conform to the legislation. It is rather the converse. The legislation in question has all along merely been concerned to reflect or implement the common law. All one is therefore looking to ensure is that between the Act and the development sought to be achieved there is harmony.

Pursuing this line of argument, Howie P proceeded to formulate a substitute for jurisdictional arrest:[30]

> In my view it would suffice to empower the court to take cognisance of the suit if the defendant were served with the summons while in South Africa and, in addition, there were an adequate connection between the suit and the area of jurisdiction of the South African court concerned from the point of view of the appropriateness and convenience of its being decided by that court. Appropriateness and convenience are elastic concepts which can be developed case by case. Obviously the strongest connection would be provided by the cause of action arising within that jurisdiction.'

And also, significantly, the doctrine of *forum (non) conveniens* was introduced by name:[31]

> And if the plaintiff decides in favour of suing here it is open to the defendant to contest, among other things, whether the South African court is the *forum conveniens* and whether there are sufficient links between the suit and this country to render litigation appropriate here rather than in the court of the defendant's domicile.

At this point two observations may be made: (1) according to Howie P, the mere physical presence of the foreign defendant in the jurisdictional area of the court would not suffice to establish jurisdiction – there must be an adequate connection

attachment has been so eroded that the value of attached property has sometimes been "trifling." However, as I have said, effectiveness is largely for the plaintiff to assess and to act accordingly.'

[26] ibid [55].

[27] 59 of 1959.

[28] *Bid Industrial Holdings* [53].

[29] ibid [54].

[30] ibid [56].

[31] ibid [55].

between the case and the court in order to render the court appropriate and convenient to hear the matter; and (2) the judgment omits reference to *Spiliada Maritime Corp v Cansulex Ltd*,[32] arguably the international *locus classicus* on *forum (non) conveniens*.

An analysis of Lord Goff's speech in *The Spiliada* will illustrate the crucial relevance of this case to the *Bid Industrial Holdings* scenario and why reference to it would have been useful and instructive, because of the clear distinction made in *The Spiliada* between *forum conveniens* and *forum non conveniens* in the jurisdictional context.

III. *Spiliada Maritime Corp v Cansulex Ltd*

Lord Goff of Chievely's speech in *The Spiliada* has become the authoritative statement on *forum non conveniens*, yet it is seldom realised that *The Spiliada* did not concern a case of *forum non conveniens* – in fact, it was a case of *forum conveniens*. The plaintiffs (appellants in the House of Lords) had obtained leave to serve proceedings 'outside the jurisdiction' on the defendants (respondents in the House of Lords) in British Columbia in order to establish jurisdiction in the English court.[33] An application by the defendants to set aside such leave was refused by Staughton J, but this was reversed on appeal to the Court of Appeal, hence the appeal by the plaintiffs to the House of Lords.[34]

At the outset, Lord Goff pointed to the crucial distinction between *forum non conveniens* (pursuant to jurisdiction founded as of right) and *forum conveniens* (service out of the jurisdiction pursuant to obtaining leave from the court):[35]

> [I]t is perhaps opportune to review the position at this stage, and in particular to give further consideration to the relationship between cases where jurisdiction has been founded as of right by service of proceedings on the defendant within the jurisdiction, but the defendant seeks a stay of the proceedings on the ground of forum non conveniens, and cases where the court is invited to exercise its discretion, under R.S.C., Ord. 11, to give leave for service on the defendant out of the jurisdiction [*forum conveniens*].

Regarding *forum non conveniens*, Lord Goff was clear that it was not mere practical convenience that was decisive in those cases; rather it was the suitability or appropriateness of the particular jurisdiction or forum, determined with reference to the principles set out by him. These principles have become a 'codified' version

32 [1987] AC 460 (HL) ('*The Spiliada*').

33 Under the then RSC, Ord 11, r 4(2): 'No such leave shall be granted unless it shall be made sufficiently to appear to the court that the case is a proper one for service out of the jurisdiction under this Order.' The specific ground upon which leave was sought, was RSC, Ord 11 r 1(1)(f)(iii) under which the action brought was one for the recovery of damages for breach of a contract governed by English law.

34 *The Spiliada* 466B–C.

35 ibid 473H–474A.

of *forum non conveniens* and have been cited numerous times in subsequent court cases across the Anglo-common law world. Suffice here to simply quote the basic principle:[36]

> The basic principle is that a stay will only be granted on the ground of forum non conveniens where the court is satisfied that there is some other available forum, having competent jurisdiction, which is the appropriate forum[37] for the trial of the action, i.e. in which the case may be tried more suitably for the interests of all the parties and the ends of justice.

Turning to *forum conveniens*, Lord Goff clearly distinguished this from *forum non conveniens*. In *forum non conveniens* cases the burden of proof is on the defendant to prove that there is another competent, clearly more appropriate forum to hear the matter. Once the defendant has proven this, a stay of proceedings will normally be granted 'unless there are circumstances by reason of which justice requires that a stay should nevertheless not be granted'.[38] The burden of proof then shifts to the plaintiff to prove, for example, that it will not obtain justice in the foreign jurisdiction.[39] On the other hand, in *forum conveniens* cases, the burden is on the plaintiff to persuade the court to exercise its discretion to grant leave to serve the defendant with process abroad. In this context, the plaintiff must make it 'sufficiently to appear to the court that the case is a proper one for service out of the jurisdiction'.[40] Historically this was labelled 'exorbitant jurisdiction',[41] effectively seeking to subject a foreign defendant, 'who owes no allegiance here, to the inconvenience and annoyance of being brought to contest his rights in this country'[42] and therefore the burden on the plaintiff is a particularly heavy one.[43]

Lord Goff pointed out that *forum conveniens* and *forum non conveniens* had a common goal:[44]

> It seems to me inevitable that the question in both groups of cases must be, at bottom, that expressed by Lord Kinnear in *Q Sim v. Robinow*, 19 R. 665, 668, viz. to identify the forum in which the case can be suitably tried for the interests of all the parties and for the ends of justice.

[36] ibid 476C; for the full set of principles, see 476C–478F.

[37] Lord Goff emphasised (*The Spiliada* 477E): 'In my opinion, the burden resting on the defendant is not just to show that England is not the natural or appropriate forum for the trial, but to establish that there is another available forum which is clearly or distinctly more appropriate than the English forum.'

[38] *The Spiliada* 478D.

[39] ibid 478D–E.

[40] Under the then RSC, Ord 11, r 4(2).

[41] Lord Goff preferred 'extraordinary' to 'exorbitant', which according to him was, 'as used in the present context, an old-fashioned word which perhaps carries unfortunate overtones': *The Spiliada*, 481E–F. See also Abela v Baadarani [2013] UKSC 44 [53], per Lord Sumption.

[42] *The Spiliada* 481C, citing Pearson J in *Société Générale de Paris v Dreyfus Brothers* (1885) 29 Ch D, 239, 242–43.

[43] *The Spiliada*, citing Ackner LJ in *Ilyssia Compania Naviera SA v Bamaodah* [1985] 1 Lloyd's Rep, 107, CA, 113.

[44] *The Spiliada* 480G.

Similar factors and considerations may play a role in determining the appropriate forum, for example, availability of witnesses and evidence,[45] multiplicity of proceedings, litigation costs, applicable law, places of business of the respective parties, location of assets for enforcement purposes, and any other significant connections or considerations in respect of a particular jurisdiction. However, although both *forum conveniens* and *forum non conveniens* concern the appropriateness of the forum, as well as considerations of justice,[46] the point of departure and burden of proof are different. *Forum conveniens* is invoked by the plaintiff to prove the appropriateness of the home forum in order to serve the foreign defendant abroad, while *forum non conveniens* may be invoked by the defendant after having been served as of right within the jurisdiction while present there. *Forum conveniens* is about the establishment or *existence* of jurisdiction, while *forum non conveniens* concerns the *exercise* of jurisdiction (jurisdiction already exists in at least one forum).[47]

Reference to *The Spiliada* in *Bid Industrial Holdings* would have assisted greatly to distinguish between *forum conveniens* and *forum non conveniens* as these two represent different jurisdictional contexts in respect of the appropriateness of forum.

In the case of *Multi-Links Telecommunications Ltd v Africa Prepaid Services Nigeria Ltd*[48] reference was made to both *Bid Industrial Holdings* and *The Spiliada*, yet the distinction between *forum conveniens* and *forum non conveniens* was, once more, not acknowledged.

IV. *Multi-Links Telecommunications Ltd v Africa Prepaid Services Nigeria Ltd*

The case concerned issues leading up to the conclusion of and the subsequent effect of a Super Dealer Agreement (SDA), as well as a number of other related issues. The proceedings before Fabricius J involved a South African plaintiff (Telkom SA), a Nigerian plaintiff (Multi-Links) and six defendants, one of which was a foreign (Nigerian) company, African Prepaid Services Nigeria (APSN).[49] The crucial issue was the jurisdiction of the South African court over APSN as a foreign defendant. Proceedings were served on APSN's South African attorneys in South Africa, by

[45] Virtual options may now assist in this regard.

[46] The plaintiff may also invoke considerations of justice for purposes of *forum conveniens*.

[47] It is possible to have proceedings pending in two jurisdictions at the same time.

[48] 2014 3 SA 265 (GP) ('*Multi-Links*').

[49] The SDA was central to all the claims. It was concluded between Multi-Links and African Prepaid Services (APS), a South African company, in 2008. Although Telkom SA was not a party to the SDA, it was integral to the conclusion of it, Multi-Links having been a subsidiary of Telkom SA from 2007 to 2011: *Multi-Links* [2]. APSN was not involved in the conclusion of the SDA; it was established in 2009 to take assignment of APS's rights and obligations under the SDA: *Multi-Links* [4].

way of its alleged consent to have its South African attorneys accept service on its behalf.[50] However, submission to jurisdiction by APSN on the basis of *domicilium citandi et executandi* could not be established at that stage, due to lack of sufficient ventilation and evaluation of relevant facts.[51]

There was also no attachment of any asset belonging to APSN to found or confirm jurisdiction.[52] In challenging the jurisdiction of the court over it, APSN relied on the dictum by Harms JA in *Tsung v Industrial Development Corporation of SA Ltd*:[53]

> [I]f the defendant is a peregrinus and whether or not the court has jurisdiction over the cause, eg because the cause of action arose within the jurisdiction or jurisdiction exists *ratione delictus* or *ratione contractus*, an attachment or arrest is essential for the exercise of jurisdiction: a recognised *ratio jurisdictionis* by itself will not do.

In response, the plaintiffs relied on the judgment in *Bid Industrial Holdings*, arguing that APSN's argument – that only attachment of property was sufficient to establish jurisdiction over a foreign defendant – was flawed.[54] Following *Bid Industrial Holdings*, arrest of a foreign defendant was rendered unconstitutional and therefore abolished and, where attachment of property was not possible, jurisdiction could be established

> if the summons were served on the defendant while in South Africa, and there were sufficient connection between the suit and the area of jurisdiction of the court concerned, so that disposing the case by that court was appropriate and convenient.[55]

In terms of 'appropriateness and convenience',[56] a number of factors pointed towards the court assuming jurisdiction over APSN: it concluded the agreement as an *incola* of the court;[57] it agreed to arbitration in South Africa; it nominated a *domicilium citandi et executandi* within the area of the court's jurisdiction; it agreed to South African law as the governing law of the SDA and any disputes arising therefrom; it invoked the arbitration clause and even extended the terms of reference to include the special plea; it was controlled by the first and second defendants who were both domiciled within the jurisdictional area of the court; it was cited as co-defendant with another defendant who was domiciled and ordinarily resident in the jurisdictional area of the court; the factual events on which Telkom SA and Multi-Links relied had occurred within the court's jurisdiction and involved all the defendants in the action; the defendants were sued jointly and

[50] ibid [2].
[51] ibid [21].
[52] ibid [6].
[53] 2006 (4) SA 177 (SCA) [3].
[54] ibid [10].
[55] ibid [11].
[56] ibid [15].
[57] Although APSN had not been involved in the conclusion of the agreement, the rights and obligations of APS were assigned to it. According to Fabricius J, 'these negotiations were expressly conducted on its behalf as a company "to be formed"': ibid [15].

severally; and any judgment in favour of the plaintiffs could be executed effectively in South Africa.[58]

Fabricius J then referred to *The Spiliada*, quoting Lord Goff's exposition of the principles governing *forum non conveniens*.[59] He also referred to section 7 of the Admiralty Jurisdiction Regulation Act[60] and relevant admiralty cases that had applied the doctrine of *forum non conveniens*.[61] Although Fabricius J recounted the facts of *The Spiliada* and the jurisdictional issue being concerned with service abroad – in other words *forum conveniens* – the distinction between *forum conveniens* and *forum non conveniens* was not acknowledged at all.

Fabricius J proceeded:[62]

> [I]t seems to me that one must determine the forum most suitable for the ends of justice, and because pursuit of the litigation in that forum is most likely to secure those ends. The appropriate or natural forum is that with which the action has the most real and substantial connection. In that context then, the court would look to all the connecting factors, including all background facts, convenience, experts, the law governing the relevant transaction or action, the place where the parties reside or carry on business, etc.

In the final analysis, Fabricius J decided that APSN was not entitled to an order declaring that the court did not have jurisdiction over it.[63]

Although *Multi-Links* only concerned the possible attachment of assets (and not arrest of the defendant) the principles regarding appropriateness of forum are the same – in fact, Fabricius J endorsed the decision in *Bid Industrial Holdings* and also added the authority of *The Spiliada* to the debate. However, it is clear that *Multi-Links* also did not distinguish between *forum conveniens and forum non conveniens* in the jurisdictional context.

V. Current State of *Forum (Non) Conveniens* in South Africa

As explained in the introduction of this chapter, South African law is classified as a mixed or hybrid system of law, drawing upon several influences from other legal traditions, as well as being grounded in a constitutional democracy. And, even

[58] ibid.
[59] ibid [18], as summarised by Forsyth, *Private International Law*, 5th edn (Juta, 2012) 188.
[60] 105 of 1983, S 7(1)(a): 'A court may decline to exercise its Admiralty jurisdiction in any proceedings instituted or to be instituted, if it is of the opinion that any other court in the Republic or any other court or any arbitrator, tribunal or body elsewhere will exercise jurisdiction in respect of the said proceedings and that it is more appropriate that the proceedings be adjudicated upon by any such other court or by such arbitrator, tribunal or body.'
[61] *Multi-Links* [19].
[62] ibid [23].
[63] ibid [23].

though the law of civil procedure is largely based on English law, also bearing in mind the adversarial nature of South African court proceedings, the substantive law relating to jurisdiction is firmly rooted in Roman law. Many of these doctrines, rules and principles were further developed in Dutch law, culminating in a strong Roman–Dutch law tradition that forms the foundation of the South African law relating to jurisdiction. It is also interesting to note that most Continental civil law countries do not know the Anglo-common law doctrine of *forum (non) conveniens* and that the European Union Brussels Regime does not allow for its application.[64] However, in South Africa, the Constitution has intervened: jurisdictional arrest was declared unconstitutional and *forum (non) conveniens* entered the scene. But what exactly was decided in *Bid Industrial Holdings* and what is the current state of *forum (non) conveniens* in South African law?

A. Roman–Dutch Law: The Basis of Jurisdiction

As the basis of jurisdiction in South African law, Roman–Dutch law informs the adoption of the doctrine of *forum (non) conveniens*. Two points are particularly evident from Howie P's judgment.

First, the jurisdiction of South African courts is very heavily dependent on the establishment of a concrete link between the jurisdictional area of the court and the parties involved in the dispute or the occurrence that gave rise to the dispute.[65] Examples of these links, known as jurisdictional connecting factors (*rationes jurisdictionis*), are: residence; domicile (*ratione domicilii*); creation, performance or breach of a contract (*ratione contractus*); commission of a delict (*ratione delicti commissi*); *ratione rei gestae*; cohesion of causes (*ratione causae continentia*); location of property (*ratione rei sitae*); and attachment of property.[66] A South African court will not assume jurisdiction in a case unless there is a proper jurisdictional connecting factor that links the court with the case.[67]

Second, in addition to the jurisdictional connecting factors, the doctrine of effectiveness used to play an important role in the assumption of jurisdiction: 'A Court can only be said to have jurisdiction in a matter if it has the power not only of taking cognisance of the suit but also of giving effect to its judgment'.[68] The doctrine of effectiveness finds expression in the rule that the plaintiff should sue the defendant in its place of domicile (*actor sequitur forum rei*) – this comes

[64] See *Owusu v Jackson* (Case C-281/02) [2005] ECR I-1383, where the ECJ held that the English courts could not decline jurisdiction on the basis of *forum non conveniens* pursuant to Art 2 of the Brussels Convention on Jurisdiction and the Enforcement of Judgments in Civil and Commercial Matters 1968, even if the jurisdiction of no other Member State was in issue.

[65] Forsyth, *Private International Law* (2012) 169.

[66] ibid 203ff.

[67] Per Harms JA in *Tsung v Industrial Development Corporation of SA Ltd* 2006 (4) SA 177 (SCA) [3].

[68] Viljoen JA in *Veneta Mineraria Spa v Carolina Collieries (Pty) Ltd (In Liquidation)* 1987 (4) SA 883 (A), 893E.

straight out of the *Corpus Iuris Civilis*[69] and is also the bedrock of the European Union Brussels Regime.[70] The underlying ratio of this rule is that the court of the domicile of the defendant has effective control over the defendant and this will ensure greater potential for the enforcement of the judgment. However, as acknowledged by Howie P himself in *Bid Industrial Holdings*:[71]

> As to the principle of effectiveness, despite its having been described as 'the basic principle of jurisdiction in our law' it is clear that the importance and significance of attachment has been so eroded that the value of attached property has sometimes been 'trifling'. However, as I have said, effectiveness is largely for the plaintiff to assess and to act accordingly.

These Roman–Dutch law influences can clearly be seen throughout Howie P's judgment and feature prominently in the formulation of the 'substitute practice',[72] designed to fill the gap left by the abolition of jurisdictional arrest as a way to establish jurisdiction.

B. Anglo-Common Law: *Forum (Non) Conveniens*

In order to analyse the decision in *Bid Industrial Holdings*, the following passages from Howie P's judgment are crucial and bear repeating:[73]

> In my view it would suffice to empower the court to take cognisance of the suit if the defendant were served with the summons while in South Africa and, in addition, there were *an adequate connection between the suit and the area of jurisdiction of the South African court concerned from the point of view of the appropriateness and convenience of its being decided by that court*. Appropriateness and convenience are elastic concepts which can be developed case by case. Obviously the strongest connection would be provided by the cause of action arising within that jurisdiction.

And:[74]

> And if the plaintiff decides in favour of suing here it is *open to the defendant to contest, among other things, whether the South African court is the forum conveniens* and whether there are sufficient links between the suit and this country to render litigation appropriate here rather than in the court of the defendant's domicile.

Now, bearing in mind the clear distinction drawn by Lord Goff between *forum conveniens* and *forum non conveniens* in *The Spiliada*,[75] it seems as if Howie P was,

[69] D 2.3.12; 3.3.19-20; C 3.13.2.

[70] Regulation (EU) No 1215/2012 of the European Parliament and of the Council of 12 December 2012 on jurisdiction and the recognition and enforcement of judgments in civil and commercial matters (Brussels recast), Art 4(1).

[71] *Bid Industrial Holdings* [57].

[72] ibid [51].

[73] ibid [56] (emphasis added).

[74] ibid [55] (emphasis added).

[75] See *The Spiliada* 480G–481C, and discussion under III. *Spiliada Maritime Corp v Cansulex Ltd*. For South African commentary on *forum (non) conveniens*, see, eg, Taitz, 'Jurisdiction and

in the first instance, seeking to introduce *forum conveniens* as a means to establish jurisdiction: a plaintiff could serve proceedings on a foreign defendant, while present in the jurisdictional area of the court, provided that there was 'an adequate connection between the suit and the area of jurisdiction of the South African court concerned from the point of view of the appropriateness and convenience of its being decided by that court'.[76] He goes further and says that 'the strongest connection would be provided by the cause of action arising within that jurisdiction'.[77]

This very closely resembles the approach followed in English law (and other Anglo-common law jurisdictions) when serving a foreign defendant *abroad* in order to establish jurisdiction in the plaintiff's home forum. There must be a jurisdictional connecting factor that links the dispute to the plaintiff's home forum and, amongst other things, that forum must also be the appropriate forum in which to bring the case.[78] What is interesting is that the traditional South African jurisdictional connecting factors, such as creation, performance or breach of a contract (*ratione contractus*); commission of a delict (*ratione delicti commissi*); and location of property, are very similar to those required in English law (and other Anglo-common law jurisdictions) for service of proceedings abroad on a foreign defendant in order to establish jurisdiction in the plaintiff's home forum.[79] An English claimant would rely on those connections to prove that the English court is *forum conveniens*, in other words that the English court is the appropriate forum to hear the dispute.

However, whereas *forum conveniens* in its Anglo-common law context applies in respect of serving a foreign defendant *abroad*, Howie P uses it for serving a foreign defendant *in South Africa*. This begs the question: is this indeed a form of *forum conveniens*?

When Howie P talks about *forum conveniens*, in the sense that the foreign defendant may contest the appropriateness of the South African forum, it seems to be aligned with the doctrine of *forum non conveniens* as set out by Lord Goff in *The Spiliada*: the burden of proof rests on the defendant to prove that there is

forum conveniens – A New Approach?' (1980) 43 *Journal of Contemporary Roman Dutch Law* 187; Spiro, '*Forum non conveniens*' (1980) 13 *Comparative and International Law Journal of Southern Africa* 333; Taitz, 'Jurisdiction and *forum conveniens*: A Reply' (1981) 44 *Journal of Contemporary Roman Dutch Law* 372; Schulze, '*Forum non conveniens* in Comparative Private International Law' (2001) 118 *South African Law Journal* 812; and Eiselen, 'Goodbye Arrest *ad fundandam*, Hello *forum non conveniens*?' (2008) 2008 *Journal of South African Law* 794.

[76] *Bid Industrial Holdings* [56].

[77] ibid.

[78] In cases where the leave of the court is required to serve proceedings on a foreign defendant abroad, the court will exercise its discretion with reference to the appropriateness of the forum (*forum conveniens*): Torremans (ed), *Cheshire, North and Fawcett: Private International Law*, 15th edn (OUP, 2017) 364ff.

[79] Also known as 'jurisdictional gateways': Civil Procedure Rules, r 6.37: see further, Torremans (ibid) 334ff. The grounds for service out of the jurisdiction are set out in PD 6B and include, eg, a claim in respect of a contract that was made or breached within the jurisdiction (para 3.1(6)(a) and (7)); or a claim in tort where damage was or will be sustained within the jurisdiction, or where such damage results from an act committed, or likely to be committed, within the jurisdiction (para 3.1(9)(a) and (b)); or where the subject matter of a claim relates to property within the jurisdiction (para 3.1(11).

another competent, clearly more appropriate forum to hear the matter[80] – in this case the court of the defendant's domicile.[81] Normally *forum non conveniens* is available to a defendant who has been served by the plaintiff in the plaintiff's home jurisdiction, and in Anglo–common law jurisdictions, this kind of service will be based on mere presence in the jurisdiction (jurisdiction as of right) – no additional connection is required.[82] The defendant's subsequent application will be for a stay of proceedings, since jurisdiction already exists. Again, looking at Howie P's dictum, he insisted on an adequate connection or sufficient link between the court and the dispute in order to establish jurisdiction over a foreign defendant present in the plaintiff's home forum, which is not a requirement in Anglo–common law systems. This requirement seems to hark back to the requirement of jurisdictional connecting factors in South African law, as well as a lingering affection for or attachment to the doctrine of effectiveness.

But there is also a niggle in the dictum of Howie P when he says that

> it is open to the defendant to contest, among other things, whether the South African court is the *forum conveniens* and whether there are sufficient links between the suit and this country to render litigation appropriate here rather than in the court of the defendant's domicile.[83]

Is this really the *Spiliada* version of *forum non conveniens*? The focus seems to be on the appropriateness of the South African forum (as would be the case in a true *forum conveniens* inquiry), rather than the appropriateness of the foreign defendant's domiciliary forum. Dare one whisper that this might open the door to the Australian version of *forum non conveniens* where the defendant has to prove that the Australian forum is clearly inappropriate?[84]

On the other hand, if this was only a *forum conveniens* inquiry, the defendant would not carry the burden of proof. When a foreign defendant is served abroad in Anglo–common law jurisdictions, any protest to the appropriateness of the plaintiff's home forum must be addressed by the plaintiff – in other words, the plaintiff must prove that its home forum is the appropriate forum. The defendant only carries the burden of proof in the context of *forum non conveniens*, pursuant to jurisdiction having been established as of right through service in the plaintiff's home jurisdiction.

So, Howie P's judgment is not crystal-clear, and *Multi-Links* did not clarify it any further. The problem is that neither Howie P nor Fabricius J distinguished clearly between *forum conveniens* and *forum non conveniens* – *The Spiliada* was not referred to in *Bid Industrial Holdings* at all and, while it was referred to in *Multi-Links*, the significance of this distinction, so masterfully set out by Lord Goff, was not appreciated. The result is that we have no clear direction as to what *forum*

[80] *The Spiliada* 476C–478E.
[81] *Bid Industrial Holdings* [55].
[82] Torremans, *Cheshire, North and Fawcett* (2017) 324.
[83] *Bid Industrial Holdings* [55].
[84] *Voth v Manildra Flour Mills Pty Ltd* (1990) 171 CLR 538.

(non) conveniens truly means for South African law – do we have *forum conveniens* and *forum non conveniens*, or perhaps a *sui generis* form of *forum conveniens*? It is clear that both *Bid Industrial Holdings* and *Multi-Links* were focused on the establishment of jurisdiction (*forum conveniens*) and not on a stay of proceedings (*forum non conveniens*).

VI. Conclusion

Bid Industrial Holdings is an important landmark in South African private international law. It brings together a wealth of different influences and traditions, only to be found in a hybrid or a mixed system of law. Arrest of a foreign defendant to found or confirm jurisdiction originated from Roman–Dutch law and it was declared unconstitutional in terms of several sections of the Bill of Rights in the Constitution of the Republic of South Africa, 1996. In an interesting twist, the lacuna occasioned by the abolition of jurisdictional arrest of a foreign defendant, was filled by an Anglo–common law doctrine, namely *forum (non) conveniens.*

In the words of Christopher Forsyth, this may 'lead the law of jurisdiction right away from its Roman–Dutch roots'.[85] Or, will those Roman–Dutch roots be incorporated into the new substitute practice in the sense of adequate connections or sufficient links to allow service on a foreign defendant present in the jurisdiction before triggering a plea of *forum non conveniens*? Only time will tell but, in the meantime, it is important to bear in mind Lord Goff's observation that *forum conveniens* and *forum non conveniens* have a common goal – that is, 'to identify the forum in which the case can be suitably tried for the interests of all the parties and for the ends of justice'.[86] Courts will do well to remember this when assuming jurisdiction in cross-border disputes.

[85] Forsyth (n 59) 203.
[86] *The Spiliada* 480G.

11

Re Flightlease and Common Law Judgment-Recognition in Ireland

MÁIRE NÍ SHÚILLEABHÁIN

I. Introduction

In *Re Flightlease*[1] the Irish Supreme Court grapples with the common law rules for recognition and enforcement of foreign judgments *in personam*, and considers whether Irish law should follow the Canadian courts in adopting a 'real and substantial connection' test for recognition.[2] Ultimately, the Irish Supreme Court follows the Irish High Court[3] in refusing to adopt the Canadian approach, and in adhering to the traditional common law grounds for recognition (presence in the country of origin at the time of service of proceedings, or submission to the court of origin). In this chapter, these common law principles requiring either presence, or submission, are variously referred to as the 'traditional common law criteria', the 'traditional common law grounds for recognition', the 'traditional common law rules', or in cognate terms.

The *Flightlease* case merits detailed discussion (and inclusion in this volume) for a variety of reasons: first and foremost, because judgment-recognition is one of the few areas where the common law retains a significant role in the Irish conflict of laws (jurisdiction and choice of law having been largely subsumed by EU Regulations). While the common law rules do not apply to judgments from other EU Member States,[4] they still govern the recognition and enforcement of

[1] *In the matter of Flightlease (Ireland) Limited (in voluntary liquidation) and in the matter of an application for directions pursuant to s 280 of the Companies Act 1963; Paul McCann and Stephen Akers, Joint Liquidators* [2012] IESC 12, [2012] 1 IR 722 ('*Flightlease*').

[2] *Morguard Investments Ltd v De Savoye* (1991) 76 DLR (4th) 256 ('*Morguard*'); *Beals v Saldanha* 2003 SCC 72, [2003] 3 SCR 416 ('*Beals*').

[3] [2006] IEHC 193.

[4] Intra-EU enforcement of judgments 'in civil and commercial matters' is governed by the Brussels I Recast Regulation (Regulation (EU) No 1215/2012 of the European Parliament and of the Council of 12 December 2012 on jurisdiction and the recognition and enforcement of judgments in civil and commercial matters [2012] OJ L351/1). The 2007 Lugano Convention [2007] OJ L339/3 provides a very similar regime for recognition and enforcement of judgments from Iceland, Norway and Switzerland.

judgments from the rest of the world – and this includes some of Ireland's main trading partners.[5] The *Flightlease* judgment is also significant insofar as it focuses on one of the most widely criticised aspects of the Irish conflict of laws[6] – and arguably one of the most unsatisfactory elements of the common law conflict of laws more generally.[7] The common law conflict of laws prides itself on its commitment to individual justice and the avoidance of inflexible generalised rules[8] – but these virtues are conspicuously absent in this area where the common law has cleaved to long-standing rules of little merit. The *Flightlease* judgment is also notable for its engagement with case law and literature from other common law countries and it raises important questions as to the role and limits of the common law in the development of the conflict of laws.

This chapter will begin with a discussion of the Irish common law prior to *Flightlease* (examining the logic and theoretical underpinnings of the earlier judicial support for the traditional common law position) before moving on to consider first the Irish High Court judgment and then the judgments of the Supreme Court in *Flightlease* itself. The chapter will conclude with an analysis of the ongoing significance of *Flightlease* and of the Irish courts' adherence to the traditional common law criteria, taking account of subsequent legal, economic and geopolitical developments.

II. Irish Law Prior to the *Flightlease* Litigation: *Rainford*

A. *Rainford* in Outline

Prior to *Flightlease*, it seems there was only one reported decision on the common law criteria for foreign judgment-recognition in Ireland.[9] This was the case of *Rainford v Newell-Roberts*,[10] an Irish High Court decision of 1961.

The *Rainford* case concerned a debt incurred and discharged by a medical partnership located near Birmingham, England and subsequent attempts to compel a contribution towards satisfaction of that debt by the defendant, a former partner

[5] See (n 98).

[6] See Newman, 'Enforcement of Foreign Judgments in Non-Convention Cases' (2000) 5 *Bar Review* 354; Kenny, '*Re Flightlease*: The "Real and Substantial Connection" Test for Recognition and Enforcement of Foreign Judgments Fails to Take Flight in Ireland' (2014) 63 *ICLQ* 197, 197–200.

[7] See Hill and Ní Shúilleabháin, *Clarkson & Hill's Conflict of Laws*, 5th edn (OUP, 2016) 179; *Morguard* (n 2) 268–70; *Beals* (n 2) [20]ff.

[8] Hartley, 'The European Union and the Systematic Dismantling of the Common Law of Conflict of Laws' (2005) 54 *ICLQ* 813, 813–15.

[9] *Dyer v Dolan* (10 June 1993, unreported) is also cited in *Flightlease*. *Rainford, Boston and Graham v Newell-Roberts* [1962] IR 95 ('*Rainford*') appears to have been the only previous reported judgment considering the conditions for recognition of ordinary civil and commercial judgments *in personam*.

[10] *Rainford* (ibid).

at the practice.[11] Having resigned from the practice, the defendant had moved to Ireland and refused to comply with the requests of the remaining partners (the plaintiffs) for voluntary payment. Having failed to settle the matter amicably, the plaintiffs commenced proceedings in the English High Court and obtained permission to serve the defendant in Ireland pursuant to Order 11 of the English Rules of Court. The defendant entered no appearance and in 1958 an English judgment was entered against him for £971. The plaintiffs then applied to the Irish High Court for recognition and enforcement of this English judgment in Ireland, but this was denied on the basis that the Irish common law recognition principles required either presence in England at the time of service, or submission to the English court, in order to justify recognition of the English judgment in Ireland, and neither of these requirements had been met.[12] The plaintiffs had argued that the defendant's British nationality should justify recognition of a British (English) judgment in Ireland, and that 'nationality' should be considered a sufficient connection to the court of origin for the purposes of judgment-recognition, but it was determined by the Irish High Court that 'nationality' was not a relevant connection in determining the recognition of foreign judgments under the common law as it applied in Ireland; only 'presence' or 'submission' would suffice.

B. Legal Reasoning in *Rainford*

There were various obiter dicta in the early English case law supporting the use of 'nationality' as a basis for judgment-recognition at common law, and these English cases were cited by Davitt P, the Irish High Court judge deciding *Rainford*.[13] However, having cited these cases, Davitt P preferred to focus his attention on the views of English text-writers, in particular, *Dicey* and *Cheshire*. While *Dicey* (in the early editions) had expressed support for the view that the judgment-debtor's nationality would be a sufficient connection to the court of origin as to warrant recognition of the judgment under the common law,[14] *Cheshire* did not agree[15] and Davitt P preferred 'with considerable diffidence' the views of *Cheshire*.[16]

[11] In fact the debt in question was owed by the partnership to the Revenue but there was no suggestion that this affected the recognition of the judgment at hand (which was in favour of the plaintiff partners and not the Revenue) although it is widely accepted that foreign revenue judgments are excluded from recognition under the common law rules: see Collins (ed), *Dicey, Morris & Collins, The Conflict of Laws*, 15th edn (Sweet & Maxwell, 2012) 673; *Clarkson & Hill* (2016) 180.

[12] *Rainford* (n 9) 100–01, 104.

[13] Davitt P cited a number of English authorities containing supportive dicta including *Schibsby v Westenholz* (1870) LR 6 QB 155, 161; *Emanuel v Symon* [1908] 1 KB 302, 309.

[14] *Rainford* (n 9) 98–99.

[15] ibid 100–01.

[16] ibid 104.

Cheshire (in the extracts quoted in *Rainford*) had argued: 'the criterion by which the competence of an English court is tested must also be adopted when the inquiry relates to the competence of a foreign court'[17] – in other words, that the English common law judgment-recognition criteria should mirror the domestic jurisdictional requirements in England (traditionally based on presence and submission).[18] Noting that English courts did not base their own jurisdiction on nationality, Davitt P agreed that it seemed 'strange that nationality should be accepted as a basis of jurisdiction in the case of a foreign judgment, when it is clearly not so in the case of the Courts in England itself'.[19] Applying *Cheshire*'s logic in the Irish context, where, as in England, domestic jurisdiction could not be derived from a defendant's nationality, Davitt P thus concluded that the defendant's British nationality did not justify recognition in Ireland of the judgment obtained by the plaintiffs in England.

Towards the end of his judgment, Davitt P acknowledged that the English jurisdictional rules which had been deployed here (Order 11 of the Rules of Court) were replicated in Irish law.[20] This had caused him to think perhaps that 'the principle of the comity of Courts' would oblige him to recognise the English judgment;[21] however, noting that there would be 'no reciprocity' and that English courts would not recognise foreign judgments founded on rules of court akin to the English Order 11,[22] he retreated to a position of non-recognition.[23]

C. Critical Analysis of the Reasoning in *Rainford*

Davitt P's closing remarks (outlined above) expose two flaws in his reasoning. If submission and presence are adopted as judgment-recognition criteria precisely because they were accepted as bases for domestic jurisdiction in Ireland, then an expansion in domestic jurisdiction (via Order 11 and its predecessors) should trigger a corresponding expansion in the recognition criteria. So 'reciprocity' in the sense of providing recognition for judgments emanating from foreign countries using the very same jurisdictional criteria[24] seemed to be intrinsic to Davitt's acceptance of presence and submission – but Davitt P abandons this logic when he considers the English Order 11 and its

[17] ibid 100.

[18] This rationalisation is not supported by the modern English jurisprudence on judgment-recognition: see *Rubin v Eurofinance SA and others* [2012] UKSC 46, [2013] 1 AC 236 [126].

[19] *Rainford* (n 9) 102–03.

[20] ibid 104.

[21] ibid.

[22] Citing *Phillips v Batho* [1913] 3 KB 25, 29–30. In modern English law, the equivalent rules are to be found in CPR r 6.36 and CPR PD 6B para 3.1.

[23] *Rainford* (n 9) 104–05.

[24] 'Reciprocity' in this sense is discussed (and rejected) by the UK Supreme Court in *Rubin* (n 18) [127]. This kind of 'reciprocity' is referred to approvingly by the Canadian Supreme Court in *Beals* (n 2) [29].

Irish equivalent. Indeed, in his deliberations on Order 11, Davitt P uses the word 'reciprocity' in a different sense, approximating to mutual recognition: and he declines to recognise an English judgment founded on the English Order 11 because an English court would not reciprocate in recognising an Irish judgment founded on the equivalent Irish rule of court.[25] This reliance on 'reciprocity' (in the sense of mutual recognition) is also unconvincing because it is not a prerequisite to reliance on presence and submission. Of course, one can readily appreciate the benefits of such mutuality (and the undesirability of unilateral recognition which is not reciprocated[26]), but this had never been demanded for common law recognition based on presence or submission and so it was unclear as to why it should present a barrier in the context of a foreign use of Order 11 (or its equivalent).

In summary, Davitt P in *Rainford* made Irish recognition of foreign judgments contingent on submission to or presence in the jurisdiction of the court of origin, and thus Irish law (prior to *Flightlease*) was aligned to the English common law as subsequently laid down in *Adams v Cape Industries*.[27] As has been seen, however, the rational basis for Davitt P's approval of these criteria within the Irish common law was not entirely clear and the reasoning was not wholly persuasive.

D. Theoretical Foundation for Recognition Policy

As discussed above, Davitt P toyed with various (conflicting) ideas of reciprocity in his judgment in *Rainford*. He also made reference to comity – although in the end he concluded that 'the principle of the comity of Courts is not the one to apply'.[28]

In his judgment, Davitt P also appeared to approve of the 'obligation theory'[29] which has often been described as the theoretical basis for the traditional common law treatment of foreign judgments[30] (although more recently its significance has been questioned by courts[31] and commentators[32]). According to the 'obligation theory', recognition is justified in circumstances of presence and submission because both connections create an obligation of obedience to the court of origin.[33]

[25] *Rainford* (n 9) 104.
[26] See the judgment of O'Donnell J in *Re Flightlease* (n 1) [86].
[27] *Adams and others v Cape Industries plc* [1990] 1 Ch 433, 515ff.
[28] *Rainford* (n 9) 104.
[29] *Rainford* (n 9) 100, 104. It has been suggested on this basis that *Rainford* adopts the 'obligation theory' into Irish law: see Newman, 'Enforcement of Foreign Judgments' (2000) 355; Biehler, McGrath and McGrath, *Delany and McGrath on Civil Procedure*, 4th edn (Round Hall, 2018) [26.10].
[30] See eg McClean and Ruiz Abou-Nigm, *Morris: The Conflict of Laws*, 9th edn (Sweet & Maxwell, 2016) 237; *Clarkson & Hill* (n 7) 169–70.
[31] *Rubin* (n 18) [9].
[32] See Torremans (ed), *Cheshire, North & Fawcett Private International Law*, 15th edn (OUP, 2017) 526; Newman (n 6) 356.
[33] *Cheshire, North & Fawcett* (ibid) 528.

This theory is, however, open to the criticism that it fails to explain why *other* connections do not create any 'obligation' and in the end this 'obligation theory' is more descriptive than expository.[34]

Davitt P did not attempt to reconcile these various theories of recognition and enforcement, and, as a consequence, his judgment is somewhat lacking in conviction. As will be explained later in this chapter, it is now arguable that as Contracting States to the European Convention on Human Rights (ECHR), both Ireland and the UK owe obligations to facilitate foreign-judgment recognition as a matter of human rights law, and in time, this might provide a more satisfactory conceptual framework for judgment-recognition than the ideas of comity, and reciprocity and obligation, which were under consideration in *Rainford*. Of course, at the time *Rainford* was being decided (in 1961), the ECHR and human rights law were in their infancy and one would not have expected Davitt P to conceive of foreign judgment-recognition in terms of human rights obligations.

E. *Rainford*: Sleepwalking into Unjust Judgment-Recognition Practices?

In *Rainford*, while the 'nationality' criterion was assessed (and rejected) on its merits (insofar as connections of nationality may be tenuous and long since abandoned),[35] 'presence' and 'submission' were endorsed within the Irish common law without any such evaluation of their appropriateness as common law recognition criteria. *Rainford* has since been described as a case which 'starkly illustrated' the 'gross shortcomings' of the Irish (and common law) criteria on judgment-recognition.[36] England was clearly the natural forum for the action in *Rainford* and yet the plaintiffs, who had secured a judgment in England, were denied recognition and enforcement in Ireland. There appeared to be no compelling reason for this injustice to the plaintiffs, who were now put to the trouble of commencing *de novo* in Ireland[37] (if indeed they were not statute-barred by this time).

In these circumstances, *Rainford* creates an impression of judicial passivity (and conceptual confusion) in the face of manifest injustice in the domain of judgment-recognition. There is a sense of uncritical affirmation of the pre-existing common law judgment-recognition criteria based on presence and submission, and a reluctance to consider whether an expansion in the grounds for common law judgment-recognition might be required for the avoidance of injustice.

[34] ibid 526; Rogerson, *Collier's Conflict of Laws*, 4th edn (CUP, 2013) 219; Ho, 'Policies Underlying the Enforcement of Foreign Commercial Judgments' (1997) 46 *ICLQ* 443, 443–44. But see also Briggs, 'Recognition of Foreign Judgments: a Matter of Obligation' (2013) 129 *LQR* 87.

[35] *Rainford* (n 9) 101.

[36] Newman (n 6) 356.

[37] ibid.

III. *Flightlease* in the Irish High Court

A. *Flightlease* in Outline

The *Flightlease* case arose in the context of the insolvency of two related companies, Flightlease, an Irish company in liquidation, and SwissAir, a Swiss company, also in liquidation. SwissAir had made payments to Flightlease which were alleged to have been unlawful under Swiss law, and SwissAir had commenced Swiss proceedings for recovery of this money. At the time of the commencement of the Swiss action, the liquidators of Flightlease were proposing to distribute the Flightlease assets as part of a wind-down agreement, and so, when they were notified of the Swiss proceedings, they sought guidance from the Irish High Court as to whether any resulting Swiss judgment would be entitled to recognition and enforcement in Ireland. The provision of guidance of this kind was permitted by section 280 of the Companies Act 1963, which allowed liquidators to seek determinations on any relevant question of law arising in the winding up. This section 280 application was of value to Flightlease insofar as it would establish whether Flightlease needed to defend the Swiss action (or whether in the alternative it could continue with the distribution of assets), and it was of value to SwissAir in signalling whether it was worthwhile continuing with the Swiss action.[38]

Flightlease was no longer present in Switzerland at the time of commencement of the Swiss proceedings,[39] nor had it (to date) submitted to the jurisdiction of the Swiss court; and therefore it was argued by the Flightlease liquidators, in reliance on the traditional common law recognition criteria, that the Swiss judgment would not be entitled to recognition and enforcement in Ireland.[40] The SwissAir liquidators contended, however, that the Irish courts should apply the Canadian 'real and substantial connection test' and it was clear on the facts that there was a connection of this kind to Switzerland (at the time of the relevant transaction, Flightlease had a fixed place of business in Switzerland where a significant number of the company's commercial decisions were made by Swiss board members).[41]

Flightlease had also argued that the Swiss judgment as a judgment in bankruptcy would not be entitled to be recognised at common law as a judgment *in personam*, but this contention was rejected by the High Court and it was held that any determination concerning the entitlements or liabilities of the insolvent person or entity are properly characterised as judgments *in personam*.[42]

[38] *Flightlease* (HC) (n 3) [1.4]–[1.5].

[39] ibid [4.5] defining presence in accordance with *Okura & Co Ltd v Forsbacka Jernverks AB* [1914] 1 KB 715 and *Adams v Cape Industries* (n 27).

[40] While Swiss judgments are ordinarily entitled to recognition under the Lugano Convention (see n 4), matters of insolvency are excluded from the scope of that Convention (Art 1(2)(b)).

[41] *Flightlease* (HC) (n 3) [2.4], [4.3].

[42] ibid [3.3].

B. The Irish High Court in *Flightlease*: Analysis of Common Law Judgment-Recognition Policy

On the principal question, as to the appropriate recognition criteria to be applied, Clarke J, giving judgment for the Irish High Court, started by citing *Rainford*, and noted its support for recognition based on presence or submission, a position which Clarke J subsequently referred to as 'Dicey Rule 36'.[43] He went on to describe the Canadian Supreme Court's rejection of the traditional common law criteria (in *Morguard v de Savoye*[44] and *Beals v Saldanha*[45]) and quoted at length from *Morguard* as to the reasons for moving to a 'real and substantial connection test'.[46] Clarke J thus acknowledged the Canadian courts' emphasis of comity and the need 'to facilitate the flow of wealth, skills and people across state lines in a fair and orderly manner' in 'our highly complex and interrelated world' and the interest in promoting 'suitable conditions of interstate and international commerce' and 'security of transactions'.[47] He also referred to the Canadian criticisms of the traditional common law approach: citing La Forest J in *Morguard* as to the parochialism and anachronism of the common law and the inappropriateness in the modern world of rules tailored for the protection of English defendants in the nineteenth century (when travel and communication were very difficult and there was an orthodoxy of suspicion of foreign legal orders).[48] However, having quoted from the *Morguard* judgment, Clarke J did not engage further with the reasoning of the Canadian courts; instead, he immediately shifted his focus to the *negative* repercussions of the Canadian approach and he concluded that the adoption of the Canadian test 'would have the potential to do more harm than good'.[49]

In this context, Clarke J was concerned, in particular, with the transitional effect of a widening of the common law recognition criteria and the impact on those who had been advised to ignore an overseas action and had been assured (in reliance on the narrowness of the traditional common law rules) that the overseas judgment would not be entitled to recognition and enforcement in Ireland.[50] This is a reasonable concern – and the Canadian jurisprudence provides real-life

[43] ibid [5.1]. Clarke J was referring to Collins (ed), *Dicey, Morris & Collins, The Conflict of Laws*, 14th edn (Sweet & Maxwell, 2006) 588ff and its summation of the traditional common law criteria based on presence and submission.

[44] *Morguard* (n 2).

[45] *Beals* (n 2).

[46] *Flightlease* (HC) (n 3) [5.3]–[5.6].

[47] ibid [5.5] referring to *Morguard* (n 2) 269–70. (La Forest J in *Morguard* was, in turn, drawing on other case law and on academic literature: Von Mehren and Trautman, 'Recognition of Foreign Adjudications: a Survey and a Suggested Approach' (1968) 81 *Harvard Law Review* 1601; Yntema, 'The Objectives of Private International Law' (1957) 35 *Canadian Bar Review* 721).

[48] *Flightlease* (HC) (n 3) [5.5] referring to *Morguard* (n 2) 269–70.

[49] ibid [5.16].

[50] ibid [5.12] ff.

examples of defendants who had so acted, only to find themselves bound by a foreign judgment having lost the opportunity to raise a defence.[51] Nonetheless it is important to keep the scale of this problem in perspective and to recognise that the Irish High Court could have taken steps to mitigate such concerns. As O'Donnell J in the Irish Supreme Court in *Flightlease* observed, the number of defendants affected by transitional retrospectivity is likely to be very low.[52] In reality, few businesses can afford to rely on a guarantee of Irish non-recognition: for so long as they have business interests and assets in other states, Irish law cannot guarantee a shelter from the foreign judgment.[53] Also, while it is very unusual for judges to revise the common law on a prospective basis only, this can be done even in the domain of private law[54] and in view of the implications for plaintiffs (such as in *Rainford*), it is arguable that the Irish courts should have given serious consideration to 'prospective overruling' in *Flightlease*. In the alternative, a flexible 'natural justice' defence[55] could also provide some protection for 'transitional' defendants who acted on the faith of the existing law. Such transitional concerns would, in any event, peter out over time and did not arise at all in the case at hand because Flightlease was in the fortunate position of being able to seek *advance* reassurance as to the status of the Swiss judgment.

In refusing to follow the Canadian example, Clarke J also relied on the lack of consensus in favour of the Canadian approach in the common law world and the absence of a 'broad acceptance in the common law world of a new direction'.[56] Kenny has criticised this reasoning, pointing to the fact that the Canadian approach had not yet been considered in other common law courts.[57] For Kenny, there is no consensus either for or against a development in such circumstances, and no significance should be attached to the lack of judicial deliberation elsewhere.[58] Also, as Kenny pointed out, if all common law courts adopted this attitude, 'a consensus on change could never develop, precisely because a consensus had not previously developed'.[59] Clarke J also referred to the existence of academic commentary cautioning against the Canadian approach but did not provide further detail as to the nature of such commentary (or as to the identity of the relevant commentators).[60]

[51] See eg *Beals* (n 2); see also *Moses v Shore Boat Builders* 1993 CanLII 2276 (BC CA), (1993) 106 DLR (4th) 654 ('*Moses*').

[52] *Flightlease* (SC) (n 1) [79].

[53] ibid.

[54] See *Royal Bank of Scotland v Etridge (No 2)* [2001] UKHL 44, [2002] 2 AC 773; *In Re Spectrum Plus Ltd (in liquidation)* [2005] UKHL 41, [2005] 2 AC 680; *Murphy v Att Gen* [1982] IR 241; also Arden, 'Prospective Overruling' (2004) 120 *LQR* 7; Sheehan and Arvind, 'Prospective Overruling and the Fixed-Floating Charge Debate' (2006) 122 *LQR* 20.

[55] See *Beals* (n 2) [258]–[264] (LeBel J).

[56] *Flightlease* (HC) (n 3) [5.9], [5.16].

[57] Kenny, '*Re Flightlease*' (2014) 207.

[58] ibid.

[59] ibid.

[60] *Flightlease* (HC) (n 3) [5.9].

C. The Irish High Court in *Flightlease* and Theories of Judgment-Recognition

While Clarke J had referred to the 'comity' theory in quoting from *Morguard*, he did not expand on the theoretical basis for judgment-recognition policy in Ireland and did not rely on the 'obligation theory' in justification of Dicey Rule 36. Major J in *Beals* had referred approvingly to the idea of jurisdictional reciprocity – in the sense of recognising judgments from legal orders with the same jurisdictional rules and viewing judgment-recognition as a mirror image of domestic jurisdiction[61] – but Clarke J did not make express reference to this aspect of the Canadian jurisprudence.

D. Concluding Remarks on the Irish High Court Judgment in *Flightlease*

Clarke J did not provide wholly convincing justifications for his refusal to depart from Dicey Rule 36 and did not consider the theoretical underpinnings of the traditional common law approach, as applied in Ireland. The focus of the Irish High Court judgment was on the disadvantages of the Canadian approach, but there was no direct discussion of the countervailing disadvantages of Rule 36 (beyond that contained in the extract from *Morguard*) and, to that extent, the reasoning of the court seems somewhat lopsided. It is regrettable that Clarke J did not engage further with the reasoning in *Morguard* and *Beals* – and did not dwell on the impact on plaintiffs of Dicey Rule 36.

IV. *Flightlease* in the Irish Supreme Court

A. The Majority Judgment in the Supreme Court (Finnegan J)

Finnegan J gave the majority judgment in the Irish Supreme Court, upholding the decision of Clarke J, and deciding, for similar reasons, that Irish law should continue to apply the traditional recognition criteria based on presence and submission only. He agreed with Clarke J that the Swiss judgment would be a judgment *in personam* (notwithstanding its associations with bankruptcy proceedings)[62] and he shared Clarke J's concerns with respect to transitional retrospectivity and the absence of a common consensus in the common law world in favour of the

[61] See *Beals* (n 2) [29].
[62] *Flightlease* (SC) (n 1) [58]–[67].

Canadian approach.[63] Like Clarke J, Finnegan J exhibited a strong commitment to Dicey's account of the common law,[64] and a disinclination to engage with the theories of judgment-recognition. Indeed, while Finnegan J provided a lengthy account of the proceedings and of the parties' submissions, he was notably brief in stating his reasons for declining to follow the Canadian lead.[65]

Finnegan J goes beyond the reasoning of Clarke J in two important respects. First, he argues that this is an area best handled by legislation, and ideally an international convention.[66] In Finnegan J's view, piecemeal development through case law is suboptimal given the particular need for legal certainty in this domain.[67] He points out that even many years on, the Canadian courts are still working through the implications of the new test – and considering the creation of new defences to recognition.[68] Having stated a preference for international and legislative solutions, Finnegan J goes further and states his opinion that it would 'exceed the judicial function to re-state the common law' as suggested by SwissAir.[69] This very strong statement of judicial reticence is criticised by Kenny, who points out that there was no clear reason why the adoption of the Canadian reform would constitute an impermissible development of the common law.[70] The pre-existing law was judge-made and there would be no interference with any legislation.[71] If the legislature was dissatisfied with the adoption of a 'real and substantial connection' test, it could legislate for its removal. Further, as Kenny points out, this 'unnecessarily narrow view of the judicial function' will inevitably lead to the ossification of pre-existing common law rules, irrespective of their intrinsic merits.[72]

B. The Concurring Judgment of O'Donnell J

O'Donnell J's concurring judgment is more nuanced and wide-ranging. Unlike his judicial brethren, O'Donnell J directs his attention to the logic and (de) merits of the pre-existing common law rules and their impact on plaintiffs. He is critical of the narrowness of those traditional rules, and emphasises their tendency to compel a second action in another (less appropriate) forum, leading to a

[63] ibid [68].

[64] ibid.

[65] ibid [68]–[70].

[66] *Flightlease* (SC) (n 1) [69]. Finnegan J does not explicitly refer to the Hague Conference, but it is likely that he had the Hague Judgments Project (which was then ongoing) in mind. This chapter later contains a discussion of the 2019 Hague Judgments Convention which (eventually) emerged from this project.

[67] ibid.

[68] ibid.

[69] ibid [69]–[70].

[70] Kenny (n 6) 208. But see the views of Professor Briggs, cited by O'Donnell J in *Flightlease* (SC) (n 1) [86]–[87], arguing, as a matter of English law, that the adoption of the Canadian approach 'would require legislation' (Briggs, *Conflict of Laws*, 2nd edn (OUP, 2008) 138). These views are echoed in Briggs, *Conflict of Laws*, 4th edn (OUP, 2019) 140. See also *Rubin* (n 18) [129].

[71] Kenny (n 6) 208.

[72] ibid.

duplication of proceedings and the unnecessary inconveniencing of plaintiffs who acted entirely reasonably in litigating in the first (foreign) forum.[73] He notes that on the facts here, the adherence to Dicey Rule 36 may force SwissAir to pursue their claim in Ireland, resulting in an Irish court hearing a case governed by Swiss law, and based on the evidence of Swiss-resident witnesses, in circumstances where the Swiss courts would likely be much better placed to hear the case.[74] O'Donnell J also points to the risk of inconsistent decisions in the event of such duplication (and the inevitable confusion which follows)[75] and to the wasting of the parties' money[76] and of scarce court time and resources.[77]

However, citing academic commentators including Blom and Edinger, Briggs and Castel,[78] O'Donnell J also acknowledges the need for certainty and predictability in framing the law on judgment-recognition, and he observes that while the traditional common law rules have very little inherent merit, they are at least predictable.[79] He recognises that while in this case, the would be judgment-debtor was able to seek advance confirmation of (non)-recognition (pursuant to section 280 of the Companies Act 1963), most defendants will not have that luxury, and will have to make a decision at the time of service of the foreign proceedings as to whether to defend or not.[80] Where recognition and enforcement are based on presence and submission, this task is relatively straightforward; it is infinitely more difficult if recognition is based on a 'real and substantial connection', a much more open-textured criterion.[81] At such an early stage in the action, the party forced to make such a choice may have 'only partial information and little time'.[82]

In the end, O'Donnell J concurs with the rest of the Irish Supreme Court, supporting the continued application of the traditional common law rules and refusing to incorporate the Canadian test into Irish law. However, he arrives at this conclusion 'with no particular enthusiasm'[83] and agrees with the Canadian courts that wider recognition criteria are necessary to support global trade.[84] He thinks the Canadian approach 'offers substantially more in terms of inherent merit' but extracts a 'much heavier price in terms of uncertainty and unpredictability'[85] and ultimately these latter considerations are prioritised by O'Donnell J.

[73] *Flightlease* (SC) (n 1) [76]–[77], [81].
[74] ibid [76], [81].
[75] ibid [76].
[76] ibid [81].
[77] ibid [78].
[78] ibid [84]–[89] citing (amongst others) Blom and Edinger, 'The Chimera of the Real and Substantial Connection Test' (2005) 38 *University of British Columbia Law Review* 373; Briggs, 'Crossing the River by Feeling the Stones: Rethinking the Law on Foreign Judgments' (2004) 8 *Singapore Year Book of International Law* 1; JG Castel, 'The Uncertainty Factor in Canadian Private International Law' (2007) 17 *McGill Law Journal* 555.
[79] *Flightlease* (SC) (n 1) [74], [77], [83].
[80] ibid [80]–[85].
[81] ibid [88]–[90].
[82] ibid [85].
[83] ibid [74].
[84] ibid [77]–[78].
[85] ibid [83].

C. An Alternative Approach?

The Irish Supreme Court in *Flightlease* was presented with a binary choice between the very conservative common law criteria and the 'radical'[86] test adopted in Canada, but one wonders whether it might have been possible to take some steps towards widening the judgment-recognition criteria without going as far as the Canadian Supreme Court did, and without sacrificing legal certainty to the same extent. While *Beals* and *Morguard* allow for recognition on the basis of a 'real and substantial connection' (and therefore recognition even if there are other fora with an equivalent connection), a 'most connected forum' test would allow for recognition and enforcement in those (relatively clear-cut[87]) cases where really there is only one obvious forum for the dispute and where the case was litigated there.[88] The common law's denial of recognition is most egregious in these kinds of cases[89] (which would include *Rainford* and *Morguard*) and so a revised rule in those terms might address the most significant injustices wrought by the traditional common law rules (without imposing such a significant burden of uncertainty).

V. Subsequent Developments Post-*Flightlease*

At the time of the *Flightlease* litigation, and thereafter, there was a widely held view (both amongst judges and commentators) that an international convention was the ideal solution to problems with judgment-recognition but extremely unlikely to emerge in practice.[90] The Hague Judgments Project had commenced in 1992[91] and, after 20 years, there was still no sign of a new Convention. Nonetheless, following renewed efforts, a Working Group produced a proposed draft Convention in 2015,[92] culminating in agreement on a new Hague Judgments Convention in 2019. The Convention is not yet in operation, but the EU has decided in favour of accession,[93] and the literature expresses optimism as to the

[86] ibid [87]; O'Donnell J citing Briggs *Conflict of Laws* (2008) 138.

[87] See *Moses* (n 51) [11] distinguishing the case at hand (where there were 'real and substantial connections' to two fora) from 'easy' cases like *Morguard* where the case was brought in 'the only reasonable place for the action'. See also Blom and Edinger, 'Chimera' (2005) 376–77 arguing that a test of comparative connectedness is always easier to apply than a test of sufficient connectedness.

[88] See *Moses* (n 51) [11] referring to the 'territory with the most significant contacts'.

[89] *Clarkson & Hill* (n 7) 179.

[90] *Flightlease* (SC) (n 1) [69], [77], [86]–[90], citing Briggs and Rees, *Civil Jurisdiction and Judgments*, 5th edn (Informa, 2009) [7.56]; Kenny (n 6) 209, 211.

[91] Garcimartín and Saumier, 'Explanatory Report on the Convention of 2 July 2019 on the Recognition and Enforcement of Foreign Judgments in Civil or Commercial Matters' (22nd Session, The Hague, 2020) 44.

[92] ibid 45.

[93] See EU Commission, 'Proposal for a Council Decision on the accession by the European Union to the Convention on the Recognition and Enforcement of Foreign Judgments in Civil or Commercial Matters' COM (2021) 388 final. The Council of the EU adopted a decision in favour of accession on 12 July 2022: see www.consilium.europa.eu/en/press/press-releases/2022/07/12/convention-on-the-recognition-of-judgements-council-adopts-decision-on-eu-accession.

prospect of a new dawn of widescale international cooperation on judgment-recognition.[94] The Preamble to the Convention indicates that its primary objective is to 'promote effective access to justice' and these sentiments are echoed in the EU Commission's assessment of the Convention from the perspective of the protection of fundamental rights.[95]

Given the EU's imminent accession, it is likely that, in the near future, Irish recognition of judgments from non-EU countries will depend – to some extent at least – on the new, much wider, criteria laid down in the 2019 Convention. The 2019 Convention allows (in Article 15) for the continuation of existing domestic recognition criteria, but requires these to be supplemented by the Convention criteria laid down in Article 5. Article 5 requires recognition of judgments obtained in the country of the defendant's habitual residence or principal place of business; and for recognition of certain tort judgments obtained in the country where the initiating event occurred; and for recognition and enforcement of contract judgments obtained in the place of performance of the obligation in question (amongst others). These criteria fill a lot of the gaps left by the common law – and they achieve many of the positive effects of the 'real and substantial connection' test[96] without creating so much uncertainty. Under Article 5 of the 2019 Convention, a series of specific concrete criteria are deployed instead of an indeterminate catch-all standard (as per the Canadian common law). Aside from the benefits for incoming judgments, the 2019 Convention will also enhance the recognition of Irish judgments overseas. Indeed, it is this aspect of the Convention that was emphasised by the EU Commission in recommending accession: the EU focus is not so much on the improved treatment of incoming judgments, as was the concern in *Morguard* and *Beals*, but primarily on enhanced worldwide recognition for judgments pronounced in EU Member States.[97]

From an Irish perspective, the 2019 Convention will be particularly valuable if it is ratified by the US and the UK, two of Ireland's most significant trading partners.[98]

[94] Stewart, 'The Hague Conference Adopts a New Convention on the Recognition and Enforcement of Foreign Judgments in Civil or Commercial Matters' (2019) 113 *The American Journal of International Law* 772, 774, 781–82; Nielsen, 'The Hague 2019 Judgments Convention – From Failure to Success?' (2020) 16 *Journal of Private International Law* 205, 246.

[95] EU Commission (n 93) 7.

[96] See Garcimartín and Saumier, 'Explanatory Report' (2020) 48: many of the stated aims of the 2019 Convention are very closely aligned to the objectives of the 'real and substantial connection' test as outlined in *Morguard* and in O'Donnell J's concurring judgment in *Flightlease*; eg promotion of global trade, avoidance of duplication, and reduction in cost of cross-border litigation.

[97] EU Commission (n 93) 1, 4, 6. But see also Impact Assessment SWD (2021) 192 final where there is some focus on the improvement of judgment-recognition for incoming judgments: interestingly Ireland is ranked towards the liberal end of the spectrum for ease of recognition for incoming non-EU judgments and it seems the majority of EU Member States have even more restrictive national judgment-recognition rules as things currently stand – see Impact Assessment, 26.

[98] See eg the Central Statistics Office report on 'Ireland's Trade in Goods 2020' indicating that the US is Ireland's biggest export market, followed by Belgium, then Germany, then the UK – while the UK and then the US are the countries from which Ireland imports most: see further www.cso.ie/en/releasesandpublications/ep/p-ti/irelandstradeingoods2020/toptradingpartners.

Ireland had previously enjoyed an arrangement of mutual recognition of judgments with the UK (whilst it was still an EU Member State) – and in the absence of the continuation of this arrangement through the 2007 Lugano Convention (which seems, at present, very unlikely[99]), the 2019 Hague Convention will provide a reasonably satisfactory alternative (and certainly a vast improvement on the traditional common law rules which would lead to frequent non-recognition of judgments as between the two countries).[100] There is significant support for ratification of the 2019 Convention within the UK – and it is seen as a useful mechanism for bridging some of the regulatory gaps left by Brexit.[101]

Since the US is already generous in its recognition of foreign judgments,[102] ratification of the 2019 Convention will work to its advantage: ensuring a more balanced mutuality and improving overseas recognition for judgments pronounced in US courts. As a consequence, Stewart anticipates 'support – perhaps even enthusiasm – from the US business and legal communities';[103] although he also warns of potential difficulty with ratification and consistent application in the absence of coordination between federal and state authorities.[104] The US has already signed the 2019 Convention, but has not yet ratified it.[105]

VI. Final Remarks

The Irish case law has been consistent in supporting common law judgment-recognition based on presence and submission (if not on the underlying theory) and in *Flightlease*, the Irish Supreme Court refused to sanction recognition based on a 'real and substantial connection'. Since *Rainford* (and with the notable exception of O'Donnell J in *Flightlease*) there has been a tendency to accept the traditional common law recognition rules without examining their merits.[106] As Kenny argues, this reflects a perception of the existing common law as 'a background reality' and not as judge-made law which is being consciously retained

[99] See EU Commission, 'Communication from the Commission to the European Parliament and the Council: Assessment on the Application of the United Kingdom of Great Britain and Northern Ireland to accede to the 2007 Lugano Convention' COM (2021) 222 final.

[100] The 2005 Hague Choice of Court Convention applies as between Ireland and the UK allowing for recognition of judgments granted by a court nominated in an exclusive jurisdiction agreement – but all remaining judgments are at present dependent on common law recognition.

[101] Beaumont, 'Some Reflections on the Way Ahead for UK Private International Law After Brexit' (2021) 17 *Journal of Private International Law* 1, 4–5; Dickinson, 'Walking Solo – A New Path for the Conflict of Laws in England' (19 January 2021), available at www.law.ox.ac.uk/business-law-blog/blog/2021/01/walking-solo-new-path-conflict-laws-england.

[102] J Walker, 'The Great Canadian Comity Experiment Continues' (2004) 120 *LQR* 365, 365–66.

[103] Stewart, 'The Hague Conference' (2019) 782.

[104] ibid 782–83.

[105] See the Status Table at www.hcch.net/en/instruments/conventions/status-table/?cid=137.

[106] See (in a similar vein) Le Forest J in *Morguard* (n 2) 268 expressing criticism of the 'unthinking' adoption of the common law rules for inter-provincial recognition and enforcement in Canada.

and supported.[107] *Flightlease* and *Rainford* also reveal a particular attachment to English textbooks in this area, particularly *Dicey*. The views of text-writers are not normally accorded such prominence[108] and *Flightlease* and *Rainford* raise questions as to the desirability of such deference to the views of a single commentator. *Dicey*'s Rules are treated almost as though they have the force of law,[109] and as O'Donnell J suggests, it is possible that *Dicey*'s code format has 'contributed to a creeping fossilisation of the law and a loss of some of the traditional flexibility of the common law'.[110] Swan is also critical of this method of presentation in *Dicey* and argues that it inhibits the 'proper discussion of principle'.[111] Such reliance on *Dicey* is perhaps particularly problematic in a context where legal certainty is prioritised and there is consequently a reluctance to engage in any substantial reform of the common law. This prioritisation of legal certainty – which is also relevant to other aspects of the common law conflict of laws – can result in an uncritical acceptance of the views articulated in *Dicey* and consequently a distortion of the common law methodology.[112]

In hindsight, given the subsequent adoption of the 2019 Hague Convention, the Irish Supreme Court's conservatism in *Flightlease* is more easily justified, and, in retrospect, it seems the Supreme Court may have been right to avoid a 'fundamental reorientation of the law'.[113] Nonetheless, it is possible that the 2019 Convention will be slow to attract ratifications and that the Irish common law criteria will retain a significant role, for many years to come, in determining the recognition and enforcement of judgments from countries outside the EU.[114] In that event, the extremely narrow common law criteria may come under increasing pressure. As Newman points out, Ireland presents itself as an open economy (and as a destination for foreign direct investment), and, in that context, a widening of judgment-recognition criteria may be necessary to promote confidence in commercial arrangements.[115] From this perspective, the narrow common law criteria may be perceived negatively as a form of protectionism and as a mechanism for the evasion of obligations assumed overseas by Irish residents and Irish businesses.[116] Also, while the common law criteria are generally criticised for

[107] Kenny (n 6) 209.

[108] See Byrne et al, *Byrne and McCutcheon on the Irish Legal System*, 7th edn (Bloomsbury Professional, 2020) [12.95].

[109] See ibid [12.95] emphasising that textbooks, unlike case law and legislation, lack 'the force of law'.

[110] *Flightlease* (SC) (n 1) [77].

[111] Swan, 'How Should a Court Approach the Recognition or Enforcement of a Foreign Judgment?' (2007) 29 *Dublin University Law Journal* 443, 445.

[112] See the judgment of Clarke J at [4.1] referring to a generalised reliance on *Dicey* 'as representing the common law in this jurisdiction': *Flightlease* (HC) (n 3).

[113] *Flightlease* (SC) (n 1) [87]–[88], O'Donnell J referring to the words of Briggs (2008) (n 70) 138.

[114] eg if the 'federalism considerations' hamper US ratification of the 2019 Convention, in the same way as they frustrated ratification of the 2005 Hague Choice of Court Convention: Stewart (n 94) 783.

[115] Newman (n 6) 354, 358.

[116] ibid 354. Conversely, however, it might be argued (as it was in relation to Canada) that the widening of recognition criteria exposes local assets to opportunistic foreign lawsuits, and, to that extent, discourages inward trade and investment: see Walker, *Canadian Comity* (2004) 366, 369; Atrill, 'The Enforcement of Foreign Judgments in Canada' (2004) 63 *CLJ* 574, 575–76.

their restrictiveness, in truth they are at once too narrow and too wide insofar as they allow for recognition and enforcement based on transient presence.[117] It is therefore equally possible that an Irish resident, who has been subjected to tag jurisdiction abroad, may challenge the rationality of Dicey Rule 36 from that perspective.[118]

Even if the 2019 Convention is a resounding success, and the *Flightlease* ruling recedes into insignificance in the domain of judgment-recognition, the assumptions underpinning *Flightlease* may yet prove problematic in other domains of the common law conflict of laws. Finnegan J in *Flightlease* appeared to take the view that international agreements were generally preferable to common law solutions right across the conflict of laws.[119] And indeed, it was noteworthy that the same sense of judicial reticence and deference to legislative solutions re-emerged in 2015 in *H v H*[120] when the Irish Supreme Court was asked to widen the common law criteria for foreign divorce recognition and declined to do so. In this domain, no legislative solution has been forthcoming, leaving spouses dependent on common law rules which were acknowledged to be 'potentially very unsatisfactory'.[121]

The success of the 2019 Hague Convention will determine the future relevance of the Irish common law rules on judgment-recognition. If the common law rules retain practical importance, it is hoped that the Irish courts will be able to move beyond the passivity that was in evidence in *Flightlease* and to recapture some of the reforming zeal that was previously brought to bear on the common law conflict of laws.[122] If the 2019 Convention is applicable to some of Ireland's main trading partners but not to others, the Irish courts might even consider drawing on the Hague Convention criteria as an inspiration for reform of the common law. This kind of 'cross-fertilisation' has informed the development of the common law in other domains[123] and might allow, for example, for common law recognition based on the locus of the tort (for tort judgments) or the place of contractual performance (for contract judgments).[124] Incremental – and concrete – extensions of that kind would be preferable to an all-encompassing

[117] Kenny (n 6) 200.

[118] See *Clarkson & Hill* (n 7) 178–79.

[119] *Flightlease* (SC) (n 1) [69].

[120] *H v H* [2015] IESC 7, [2015] 1 ILRM 453.

[121] Per Clarke J at [3.9]. See further Ní Shúilleabháin, 'Foreign Divorce Recognition and Residence: A Critical Analysis of H v H' (2017) 57 *Irish Jurist* 162.

[122] See eg *W v W* [1993] 2 IR 476 (a divorce recognition case).

[123] See eg *Showlag v Mansour* [1995] 1 AC 431; also Fawcett, 'Cross-Fertilization in Private International Law' (2000) 53 *Current Legal Problems* 303.

[124] Both Dickinson, 'Walking Solo' (2021) and Beaumont, 'Some Reflections' (2021) highlight the particular value of these Hague recognition criteria (laid down in Art 5(1)(g) and (j)), although they do not advocate for their incorporation into the common law, as the author does. Dickinson argues for legislative reform to allow for recognition on these grounds. However, if that is a realistic prospect in the UK, where there is some history of statutory intervention into the common law conflict of laws

but highly uncertain 'real and substantial connection' test, and allow for a better balancing of party interests.[125] Common law alignment with the Hague recognition grounds could bring welcome simplicity and conceptual consistency to the conflict of laws – whilst also allowing the common law to benefit from the interpretative jurisprudence on the 2019 Hague Convention.

Finally, it is suggested that the 2019 Hague Judgments Convention may also provide inspiration for a new conceptualisation of common law judgment-recognition, allowing Irish courts to move beyond the theoretical opacity of *Flightlease* (and the conceptual muddle of *Rainford*). As noted above, the 2019 Convention conceives of recognition and enforcement of foreign judgments as a question of 'access to justice'. In recommending accession to the 2019 Convention, the EU Commission also referred to the Convention's enhancement of 'the right to property in the EU'.[126] This rights-based rhetoric reflects the idea – accepted by the European Court of Human Rights for many years – that judgment-debts are possessions deserving of protection under the ECHR right of property (Article 1 of Protocol 1)[127] and that non-enforcement of a judgment implicates Article 6 ECHR, the fair trial right.[128] The Strasbourg court has yet to develop these interpretations in the cross-border context, and to date there has been no clear confirmation that the ECHR creates positive obligations with respect to the recognition of foreign judgments.[129] Nonetheless the 2019 Hague Convention appears to give an international imprimatur to a rights-based theory of judgment-recognition and the common law may follow suit. Indeed, the Constitutional Court of South Africa has referred to a constitutional right of access to the courts in justification of an expansion in its common law principles on foreign judgment-recognition.[130] Invoking section 34 of the South African Constitution, which guarantees a right to a fair hearing, the Court opined that execution of court orders is a crucial component of access to justice, and that this includes foreign court orders.[131] Thus, even within the common law world, recent authority provides some support for a rights-based conceptualisation of foreign judgment-recognition.

(eg in the Private International Law (Miscellaneous Provisions) Act 1995), it is a far less likely prospect in Ireland, where there is no such history of homegrown statutory activism in this area).

[125] The 'most connected forum' test, outlined above (see text to n 88), might also offer a workable solution.

[126] EU Commission (n 93) 7.

[127] See eg *Agrokompleks v Ukraine* App No 23465/93 (ECHR, 6 October 2011) [166]; Fawcett, Ní Shúilleabháin and Shah, *Human Rights and Private International Law* (OUP, 2016) 819–20.

[128] Fawcett, Ní Shúilleabháin and Shah (ibid) 171–85, 396–98, 402–03.

[129] ibid 402–03, 820.

[130] *Government of Republic of Zimbabwe v Fick* [2013] ZACC 22, 2013 (5) SA 235 (CC) [60]–[64].

[131] ibid.

12

Vizcaya Partners Limited v Picard

Implications for the Recognition and Enforcement of Foreign Judgments at Common Law and Beyond

ANTHONY KENNEDY AND ANDREW MORAN

I. Introduction

For many reasons, exploring the judgment of the Privy Council in *Vizcaya Partners Limited v Picard*[1] is a perfect way to bring this collection to a close. It meets each criterion which may be used to determine a case of significance within the study of the common law jurisprudence of the conflict of laws. Factually, the case dealt with the fallout from an international fraud of epic proportions.[2] Statistically, the judgment amounted to something of an oddity, handed down, as it was, despite the fact that the parties had settled by the time the Privy Council gave its advice.[3] Legally, and concerning as it did primarily the content and scope of the rule that a foreign default judgment is enforceable against a judgment debtor who has agreed to submit to the jurisdiction of the foreign court, *Vizcaya* settled a long-running controversy: whether an agreement to submit must be express or could be implied or inferred.[4] There can be no doubt that *Vizcaya* well merits its place in a collection such as this.

Yet, it is the fact that it weaves together several of the strands of thought already laid out by other contributors to this volume which justifies its place at the end of this collection. After all, the judgment of the Privy Council clearly illustrates

[1] [2016] UKPC 5, [2016] 3 All ER 181 ('*Vizcaya*').

[2] As Lord Collins, giving judgment on behalf of the Privy Council, made clear in *Vizcaya* [1], the origin of the case was the fraudulent Ponzi scheme operated by Bernard Madoff, through his New York company Bernard L Madoff Investment Securities LLC.

[3] *Vizcaya* [9]. The Privy Council delivered its advice after the settlement was approved by the New York Bankruptcy Court and delivered it, notwithstanding the parties' settlement, because it raised 'issues which are not only of general importance, but which are of international importance in other common law countries'.

[4] ibid [3]–[4].

the common law's[5] ability to evolve over time and to shape conclusions to ensure that they accord with principle. At the same time, one may wonder as to the size of the territory over which the common law will continue to exert an influence in the future. That question is especially important in the light of the range of international instruments and statutory interventions, both present and forthcoming, which might seek to narrow or even to wipe out entirely the common law's domain.

To explain properly the significance of the judgment in *Vizcaya*, this chapter proceeds as follows. First, it considers the law as it stood prior to *Vizcaya* before moving on to explore the facts of, and judgments in, the case itself. Next, it analyses the reasoning of, and the conclusions reached in, *Vizcaya* to ascertain exactly how and why the case is significant for the future development of the common law governing the recognition and enforcement of foreign judgments. An overall conclusion then follows.

II. The Common Law Prior to *Vizcaya*

A. An Overview

Almost three and a half years before *Vizcaya*, the United Kingdom Supreme Court took the opportunity, in *Rubin v Eurofinance SA*,[6] to clarify the common law on the recognition and enforcement of foreign judgments. In particular, the Supreme Court reaffirmed the circumstances in which a foreign court would have jurisdiction to give a judgment *in personam* capable of enforcement or recognition as against the judgment debtor.

In essence – and the essence of the decision in *Rubin* suffices for present purposes – the Supreme Court held that the foreign court would have jurisdiction where the person against whom the judgment was given was: (i) present in the foreign country at the time proceedings commenced; (ii) claimed, or counterclaimed, in the proceedings in the foreign court; (iii) submitted to the jurisdiction of the foreign court by voluntarily participating in proceedings in the foreign court; or (iv) had, before the commencement of the proceedings, agreed to submit to the jurisdiction of the foreign court in respect of the subject matter of proceedings.

[5] The case reached the Privy Council by way of appeal from the courts of Gibraltar. Strictly speaking, therefore, it demonstrates the flexibility of the Gibraltarian common law but there is no material difference between that and English common law on the relevant points.

[6] [2012] UKSC 46, [2013] 1 AC 236 ('*Rubin*'). As it transpired, the trustee in bankruptcy in *Vizcaya*, in his capacity as a party to proceedings in Gibraltar and in the Cayman Islands, intervened in the appeal in *Rubin*: *Vizcaya* [2]. For a discussion of the development of the Irish common law principles governing recognition and enforcement of foreign judgments, please see Associate Professor Ní Shúilleabháin's contribution to this collection.

In so doing, the Supreme Court gave its approval to what had become known as the '*Dicey* rule',[7] reaffirming orthodoxy in the process.

Vizcaya concerned the ambit of ground (iv) set out in the previous paragraph. The Privy Council was required to determine whether the agreement to submit had to be express or whether it could exist implicitly. As will be seen momentarily, *Vizcaya* was not the first case required to answer this question. By the time the Privy Council handed down judgment, several judges of varying seniority had attempted to answer it. Despite their best efforts, however, no clear and authoritative answer had been reached. It is to those various attempts that attention must now turn.

B. *Dicey*'s Original Position

The first edition of *Dicey*[8] asserted that parties to a contract 'may make it one of the express or implied terms of the contract that they will submit in respect of any alleged breach thereof, or any matter having relation thereto, to the jurisdiction of a foreign court'.[9] In successive editions of *Dicey*, it was said that four cases, each concerned with the enforcement of a default judgment handed down by a foreign court against a shareholder of a foreign partnership or company, supported that proposition.[10]

First in time was the decision of the Court of Exchequer in *Valleé v Dumergue*,[11] where the claimant liquidator brought an action based on a French judgment against the defendant in England. In finding for the claimant, Alderson B held that, in circumstances where the defendant agreed that notice of the French proceedings ought to be given to him in a particular way and where notice was so given, there was nothing contrary to natural justice in the defendant being bound by a French judgment which concluded those proceedings.[12] Perhaps because Alderson B conceived of the case before him as giving rise to questions pertaining to natural justice, he did not explore the question of whether the defendant had submitted to the French court at all. In consequence, and taken at its highest, the only support which *Valleé* offered for the proposition that an agreement to submit could be implicit was rooted in what the judgment did not say, rather than what it did.

Next came the decisions in *Bank of Australasia v Harding*[13] and *Bank of Australasia v Nias*,[14] which may be taken together given that they concerned

[7] ibid [7]. The '*Dicey* rule' could, at the time *Rubin* was handed down, be found in Collins (ed), *Dicey, Morris & Collins, The Conflict of Laws*, 15th edn (Sweet & Maxwell, 2012) vol 1, 14R-054.

[8] *Conflict of Laws*, 1st edn (Stevens & Sons, 1896) 377.

[9] This formulation was maintained until the 8th edition of the work.

[10] *Dicey* did cite other cases too but the discussion of these four cases is sufficient for present purposes.

[11] (1849) 4 Ex 290 ('*Valleé*').

[12] ibid 302–03.

[13] (1850) 9 CB 661 ('*Harding*').

[14] (1851) 16 QB 717 ('*Nias*').

largely the same subject matter. Both offered much more meaningful support for the proposition that an agreement to submit could be implicit. In each case the claimant sought to enforce in England a judgment of the New South Wales Supreme Court against the defendant (resident in England), who was either a member or shareholder of the Bank of Australia. The New South Wales Legislative Council had passed legislation[15] authorising actions against members and shareholders of the bank naming the chairman as representative defendant. The courts held that the New South Wales judgments were enforceable against the defendants in England. In *Harding*, Cresswell J concluded that the defendant:

> [W]as a member of a company who must be taken to have been a consenting party to the passing of the [New South Wales legislation]. He must, therefore, be regarded as having agreed that suits upon contracts entered into by the company might be brought against the chairman, and the chairman should for all purposes represent him in such actions.[16]

Similarly, in *Nias*, Lord Campbell CJ was content simply to state: (i) the New South Wales legislation was passed for the benefit of the bank; and (ii) the defendant was a shareholder of the bank when the legislation was passed and when the promises were made by the bank, on which the action against the chairman was commenced. As a result, he determined that the New South Wales judgment could be enforced against the defendant in England.[17]

Of the two, *Harding* offered the greater support for the notion that an agreement to submit could be implicit. The court's consideration of what a person may 'be regarded as having agreed' is redolent of modern phrases to describe the circumstances in which terms may be implied in fact[18] (in particular) or in law into a contract. That said, and not unsurprisingly, the cases did not seek to lay down any general principles governing when a person may be taken to have agreed impliedly to submit to the jurisdiction of the foreign court. The courts were content simply to decide the matters before them.

The final case relied on by *Dicey* was *Copin v Adamson*.[19] The claimant sought to enforce against the defendant, a shareholder in a bankrupt French company, a French default judgment for unpaid calls on shares. To demonstrate that the French court had jurisdiction, the claimant referred to the articles of association, by which the defendant was bound. These provided: 'all disputes arising during

[15] The Bank of Australia Act 1833, which Wilde CJ assumed in *Harding* at 685 to have 'been obtained at the request of the parties' and which Lord Campbell CJ in *Nias* at 733 held was for the 'benefit of the Bank of Australia'.

[16] *Harding* 667.

[17] *Nias* 733. Lord Campbell CJ also confirmed that there was nothing 'repugnant to the law of England, or to the principles of natural justice, in enacting that actions on such contracts [as were at issue in the case], should be brought against the chairman whom [the shareholders] have appointed to represent them'.

[18] *Marks & Spencer plc v BNP Paribas Securities Services Trust Co (Jersey) Ltd* [2015] UKSC 72, [2016] AC 742.

[19] 1 Ex D 17 ('*Copin*').

the liquidation of the company between the shareholders of the company [and the administrators] … should be submitted to the jurisdiction of the French Court'. The Court of Appeal, endorsing the decision of the court below to allow enforcement of the default judgment, held that the defendant was bound by the articles of association of the company.

Properly analysed, *Copin*, like its counterpart *Valleé*, offered no real support for the suggestion that an agreement to submit could be implied. Lord Cairns LC thought that the case was one of express submission to the jurisdiction of the French court, as reflected by his comment that the question 'whether, without any express averment, by the law of France as by that of every civilized country, the shareholder would not be bound by all the statutes and provisions of the company in which he was a shareholder'[20] did not arise in the case before him.[21]

C. *Dicey*'s Position Open to Question

From the foregoing discussion, it is clear that there was at least some authority to substantiate the proposition that a party could impliedly agree to submit to the jurisdiction of the foreign court when the first edition of *Dicey* was published. However, other, and more persuasive, authority handed down closer to the date of that first edition's publication seemed to stand against the proposition.

In 1894, roughly two years before the publication of the first edition of *Dicey*, the Privy Council handed down judgment in *Sirdar Gurdyal Singh v Rajah of Faridkote*.[22] The Rajah sought to enforce two judgments from the Civil Court of Faridkote in the courts of Lahore. He argued that the defendant had impliedly submitted to the jurisdiction of the Faridkote court: the defendant, by becoming state treasurer in Faridkote, 'must be deemed to have agreed to be bound by the jurisdiction of that state as accounting for money due from him to that state in respect of that office'.[23] The argument was swiftly and soundly rejected by the Earl of Selbourne (giving the advice of the Privy Council):

> [On the question] whether an obligation to accept the *forum loci contractus*, as having, by reason of the contract, a conventional jurisdiction against the parties in a suit founded upon that contract for all future time, wherever they might be domiciled or resident was generally to be implied … such obligation, unless expressed, could not be implied.[24]

In 1907, the year before the second edition of *Dicey* was published, the Court of Appeal decided *Emanuel v Symon*.[25] The claimants brought an action against the

[20] ibid 19.

[21] The first edition of *Dicey* (n 8) lends support to the proposition that *Copin* is a case of express submission: it is cited therein for exactly that proposition.

[22] [1894] AC 670 ('*Sirdar*').

[23] *Sirdar* 680, taken from the argument of Finlay QC.

[24] ibid 686.

[25] [1908] 1 KB 302 ('*Emanuel*').

defendant in England on a default judgment obtained in the Supreme Court of Western Australia. Reversing the judge at first instance,[26] the Court of Appeal determined that the Western Australian court did not have jurisdiction over the defendant. The case is interesting for three reasons. First, Lord Alverstone CJ felt able to distinguish *Copin*, on which the judge at first instance had relied, on the basis that it dealt with express, rather than implied, submission to the jurisdiction of the foreign court;[27] no mention was made by any member of the court of *Harding* or *Nias*. Second, during the course of the argument, the claimants submitted that when 'persons agree to become partners in a business or transaction which can only be carried on or effected in a foreign country, there is necessarily implied an agreement to submit to the jurisdiction of the foreign courts'.[28] In response, Kennedy LJ intervened by saying: 'such an agreement, in order to be binding, must be express. It is not to be implied,' and relied on the decision in *Sirdar*.[29] Third, and perhaps most importantly, in his judgment in the case, Kennedy LJ held that the Privy Council in *Sirdar* had decided that an obligation 'to accept the *forum loci contractus* … is not to be implied from the mere fact of entering into a contract in a foreign country'.[30]

Read in conjunction with his remarks in argument and his reliance on the judgment in *Sirdar*, one might have been tempted to say that Kennedy LJ's judgment in *Emanuel* rejected the proposition that one could impliedly agree to submit to the jurisdiction of the foreign court. However, reading the words of the judgment alone, one may equally conclude that Kennedy LJ's judgment did not, in fact, go as far as that. By contrast, so the argument could go, all he decided was that the 'mere' fact of entering a contract in a foreign country did not support the implication that the defendant had agreed to submit to the jurisdiction of the courts of that country.

D. More Modern Authorities

The question whether a person could impliedly agree to submit to the jurisdiction of a foreign court returned for discussion in England in a series of first instance decisions between 1961 and 1989.

First, in *Blohn v Desser*,[31] the claimant brought an action in England against the defendant on an Austrian judgment. After citing the judgment of Buckley LJ

[26] Channell J, who had held that by entering into a partnership in Western Australia relating to real estate there the defendant had impliedly agreed to submit to the jurisdiction of the Western Australian court as to disputes arising during the continuance and on the termination of the partnership: *Emanuel* 304).

[27] *Emanuel* 306. It is submitted that Lord Alverstone CJ was correct to distinguish *Copin* in this way.

[28] ibid 305.

[29] ibid.

[30] ibid 314.

[31] [1962] 2 QB 116 ('*Blohn*').

in *Emanuel*, Diplock J held that it was 'clear law' that an agreement 'to submit to the forum in which the judgment was obtained may be express or implied'.[32] He proceeded to find that the defendant had impliedly submitted to the jurisdiction of the Austrian court because she had become a partner in a foreign firm with a place of business in Austria, had appointed an agent resident in Austria to conduct business on behalf of the partnership in Austria and permitted those matters to be notified to persons doing business with the firm by registration in a public register.

Given the state of the authorities up to that point in time, it was, perhaps, a little optimistic of Diplock J to conclude that the law was 'clear' and even more optimistic to find that it was clearly supportive of the conclusion that agreements to submit to the jurisdiction of the foreign court could be implied. It is true that the first seven editions of *Dicey* had said that the agreement could be implicit; however, without considering in detail the reasoning in *Sirdar* or the wording of Kennedy LJ's judgment (definitely) and Alverstone CJ's judgment (probably) in *Emanuel* (none of which Diplock J cited),[33] it is difficult to see how Diplock J arrived at the conclusion he did.[34]

Just short of three years after *Blohn*, Mocatta J, in *Sfeir & Co v National Insurance Company of New Zealand*,[35] considered the registration of a judgment of the High Court of Ghana under the Administration of Justice Act 1920. Without reference to *Blohn*,[36] Mocatta J determined[37] that an implied submission or agreement to submit could satisfy the words of section 9(2)(b) of the Administration of Justice Act 1920 ('submit or agree to submit to the jurisdiction [of the foreign court]') but that, in the case before him, there was, in fact, no implied agreement so to submit. In his view, such agreement could only be implied where such implication was 'necessary',[38] which threshold had not been passed on the facts.

Perhaps somewhat surprisingly in the light of *Blohn* and *Sfeir*, the eighth edition of *Dicey*[39] moved away from the form of words which had been employed in the first seven editions and instead provided: 'Although it has been said that an agreement to submit to the jurisdiction of a foreign court may be express or implied,[40] English judges have generally been reluctant to imply such an agreement'.

[32] ibid 123.

[33] *Harding* and *Nias*, the authorities which, as has been illustrated above, did actually support the proposition that an agreement to submit could be implicit, were cited by counsel for the claimant but not by Diplock J in his judgment.

[34] See, in this respect, the criticism of *Blohn* by Scott J in *Adams v Cape Industries* [1990] Ch 433, 465–66.

[35] [1964] 1 Lloyd's Rep 330 ('*Sfeir*'). In the interests of fairness, Lord Collins in *Vizcaya* [49] said it was 'understandable' why Diplock J took the view that he did.

[36] Or, indeed, any other case or textbook.

[37] *Sfeir* 339–40.

[38] ibid 340.

[39] By then: Morris (ed), *Dicey & Morris, The Conflict of Laws*, 8th edn (Stevens & Sons, 1967) 979.

[40] For the proposition that an agreement to submit could be implicit, *Dicey* did refer to the judgments of *Blohn* and *Sfeir*, but that makes the change of formulation all the more surprising. *Dicey* noted that *Blohn* had been 'severely criticised extra-judicially', citing Lewis, 10 ICLQ 583, Cohn, 11 ICLQ 583 and Carter, 38 BYIL 493.

The case law then took one final turn. In *Vogel v R & A Kohnstamn Limited*,[41] Ashworth J decided that *Sirdar* and *Emanuel* established the following principle:

> [A]n implied agreement to assent to the jurisdiction of a foreign tribunal is not something which the courts of this country have entertained as a legal possibility. Recognising that such an agreement may be made expressly they have in terms decided that implication is not to be relied upon.[42]

In consequence, in Ashworth J's view, the statements to the contrary in both *Blohn* and *Sfeir* were incorrect, and he declined to follow them. In the light of *Vogel*, the ninth edition of *Dicey* simply provided: 'It may be laid down as a general rule that an agreement to submit to the jurisdiction of a foreign court must be express: it cannot be implied'.[43]

Against this background, one might well have every sympathy for Ashworth J's observation that the problem of whether an agreement to submit to the jurisdiction of the foreign court could be implied was 'lamentably bedevilled by the fact that not every decided case … sings the same tune'.[44] Never were truer words spoken. This was the background, then, against which the Privy Council gave judgment in *Vizcaya*.

III. *Vizcaya*

A. Facts

The case itself arose out of a fraudulent Ponzi scheme run by Bernard Madoff, through his New York company, Bernard L Madoff Investment Securities LLC (BLMIS). Vizcaya Partners Limited, a British Virgin Islands company which carried on business as an investment fund, had invested about US$328m with BLMIS between January 2002 and December 2008. The contractual documents which governed Vizcaya Partners' relationship with BLMIS were entered into on Vizcaya Partners' behalf by a custodian bank (Safra). For present purposes, the most relevant of the contractual documents was the customer agreement. This had been written on BLMIS headed note paper and had been signed by Safra as the custodian for and on behalf of Vizcaya Partners in March 2005.

Three clauses from the customer agreement fall to be considered. First, and most pressingly, clause 10 provided: 'This agreement shall be deemed to have been made in the state of New York and shall be construed, and the rights and

[41] [1973] QB 133 ('*Vogel*').

[42] ibid 145.

[43] Morris (ed), *Dicey & Morris, The Conflict of Laws*, 9th edn (Stevens & Sons, 1973) 999. For the proposition just given, *Dicey* cited *Sirdar*, *Emanuel* and *Vogel*, noting that the latter had declined to follow *Blohn* and *Sfeir*. The formulation given in the main text was repeated as para 14-079 in the 15th edition (n 8) but the paragraph has been altered in the light of the judgment in *Vizcaya*.

[44] *Vogel* 144.

liabilities of the parties determined, in accordance with the laws of the state of New York.' Second, by clause 12, the parties agreed that arbitration would be final and binding on them and that they waived 'their right to seek remedies in court, including the right to jury trial'. Third, by clause 13, the parties agreed:

> All controversies which may arise between us concerning any transaction or the construction, performance or breach of this or any other agreement between us pertaining to securities and other property, whether entered into prior, on or subsequent to the date hereof, shall be determined by arbitration under this agreement [and] shall be construed pursuant to the Federal Arbitration Act and the laws of the state [of New York], before the American Arbitration Association.

Following instructions given by Safra, BLMIS transferred to Vizcaya Partners a total of US$180m between August and October 2008. The funds were then credited to Vizcaya Partners' account with Safra in Gibraltar. Part of the funds were subsequently transferred on to Vizcaya's own shareholders and then to their own respective shareholders, and some of the funds (about US$74m) remained in bank accounts in Gibraltar. However, the fraud which Madoff had perpetuated came to light shortly thereafter and Picard was appointed trustee in BLMIS's liquidation in the New York Bankruptcy Court.

In April 2009, the trustee commenced a civil action in the New York Bankruptcy Court against Safra and Vizcaya Partners, the purpose of which was to avoid and recover the transfers to Vizcaya. The New York proceedings were based upon the exercise of various statutory avoidance powers conferred on a trustee in bankruptcy by the US Bankruptcy Code.

On 6 August 2010, the New York Bankruptcy Court entered a judgment in default of appearance in the sum of US$180m against Vizcaya. That judgment recognised that the New York Bankruptcy Court had determined that the trustee had made a proper prima facie showing of personal jurisdiction over the defaulting defendants.

The trustee then sought to enforce, at common law, the default judgment against Vizcaya Partners in Gibraltar. In response, Vizcaya Partners made an application for summary judgment, contending, in essence, that the trustee had no real prospect of succeeding in the enforcement action: the New York Bankruptcy Court, it was said, had no jurisdiction over Vizcaya Partners.

B. The Judgments of the Courts in Gibraltar

Before both the Supreme Court of Gibraltar[45] and the Gibraltar Court of Appeal,[46] Vizcaya Partners sought summary judgment on the following grounds. First, the trustee's case had been inadequately pleaded; second, Vizcaya Partners was not

[45] 2013–14 Gib LR 209.
[46] 2015 Gib LR 282.

subject to the jurisdiction of the New York Bankruptcy Court because it had not been present in New York at the relevant point in time; and, third, Vizcaya Partners had not submitted to the jurisdiction of the New York Bankruptcy Court.

By the time the case came before the Privy Council, only the third of these grounds was still in issue. Thus, this chapter has nothing to say about the arguments in respect of, or conclusions reached on, the first and the second grounds; the focus of what follows below is on the question whether Vizcaya Partners submitted, by way of agreement, to the jurisdiction of the New York Bankruptcy Court.

Before the Gibraltar Supreme Court,[47] the trustee argued that the customer agreement 'was subject to New York law and jurisdiction, and that the effect and construction of the agreement and the general factual matrix underpinning the BLMIS/Vizcaya [Partners] relationship is such that it constitutes submission by agreement'. As might be expected, the trustee sought to lay stress on the wording of clause 10 of the customer agreement and, in particular, on the use of 'determined', which, in the trustee's submission, meant that clause 10 went 'beyond a choice of law clause [and] is also capable of being interpreted as a New York jurisdiction clause'.[48]

In response, Vizcaya Partners submitted that the customer agreement contained no agreement to submit to the jurisdiction of the New York Bankruptcy Court.[49] Not only, it was argued, did clause 10 speak to choice of law and not to jurisdiction, but clause 12 contained a waiver of the parties' rights to seek 'remedies in court', such that 'no reliance [could] be placed upon the customer agreement as an agreement to submit to the jurisdiction of the New York Bankruptcy Court'.[50] Vizcaya Partners further submitted that, as a matter of English law[51] – which law governed, in Vizcaya Partners' submission, the question whether there was an agreement to submit – there had to be an express agreement to submit to the jurisdiction of a foreign court.[52]

Dudley CJ rejected Vizcaya Partners' submissions. In so doing, he identified the 'possible flaw' therein as being the 'contention that determination of whether there is an agreement to submit to the New York Bankruptcy Court is a matter of [English] law and not New York law'.[53] Dudley CJ held that, for the purposes of the summary judgment application, the trustee could reasonably argue that New York law governed the jurisdiction agreement and, further, that, on the state of the expert evidence then before the court regarding the question of how

[47] 2013–14 Gib LR 209 [9]. The Court of Appeal does not suggest that the trustee's submissions were different on appeal: 2015 Gib LR 282 [34].

[48] ibid.

[49] ibid [13]. Vizcaya Partners repeated this submission in the Court of Appeal: 2015 Gib LR 282 [43].

[50] ibid, which submission was again repeated in the Court of Appeal: 2015 Gib LR 282 [43].

[51] Vizcaya Partners' submission on this point was that Gibraltarian common law was the same as English common law in this respect: 2015 Gib LR 282 [43].

[52] 2013–14 Gib LR 209 [13].

[53] ibid [14].

clause 10 would be interpreted by a New York court, the trustee did have a real prospect of demonstrating that Vizcaya Partners submitted to the jurisdiction of the New York Bankruptcy Court.

On appeal, the Court of Appeal agreed with Dudley CJ's rejection of Vizcaya Partners' submissions.[54] Potter JA, giving a judgment with which the other members of the court agreed, began by clarifying that clause 10 of the customer agreement 'unequivocally identified' New York law as the governing law of the agreement, which law was to be applied in order 'to make the definitive assessment of whether or not the clause also amounts to an agreement to submit to the jurisdiction' of the New York Bankruptcy Court.[55] Next, Potter JA held that there was 'uncontradicted (though untested)' expert evidence before the court to the effect that, 'by agreeing to a contract governed by the law of New York and involving a transaction of business in New York by an agent (BLMIS), a party [Vizcaya Partners] submits to the specific jurisdiction of the New York courts for adjudication of matters arising out of that contract'.[56] Finally, Potter JA emphasised that the court, on the present facts, was confronted with a clause – in the form of clause 10 of the customer agreement – which was not a 'simple choice of law clause'.[57] In consequence, Vizcaya Partners' reliance on the conclusions on the absence of implicit agreement in cases like *Sfeir* was inapposite; Dudley CJ had been right to hold 'that the question of whether or not clause 10 was properly to be interpreted as submission by agreement to the [New York Bankruptcy Court] was well arguable', required expert evidence to resolve and was unsuitable for determination using the summary judgment procedure.[58]

C. The Judgment of the Privy Council

In its appeal to the Privy Council, Vizcaya Partners contended that whether or not the customer agreement contained a jurisdiction agreement was a question of contractual construction.[59] Further, and seemingly modifying slightly its submissions as they had been presented before the courts below, Vizcaya Partners argued that an agreement to submit to the foreign court had to be 'express or at any rate is not to be implied from' (in combination or individually) the fact that the contract was governed by a foreign law, the contract had to be performed in a foreign country, the contract was made in a foreign country and/or that the foreign law conferred jurisdiction on the foreign court.[60] Vizcaya Partners also made various

[54] 2015 Gib LR 282 [65].
[55] ibid [59].
[56] ibid [62].
[57] ibid [59].
[58] ibid [64]–[65].
[59] *Vizcaya* [27].
[60] ibid [27].

criticisms of the judgment of the Court of Appeal, arguing, in summary, that the question of whether there was an agreement to submit was a question for English law to determine and that, on the facts of this case, there was no agreement to submit to the jurisdiction of the New York Bankruptcy Court in any event.[61]

In response, the trustee was content to accept that English law had not yet provided a clear answer to the question whether an agreement to submit to the jurisdiction of the foreign court could be implied or whether it had to be express.[62] In seeking to uphold the decision of the Gibraltar Court of Appeal, the trustee was not seeking to equate a simple choice of law with a choice of jurisdiction; rather, and most simply put, the trustee argued that New York law governed the construction of clause 10 of the customer agreement and so governed the question whether, by that clause, Vizcaya Partners had agreed to submit to the jurisdiction of the New York Bankruptcy Court.[63]

Lord Collins began his analysis by reviewing the case law set out in section II of this chapter; he referred also to the decisions of the Alberta Appellate Division in *Mattar v Public Trustee*,[64] which applied *Sirdar* and *Emanuel*, and of the New South Wales Court of Appeal in *Dunbee Ltd v Gilman & Co (Australian) Pty Ltd*,[65] which merely noted the conflicting authorities on the question of whether an agreement to submit could be implicit but did not seek to resolve the tension between them. Given, therefore, that the cases did not provide one uniform answer to the question under consideration, Lord Collins concluded that it was 'necessary to step back and consider the question as a matter of principle and authority'.[66]

Considering the matter thus yielded the following points:[67] (i) the court had to determine whether the judgment debtor had agreed to submit to the jurisdiction of the foreign court; (ii) that agreement did not have to be contractual in nature;[68] (iii) it was commonplace that a contractual agreement or consent may be implied or inferred; (iv) there was no reason in principle why the position should be any different in the case of a contractual agreement or consent to submit to the jurisdiction of a foreign court; and (v) properly interpreted, the authorities said to preclude an implied agreement to submit to the jurisdiction of a foreign court (especially *Sirdar*) meant only that there had to be an actual agreement or consent.

[61] ibid [28]. Vizcaya Partners also argued, by way of fallback position one suspects, that even if there had been an agreement to submit to the jurisdiction of the New York Bankruptcy Court, it could only have been intended to relate to contractual disputes between the parties and not to statutory avoidance claims made in insolvency proceedings by the trustee in bankruptcy of one of them.

[62] ibid [31].

[63] ibid [29].

[64] [1952] 3 DLR 399 ('*Mattar*').

[65] [1968] 2 Lloyd's Rep 394 ('*Dunbee*'). Vizcaya Partners had placed reliance on this case before the Gibraltar Court of Appeal.

[66] *Vizcaya* [55].

[67] ibid [65].

[68] Relying on *SA Consortium General Textiles v Sun and Sand Agencies Ltd* [1978] QB 279.

It followed, so concluded the Privy Council,[69] which accepted Vizcaya Partners' submissions on this point, that because it was necessary to find an actual agreement, that agreement could not be inferred or implied from matters such as: (i) the mere fact that the defendant was a shareholder in a foreign company or a member of a foreign partnership;[70] (ii) the fact that the contract was made in the foreign country;[71] (iii) the fact that the contract was governed by the law of the foreign country;[72] (iv) the fact that the contract was performed in a foreign country;[73] or (v) the fact that the result of the contract being governed by the foreign law gave the foreign court jurisdiction under its own law.[74]

Before seeking to apply these principles to the facts of the case, the Privy Council provided some more general guidance on the implication of terms in the sphere of the conflict of laws. The starting point[75] was a simple one: the characterisation of whether there had been a submission to the jurisdiction of the foreign court for the purposes of enforcement of foreign judgments depended on English law. Yet, in the present context, there simply had to be an agreement to submit to the jurisdiction of the foreign court, which agreement may arise through an implied term. Terms could either be implied in fact or in law. In the former case,[76] and seemingly accepting the submissions of the trustee on this point, the Privy Council determined that this depended on the construction of the contract in the light of the circumstances, such that, where the contract was governed by foreign law, questions of interpretation were governed by that foreign law. In consequence, an expert was required to prove the rules of construction of the foreign law. By contrast, where the court was concerned with a term implied in law, the expert had to give a view as to whether a particular term would be implied by the law in question.[77]

Finally, then, Lord Collins sought to apply the identified principles and guidance to the facts of the case before the Privy Council. While it was conceptually possible that Vizcaya Partners could have impliedly agreed to submit to the jurisdiction of the New York Bankruptcy Court, the trustee's expert evidence did not demonstrate that it was sufficiently arguably that Vizcaya Partners had done so in this case. Indeed, as Lord Collins held:

> [E]ven as a matter of New York law the evidence does not state that a choice of law carries with it an agreement to the jurisdiction of the New York court, since it only does so, according to the evidence, if there is also a transaction of business in New York.[78]

[69] *Vizcaya* [58].
[70] Citing, in support, *Copin* and *Emanuel* and holding that *Blohn* was wrongly decided on this point.
[71] Citing, in support, *Sirdar, Emanuel* and *Vogel.*
[72] Citing, in support, *Sfeir* and *Vogel.*
[73] Citing, in support, *Sfeir* and *Vogel.*
[74] Citing, in support, *Dunbee.*
[75] *Vizcaya* [61], citing *Rubin.*
[76] ibid [60].
[77] ibid [61]. On questions relating to proof of foreign law in English courts, see the judgment of Lord Leggat in *FS Cairo (Nile Plaza) LLC v Brownlie* [2021] UKSC 45, [2021] 3 WLR 1011.
[78] ibid [69].

Instead, the trustee's expert evidence simply suggested that the New York Bankruptcy Court took jurisdiction over Vizcaya Partners on the basis of section 302(a)(1) of the Civil Practice Law and Rules;[79] it did not suggest that there was a term implied either in fact or in law into the customer agreement that Vizcaya Partners had consented to the jurisdiction of the Bankruptcy Court.[80] By way of a final point, the Privy Council expressed the view that even if there had been an implied agreement, the scope of which would have been a matter for New York law, there was nothing in the trustee's expert evidence to suggest that any implied submission would apply to the avoidance proceedings which the trustee had brought.[81]

In consequence, the Privy Council advised that Vizcaya Partners' appeal ought to be allowed.

IV. The Significance of the Reasoning in *Vizcaya*

While the conclusions reached in *Vizcaya*, and the reasoning behind them, are significant for several reasons, in the context of this collection three points in particular stand out. They are addressed in this section.

A. Agreement to Submit to the Jurisdiction of the Foreign Court can be Implied

It is submitted that the proposition for which *Vizcaya* stands as authority, viz an agreement to submit to the jurisdiction of the foreign court may be implied, is entirely correct as a matter of principle. Indeed, in circumstances where the decisions in *Harding* and *Nias* were considered correct (and none of *Sirdar*, *Emanuel* or *Vogel* – authorities believed to demonstrate that an agreement to submit could not be implied – called into question their correctness), anything other than the position at which the Privy Council arrived would have been illogical and impossible to defend on a principled basis. Indeed, even those international instruments, like the Commonwealth Secretariat's Model Law on the Recognition and Enforcement of Foreign Judgments, which, if in force, would reverse the conclusion in *Vizcaya* offer no principled justification for so doing.[82]

As noted at the beginning of this chapter, the Privy Council's settling such a long-running controversy is significant in and of itself, at least as far as English

[79] ibid. The New York legislation was referred to throughout *Vizcaya* as the 'long arm statute'.
[80] ibid [70].
[81] ibid [74].
[82] See clause 5(a), which would require an 'express agreement' by the judgment debtor to the jurisdiction of the foreign court. Nothing in the explanatory comments to clause 5(a) explains why express agreement should be required.

law is concerned. Not only is it now clear that, for the purposes of the English common law, an agreement to submit to the jurisdiction of the foreign court may be implied, it is equally clear that the existence of such an agreement may either demonstrate (for the purposes of section 9 of the Administration of Justice Act 1920) or provide a ground on which it may be deemed (for the purposes of section 4(2) of the Foreign Judgments (Reciprocal Enforcement) Act 1933) that the foreign court had jurisdiction when an English court is required to consider whether a foreign judgment may be registered in England.[83]

The principle endorsed in *Vizcaya* is likely to have implications for courts in other common law jurisdictions as well.[84] It may, for instance, encourage courts in Canada to consider again whether cases like *Mattar*, which seemingly placed such heavy reliance on *Sirdar* and *Emanuel*, were correctly decided. It may be looked on by South African courts as a conclusion which ought to have been reached long ago and as a reason to continue to decide the question as they have done for the last 40 or so years.[85] It likely offers Australian courts the chance to resolve the question which was left unresolved by the New South Wales Court of Appeal in *Dunbee*, the answer to which carries importance not only from a common law perspective but also for the purposes of section 7 of Australia's Foreign Judgments Act 1991.[86]

For English courts and those other common law courts which decide to follow *Vizcaya*, the next question of no little significance will be to identify the precise circumstances in which it will be legitimate to conclude that an implied agreement to submit exists. Both English[87] and South African[88] authority, for instance, conclusively demonstrate that an implicit agreement should not be found 'loosely or lightly'.[89] The point is in any event put beyond doubt by the Privy Council in *Vizcaya*, given the enumeration by Lord Collins of the factors which do not give rise to the implication. This is all as it should be but, it is submitted, at the same time, the principle endorsed in *Vizcaya* is sensible; its proper application

[83] *Vizcaya* [5], where Lord Collins held that these statutory schemes 'are based on the common law and fall to be interpreted in accordance with the common law'. The principle which emerges from *Vizcaya* chimes with the conclusions of Mocatta J in *Sfeir*, which was concerned with an application for registration of a judgment under the Administration of Justice Act 1920: *Sfeir*, 334.

[84] One of the reasons why Lord Collins thought the question at the heart of *Vizcaya* an 'important practical' one: ibid [5].

[85] *Standard Bank v Butlin* 1981 (4) SA 158 (D), 161 ('*Butlin*').

[86] In this respect, see Lee and Ford, 'Can submission to the jurisdiction under the common law be implied? An Australian perspective on the Privy Council decision in *Vizcaya Partners*' (2016) 9 *Corporate Rescue and Insolvency* 55–57. Contrary to the view put forward by Lee and Ford, however, it is submitted that the decision in *Privatbrauerei Erdinger Weissrau Werner Brombach GMBH v World Brands Australia Pty Ltd* [2016] WASC 9 [30], a case concerned with the incorporation of express terms, does not substantiate the view that Australian courts would follow *Vizcaya*.

[87] *Sfeir* 340.

[88] *Butlin* 165, where the court determined that agreement in the form of a *domicilium citandi et executandi* clause to service of process in modern day Zimbabwe could never 'support the inference of a submission to jurisdiction'.

[89] Briggs, *Civil Jurisdiction and Judgments*, 7th edn (Routledge, 2021) 776.

correctly clarifies (and probably extends, at least as a matter of English law) the circumstances in which a foreign judgment may be enforced. In consequence, courts ought not to set the bar for implication so high as to remove the potential application of that principle altogether.

Difficulty therefore stems from the fact that the Privy Council provided little guidance – not *no* guidance, though, given the endorsement of *Harding* and *Nias* – as to when an implied agreement may be found. It would be a pity, given that *Vizcaya* demonstrates the utility of considering the jurisprudence of other common law courts, for the courts of Australia, England, South Africa, and cognate common law jurisdictions to work out in splendid isolation when an implied agreement may legitimately be found. Little good can come of that. In the light of the advice of the Privy Council in *Vizcaya*, one may stand back and opine that, at present, 'it is not easy to say when such an agreement will be implied', it is equally true that 'a common lawyer never says never',[90] especially when they take into account the views of their friends.

B. Which Law Governs the Question of Implication

In seeking to identify the circumstances in which an implicit agreement to submit to the jurisdiction of the foreign court may be found, the Privy Council in *Vizcaya* was clear that the question whether the foreign court had jurisdiction was a matter of English private international law.[91] However, the Privy Council was equally clear that an agreement arising by virtue of an implied term had to be construed in accordance with the law which governed the agreement.[92] In other words, the issue of construction was not to be resolved by considering how 'English law eyes' would interpret the clause.[93]

This aspect of the Privy Council's reasoning has been criticised on grounds of principle. The point has been put that the question whether an agreement on jurisdiction exists is properly characterised as a question of consensus, such that 'the implication of a jurisdiction agreement is most naturally subject to the law of the forum and not to the law of the host contract'.[94] It has also been said that the approach which the Privy Council took in *Vizcaya* on this point was different to that in *Sfeir* and in *Vogel*, which 'decided the implication of [agreement to the foreign court's] jurisdiction [question] by reference to English law, even where the governing law of the contract was allegedly foreign'.[95]

[90] Briggs, *The Conflict of Laws*, 4th edn (OUP, 2019).

[91] *Vizcaya* [59]. See also *Public Joint Stock Co Rosgosstrakh v Starr Syndicate Ltd* [2020] EWHC 1557 (Comm), [51] ('*PJSC*').

[92] *Vizcaya* [60].

[93] *PJSC* [53].

[94] Kupelyants, 'Implication of Jurisdiction Agreements' (2016) 72 *CLJ* 216, 217.

[95] ibid 217. See also Driscoll, 'Common Law Recognition of Foreign Judgments by English and Commonwealth Courts: What are you Implying?' (2016) 31 *Butterworths Journal of International Banking and Financial Law* 396.

One may deal with the second point relatively quickly: the Privy Council's reasoning did not have to chime with either *Sfeir* or *Vogel* because those cases did not bind it. More than that, though, one could point out that in *Sfeir*, Mocatta J made it plain that he reached his conclusion 'without determining what the proper law of the contract was or whether it was other than that of Ghana';[96] and that, in *Vogel*, Ashworth J merely concluded that the contract was 'not made within the foreign jurisdiction [and was] not to be performed there'.[97]

With respect to the first point, there is a certain tension between the exclusively English law approach adopted in *Harding* (where the implied agreement arose from the fact that the defendant was a member of a company who must be taken to have been a consenting party to the passage of the New South Wales legislation) and the requirement to interpret the relevant contractual term according to its governing law set out in *Vizcaya*. However, it is submitted, that tension may be explained away – as Lord Collins sought to do – by keeping in mind generally the context of each case and, specifically that in *Vizcaya* the issue was whether there was an implied term in a contract by which Vizcaya Partners had agreed to submit to the jurisdiction of the New York Bankruptcy Court. An approach which pays appropriate regard to the context of the cases considers that where parties, as in *Vizcaya*, agree[98] upon the law which governs their contract, their expectation would be that any agreement between them would be construed in the light of that law. *Vizcaya* simply gives effect to such an expectation.

Before leaving this part of the discussion, it is appropriate to observe that the entry into force of international instruments, such as the Hague Convention on Choice of Court Agreements,[99] does not obviate the need for the common law to continue to explore questions such as whether there can be an implied agreement to submit to the jurisdiction of the foreign court and, if there can, what law governs the implication. Accession to, and ratification of, the various instruments is not as widespread as it might be and, in any event, *Vizcaya* gives ready answers to questions which are elsewhere left partially or completely unaddressed. By way of example, Article 3 of the Hague Convention on Choice of Court Agreements does not say in terms that the parties must expressly agree to the exclusive jurisdiction of the court in question[100] or provide explicit guidance as to the law to be applied in order to determine whether there is a jurisdiction agreement at all.[101]

[96] *Sfeir* 340.

[97] *Vogel* 147.

[98] Which, one might think, would happen in the majority of commercial cases.

[99] 30 June 2005. One might make a similar point about the Hague Convention on the Recognition and Enforcement of Foreign Judgments in Civil or Commercial Matters, 2 July 2019.

[100] Compare with clause 5(a) of the Commonwealth Secretariat's Model Law on the Recognition and Enforcement of Foreign Judgments (n 82).

[101] It would appear to be national law, at least according to the report of Professors Hartley and Dogauchi, which is reproduced in Hartley, *Choice-of-Court Agreements under the European and International Instruments*, 1st edn (OUP, 2013) [93]–[115]. However, Art 23 requires courts, when interpreting the Convention, to have regard to 'its international character and to the need to promote uniformity in its application'.

In consequence, even those common law countries whose courts follow *Vizcaya* and whose legislatures either have given effect to or come to give effect to international instruments which concern jurisdiction clauses or the recognition and enforcement of foreign judgments will still need to grapple with the question of what law ought to govern the implication of any agreement to submit to the jurisdiction of the foreign court. This is territory over which the common law continues to exert its influence.

C. Why a Party who Submits to the Jurisdiction of the Foreign Court is Bound

On the face of it, to say that the Privy Council reached a conclusion as to why, theoretically, a party who submitted by way of (implied) agreement to the jurisdiction of the foreign court is bound by the judgment of the foreign court is slightly odd. There were, after all, no sweeping statements as to the theoretical basis for the recognition and enforcement of foreign judgments. That is hardly surprising because Lord Collins appeared to have done what work there was to do (in his view) in *Rubin*, holding: 'where a court of competent jurisdiction has adjudicated a certain sum to be due from one person to another, a legal obligation arises to pay that sum, on which an action of debt to enforce the judgment may be maintained'.[102] Yet, one must tread carefully. *Vizcaya* is authority for the proposition that the conceptual basis of submission – or, in other words, the reason why the judgment of the foreign court is said to bind a party – cannot be rooted in contract.[103]

If the obligation theory, which was repeated by the Supreme Court in *Rubin* and uncontradicted by the Privy Council in *Vizcaya*, correctly explains why, theoretically, foreign judgments may be enforced at common law, nothing in either judgment adequately explains how the obligation comes to arise. That 'if' is, in any event, a big 'if'. Despite admirable defences of obligation theory,[104] it is no longer in vogue in several places within the common law world.[105] Scholars continue to debate whether there is one overarching theory which explains why foreign judgments ought to be enforced,[106] and, if there is, what its shape is and how it operates.[107]

[102] *Rubin* [9].

[103] Dickinson, 'Foreign Submission' (2019) 135 *LQR* 294, 316–17.

[104] Briggs, 'Recognition of Foreign Judgments: A Matter of Obligation' (2013) 129 *LQR* 87.

[105] See, by way of example, the judgment of the South African Constitutional Court in *Government of the Republic of Zimbabwe v Fick* [2013] ZACC 22, 2013 (5) SA 325 (CC) and *Beals v Saldanha* 2003 SCC 72, [2003] 3 SCR 416.

[106] See, for example, Dickinson (n 103) 317, who argues that cases where the parties have formally participated in proceedings before the foreign court ought to be distinguished from cases in which there is an expressed or implied agreement to be bound by a foreign court's adjudication.

[107] For a relatively new offering in this field, see Okoli, *Promoting Foreign Judgments: Lessons in Legal Convergence from South Africa and Nigeria*, 1st edn (Kluwer, 2019), where the author promotes a theory of 'qualified obligation'.

The task of identifying the true reason or reasons why a foreign judgment ought to be enforced remains a vitally important one: where theory is forgotten, little good is achieved.[108] *Vizcaya* thus aids the quest for theoretical explanation in two ways. First, it added nothing to the statement in *Rubin* that, at least as far as English common law was concerned, obligation theory ruled the roost. In consequence, it did nothing to ameliorate the criticisms of that theory and so neither stymied nor resolved the theoretical debate conclusively in favour of obligation theory. Second, and as stated already, it clarified that the agreement to submit to the jurisdiction of the foreign court did not have to be contractual in nature. In consequence, if, in keeping with obligation theory, an obligation arises, *Vizcaya* confirms that it does not arise from a contract yet does not set out the source of the obligation. More widely, *Vizcaya*, confirms the proposition that the concept of submission cannot be explained through a contractual lens and so, as Professor Dickinson has written, it remains 'necessary to seek another explanation for the conclusion that a party who "submits" to the jurisdiction of a foreign court is bound by its judgment'.[109]

Of course, if the Hague Convention on the Recognition and Enforcement of Foreign Judgments in Civil or Commercial Matters[110] gains widespread traction, that will decrease the need to identify clearly the theoretical basis for the enforcement of foreign judgments. Until then, there remains room for scholars to conceptualise precisely why, at common law, judgments should be enforceable outside the territory of the court which rendered them.

V. Conclusion

In simple terms, *Vizcaya*'s central significance is its conclusion that a party may impliedly agree to submit to the jurisdiction of a foreign court. That conclusion is surely correct as a matter of principle, and it may well be the case that those common law courts across the oceans which have hitherto taken no view, or a different view, see in *Vizcaya* an opportunity to change course. Irrespective of whether *Vizcaya* is taken up by (more of) the common law world, it is submitted that the Privy Council's decision and the reasoning behind it demonstrates, at least in certain senses, the enduring flexibility and utility of the common law to answer questions with which other international instruments do not appear equipped to deal.

Of course, *Vizcaya* also leaves questions of no little importance without an answer. It is not altogether clear when exactly an implied agreement to submit can be found; the correct theoretical basis on which foreign judgments may be enforced at common law remains open to debate. Notwithstanding the increased

[108] Briggs, 'Recognition of Foreign Judgments' (2013) 100.
[109] Dickinson (n 103) 316.
[110] See (n 99).

number of international instruments which now seek, or will seek, to regulate the circumstances in which a judgment of a foreign court may be enforced, the questions left unaddressed by *Vizcaya* are likely to be questions with which common law courts will need to grapple for some time to come.

In completing that task, common law courts will be carrying out work of a similar nature to that chronicled in this collection. They, in other words, will be bolstering ever further the significance of the common law jurisprudence of the conflict of laws.

INDEX

academic scholarship
- foreign marriages, English choice of law rules on 2–8
- Ireland, common law recognition of foreign judgments in 215, 218
- submission to jurisdiction 242

act of state doctrine 175–6, 181–9
- common law 181–7
- non-justiciability, principle of 175–6, 181–5
- public policy exception 175–6, 181, 184–5, 189
- Westphalian value 188–9

Admiralty law 146–8
affinity marriages, prohibitions on 7, 8, 9–16, 20
African customary or indigenous law 191
Allason, Rupert (Nigel West) 112
apartheid 191
appeals 45–6, 61–4
applicable law 2–8, 175–6, 178
- Australia 114
- choice of law 37, 40–1
- foreign marriages, choice of law rules on 16–21
- legal certainty 41
- party autonomy 87

arbitration 85, 90–1, 109
Armstrong, Robert 117, 121–3
arrest of foreign defendants to found or confirm jurisdiction, constitutionality of (*Bid Industrial Holdings (Pty) Ltd v Strang and another* (South Africa) 191–206
- Anglo-common law 191–8, 202, 203–6
- attachment 200–1, 203
- Bill of Rights, interpretation of 191–2, 206
- connecting factors 196–7, 203–5
- Constitution 191–2, 195, 202, 206
- detention 194–5
- domicile 200–1, 203–5
- effectiveness, principle of 195–6, 203–5
- facts 193–4
- *forum non conveniens* 192, 195–206
  - current state in South Africa 201–6
  - *forum conveniens* distinguished 197–9, 201, 203–6
  - *Multi-Links Telecommunications Ltd* decision 199–201
  - *Spiliada* decision 197–9, 201, 203–6
  - stay of proceedings 197–8, 205–6
  - suitability or appropriateness 197–201, 204–5
- freedom and security of the person, right to 195
- mixed or hybrid legal system, South Africa as 191–2, 201–2, 206
- *Multi-Links Telecommunications Ltd* decision 199–201
- physical presence in jurisdiction, service based on 195–7, 204–6
- reasoning 194–7
- residence 196
- Roman-Dutch law 191–2, 194, 202–3, 206
- service on basis of temporary presence in jurisdiction 195–6
- service out of the jurisdiction 197, 199–201, 204
- substitute practice 195–6, 203, 206
- Supreme Court of Appeal 193–206

attachment 200–1, 203
Australia *see also* ***Spycatcher*** **case (Australia)**
- appeals 63–4
- applicable law 114
- Australia Acts 1986 113–14
- Balfour Declaration of 1926 113, 125
- *Bonython v Commonwealth of Australia*, proper law rule in 65–83
- *Breavington v Godleman* 139–42, 152, 159, 163
- choice of law 139–43
  - express 34–5, 37–8, 41
  - tort 152, 159, 163, 168
- colonial relationship with UK 113–14
- common law 63–4, 152, 159, 163, 168, 187
- Constitution 143, 186–7
- customary international law 187

dualism 186
Foreign Judgments Act 1991 239
forum non conveniens 114–15
Hague Marriage Convention 22
High Court of Australia 19, 35, 38, 64–76, 81, 113–14, 117, 118, 123, 129–35
illegality 37
jurisdiction, agreements to submit to 239–41
nationalism 111, 113–17, 120
non-justiciability, principle of 183
Privy Council, Judicial Committee of the 63–4, 113–14
proper law rule 65–83
proportionality 179–80
public international law 186–7
public policy 34–5, 41, 178
Queen as Head of State 116
renvoi 38
republicanism 116, 125
Statute of Westminster 1942 113
tort, choice of law rules on 152, 159, 163, 168

autonomy *see* **party autonomy**

bailment, rights and duties of a common carrier in 26–7, 30
Balfour Declaration of 1926 113, 125
bans on publications *see* ***Spycatcher*** **case (Australia)**
Beaumont, Paul R 134
Bid Industrial Holdings (Pty) Ltd *see* **arrest of foreign defendants to found or confirm jurisdiction, constitutionality of (*Bid Industrial Holdings (Pty) Ltd v Strang and another* (South Africa)**
bills of lading 25–9
clause paramount 25–6, 40
express choice of law 25–9, 30, 36, 40
Hague Rules, incorporation of 25–6, 30, 36
illegality 25–30
Newfoundland Carriage of Goods Act 1932 25–9
Black, Vaughan 146
Blom, Joost 218
Blunt, Anthony 112
Bonython v Commonwealth of Australia *see* **proper law rule in *Bonython v Commonwealth of Australia***
M/S Bremen v Zapata Off-shore Company *see* **party autonomy in United States (*M/S Bremen v Zapata Off-shore Company*)**
Briggs, Adrian 82, 218
Brook v Brook *see* **foreign marriages, choice of law rules on (*Brook v Brook*) (English law)**
Burge, William 6
Bush, George HW 93

Caldwell, Bill 120–1, 124, 130
Canada *see also* **Canada, recognition and enforcement of interprovincial judgments in (*Morguard Investments v De Savoye*); Canadian common law choice of law rule for torts (*Tolofson v Jensen*)**
act of state doctrine 183
common law 63–4
express choice of law 33, 37, 38–9, 41
Newfoundland Carriage of Goods Act 1932 25–9, 37
Privy Council 63–4
public policy 41, 178
renvoi 38–9
submission to jurisdiction 239–40
Canada, recognition and enforcement of interprovincial judgments in (*Morguard Investments v De Savoye*) 137–50
academic commentary 215
Admiralty law 146–8
Alberta 144–6
Australia 139–43
choice of law clauses 138, 139–50, 155–6, 167–9
civil law jurisdiction, Québec as a 142
comity 214, 216
common law 137–8, 142–3, 214–15
Constitution 139, 142–3
Constitution Act 1867 139
contract 138, 149
division of powers 139
exclusive jurisdiction 142
foreign judgments, recognition and enforcement of 137–8
forum non conveniens 137
forum shopping 140
geographically complex facts 138–9
lex fori 142, 147–8
lex loci delicti 140, 144

limitation periods 149
maritime liens, priority of 147–8
Moran v Pyle National (Canada) Ltd 138, 143, 148, 150
Ontario 140–6, 148
Québec 141–3, 148
real and substantial connection test 156, 207, 213–21
restrained or responsible assertion of jurisdiction 138
Saskatchewan 148
service out of the jurisdiction 137–8
tort 138, 140, 143–4, 149
uniformity 139–46, 150

Canadian common law choice of law rule for torts (*Tolofson v Jensen*) 151–70
Australia 152, 159, 163, 168
before *Tolofson*, common law 151–3
British Columbia 151, 153, 161
choice of law 154, 156–62, 164–70
comity 156–7
constitutional issues 159–63, 169
constitutional law, public international law and private international law, interplay of 156–62
damages 152
defamation 166, 170
evolution of private international law principles 163–6
extraterritoriality 159
federalism 156, 159, 169
forum non conveniens 157
geographically distributed torts 164–6
gratuitous passenger rule 153, 155, 157–8, 161
Hague Convention on Traffic Accidents 158, 164
Hunt v T&N plc 155–6, 167
injustice exception 163–4
interprovincial cases 151–70
jurisdiction 154, 156–8, 160, 164–8
lex fori 152–3, 157–8, 164
lex loci delicti 152, 154, 158–9, 161–9
limitation periods 153, 155, 163, 169–70
procedural, as 155, 167
substantive, as 155, 163, 167
Lucas v Gagnon 151–4, 161, 168
motor vehicle negligence cases 151–70
Morguard Investments case 155–6, 167–9
non-Canadian authorities 162–3
Ontario 151–4, 157–8, 161–2, 164–6
Phillips v Eyre 151–2, 154
provincial tort laws 152–70
public policy 158
real and substantial connection 156
Québec 152, 154, 168
Saskatchewan 153, 155, 161
sovereignty 160
sufficient connection test 162
Supreme Court of Canada
territorial principle 156, 157–60, 167–9
Thomson v Thomson 155
wilful or wanton misconduct 153, 155, 157–8, 161

capacity to marry 1–2, 7, 8, 9–20
dual domicile theory 1, 17, 19–20
intended matrimonial home theory 1–2, 19

Castel, Jean-Gabriel 218

cause, law of the (*lex causae*) 149, 177, 180

celebration of marriage, law of the (*lex loci celebrationis*) 1–22

certainty
commercial certainty 30, 41
legal certainty 41, 217–19, 222

Cheshire, GC 1–2, 30, 32, 74, 143, 209–10

children, legitimacy of 9–15

choice of forum clauses 88

choice of law
arbitration agreements under New York Convention 1958 109
Australia 139–43
bifurcated choice of law 1–2, 6, 15, 16–21
Brussels I (Recast) Regulation 99
business-to-business choice of court agreements 101–2
Canada
common law choice of law rules for torts 151–70
recognition and enforcement of interprovincial judgments 138, 139–40
characterisation 175
clauses 88, 138, 139–50, 234–7, 241
common law 99–108, 151–70
conversion 175
double actionability 174–5
enforcement 100, 103–6
exceptions to enforcement 100, 103
exclusive choice of court agreements 88–9, 99, 101–7
express choice of law 23–42
foreign marriages, choice of law rules on 1–22
forum non conveniens 103–8

Hague Convention on Choice of Court Agreements 2005 86–7, 109
Hague Convention on Traffic Accidents 158, 164
lex situs rule 175
non-exclusive, interpretation as 92, 103–4, 106
ouster doctrine 89–92, 95, 98, 109
party autonomy in United States 86–92, 94–109
public policy 28, 31–6, 39–41, 100, 103, 158
recognition and enforcement of judgments 234–7, 241
torts 151–70, 174–6
Christianity 7, 11–12, 14, 16, 18, 21
Churchill, Winston 171
civil law systems 48, 50, 60–1, 86, 89
clause paramount 25–6, 40
Codd, Michael 122, 128
colonialism 113–14, 191
comity
Canada 156–7, 214, 216
choice of law rules 29–30, 40–1, 156–7
Ireland, common law recognition of foreign judgments in 210–11, 214, 216
lex loci celebrationis 11
non-justiciability, principle of 183
public policy 40–1
recognition and enforcement of judgments 210–11, 214, 216
commercial certainty 30, 41
common carriers 25–7
common law
act of state doctrine 181–7
arrest of foreign defendants to found or confirm jurisdiction, constitutionality of 191–8, 202–6
Australia 63–4, 71, 73–83, 118–19, 134–5, 187
Canada
choice of law rule for torts 151–70
Privy Council 63–4
recognition and enforcement of interprovincial judgments in 137–8, 142–3, 214–15
choice of court
agreements 99–108
express 23–4, 33, 36, 40–1
civil law systems 48, 50
Commonwealth states 62–4
English law 151–2, 171–2, 177, 180–9, 191–8, 202
federal common law 43–64, 86
interjurisdictional interpretation 46, 62–4
Ireland, common law recognition of foreign judgments in 207–24
lex celebrationis 2, 8, 10, 19, 21–2
party autonomy in United States 85–7, 92, 96–108
proper law rule in Australia 71, 73–83
public international law 171
recognition and enforcement of judgments 137–8, 142–3, 207–44
separation of powers 182–3
South Africa 191–8, 202–6
United States
party autonomy 85–7, 92, 96–108
state law precedents in federal courts, status of 43–64, 86
Commonwealth states
Australia, *Spycatcher* case in 112–13, 125
common law 62–4
Erie problems 62–4
interjurisdictional interpretation of common law 46, 62–4
Privy Council appeals 46, 62–4
confidentiality 123–4, 126–30, 134
connecting factors *see also* **domicile (*lex domicilii*); real and substantial connection test**
arrest of foreign defendants to found or confirm jurisdiction, constitutionality of 196–7, 203–5
close connection and express choice of law 31–2, 37
closest and most real connection 69, 73–80, 82–3
express choice of law 31–2, 37
foreign marriages, English choice of law rules on 19–20, 21–2
forum non conveniens 196–7, 203–5
habitual residence 102, 220
Ireland, common law recognition of foreign judgments in 207, 213–21, 224
most substantial connection 74
nationality 209–10, 212
renvoi 69
residence 102, 196, 220
service out of the jurisdiction 204
sufficient connection test 162
consanguinity (blood relationships), marriages prohibited on grounds of 7, 8, 9, 10, 14, 16–17, 20

constitutions/constitutional law
arrest of foreign defendants to found or confirm jurisdiction, constitutionality of 191–206
Australian Constitution 135, 143, 186–7
Canada
choice of law rules for torts 159–63, 169
recognition and enforcement of interprovincial judgments in 142–3
choice of law rules for torts 159–63, 169
public and private international law, interplay with 156–62
South Africa 191, 224
United States, status of state law precedents in federal courts in 47
consumer contracts 102
contract
Canada, recognition and enforcement of interprovincial judgments in 138, 149
consumer contracts 102
employment contracts 102
foreign law, governed by 35–6
freedom of contract 87
insurance contracts 102
intention of parties 23–4, 27
lex loci contractus 16, 18, 23–4, 27, 34
lex loci solutionis 68–9, 72–3
proper law rule
Australia 69–83
English law 27–9, 36
validity of contracts under law of forum 23, 33, 35–7
conversion 174–5
crime
foreign penal law, enforcement of 118–19, 124, 126–7, 131, 133
fraud 100, 103, 225–44
Currie, Brainerd 142
custom
commercial custom 54–5
international law 184, 187
legal systems, jurisdictions with customary 48, 191

damages 152, 173–4
Darke, Rowan 120–1, 124
Dawson, Daryl 131, 133
Deane, William 130–1, 133
debentures, repayment of 65–83
defamation 166, 170
default judgments 173–4, 225, 227, 230, 233
democracy 171, 189
Dicey, AV 1, 20–1, 69, 73, 78, 119–20, 128, 209, 214, 216–18, 222–3, 227–32
Dickinson, Andrew 243
diversity jurisdiction 43–64
domicile (*lex domicilii*)
dual domicile theory 1, 17, 19–21
foreign marriages, English choice of law rules on 1–6, 8, 12, 15, 16–21
forum non conveniens 200–1, 203–5
lex loci celebrationis 8, 15, 17–21
double actionability rule 174–7
dualism 186

Edinger, Elizabeth 218
effectiveness, principle of 100, 195–6, 203–5
employment contracts 102
enforcement of judgments *see* **Canada, recognition and enforcement of interprovincial judgments in (*Morguard Investments v De Savoye*)**
English law
Australia
anti-British sentiment in 116–17, 135
Spycatcher case 111–35
Brexit 32, 221
Carriage of Goods by Sea Act 1924 25, 39–40
Carriage of Goods by Sea Act 1971 35, 40
common law 151–2, 171–2, 177, 180–9, 191–8, 202
express choice of law 30–3, 37–8
foreign marriages, choice of law rules on (*Brook v Brook*) 1–22
forum non conveniens 174, 197–9, 201, 203–6
Gibraltar 233–5
Hague Judgments Regulation 220–1
Ireland, enforcement of judgments in 208–12
Kuwait Airways Nos 4 and 5 171–89
lex loci delicti 162
Phillips v Eyre 151–2, 154
proper law of contract 27–9, 36
recognition and enforcement of judgments 226–7
renvoi 37–8
South Africa 191–2
submission to jurisdiction 239–41
Vita Foods Products decision 30–3, 37–8

equality
apartheid 191
arrest of foreign defendants to found or confirm jurisdiction, constitutionality of 195
Erie Railroad Company v Tompkins *see* **United States, status of state law precedents in federal courts in (*Erie Railroad Company v Tompkins*)**
European Convention on Human Rights (ECHR) 212, 224
European Union
Brexit 32, 221
Brussels regime 99, 101–2, 203
business-to-business choice of court agreements 101–2
consumer contracts 102
forum non conveniens 202–3
Hague Judgments Convention, accession to 219–20, 224
Rome Convention 1980 31–2, 36–7, 80, 82
Rome I Regulation 31–2, 36, 38
Rome II Regulation 80
expert evidence 234–5, 238
extraterritoriality 9–15, 113, 159

fair hearing, right to a 224
Falconbridge, John D 37–9
federalism 156, 159, 169 *see also* **United States,** status **of state law precedents in federal courts in (*Erie Railroad Company v Tompkins*)**
fiduciary duties 124, 126, 128–9
Flightlease, Re *see* **Ireland, common law recognition of foreign judgments in (*Re Flightlease*)**
foreign governments, enforcement of governmental interests by 113–35
foreign judgments, recognition and enforcement of *see* **recognition and enforcement of foreign judgments**
foreign marriages, choice of law rules on (*Brook v Brook*) (English law) 1–22
affinity (relationships by marriage) 7, 8, 9–16, 20
ecclesiastical court, challenges in the 9, 14
inheritance 9–15
legitimacy of children 9–15
Lord Lyndhurst's Act 1835 7, 9–15
after *Brook* 16–21
applicable law
after *Brook* 16–21
before *Brook* 2–8, 21
background to *Brook* 9–15
before *Brook* 2–8, 21
bifurcated choice of law 1–2, 6
essential validity of marriage 1–2, 6, 15, 16–21
formal validity of marriage 1–2, 6, 15, 16–17, 19
capacity 1–2, 7, 8, 9–20
dual domicile theory 1, 17, 19–20
intended matrimonial home theory 1–2, 19
case law, influence of 2–8
Christianity 7, 11–12, 14, 16, 18, 21
consanguinity (blood relationships) 7, 8, 9, 10, 14, 16–17, 20
deceased wife's sisters, marriage to 7, 9–21
domicile 1–6, 8, 12, 15, 16–21
dual domicile theory 1, 17, 19–21
essential validity 18, 21
incestuous marriages 12, 15, 16–21
lex loco celebrationis 8, 15, 17–21
separate domiciles 17
essential validity of marriage 1–2, 6, 15, 16–22
evasion of the law 2, 5–6, 9–15, 21
extraterritoriality 9–15
form-capacity distinction 2
formal validity of marriage 1–2, 6, 15, 16–17, 20–2
Hague Marriage Convention 1978 22
incestuous marriages 7, 8, 9–22
affinity (relationships by marriage) 7, 8, 9–16, 20
Christianity 7, 11–12, 14, 16, 18, 21
consanguinity (blood relationships) 7, 8, 9, 10, 14, 16–18, 20
deceased wife's sisters, marriage to 7, 9–21
domicile 8, 12, 15, 16–21
inheritance 9–15
legitimacy of children 9–15
lex loci celebrationis 7, 8, 10–22
Lord Lyndhurst's Act 1835 7, 9–16, 21
inheritance 9–15
intended matrimonial home theory 1–2, 19, 21–2
legitimacy of children 9–15

lex loci celebrationis (law of the place of celebration) 1–22
lex loci contractus 16, 18
Lord Lyndhurst's Act 1835 7, 9–16, 21
extraterritorial effect 9–15
evasion 9–15
inheritance 9–15
interpretation 10–13
legitimacy of children 9–15
personal statute, as a 10, 12–13
public policy 11–13, 15, 16–17, 21
real and substantial connection test 19–20, 21–2
Royal Marriages Act 1772 7–8, 11, 13
scholars, influential role of 2–8
Scotland between English people, validity of marriages in 5
Scottish courts to dissolve English marriages, jurisdiction of 3–5
symbolic value of *Brook* 2
validity of foreign marriages 1–22
foreign penal law, enforcement of 118–19, 124, 126–7, 131, 133
foreign revenue laws, enforcement of 118–19, 126, 128, 131, 133
forfeiture laws 118–20
Forsyth, Christopher 206
forum, law of the *see* ***lex fori***
forum non conveniens
arrest of foreign defendants to found or confirm jurisdiction, constitutionality of 192, 1955–206
attachment 200–1, 203
Australia 114–15
burden of proof 198–9, 205
Canada 137, 157
choice of law 103–8, 157
common law 197–8, 202, 203–6
connecting factors 196–7, 203–5
domicile 200–1, 203–5
effectiveness, principle of 100, 195–6, 203–5
English law 174, 197–9, 201, 203–6
EU law 202–3
exorbitant jurisdiction 198
forum conveniens distinguished 197–9, 201, 203–6
party autonomy in United States 86–8, 91, 95–9, 100, 103–8
public interest 88
Roman-Dutch law 202–3
service out of the jurisdiction 197, 199–201, 204
Spiliada decision 197–9, 201, 203–6
stay of proceedings 88, 197–8, 205–6
substantial inconvenience 100
suitability or appropriateness 197–201, 204–5
forum shopping 47, 51–2, 140, 152
fraud 100, 103, 225–44
freedom and security of the person, right to 195
freedom of movement 195
French law of marriages 7–8

Gibraltar 233–5
good faith 33–4
Gorton, John 118
governing law 226, 235, 240–2
Griffith, Gavan 121
Gummow, Bill 121, 124
Gutteridge, HC 39

habitual residence 102, 220
Hague Conference on Private International Law 188
Hague Convention on Choice of Court Agreements 2005 86–7, 109, 241
Hague Convention on Recognition and Enforcement of Foreign Judgments in Civil or Commercial Matters 243
Hague Convention on Traffic Accidents 158, 164
Hague Marriage Convention 1978 22
Hague Rules 25–6, 30, 32, 35–6, 39–42
Hague-Visby Rules 35, 40
Hanley, Michael 112
Harriman, Averell 93
Hawke, Bob 121, 129
Hollis, Roger 112
Hong Kong 178, 180
Hooper, David 115
Hosack, John 3, 7
Huber, Ulrik 6, 11, 15
Hughes, Thomas 117
Hughes, Tom 117, 130
human dignity 195
human rights
applicable law 178
common law 187
European Convention on Human Rights (ECHR) 212, 224

fair hearing, right to a 224
freedom and security of the person, right to 195
property, right to 224
public policy 178, 184
Russian invasion of Ukraine 171
South African Bill of Rights, interpretation of 191–2, 206
torture 184

illegality 23, 25–30, 35–7
***in personam* judgments** 207, 213, 216, 226, 233
***in rem* jurisdiction** 95
incestuous marriages 7, 8, 9–22
inconsistent judgments 218
indigenous law 191
inheritance 9–15
injunctions 120, 122, 126–7, 130
insolvency 213–24
insurance contracts 102
international law *see* **public international law**
Internet 166
Iraq *see* ***Kuwait Airways Nos 4 and 5* (England)**
Ireland, common law recognition of foreign judgments in (*Re Flightlease*) 207–24
academic commentary 215, 218
alternative approach 219
before *Flightlease* judgment 208–12
Brexit 221
Canada 207, 213–21
Cheshire, reliance on 209–10
comity 210–11, 214, 216
connecting factors
nationality 209–10, 212
real and substantial connection test 207, 213–21, 224
Dicey, reliance on 209, 214, 216–18, 222–3
English judgments, enforcement of 208–12
European Convention on Human Rights (ECHR) 212, 224
habitual residence 220
Hague Judgments Convention 219–24
EU, accession of 219–20, 224
United Kingdom, relationship with 220–1
High Court 207–16
in personam judgments 207, 213, 216
inconsistent judgments, risk of 218
insolvency 213–24
justice 208, 212, 220
legal certainty 217–19, 222
nationality 209–10, 212
natural justice 215
obligation theory 211–12, 215
outline of *Flightlease* 213
policy, analysis of 211–12, 214–15
presence in country of origin 207, 209–14, 216, 218, 221
principal place of business 220
Rainford decision 208–12, 214, 219, 221–2
critical analysis 210–11
English judgments, enforcement of 208–12
legal reasoning 209–11
outline 208–9
real and substantial connection test 207, 213–21, 224
reciprocity 210–11, 216
service of proceedings
out of the jurisdiction 209
presence at time of service 209
submission to court of origin 207, 209–14, 216, 218, 221
subsequent developments 219–21
Supreme Court 207–8, 216–19, 221
Swiss judgments 213–24
theoretical foundation for recognition policy 211–12, 216–17, 224
traditional common law criteria 207–8, 216–19, 221–4
transitional retrospectivity 214–17
United States 221
unjust recognition practices 212

judgments *see also* **recognition and enforcement of foreign judgments**
default judgments 173–4, 225, 227, 230, 233
registration 239
summary judgments 233–5
Judicial Committee of the Privy Council *see* **Privy Council, Judicial Committee of the judiciary**
activism 124–5, 131
conservatism 114, 131, 133
jurisdiction *see also* **physical presence in jurisdiction; service out of the jurisdiction**
agreements to submit
express 225, 227, 229–32, 234–5, 241
implied 225, 227–32, 235–44

arrest of foreign defendants to found or confirm jurisdiction, constitutionality of 192–206
Australia, *Spycatcher* case in 118, 128–35
Canada, choice of law rules for torts in 154, 156–8, 160, 164–8
diversity jurisdiction 43–64, 86, 91, 108
exorbitant jurisdiction 198
extraterritoriality 9–15, 113, 159
freedom of contract 87
in rem jurisdiction 95
party autonomy in United States 86, 91, 108
prescriptive jurisdiction 160
restrained or responsible assertion of jurisdiction 138, 156
submission to jurisdiction 207, 209–14, 216, 218, 221
express agreements 225, 227, 229–32, 234–5, 241
implied agreements 225, 227–32, 235–44
territorial principle 156, 157–60, 167–9

jus cogens 184, 187

justice
choice of law rules for torts 163–4
Ireland, common law recognition of foreign judgments in 208, 212, 220
natural justice 215, 227

justiciability *see* **non-justiciability, principle of**

Kahn-Freund, Otto 17
Kenny, David 215, 217, 221–2
Kirby, Michael 124–6, 128–9, 131, 134

***Kuwait Airways Nos 4 and 5* (England)** 171–89
act of state doctrine 175–6, 181–9
applicable law, Iraqi law as 175–6
background 172–3
causation 174
choice of law 174–6
Commercial Court 173–4
common law 171–2, 177, 180–9
conversion 174–5
damages 173–4
default judgments 173–4
delivery up 173
domestic law, private international law as 188
double actionability rule 174–7
dualism 186
forum non conveniens 174
House of Lords 175–81, 189
human rights 171, 178, 184, 187
non-justiciability, principle of 172, 174–6, 181–5, 187–8
Operation Desert Storm 173–4
procedural history 173–4
public international law 171, 175–80, 185–8
private international law, interaction with 185–8
public policy exception to application of foreign law 175–80, 184–6
public policy exception to application of foreign law 171, 174–81
act of state doctrine 175–6, 181, 184–5, 189
breaches of international law 175–80, 184–6
double actionability rule 177
human rights 178, 184
non-justiciability, principle of 187–8
private international law 177–81
transnational public policy 179
Resolution 369 of Revolutionary Command Council (RCC) of Iraq 172, 174–6, 178
sanctions 173
Security Council resolutions 172–4, 176, 185, 189
state immunity 174, 181, 189
Supreme Court 183–4
tort 171, 174–7
war crimes 171
wrongful interference with goods 173

Laws, John 124, 130
legal certainty 41, 217–19, 222
legitimacy of children 9–15
lex causae 149, 177, 180
lex domicilii *see* **domicile (*lex domicilii*)**

lex fori
Canada 142, 147–8, 152–3, 157–8, 164
choice of law 32, 34, 36, 152–3, 157–8, 164
lex causae 177
validity of contracts under law of forum 23, 33, 35–7

lex loci celebrationis 1–22
lex loci contractus 16, 18, 23–4, 27, 34

lex loci deliciti
Canada
choice of law rules for torts 152, 154, 158–9, 161–9
recognition and enforcement of interprovincial judgments in 140, 144

choice of law rules for torts 152, 154, 158–9, 161–9
public policy 177
renvoi 38–9
tort 140, 144
lex loci solutionis 68–9, 72–3
lex mercatoria 50, 179
lex situs 175–6
liberty 171, 189
limitation periods
Canada
choice of law rules for torts 153, 155, 163, 169–70
recognition and enforcement of interprovincial judgments in 149
choice of law rules for torts 153, 155, 163, 169–70
civil law countries 163
lex causae 149
procedural, as 155, 167
substantive, as 155, 163, 167
United States, status of state law precedents in federal courts in 50–2
Lord Lyndhurst's Act 1835 7, 9–16, 21

McEleavy, Peter E 134
McHugh, Michael 124–9
McWilliam, Bruce 115
Mance, Jonathan (Lord Mance) 182
mandatory rules 31, 33, 35–7, 40
Mann, FA 32, 182, 185–6
maritime liens, priority of 147–8
marriage *see* **foreign marriages, choice of law rules on (*Brook v Brook*) (English law)**
Mason, Anthony 114–15
media 111–12, 115–17, 120, 122
merchant law 50, 179
Mills, Alex 188
Morguard Investments v De Savoye *see* **Canada, recognition and enforcement of interprovincial judgments in (*Morguard Investments v De Savoye*)**
Morris, John 30, 31–3, 39, 41
Müller, Horst 6

Napoleonic Code 7–8
national security *see* ***Spycatcher*** **case (Australia)**
nationalism 111, 113–17, 120
nationality as a connecting factor 209–10, 212
natural justice 215, 227
natural law 7, 8, 9–19, 46–7
Navalny, Aleksei 189
New Zealand
express choice of law 35, 37, 41
forfeiture laws 119–20
illegality 37
public law exclusion 119–20
public policy 41
Spycatcher, publication in 124
Newman, J 222
non-justiciability, principle of 172, 174, 181–5
act of state doctrine 175–6, 181–5
comity 183
definition 181–2
public policy exception 187–8
separation of powers 182–3
Norman, Henry Wylie 65
North, PM 32

Official Secrets Act 1939 123–4, 127–8, 134
O'Keefe, Roger 182
Operation Desert Storm 173–4
ouster doctrine 89–92, 95, 98, 109
overreaching 100, 103

Packer, Kerry 115
parallel proceedings 87, 95
Parker, Matthew, Archbishop of Canterbury 9
party autonomy *see also* **party autonomy in United States (*M/S Bremen v Zapata Offshore Company*)**
express choice of law 23, 30, 41
proper law rule 75–6, 81
party autonomy in United States (*M/S Bremen v Zapata Off-shore Company*) 85–109
applicable law 87
arbitration 85, 90–1, 109
background 93
Brussels I (Recast) Regulation 99, 101–2
burden of proof 98–9
business-to-business choice of court agreements 101–2
choice of court agreements 86–92, 94–109
arbitration agreements under New York Convention 109
common law 99–108
enforcement 100, 103–8
exceptions to enforcement 100, 103

exclusive 88–9, 99, 101–7
forum non conveniens 103–8
non-exclusive, interpretation as 92, 103–4, 106
ouster doctrine 89–92, 95, 98, 109
prior to *Bremen* 88–92
choice of forum clauses 88
civil law systems 86, 89
common law 85–7, 92, 96–108
diversity jurisdiction 86, 91, 108
effective remedy, denial of an 100
enforcement of choice of court agreements 100, 103, 107–8
effective remedy, denial of an 100
exceptions 100
fraud, overreaching, or unconscionable conduct 100, 103
manifestly and gravely inconvenient, where courts are 103
public policy 100, 103
substantial inconvenience 100, 103, 107
unfair, unjust or unreasonable conduct 100
Erie question 86, 108
exculpatory clauses 94–8
facts of case 94
Federal Arbitration Act 1925 85, 90–1
forum non conveniens 86–8, 91, 95–9, 100, 103–8
fraud, overreaching, or unconscionable conduct 100, 103
freedom of contract 87
habitual residence 102
Hague Convention on Choice of Court Agreements 2005 86–7, 109
jurisdiction 86–7, 91, 95, 108
legal development of case 94–9
manifestly and gravely inconvenient, where courts are 103
ouster doctrine 89–92, 95, 98, 109
parallel proceedings 87, 95
public interest 88, 101, 107
public policy 95–6, 98, 100, 103
recognition and enforcement of foreign judgments 87
Restatement (Second) Conflict of Laws 92
substantial inconvenience 100, 103, 107
unfair, unjust or unreasonable conduct 100
physical presence in jurisdiction
arrest of foreign defendants to found or confirm jurisdiction, constitutionality o) 195–7, 204–6
Ireland, common law recognition of foreign judgments in 207, 209–14, 216, 218, 221
recognition and enforcement of foreign judgments 226, 234
service 195–7, 204–6
temporary presence 195–6
Pincher, Chapman 112, 122
Pitel, Stephen 34–5, 146, 148
place of the wrong, law of the *see* ***lex loci deliciti***
place where property is situated, law of (*lex situs*) 175–6
positivism 44–5, 47, 48
Pothier, Robert-Joseph 6
Powell, Philip 121–4
precedent
Australia, *Spycatcher* case in 113, 125, 128, 133–4
United States, status of state law precedents in federal courts in 43–64
presence in jurisdiction *see* **physical presence in jurisdiction**
Privy Council, Judicial Committee of the
appeals 46, 62–4
Australia 65–83, 113–14
Bonython v Commonwealth of Australia 65–83
express choice of law 23–42
proper law rule 65–83
recognition and enforcement of foreign judgments 225–44
Vita Food Products decision 23–42
Vizcaya Partners Limited v Picard 225–44
procedure
limitation periods 155, 167
statutes 53–4, 60
substance, difference from 49–50, 53–4
uniformity 52
proper law rule in *Bonython v Commonwealth of Australia* 65–83
closest and most real connection 69, 73–80, 82–3
common law 71, 73–83
contract 69–83
debentures, repayment of 65–83
intention test 74–83
lex loci solutionis 68–9, 72–3
most substantial connection 74
party autonomy 75–6, 81
presumed intention test 74–83

Privy Council, Judicial Council of the 65–83
reasoning 67–76
reasons 70–6
Queensland 65–83
Rome Convention 1980 80, 82
Rome I Regulation 80–3
Rome II Regulation 80
renvoi 69
property, right to 224
proportionality 179–80
public interest 88, 101, 107, 126–7
public international law
Australia 186–7
common law 171
constitutional law and private international law, interplay with 156–62
customary international law 184, 187
double actionability rule 177
dualism 186
human rights 178, 184
jus cogens 184, 187
non-justiciability, principle of 187–8
private international law, interplay with 156–62, 177–81, 185–8
public policy exception to application of foreign law 175–80, 184–6
transnational public policy 179
public law exclusion 119–20, 123–4, 126–8, 133–4
public policy
act of state doctrine 175–6, 181, 184–5, 189
Australia 34–5, 41, 129, 132–3
bills of lading 28
Canada 41, 178
choice of law 28, 31–6, 39–41, 100, 103, 158
comity 40–1
double actionability rule 177
exculpatory clauses 94–8
foreign marriages, English choice of law rules on 11–13, 15, 16–17, 21
Hague Rules 40
Ireland, common law recognition of foreign judgments in 211–12, 214–15
New Zealand 41
non-justiciability, principle of 187–8
Putin, Vladimir 171

Rafferty, Nicholas 34–5, 146, 148
real and substantial connection test
Canada 156, 214, 219
choice of law 31, 156
foreign marriages, English choice of law rules on 19–20, 21–2
Ireland, common law recognition of foreign judgments in 207, 213–21, 224
reciprocity 210–11, 216
recognition and enforcement of foreign judgments
agreements to submit to jurisdiction 225, 227–44
express 225, 227, 229–32, 234–5, 241
implied 225, 227–32, 235–42
Canada, recognition and enforcement of interprovincial judgments in 137–50
choice of law clauses 234–7, 241
common law 225–44
default judgments 225, 227, 230, 233
Dicey rule 227–31
expert evidence 234–5, 238
fraud 225–44
governing law 226, 235, 240–2
Hague Judgments Convention 219–24
Hague Convention on Recognition and Enforcement of Foreign Judgments in Civil or Commercial Matters 243
in personam judgments 207, 213, 216
inconsistent judgments 218
obligation theory 242–3
party autonomy in United States 87
presence in jurisdiction 226, 234
Privy Council 225–44
registration of judgments 239
South Africa 224
submission to jurisdiction 226, 234
Swiss judgments 213–24
United Kingdom, Supreme Court in 226–7
Vizcaya Partners Limited v Picard 225–44
renvoi 28, 37–9, 41, 69, 188
residence 102, 196, 220
road accidents
Canada, choice of law rules for torts in 151–70
gratuitous passenger rule 153, 155, 157–8, 161
Hague Convention on Traffic Accidents 158, 164
wilful or wanton misconduct 153, 155, 157–8, 161
Robertson, Alan 121
Robertson, Geoffrey 115–16
Robinson, Mark 130
Roman-Dutch law 191–2, 194, 202–3, 206

Rome Convention 1980 31–2, 36–7, 80, 82
Rome I Regulation 31–2, 36, 38
Rome II Regulation 80
Royal Marriages Act 1772 7–8, 11, 13
Russia *see* **Ukraine, Russia's military aggression towards**

scholarship *see* **academic scholarship**
Scotland
- dissolve English marriages, jurisdiction of Scottish courts to 3–5
- foreign marriages, choice of law rules on 3–5, 7
- Gretna Green marriages 5
- *lex loci celebrationis* 4–5, 7
- Lord Hardwicke's Act 1753 5

Security Council (UN)
- autocratic states with permanent membership 189
- common law courts 189
- resolutions 172–4, 176, 185, 189
- sanctions 173

separation of powers 182–3
service out of the jurisdiction
- arrest of foreign defendants to found or confirm jurisdiction, constitutionality of 197, 199–201, 204
- Canada, recognition and enforcement of interprovincial judgments in 137–8
- connecting factors 204
- *forum non conveniens* 197, 199–201, 204
- Ireland, common law recognition of foreign judgments in 209
- temporary presence 195–6

Shelford, Leonard 6
Simos, Theo 120–2, 124, 127, 129, 130
South Africa *see also* **arrest of foreign defendants to found or confirm jurisdiction, constitutionality of (*Bid Industrial Holdings (Pty) Ltd v Strang and another* (South Africa)**
- access to justice 224
- African customary or indigenous law 191
- apartheid 191
- colonialism 191
- common law 191–2
- Constitution 191, 224
- Constitutional Court 191, 224
- English law 191–2
- fair hearing, right to a 224
- independence 191
- mixed or hybrid legal system 191–2, 201–2, 206
- recognition and enforcement of foreign judgments 224, 239–40
- Roman-Dutch law 191

sovereignty
- Australia, *Spycatcher* case in 113, 119–20, 125–6, 129, 134
- United States, status of state law precedents in federal courts in 47, 48–51

***Spycatcher* case (Australia)** 111–35
- account of profits 120
- anti-British sentiment 116–17, 135
- Australian Government's support of British government 121–2
- before *Spycatcher*, the law 118–20
- bicentennial celebrations 113–14, 125
- common law 118–19, 134–5
- Commonwealth
  - foreign countries to each other, as not being 125
  - place of Australia in the 112–13
- confidentiality 123–4, 126–30
  - equitable obligation 126–9, 134
  - injunctions 126–7
  - prerogative powers 123, 126–7
  - public interest 126–7
- Constitution 135
- doctrine 113, 117, 122–3, 133–5
- extraterritoriality 113
- fiduciary duties 124, 126, 128–9
- foreign governments, enforcement of governmental interests by 113–35
- foreign penal law, enforcement of 118–19, 124, 126–7, 131, 133
- foreign revenue laws, enforcement of 118–19, 126, 128, 131, 133
- forfeiture laws 118–20
- High Court of Australia 113, 117, 118, 123, 129–35
- *Huntington v Attrill* doctrine 118–19, 123, 127–8
- independence of Australia 112–13, 116, 124, 131, 134
- injunctions 120, 122, 126–7, 130
- judicial activism 124–5, 131
- judicial conservatism 114, 131, 133
- jurisdiction 118, 128–35
- Liberal Party 116–17
- Mason court 114–15, 130–1, 133–4
- media 111–12, 115–17, 120, 122
- nationalism 111, 115–17, 120

New South Wales 113, 115–17, 126, 132
Court of Appeal 129
Supreme Court 111, 120–4
New South Wales Court of Appeal 122–3, 124–9
New Zealand, publication in 124
Official Secrets Act 1939 123–4, 127–8, 134
precedents 113, 125, 128, 133–4
public domain, information in the 130
public interest 126–7
public law exclusion 119–20, 123–4, 126–8, 133–4
public policy 129, 132–3
research 113, 117, 122, 133–5
significance of *Spycatcher* 133–5
State sovereignty 113, 119–20, 125–6, 129, 134
Supreme Court of New South Wales 111, 120–4
undertakings 120, 124, 130
United States, publication in 124
state law *see* **United States, status of state law precedents in federal courts in (*Erie Railroad Company v Tompkins*)**
state security *see* ***Spycatcher* case (Australia)**
Statute of Westminster 1942 113
statute law
civil law systems 60
substantive or procedural, as 53–4, 60
United States, status of state law precedents in federal courts in 53–4, 60–1
Stewart, David 221
Story, Joseph 3, 6–7, 12–13, 15, 18
Street, Laurence 124–30, 132, 134–5
submission to jurisdiction 207, 209–14, 216, 218, 221
express agreements 225, 227, 229–32, 234–5, 241
implied agreements 225, 227–32, 235–44
substance
civil law systems 60
limitation periods 155, 167
procedure, difference from, 49–50, 53–4
statutes 53–4, 60
substantial connection test *see* **real and substantial connection test**
summary judgments 233–5
Swan, Angela 222
Swiss judgments 213–24

tax laws, enforcement of foreign 118–19, 126, 128, 131, 133
temporary presence 195–6
territorial principle 156, 157–60, 167–9
Tetley, William 39–40
Thatcher, Margaret 111, 121, 129
time limits *see* **limitation periods**
Tolofson v Jensen *see* **Canadian common law choice of law rule for torts (*Tolofson v Jensen*)**
tort 151–70, 171
Canada 138, 140, 143–4, 149, 151–70
choice of law rules for torts 151–70
conversion 174–5
double actionability rule 174–7
geographically distributed torts 164–6
lex loci delicti 140, 144
traffic accidents *see* **road accidents**
Turnbull, Lucy 117–19, 122, 126, 128, 130, 133, 135
Turnbull, Malcolm Bligh 115–21, 123–4, 125–6, 128, 130, 132–5

Ukraine, Russia's military aggression towards
Crimea and eastern provinces 187
invasion of Ukraine 171, 189
non-justiciability 187
public policy 189
unconscionable conduct 100, 103
uniformity 39–41, 51–2, 139–46, 150
United Kingdom *see* **English law**
United Nations *see* **Security Council (UN)**
United States *see also* **United States, status of state law precedents in federal courts in (*Erie Railroad Company v Tompkins*)**
anti-miscegenation law 6
Hague Judgments Convention 221
lex loci delicti 162
maritime liens, priority of 147
party autonomy 85–109
Spycatcher, publication in 124
United States, status of state law precedents in federal courts in (*Erie Railroad Company v Tompkins*) 43–64
appeals
Privy Council 46, 62–4
state courts to Supreme Court, availability of appeals from 46, 61–2
unavailability of 45
Australia 63–4
Canada 63–4
certification 51
civil law jurisdictions 48, 50, 60–1

common law 43–64
brooding omnipresence, as 46–7, 48
Commonwealth states 62–4
federal common law 43–64, 86
general common law 43–4, 46–50, 59, 62–3
interpretation 43–5, 47–51, 53–64
natural law, as 46–7
Rules of Decision Act 52
Commonwealth states
Erie problems 62–4
interjurisdictional interpretation of common law 46, 62–4
Privy Council appeals 46, 62–4
Swift approach 62–3
constitutional issues 47
content of target's courts, determination of 44
coordination problem 46, 56, 58, 64
custom 54–5
deference of interpreter courts to views of target's courts 44, 52–64
diversity jurisdiction 43–64, 86
Erie problems 44–7, 52–64
history 57–64
horizontal cases 57–9
fact approach to 54–5, 58
federal common law 43–64, 86
constitutional issues 47
customary legal systems, jurisdictions with 48
deference to state courts on cases concerning local usage 43
diversity jurisdiction 43–64, 86
Erie problems 44–7, 59–62
diversity jurisdiction 43, 47, 51–2
state's common law, federal courts' interpretation of 59–60
vertical uniformity with state courts 51–2
forum shopping 47, 51–2
limitation periods 50–2
negotiation approach 55–6, 57, 59
positivism 44–5, 47, 48
procedure 49–50, 52–4
Rules of Decision Act 47–8, 52
solution to *Erie* problems 44–6
sovereignty 47, 48–51
standards 43–5, 48–50, 54–6, 59, 62–3
state courts
appeals 46, 61–2
certification 51
civil law system in Louisiana 60–1
common law, interpretation of sister state's 57–8
diversity jurisdiction 43–64, 86
Erie problems 57–62
federal court's interpretation of state's common law 59–60
interpretation 52, 57–62
sovereignty 47, 48–51, 57
statutes, interpretation of state's 60–1
vertical uniformity with federal courts 51–2
statutes 53–4, 60–1
substance
civil law system 60
Erie questions 53
procedure, difference from 49–50, 53–4
statutes as substantive or procedural 53–4, 60
Swift v Tyson 43, 45–62
Brandeis on *Swift* 46–52, 56
fact approach 54–5, 58
target court's views, deference of interpreter court to 52–64
coordination problem 46, 56, 58, 64
custom 54–5
Erie problems 44–7, 52–64
fact approach to *Swift* 54–5, 58
highest courts, interpretation by 53–6, 60
negotiation approach 55–6, 57, 59
vertical uniformity 51–2

***Vita Food Products* decision and express choice of law (Privy Council decision)** 23–42
applicable law 37, 40–1
Australia, influence in 34–5, 37–8, 41
bailment, rights and duties of a common carrier in 26–7, 30
bills of lading 25–30, 40
clause paramount 25–6, 40
Hague Rules, incorporation of 25–6, 30, 36
illegality 25–30
Newfoundland Carriage of Goods Act 1932 25–9
public policy 28
Brexit 32
Canada, influence in 33, 37, 38–9, 41

Carriage of Goods by Sea Act 1924 25, 39–40
Carriage of Goods by Sea Act 1971 35, 40
choice of law before *Vita Food* 23–4
clause paramount 25–6, 40
close connection 31–2, 37
comity 29–30, 40–1
commercial certainty 30, 41
common carriers 25–7
common law 23–4, 33, 36, 40–1
criticism of decision 23
England and Wales, influence in 30–3, 37–8
facts of case 25–6
foreign law, where contract governed by 35–6
formal validity 37
good faith 33–4
Hague Rules 25–6, 30, 32, 35–6, 39–42
Hague Visby Rules 35, 40
illegality 23, 25–30, 35–7
intention of parties 23–4, 27, 29–31
legal certainty 41
lex loci contractus 23–4, 27, 34
lex fori 32, 34, 36
mandatory rules 31, 33, 35–7, 40
material validity 37
New Zealand, influence in 35, 37, 41
Newfoundland Carriage of Goods Act 1932 25–9, 37
party autonomy 23, 30, 41
proper law of contract, English law as the 27–9, 36
public policy 28, 31–6, 39–41
Ralli Bros principle 37, 40
real and substantial connection 31
renvoi 28, 37–9, 41
Rome Convention 1980 31–2, 36–7
Rome I Regulation 31–2, 36, 38
uniformity 39–41
validity of contracts under law of forum 23, 33, 35–7
  formal validity 37
  illegality under law elsewhere 23, 35–7
  material validity 37
Vita Food gap 30

***Vizcaya Partners Limited v Picard* on recognition and enforcement of foreign judgments** 225–44
agreements to submit 225, 227–44
  express 225, 227, 229–32, 234–5, 241
  implied or inferred 225, 227–32, 235–44
  obligation theory 242–3
  why parties are bound 242–4
before *Vizcaya*, common law 226–32
choice of law clauses 234–7, 241
claims or counterclaims in foreign court proceedings 226
common law 225–44
default judgments 225, 227, 230, 233
Dicey rule 227–31
  open to question, position as 229–30
  original position 227–9
expert evidence 234–5, 238
facts 232–3
fraud 225–44
Gibraltar courts, judgments of 233–5
governing law 226, 235, 240–2
Hague Convention on Choice of Court Agreements 241
Hague Convention on Recognition and Enforcement of Foreign Judgments in Civil or Commercial Matters 243
implied or inferred agreements to submit 225, 227–32, 235–42
in personam judgments 226, 233
natural justice 227
obligation theory 242–3
presence in jurisdiction 226, 234
Privy Council 225–43
registration of judgments 239
Rubin v Eurofinance SA 226–7
significance of reasoning 238–43
submission to jurisdiction
  agreements to submit 225, 227–44
  voluntary participation 226
summary judgments 233–5
Supreme Court (UK) 226–7
Voet, Paul 6

war crimes 171
West, Nigel (Rupert Allason) 112
Westlake, John 20, 74–6
Whitlam, Gough 116, 121
Wright, Peter 111–35

www.ingramcontent.com/pod-product-compliance
Ingram Content Group UK Ltd.
Pitfield, Milton Keynes, MK11 3LW, UK
UKHW021909150926
475560UK00003B/272

9 781509 954278